BELONGING and COMFORT

BELONGING and COMFORT

365 Meditations on the Heidelberg Catechism

REFORMED
FREE PUBLISHING
ASSOCIATION
Jenison, Michigan

©2025 Reformed Free Publishing Association

Except for the meditations from August 20 to September 2, November 19 to December 2, and December 31, all meditations are provided by

Covenant Evangelical Reformed Church
11, Jalan Mesin #04-00
Standard Industrial Building
Singapore 368813
cerc.org.sg
Adapted for publication and printed with permission.
All rights reserved.

Printed in the United States of America.

No part of this publication may be reproduced, stored in a retrieval system, or transmitted in any form or by any means—electronic, mechanical, photocopying, recording, or otherwise—without the prior written permission of the publisher. The only exception is brief quotations in reviews.

Scripture cited is taken from the King James (Authorized) Version. Italics in Scripture quotations reflect the authors' emphasis.

Cover design: Amy Zevenbergen
Interior design and typeset: Katherine Lloyd, The DESK

Reformed Free Publishing Association
1894 Georgetown Center Drive
Jenison, Michigan 49428
616-457-5970
mail@rfpa.org
www.rfpa.org

ISBN 9798987161487
Ebook ISBN 9798987161494

CONTENTS

Publisher's Foreword vii
Introduction. 1
Lord's Day 1 3

THE FIRST PART—OF THE MISERY OF MAN

Lord's Day 2 12
Lord's Day 3 18
Lord's Day 4 26

THE SECOND PART—OF MAN'S DELIVERANCE

Lord's Day 5 34
Lord's Day 6 42
Lord's Day 7 50
Lord's Day 8 59
Lord's Day 9 66
Lord's Day 10 74
Lord's Day 11 82
Lord's Day 12 90
Lord's Day 13 98
Lord's Day 14 106
Lord's Day 15 114
Lord's Day 16 122
Lord's Day 17 130
Lord's Day 18 138
Lord's Day 19 146
Lord's Day 20 154
Lord's Day 21 162
Lord's Day 22 170

Lord's Day 23 178
Lord's Day 24 186
Lord's Day 25 194
Lord's Day 26 202
Lord's Day 27 210
Lord's Day 28 218
Lord's Day 29 226
Lord's Day 30 226
Lord's Day 30 234
Lord's Day 31 242

THE THIRD PART—OF THANKFULNESS

Lord's Day 32 250
Lord's Day 33 258
Lord's Day 34 266
Lord's Day 35 274
Lord's Day 36 282
Lord's Day 37 290
Lord's Day 38 298
Lord's Day 39 306
Lord's Day 40 314
Lord's Day 41 322
Lord's Day 42 330
Lord's Day 43 338
Lord's Day 44 346
Lord's Day 45 354
Lord's Day 46 362
Lord's Day 47 371
Lord's Day 48 378
Lord's Day 49 386
Lord's Day 50 394
Lord's Day 51 402
Lord's Day 52 410

List of Contributors 419

PUBLISHER'S FOREWORD

Belonging and Comfort: 365 Meditations on the Heidelberg Catechism is a companion volume to *Believing and Confessing: 365 Meditations on the Belgic Confession* that the Reformed Free Publishing Association published in 2023. Most of the meditations in *Belonging and Comfort* originally appeared in pamphlet form. They were published by the Covenant Evangelical Reformed Church in Singapore, which kindly granted permission for republication in book format. The RFPA expresses gratitude to the CERC, as well as to the authors of the meditations.

The Heidelberg Catechism is a creed and teaching tool of many Reformed congregations all around the world. That is one of the reasons why the Catechism never stops offering occasions for instruction, meditation, and devotion. We hope that *Belonging and Comfort* will be a contribution for further learning and enjoyment of the eternal truths of the gospel of Jesus Christ that the Catechism so ably explains.

January 1 — Introduction — The Value of the Heidelberg Catechism

Read: John 14:16–18, 26–28; 15:26; 17:7–11, 13–14.

The Reformation, begun in Germany by Martin Luther, spread throughout Germany and came to a province called the Palatinate, with its capital in Heidelberg. Over this province Frederick the Wise ruled, who was persuaded of the truth of the Reformation doctrines taught by John Calvin in Geneva, a fairly short distance south of Heidelberg. Frederick was a godly and pious man and desired that the children and young people of his province learned and understood the truths of Scripture taught by Calvin.

He himself had been raised a Lutheran but had through a long time of study become convinced that the doctrines taught by Calvin were more faithful to the Scriptures. He wanted the province over which he ruled to be a province faithful to the teachings of John Calvin.

For these actions, Frederick was summoned before the emperor at the Diet of Augsburg of 1566 and told to recant his Calvinistic views. But his genuine piety, his love for the truth, and his deep sincerity made such an impression on the council that it did not care to condemn him.*

Frederick instructed a professor of theology in the University of Heidelberg, Zacharias Ursinus, and the court minister, Caspar Olevianus, to prepare a catechism which could serve Frederick's purpose. The result of their work is our wonderful Heidelberg Catechism, although before its publication in 1563 it underwent a few changes. The final form was soon adopted by churches throughout Europe. Its simplicity (understandable by children), its beauty of expression, and its theme of comfort attracted the loyalty of thousands. It became the personal confession of the faith of multitudes.

The great Synod of Dordt (1618–1619) adopted the Heidelberg Catechism as the confessional basis of the Reformed churches in the Netherlands, and so it has remained a part of the confessional heritage of the Reformed churches throughout the world. This synod also saw that the book was a wonderful tool for the systematic instruction of God's people in the whole counsel of God. And so it ordered that the Heidelberg Catechism be preached in the churches once a Sunday. Hence the Catechism has fifty-two Lord's Days. This was done so that the ministers might go through the Catechism in its entirety every year.

It is a book of instruction ideally suited to preaching with its motif of comfort for the believer in the truth God revealed in Scripture. The Catechism has been translated into many different languages and is loved by thousands in all parts of the world.

Herman Hanko

---

* You may find the story of this great man in my *Portraits of Faithful Saints* (Jenison, MI: Reformed Free Publishing Association, 1999), 191–200.

Lord's Day 1

Question 1. What is thy only comfort in life and death?

Answer. That I, with body and soul, both in life and death, am not my own, but belong unto my faithful Savior Jesus Christ; who with his precious blood, hath fully satisfied for all my sins, and delivered me from all the power of the devil; and so preserves me that without the will of my heavenly Father, not a hair can fall from my head; yea, that all things must be subservient for my salvation, and therefore, by his Holy Spirit, he also assures me of eternal life, and makes me sincerely willing and ready, henceforth, to live unto him.

Q. 2. How many things are necessary for thee to know, that thou, enjoying this comfort, mayest live and die happily?

A. Three: the first, how great my sins and miseries are; the second, how I may be delivered from all my sins and miseries; the third, how I shall express my gratitude to God for such deliverance.

January 2 — Q&A 1 — The Personal Approach of the Catechism

Read: Romans 11:5–6; Ephesians 2:8–9.

The Catechism has a very attractive feature about it: it is personal and experiential. It does not discuss the truths of Scripture from an abstract and impersonal way, such as one might find in a dogmatics; it speaks directly to the believer and insists that the believer answer out of his own experience. Notice the very first question: "What is thy only comfort in life and death?"[*]

This personal approach to the truth of Scripture means that the believer who answers these questions always looks at the truth from the viewpoint of the blessedness that truth has for him.

The Catechism has as its theme *comfort*. Added to the personal approach of the Catechism is the great theme of the comfort the truth means to the believer. The truth is comforting, and the believer is asked to explain how each truth is indeed of comfort to him. Comfort is sorely needed by the believer. In this world of sin and death, of sickness and pain, of sorrow and grief, of trouble and heartache, he is hungry for something that will comfort him. My mother, sick all her life, often said: "The best of life is nothing but weariness and sorrow."

The Roman Catholic Church, out of which God's people came at the time of the Reformation, could find no comfort in masses and candles, fastings and ceremonies, purgatory and penance. The theology of the Roman Catholic Church was one of saving oneself through the prescribed rituals of the church. But there was no comfort in it. Martin Luther tried in his years as a monk but could not find peace, though he was the most rigid observer of the church's rules. The problem was that Rome taught that man had to save himself by careful observance of all the laws and rituals of the church. Written above the gates of the Roman Catholic Church were the words: "Abandon all comfort, ye who enter here."

Imagine what a startling message the reformers brought to Europe's weary people of God! We bring you a gospel of comfort! It is not a comfort for some of your sorrows. It is not a comfort for the days of your life only. It is not a comfort for diseases in your body only. It is a comfort that will bring peace to your soul in life and death, in whatever may be your lot in life. It is an all-comprehensive comfort!

Herman Hanko

---

[*] Heidelberg Catechism Q 1, in *The Confessions and the Church Order of the Protestant Reformed Churches* (Grandville, MI: Protestant Reformed Churches in America, 2005), 83.

January 3 — Q&A 1 — Our Only Comfort

Read: Philippians 1:21–23.

What a wonderful possession we would have if in this world of sorrow we had something truly comforting! Something that is truly comforting is some truth that changes every sorrow, every pain, every disappointment in life into something very, very glorious. It is a truth that explains everything that happens to us and causes every experience in life to glow with joy. It is some proposition that erases all grief and suffering.

Comfort is, therefore, something that is able to bring peace to the heart of the child of God; it is something that can change his tears to laughter; it is something that brings hope in a hopeless world. It is a truth that we can carry with us to the cemetery when we bury a loved one, that can bring happiness in the hospital when we face surgery, that can strengthen us in our weariness when the burdens of life seem too heavy to carry. Above all, comfort is something that can completely take away these terrible sins that are an impossible burden to us in life.

It is true that the whole world needs comfort, for the whole world is plunged into misery and grief. Wars, diseases, death, natural disasters, sicknesses of every sort fill the hospitals and nursing homes, soak the battlefields with the blood of thousands of a nation's youth, force the building of prisons and houses of correction, and bring always greater grief. But the Catechism does not address the wicked world, and its discussion of an "only comfort" is not intended for it. That is the beauty of its personal approach. "What is thy only comfort?" The question is asked of the believing child of God.

The world would not accept the one truth that does bring comfort, for the world hates the truth of God and despises the Christ preached in the gospel. The assemblies of the nations would laugh in scorn if the believer would tell them where true comfort is to be found. They prefer to trust in their bank accounts, their pensions, their insurance policies, their own health and strength, their confidence in the goodness of man that will someday make this world a better place to live. So they live and die in misery, trusting in themselves and bitterly disappointed when their treasures turn to ashes before their eyes.

The believer is one in whom God works by his Holy Spirit and who has the gift of faith. He is asked by the Catechism to give an account of his comfort.

Herman Hanko

January 4 — Q&A 1 — To Belong to Jesus

Read: Psalm 100.

We may very well ask the question: "What wonderful truth can bring such blessings that it is a word for every grief not only in life, but also in death?" That is the question we are asked, after all: "What is thy only comfort in life and death?"* One would think, perhaps, that a comfort that has such great promise would be a difficult and complicated proposition that would take a rather large book to explain it all. A comfort in life? In death? In sickness? In sorrow? In trouble? In disappointment?

Our teachers in the Catechism say: No, it is not a difficult answer. It is not complicated. You do not have to read a book to have this comfort. In fact, it is so simple that a little child can understand it. No schooling is necessary to learn it. No brilliant mind is needed to believe it. It is simple, so simple that any child of God, old or young, strong or weak, intelligent or average, can easily take it as his own.

What is it that has such amazing power? Just this: I belong to Jesus. Four words, simple words, words easy to understand. Who cannot understand that? It is true that the Catechism says a few more things about it, but it all finally comes down to this: I belong to Jesus!

Notice how personal it is: I belong to Jesus. I believe this. I am absolutely convinced of it. I personally am the possession of Jesus Christ. It is an all-comprehensive comfort. I belong to Jesus "with body and soul."** Not my body only, but also my soul; that is, my mind, my will, my emotions.

"I am not my own." I do not own myself to do with myself as I please. I am not my own to try to find a way to some light in the darkness of sin, suffering, and death. My thoughts are not my own. My desires are not my own anymore. My eternal destiny is not decided by me. Even my experiences in life are not my desperate search to find a way out of the dark night of misery into the light of hope and joy. Indeed, I am not my own in all my life; but I am also not my own when I die. I belong to Jesus in all this life, but I also belong to him when I die.

And the Jesus to whom I belong is a faithful Savior. I can trust he will do what he has promised. He is one who is completely trustworthy. I belong to him!

Herman Hanko

---

* Heidelberg Catechism Q 1, in *Confessions and Church Order*, 83.
** Heidelberg Catechism A 1, in *Confessions and Church Order*, 83.

January 5 — **Q&A 1 — The Blessedness of Belonging to Jesus**

Read: Hebrews 9:24–28.

We have learned already from the Catechism that our only comfort is that we belong to our faithful Savior, Jesus Christ. But we need to know more; that is, we need to know how it is possible to belong to him and what it means to belong to him. The Catechism explains all these things. Actually, the entire remainder of the Catechism is written to explain what it means to belong to Jesus; here the Catechism gives a brief summary.

We do not belong to Jesus by virtue of our birth, for we belong to Satan and the wicked world. But our Savior, "with his precious blood, hath fully satisfied for all my sins, and delivered me from all the power of the devil."* I do not belong to Jesus because I have chosen him or accepted his invitation to believe in him. I do not belong to Jesus because I have done enough good works to merit becoming his possession. I cannot do any of these things. He purchased me. He bought me with his own blood that he shed on Calvary. He made me his possession, his treasure, his bride, his friend. The price he paid was enormous: it was the price of his own precious blood. On the cross he died for our sins, enduring the everlasting wrath of God that was our just due and that held us in bondage to sin and Satan.

He preserves us by his power so that "not a hair can fall from" our heads "without the will of [our] heavenly Father."** That is, nothing at all happens to us except it is God's will. And God is our Father, who has made us a part of his family, who loves us and supplies all our needs.

Beyond even God's directing all our lives as our Father, belonging to Christ means "that all things must be subservient to [our] salvation."*** Everything that happens in the whole history of the world and in all the history of heaven serves the purpose of saving us. That is indeed a bold statement; but it is implied in belonging to Jesus. The same is true of what happens to me individually: every pain and sorrow serves my salvation.

The Catechism also takes the time to answer for us the question: How can we be sure that all these wonderful things are true for us—for me?

Our Jesus to whom we belong also gives us that assurance by his Spirit in our hearts and even makes us ready and willing to live unto him. That is an incomparable comfort!

Herman Hanko

---

* Heidelberg Catechism A 1, in *Confessions and Church Order*, 83.
** Heidelberg Catechism A 1, in *Confessions and Church Order*, 83.
*** Heidelberg Catechism A 1, in *Confessions and Church Order*, 83.

January 6 — **Q&A 1 — Our Own Assurance of Belonging to Jesus**

Read: Romans 8:15–17

The Catechism always approaches all the doctrines contained in it from a very personal point of view. Our teachers who put the questions of the Catechism to us want not simply theological answers, but personal answers, answers that demonstrate that the truths of Scripture are very really our faith and that we know these truths to be for ourselves. The Catechism does not only talk about an only comfort, but it talks about *my* only comfort, *your* only comfort.

If we are to make the Catechism our own personal confession, it follows that we have to have the assurance in our own hearts that all these truths are true for us. How can we be sure of this? This is an important question, because many people in the church world claim never to be sure of their salvation. They live, go to church, and die without knowing whether they are children of God for whom the truth of Scripture is really theirs. This doubt is a very sad thing.

It is not only sad, however; it is a sin. Every one of us has his moments of doubt, of course. Especially when we come to understand the riches of our salvation, we ask ourselves whether it is really true that we are the heirs to such blessings. And when our sins rise up against us and we see our unworthiness, we cannot possibly imagine that we are the objects of such great love because we are such dreadful sinners. But these doubts are sins; they are sins that must be confessed at the foot of the cross of Calvary. They are sins that need to be forgiven. We may not doubt. We are commanded to believe in Jesus Christ. To doubt is to disobey Christ's command. We do not ask ourselves the question: Am I really and truly a child of God? We do not ask ourselves that question any more than we ask ourselves: Am I really a child of this man and this woman who claim to be my parents? Our parents would be rightfully angry if we would doubt their parenthood.

But Christ gives us, by his Spirit, the assurance of our salvation. This is the teaching of Romans 8:15–17. This assurance is not something we attain by our works but is a gracious gift of God through Christ for us. Let us joyfully confess this truth.

Herman Hanko

January 7 — Q&A 2 — What We Must Know to Have Comfort

Read: Luke 24:47; 1 Corinthians 6:10–11; John 17:3; Ephesians 5:8–10.

To be able to confess that we belong to Jesus, there are certain things we must know about ourselves. Question and answer 2 of Lord's Day 1 brings another question to our attention, which tells us the things we must know. Notice again how personal the Catechism is: "How many things are necessary for thee to know, that thou, enjoying this comfort, mayest live and die happily?"* Three things are important to know. They are so important that without knowing them, we cannot have comfort.

The first is that we must know "how great [our] sins and miseries are."** This is understandable. I cannot know the blessedness of having good health unless I know what it means to be sick to death. I cannot know the joy of comfort unless I know the horror of sorrow at the loss of one I love. Likewise, I cannot know any comfort if I have no sorrow. People who are happy and without sorrow do not need comfort.

We are told an important truth in this question and answer. The real misery that makes us long for comfort is not sickness or disappointment or death; it is sin. These other reasons for misery are all present in our lives because of sin. If we had no sin, we would not have misery. If we were perfect, we would not have pain and trouble. Sin is the great reality that makes us miserable. We must understand, therefore, how great our sins are.

Second, we then are ready to know the great work Christ did for us to deliver us from our sins. Only through tears clearing the blindness of our sins can we see clearly the need of Christ's cross. We can walk the way to Calvary only in a path wet with the tears of shame over our sins. There is no other way.

Finally, we have to have knowledge of how in our lives we express gratitude to God for what he has done for us. We show our gratitude by walking in obedience to his law. Disobedient children are unthankful children. We will not know any comfort when we live wickedly.

Those three things are the three chapters of the Catechism, in which the Catechism will teach us our comfort. May we humbly learn these lessons.

Herman Hanko

---

*   Heidelberg Catechism Q 2, in *Confessions and Church Order*, 84.
** Heidelberg Catechism A 2, in *Confessions and Church Order*, 84.

January 8 — Q&A 2 — The Real Reason Why We Need Comfort

Read: Psalm 51.

Lord's Day 1 ends with the question of how we are to gain for ourselves this wonderful comfort that brings us peace and happiness in life, in death, and forever. We were told that the attainment of this comfort involves knowledge. Comfort is not some sort of wishy-washy feeling that creeps up on us from we know not where. True comfort is the result of knowing some things.

Our teachers in whose classroom we are to learn about our comfort have lessons to teach us, and we must learn our lessons. There are, says our teacher, three things that are absolutely essential to know before we can really have that wonderful comfort which our souls crave. The three things we have to know are very surprising things. We would never have thought that our lessons in comfort would include that kind of knowledge that the Catechism says we need. Those three things are, you will recall: One, the knowledge of how great our sins and miseries are. Two, how we are delivered from our sins and miseries. Three, how we are to be thankful to God for deliverance from our sins and miseries.

And so the Catechism is divided into three sections, each section teaching us what is meant by these three things we need to know. The first section tells us about our sins (Lord's Days 2–4). The second section teaches us about our deliverance through Christ's work (Lord's Days 5–31). This section is the longest by far. And the third section deals with how we show our thankfulness to God (Lord's Days 32–52). It explains the ten commandments and the Lord's prayer, because we show how thankful we are for our deliverance from sin by keeping God's law and by praying.

The emphasis throughout is on the sovereignty of God in the work of salvation. This emphasis compels the Catechism to deal with some crucially important doctrines and also compels the Catechism to include questions and answers that show the errors of some Roman Catholic teachings and some Lutheran teachings.

In this way, the Catechism calls the confessing Christian to an antithetical life: in his calling to hold fast to the truth, he must reject wrong doctrine and he must hold fast to the truth.

So let us begin our study of the lessons we are to learn. We really want comfort in our lives. We want comfort more than anything else. So under the guidance of our teachers, let us set about learning our lessons.

Herman Hanko

January 9   **Q&A 2 — Why the Knowledge of Our Sin is Important for Comfort**

Read: Psalm 32.

We will probably want to ask our teachers why we have to know our sins in order to have comfort. We really would rather not think too much about our sins, and we surely are embarrassed to talk to others about them. But the reasons we have to know them are important.

The question and answer we are discussing talks about "sins and miseries."* That means that our miseries, for which we need comfort, are brought about by sin. Our miseries are problems, sicknesses, death, trouble, suffering, pain, disappointment, and many other things. All these things make us miserable.

But all these miseries are our lot in life because we are sinners. And the sins, which result in misery, are our own fault. We deserve all our misery.

Another reason for knowing our sins is that until the time we recognize that sin is at the bottom of all our misery, and that sins are our fault, we will not go to Christ and flee to his cross. If I put it into the framework of the Catechism, this means that we need to go through part one, "Of the Misery of Man," to get to part two, "Of Man's Deliverance."

Still another reason is that we can only know the forgiveness of sins in Jesus Christ when we confess our sins to God. And confession means that we are sorry for them. The Bible tells us in a thousand places how important confession of sin is. David had no peace until he confessed his sins of adultery and murder. He tells us of this in Psalm 32. John says: "If we say that we have no sin, we deceive ourselves, and the truth is not in us. If we confess our sins, he is faithful and just to forgive us our sins, and to cleanse us from all unrighteousness" (1 John 1:8–9).

When Jesus says that he came to save not righteous people but sinners (Luke 5:32), he meant exactly that he did not come to save those who think they are righteous; he came to save those who know that they are sinners.

It is not easy to admit we are sinners. It is not easy to confess that we are sinful. The three hardest words in the English language to say are: "I am sorry." We may be sorry for sin because a crime has landed us in jail. We may be sorry for sin because people have learned about it, and we are ashamed. We do not like the consequences of sin. But to be sorry for sin because we have sinned against God and against each other is the most difficult thing in all God's world to do.

Yet we must confess sins.

Herman Hanko

---

*   Heidelberg Catechism A 2, in *Confessions and Church Order*, 84.

THE FIRST PART—OF THE MISERY OF MAN

Lord's Day 2

Q. 3. Whence knowest thou thy misery?
   A. Out of the law of God.

Q. 4. What doth the law of God require of us?
   A. Christ teaches us that briefly, Matt. 22:37-40, *Thou shalt love the Lord thy God with all thy heart, with all thy soul, and with all thy mind, and with all thy strength. This is the first and the great commandment; and the second is like unto it, Thou shalt love thy neighbor as thyself. On these two commandments hang all the law and the prophets.*

Q. 5. Canst thou keep all these things perfectly?
   A. In no wise; for I am prone by nature to hate God and my neighbor.

January 10 — Q&A 3 — How We Know Our Sins

Read: Romans 7.

In the last meditation I said that it is very difficult to know our sins and confess them. We are always trying to defend our own sinful lives and justify ourselves. And if we are sorry for our sins, it is only because we are caught and suffer sin's consequences.

We must remember once again that the Catechism is talking to and instructing believers, people of God, those who are saved. "Whence knowest thou thy misery?"*— the implication is, therefore, that only a child of God can really know his sins. In other words, we need the grace of God in our hearts and the work of the Holy Spirit in order to be truly sorry for our sins. We have to learn to pray, even before we confess our sins: "Lord, give us grace to be sorry for our sins."

Yes, there is a certain regret for sin in the world, but the worldly people (and we too, often) take sins lightly, dismiss them as unimportant, and wave their hands with a gesture of indifference: "Oh, it was only a little lie." The problem is that among our sins is the sin of pride, and pride keeps us from admitting how wicked we really are. Pride is such a huge devil in the lives of men that pride even gets in the way of biblical theology. Pride is why all forms of Arminianism are so popular. Arminianism tells man that he can do something for his salvation. He can choose for Christ. He can let Christ into his heart. He can pray for Christ to help him.

But these are all efforts on the part of wicked men to salvage some tattered remains of their pride. Scripture and the Heidelberg Catechism won't let us do that. They insist that if we really want to know our deliverance in Christ, we must learn that we can do nothing good at all. True humility is required of us, and true humility comes only through grace. But even then, we still need help. And the help we need to know our sins and misery comes, says our teacher, through the law of God. James calls the law of God a mirror in which we see ourselves reflected (1:23–25).

Once again, I must emphasize that the law is a mirror only for the believer. A wicked man may look in the mirror of the law and see only a reflection of himself that looks pretty good to him. He preens in front of the mirror and is rather proud of himself. Or perhaps he doesn't want to look in the mirror at all. In our country, the Supreme Court has forbidden the ten commandments to be found in schools, in public buildings, or anywhere where people come. They are afraid that people will find it offensive. How sad!

Herman Hanko

---

* Heidelberg Catechism Q 3, in *Confessions and Church Order*, 84.

January 11 — Q&A 3 — Our Reflection in the Mirror

Read: James 1:19–27.

Paul tells us that by the law is the knowledge of sin (Rom. 3:20), and James speaks of the law as a mirror in which we see our reflection. If a natural man, that is, a worldly and sinful man, looks in the glass or mirror, he sees nothing and "goeth his way, and straightway forgetteth what manner of man he was" (James 1:23–24). But if he is a regenerated child of God, then, when he looks into the mirror, he is not a forgetful man, but "a doer of the work" and a man who "shall be blessed in his deed" (v. 25). What does this mean?

James calls the law "the law of liberty" (v. 25). He calls it that because it is a special mirror into which the believer looks. It is a mirror that has Christ in it—although the believer cannot see that immediately. And so, first of all, the believer looks into that mirror and sees himself spiritually as he truly is. And the picture is not pretty. It is a picture of a man or woman who, from a spiritual point of view, is ugly, hideous, full of running sores (Isa. 1:5–6) and whose righteousness is as filthy rags. That is the way we are spiritually.

But when we continue to look into that mirror of the law, gradually the mirror changes and there appears in the mirror a cross, planted on Calvary and on which hangs our Lord Jesus Christ, the eternal Son of God in our flesh. And then we see ourselves in the mirror of the law as well, but we see ourselves reflected in the mirror of the law as the law is fulfilled in Christ. We see ourselves as we are in Christ. And that reflection is beautiful. It is of a saint shining as bright as the sun (Matt. 13:43), wearing clothes that are the brilliantly white robes of Christ's righteousness (Rev. 6:11; 19:8), and with a body that is like the glorious body of Jesus Christ (Phil. 3:21).

So we first see ourselves as we truly are apart from Christ, and that is our sin and misery. But then we see ourselves as we are in Christ, beautiful and holy. But we have to see the first reflection before we can see the second. That is, we have to know our sins and miseries if we are to know our deliverance.

To know ourselves as we truly are is to fill our souls with grief at the thought that we have sinned against God and brought misery on ourselves because we have sinned. Then we repent of our sins, confess them to God, and flee to the cross as our only escape from misery. The path to the cross is wet with the tears of weeping sinners, and all those who are kneeling there with us at Calvary are looking to Christ alone as the only hope of their salvation.

Herman Hanko

January 12 — Q&A 4 — The Law of God as the Law of Love

Read: Galatians 5; Matt 22:37–40.

How is it possible for the law to show us our misery?

If we only look at the law as a code of outward moral conduct, then the law will not be a mirror of misery. Even worldly people may actually find that their lives are nearly conformable to God's law. They never swear; they do not work on Sunday; they do not worship idols; they usually keep the laws of the land; they do not kill anyone or be unfaithful to their wives or husbands; they do not steal or speak evil of others. From an outward point of view, they do a pretty good job of keeping the law of God. But then, so did the Pharisees of Jesus' day! And Jesus called them "whited sepulchres" (Matt. 23:27). In Matthew 22, Jesus explains why that is.

A lawyer was determined to trap Jesus in his words and find in some teaching of the Lord a reason to condemn him. He asked what the most important commandment of the law was. No matter what commandment Jesus quoted, the lawyer would be in a position to condemn him for setting one commandment above another (22:34–36).

But Jesus was aware of the fact that all the commandments were of equal importance, and that, as James says, to break one commandment is to break them all (James 2:10). Further, our Lord knew also that mere outward conformity to the law of God was as good as worthless in the sight of God. Again and again the Lord reprimanded Israel for outward conformity to the law, while their hearts were far from him (Isa. 1:10–17; Mal. 1:6–8; Matt. 5:21–42; Matt. 15:1–20, etc.).

And so the Lord did not quote one of the commandments as the lawyer thought he would. Instead, the Lord pointed to the inner demands of the law: "Thou shalt love the Lord thy God with all thy heart, and all thy soul, and with all thy mind. This is the first and great commandment. And the second is like unto it, Thou shalt love thy neighbour as thyself. On these two commandments hang all the law and the prophets" (Matt. 22:37–40). This was already a part of the law in the Old Testament (Deut. 6:5; Lev. 19:18).

So the foundation of all the commandments of God is the basic command: Love God! And love your neighbor for God's sake. If we do not love God, we cannot keep any of the commandments, no matter how closely we adhere to them outwardly. If we do not love God, we do not love our neighbor, for we must love our neighbor as ourselves, and we must love our neighbor because we love God.

Herman Hanko

January 13 — Q&A 4 — Love God and Our Neighbor

Read: Luke 10:25–37.

To love God means to seek the glory of God, to desire to live in fellowship with him, and to be obedient to him in all things. To love him with all our heart, mind soul, and strength means to love him with all our being and to love him without interruption—day and night, with every thought and desire, with every word we speak, with every gesture and activity of our bodies.

Who is my neighbor? The tribal chieftain in some Pacific Island? No. Some head-hunter in Africa? No. Some bag lady on the streets of Philadelphia? No. My neighbor is my wife, my children, my parents, my fellow saints, my classmates, my colleagues at work. My neighbor is the one I bump into in my life, the one whose path crosses mine, the one who needs me, the one who can sometimes annoy me to no end, the one who persecutes me. I must love my neighbor. This is the mirror of the law. Let us look into it.

Each one of us. This is the question our teacher asks each of us individually: "What doth the law of God require of us?"* Each one of us? What does the law require of you? Of me? Do I love God with my first thoughts on waking up? Do I love him as I am dressing, combing my hair, shaving? Do I love him when I walk to the bus stop? When I sit in the classroom? Do I love him when I go to work? When my colleague makes my life impossibly difficult? Do I love him when I am sick? When I am on my deathbed? Do I love him with every thought I think? With every desire in me? With every emotion? With every word? With every activity of my body?

What is your answer to all these questions? When the law is the mirror into which we look, then we see ourselves reflected in that perfect law of love. It is not a pretty picture that is reflected from that mirror. It is, in fact, so ugly that I shrink back in sheer horror. Who is that ugly monster there in the mirror? Why, it is a reflection of me! Why am I miserable with trouble, suffering, grief, pain, disappointment? Well, no wonder. Look at what I am! And God is a holy God who is satisfied with nothing less than perfection.

The teacher makes us learn some pretty hard lessons! And we do not like to learn them.

Herman Hanko

---

* Heidelberg Catechism Q 4, in *Confessions and Church Order*, 84.

January 14 **Q&A 5 — Prone to Hate God and My Neighbor**

Read: Romans 3:1–20.

Our rather stern and insistent teacher now asks the final question. Our teacher wants us to be sure that we know our sins and miseries, for we cannot go on in our studies until we learn this lesson. "Canst thou keep all these things perfectly?"* That is indeed the question that needs answering. We have seen ourselves in the mirror of the law, and it was not a very pretty sight. Well, what do you see?

"In no wise; for I am prone by nature to hate God and my neighbor."** I must confess it. It is true. There is no getting around it. I may wear a mask of piety and appear before others as pious and good. I may even try to fool myself. But there it is. The simple fact is that I cannot even begin to love God and my neighbor. And I don't do it either. Love him? Most of the time I am not even thinking about him! There are a few things about this question and answer that we must think about.

One is that the question talks about keeping the law "perfectly." Our first reaction to that might be that our teacher is trying to make things as tough for us as possible. Maybe we don't keep the law perfectly, but isn't God satisfied with our best efforts? And so what if we slip a little here and there? Do we have to be totally without any lapse, any slip? The answer is *yes*, we are talking about our relation to God! God demands of us that we be as holy as he is (1 Pet. 1:16). He has a right to do this as well. If he would permit "little" sins, he would not be the holy God that he is (Isa. 6:1–4). His holiness cannot tolerate even the tiniest of sins.

The second point is that to some, the word *prone* seems to be weak to describe our sins. If I say, I am prone to eat too much, then I mean that that is a danger all right, but I can successfully resist this proneness in me. But that is not the point. Here the word *prone* means that we are totally and completely pointed in the direction of sin.

The third point is that our teacher insists that we understand what this proneness means. The answer we are given is not: "No, I do not do all these things perfectly, but fail here and there;" nor is our answer simply: "No, I have to admit that I do not do all these things perfectly." The answer is horrible to contemplate: "I always do the exact opposite." It is not only, sadly enough, that I don't do what is required of me; the problem is that I do exactly the opposite of what I ought to do. I am called to love God, but I hate him. I am called to love God with all my heart and mind and soul and strength. But what do I do? I hate him with all my heart and mind and soul and strength.

That's how bad it is! Do you confess that truth? When we learn that lesson, we are ready to go on.

Herman Hanko

---

* Heidelberg Catechism Q 5, in *Confessions and Church Order*, 85.
** Heidelberg Catechism A 5, in *Confessions and Church Order*, 85.

Lord's Day 3

Q. 6. Did God then create man so wicked and perverse?

A. By no means; but God created man good, and after his own image, in true righteousness and holiness, that he might rightly know God his Creator, heartily love him, and live with him in eternal happiness to glorify and praise him.

Q. 7. Whence then proceeds this depravity of human nature?

A. From the fall and disobedience of our first parents, Adam and Eve, in Paradise; hence our nature is become so corrupt, that we are all conceived and born in sin.

Q. 8. Are we then so corrupt that we are wholly incapable of doing any good, and inclined to all wickedness?

A. Indeed we are; except we are regenerated by the Spirit of God.

January 15 — Q&A 6 — Why Are We Totally Depraved?

Read: Genesis 1.

Our teacher has instructed us in the real reason why we are miserable and in need of comfort. He has instructed us to learn this by looking into the mirror of God's law. Now that we have learned the true reason for our misery, we are ready to learn the next lesson. The next lesson is: How did we get that way? Were we always that way? The answer is: We got that way because our parents also are prone to hate God and their neighbor. But how did our parents get that way? Were *they* always that way?

And so we could trace our genealogies back as far as we want to go, but we will always find that the same thing is true: parents are always prone to hate God and their neighbor. And sin is passed on from parents to children. But what if we would trace our genealogies back to the first parents that ever lived? Were they that way too? Well, to answer that question we have to know how they came to be parents when they did not have any parents of their own. The answer is: God created them.

But if it is true that God created them, did God create them so wicked that they are prone to hate God and their neighbor? And that is the question that comes from our teacher in this Lord's Day. Is it God's fault that we are this way? Did God make a serious error when, in creating man, he created a monster of sin instead? It is not so strange that the Catechism asks this question, for when our first parents Adam and Eve were confronted by God and asked about their sin, they blamed God. Eve blamed the serpent God had made; and Adam blamed the woman God had given him (Gen. 3:12–13). So both wanted to blame God.

The Catechism is emphatic. "By no means" did God create man so wicked!* Man was created good, but he chose to be the way he is now. It is man's fault.

By implication, the Catechism condemns our tendency to always blame someone else for our sins. Adam and Eve did this in Paradise; little children do this when confronted with a sin; we all do this. It seems as if we are very skilled at figuring out who to blame for our sins, but always to escape our own responsibilities. It is a mortal disease. It keeps us from truly confessing our own sins.

Herman Hanko

---

* Heidelberg Catechism A 6, in *Confessions and Church Order*, 85.

January 16 — Q&A 6 — Man's Creation: Body, Soul, and Spirit

Read: Genesis 2.

Lord's Day 3 tells of man's creation. God himself tells us how he made man on the sixth day of the creation week. In Genesis 2:7, God says: "And the Lord God formed man of the dust of the ground, and breathed into his nostrils the breath of life; and man became a living soul."

When the Bible gives us this information about man's creation, it does not mean to say that God took several handfuls of dirt, formed a lifeless likeness of man, and then made it alive by breathing on it. When the Bible tells us that God formed man from the dust of the earth, it means that God formed man just as he formed the animals (Gen. 1:24). Although even in this act God used special care in forming man from the ground.

That all means that, first, God made man just as the animals so that he could live in this earthly creation. He was a part of it, dependent on it, related to it, and unable to live anywhere else—not even in heaven—than here in the world. But it also means that God gave man a soul that was higher than the animals. It was a soul that possessed a mind and a will, so that man was a rational and moral creature who could think, understand, figure things out, remember, and subdue the earth (1:28).

That God breathed into man the breath of life means that the kind of soul God made for man was also a soul that made it possible for man to live in relation to God. The animals could not do this; man can. He can know God through the singing of the birds and the animals whom he names. For the names he gave them were names that fit them: names that expressed the way in which God's glory was revealed through them. Thus he could glorify God and serve God in all he did. The Bible often mentions the spirit of man (see Eccl. 12:7; 1 Thess. 5:23; Luke 23:46). It would be profitable for you to take a good concordance and look up all the times the spirit of man is mentioned.

The Catechism describes man in detail because it wants us to know what wonderful creatures God made us. We must remember that after the fall we are not only sinners, but our bodies and souls are very weak. Before the fall, Adam never got sick; his powers of mind were far, far stronger than ours are; he could see perfectly and hear perfectly. He was a wonderful creation. Actually, since sin has come, our bodies and souls are wrecks of what they once were. That helps us understand our misery.

Herman Hanko

January 17 — Q&A 6 – Man in the Image of God

Read: Genesis 1:26–28; Ephesians 4:20–32; Colossians 3:1–10.

Our teacher is not finished with a description of the wonder and glory of our original creation. We are told that "God created us…after his own image, in true righteousness and holiness."[*] The word *image* here means that God created us so that we were in some way like him. We could not, of course, be as glorious as he is, for we are always finite creatures, and he is always the infinite God. But it does mean that in moral purity and sinlessness we were like him, though even then in a creaturely way.

Although the narrative in Genesis 1 does not tell us specifically what elements were a part of that image, two other places in Scripture do tell us this. They both speak of how, through Christ, we are saved in such a way that the image of God is restored in us. Ephesians 4:23–24 tells us that the restoration of the image in us is a renewal of the mind and that we are to "put on the new man, which after God is created in righteousness and true holiness."

The new man is "after God," that is, the new man is like God. We sometimes say of a young girl that she takes after her mother—meaning she is like her mother. That likeness to God is characteristic of the new man, which is created by God. And that new man is characterized by righteousness and holiness. Colossians 3:10 tells us that specifically knowledge belongs to that image: "And have put on the new man, which is renewed in knowledge after the image of him that created him." The text specifically says that in creating us in his image, God gave us true knowledge.

We surely were not created wicked. God made us as creatures that possessed true knowledge of him. And *knowledge* here means the same as it means in Genesis 4:1, where Adam is said to have known his wife. That is, he knew her in the most intimate knowledge of the covenant fellowship of marriage, for that knowing produced a son. Adam knew God in the covenant of fellowship in which God spoke to him in the cool of the day.

Adam's righteousness was his perfect conformity to the will of God in all his life and activity. And Adam's holiness was a spotless, guiltless holiness of his nature that reflected the glory of God. He was an unsurpassed creation of God who represented God's cause in God's world. That is how we were created. Consider into what a shamble we have fallen.

Herman Hanko

---

[*] Heidelberg Catechism A 6, in *Confessions and Church Order*, 85.

January 18 — Q&A 6 — Adam as Officebearer

Read: Genesis 2:18–25; Psalm 8.

When our teacher tells us that man was created in the image of God, he adds: "That he might rightly know God his Creator, heartily love him, and live with him in eternal happiness to glorify and praise him."* Adam was created with a body and soul, in the image of God, in order that he might represent God in the creation God had made. He represented God by his relation to the creation by subduing it and using the whole creation in the service of God. He was God's covenant friend who brought the creation as a sacrifice of praise to his creator. In this way, he was an office bearer.

As an office bearer, Adam was prophet, priest, and king. As prophet, Adam could know God and speak God's word in the creation. When Adam named the animals, Adam was functioning as God's prophet, knowing God's glory through and in each animal and giving a name to each animal that expressed how that animal revealed God's greatness. As priest in God's house, he dedicated the whole creation to God and brought it all as a sacrifice of praise and glory to God. As a king, Adam ruled over the creation in God's name. He ruled, not as a cruel and heartless tyrant, but as a benevolent ruler who was kind and gentle to God's world.

One can notice a certain beautiful pattern in this creation of man. Adam was created with a body, to be righteous in God's image, to rule as king; with a soul, to have the true knowledge of God as a prophet; with a spirit, to bear God's image of holiness, to be priest.

What a glorious creature Adam was! How wonderful Paradise was, where man could fully enjoy God in a creation in which was no blemish, no death, no struggle for survival, no conflict, no darkness. Only pulsing life and light; only peace and happiness; only beauty and the glorious knowledge of God. Only joyful service in God's creation.

And yet, although we are jumping ahead in our lessons, it is well to remember that God's purpose to glorify himself was in a better way than in Paradise. God was looking to Christ. Christ is God's true prophet, priest, and king in God's house, the new heavens and the new earth. And we are and will be prophets, priests, and kings with Christ forever and ever.

Herman Hanko

---

*   Heidelberg Catechism A 6, in *Confessions and Church Order*, 85.

January 19 — Q&A 6 — Adam: God's Covenant Friend

Read: Romans 5.

Image bearer, officebearer, rational moral creature—Adam was fully equipped to serve God in God's creation. But he was also God's covenant friend.

Things have become very mixed up over the years on this matter of Adam as God's covenant friend, for most theologians want to define this covenant between God and Adam as a covenant of works. A covenant of works is a covenant in which God promises Adam eternal life in heaven if Adam will be obedient to God in not eating of the tree of the knowledge of good and evil but eating instead of the tree of life. God also threatened Adam with death if Adam disobeyed. To this, Adam agreed, and so a covenant was established.

This notion of the covenant has no foundation in Scripture, and as closely as one examines Scripture, one cannot find anything like this. The whole notion of a covenant of works is based on Genesis 2:16–17, but these verses do not say a thing about a covenant; they only give the command of God to Adam to eat of all the trees of the garden except the tree of knowledge of good and evil. A command and a threat of death are not a covenant.

I briefly mention a few questions which the covenant of works forces on us. How long did Adam have to be obedient before he would merit heaven? Would his generations merit heaven with him? Was it possible that somewhere in his generations one would sin by disobeying God? What would happen then? Is it possible that an earthly man, made of flesh and blood, created to life in this material world, could somehow inherit the heavenly creation? Paul says "that flesh and blood cannot inherit the kingdom of God" (1 Cor. 15:50). The covenant of works claims they can.

But Adam did live in a covenant relation to God. That covenant was not a covenant of works that was made with Adam after his creation so that before the covenant was made, there was no covenant. No, God's covenant was made with Adam by virtue of his creation. He could be nothing else but a covenant friend of God. And so the covenant then as now is a relationship between God and Adam of friendship and fellowship in which God and Adam lived together in joyful communion.

But Adam's creation had one more aspect to it that we have to know. Our teacher here in this class on the Catechism does not speak of it specifically, but he does imply it in Lord's Days 3 and 4. And that is that Adam was created as our covenant head. He was the head of the whole human race from which the human race came, but he was also the representative head of the human race, so that what Adam did, he did on behalf of all his generations that would follow. Adam fell!

Herman Hanko

January 20 — Q&A 7 — Adam's Fall

Read: Genesis 3.

Satan was the tempter who tempted Adam and Eve to fall. He was an angel, probably the highest angel, who conspired against God and attempted to seize the heavenly creation from God. Joining him was an enormous host of angels, all of whom were banished from heaven. They, with Satan at their head, now conspired to take control of the earthly creation and use it for their sinful purposes. To take control of the earthly creation, Satan and his demons had to gain Adam to their side, for Adam was the head of the creation.

Satan tempted Eve before he tempted Adam. He called Eve's attention to the beauty of the tree of the knowledge of good and evil and lied about God: he charged God with deception when he said that God forbade eating of this one tree because he knew that if man would eat of it, man would be like God and determine for himself what was good and what was evil. Eve listened, and she took it upon herself to tempt Adam to do the same. They both disobeyed God's command. The result was that God's judgment of death came on them. God's punishment for sin was death! Death is separation from God. As we sing in Psalm 73: "To live apart from God is death."*

Death is basically total depravity. Our nature is so corrupted that it is no longer able to do any good. But that total depravity is also physical death, so that the moment we are born, we start on a road that leads to the grave. And the grave is the door to eternal death in hell.

It is a sad story, for Adam's sin opened the floodgate to hatred, war, bloodshed, and constant bitterness between men. Adam's sin opened the door to sickness, disease, suffering, pain, and the need for hospitals and cemeteries. Adam's sin opened the door to floods, tsunamis, earthquakes, volcanic eruptions, hurricanes, typhoons, and tornadoes, all of which kill hundreds of thousands. All these are part of death, dreadful death.

There are two important truths to remember in the midst of the chaos that sin brought. The first is that Adam's sin is our sin, and we can and do go to hell for that one sin of eating of the forbidden tree. We are conceived and born in sin because God is punishing us for eating of the tree he told us not to eat of. The second truth is that Adam's fall was not a mistake in God's plan. God was preparing the way for Christ. And Christ gives us salvation.

Herman Hanko

---

* No. 203:5, in *The Psalter with Doctrinal Standards, Liturgy, Church Order, and added Chorale Section*, reprinted and revised edition of the 1912 United Presbyterian *Psalter* (Grand Rapids, MI: Eerdmans, 1927; rev. ed. 1995).

January 21 — Q&A 8 — Total Depravity

Read: Genesis 4:19–24; 6:1–13.

Total depravity is one of the five points of Calvinism. It is first in the acronym TULIP. It is one of the truths that we must confess.

Many have been the attempts to deny it. Pelagianism maintains that man is born without sin, and that if he does sin, it is only because he follows a bad example. Semi-Pelagianism says that man is born sick and his sickness would be fatal unless he calls on the divine physician to heal him, but he is not dead. Roman Catholicism teaches that although man is very sinful, God will not save him unless he first performs many works of penance. The Arminians teach that man has a free will and can choose between hell and heaven, Satan and Christ. Those who hold to common grace teach that although man is totally depraved, he is not absolutely depraved. That is, although sin discolors every part of him, it does not completely spoil all of him. Synergism teaches that man can and does cooperate with God in the work of salvation.

The Bible teaches total depravity. We are so sinful that no good thing can be found in us; we are not able to do anything to please God, we cannot even want to be saved. As an old farmer told his minister in 1834, the year of the Separation in the Netherlands: "Pastor, if I had to contribute so much as a sigh of sorrow to my salvation, I would go to hell." We are as bad as we can be. We "are dead in trespasses and sins" (Eph. 2:1). This is what our teacher teaches us: "Are we then so corrupt that we are wholly incapable of doing any good, and inclined to all wickedness? Indeed we are, except we are regenerated by the Spirit of God." *

Let us never forget that this is a lesson we have to learn. We must confess before God that we are totally depraved. We must believe this so that we know that we cannot do one good thing—even pray—unless God gives us grace. This is a lesson we have to learn if we really want to learn that we are saved in Christ and by his work. If we know that we can do no good, we will not try to buy our way into heaven or persuade God to save us because we deserve it. We will only run as fast as we can to the cross of Christ and hurl ourselves into the arms of our Savior.

Herman Hanko

---

* Heidelberg Catechism Q&A 8, in *Confessions and Church Order*, 86.

Lord's Day 4

Q. 9. Doth not God then do injustice to man, by requiring from him in his law, that which he cannot perform?

A. Not at all; for God made man capable of performing it; but man, by the instigation of the devil, and his own willful disobedience, deprived himself and all his posterity of those divine gifts.

Q. 10. Will God suffer such disobedience and rebellion to go unpunished?

A. By no means; but is terribly displeased with our original was well as actual sins; and will punish them in his just judgment temporally and eternally, and he hath declared, *Cursed is every one that continueth not in all things, which are written in the book of the law, to do them.*

Q. 11. Is not God then also merciful?

A. God is indeed merciful, but also just; therefore his justice requires that sin which is committed against the most high majesty of God be also punished with extreme, that is, with everlasting punishment of body and soul.

January 22 — Q&A 9 — God's Justice in His Demand of Obedience

Read: Romans 2:1–16.

The teacher in whose classroom we are learning about our only comfort is eager to get to those lessons that speak of belonging to our faithful Savior, Jesus Christ. But he is not quite ready to take us to those lessons, for there is one more truth about our misery we have to know: the truth concerning the justice of God in relation to our sin.

The question, "Doth not God then do injustice to man, by requiring from him in his law that which he cannot perform?"*, is an important one, for many answer the question with a loud yes. It would be unjust of God, they say, if God would demand of us something we cannot do and then punish us if we do not do it. A father would be terribly unjust if he asked his son of five years old to carry a fifty kilogram bag of cement and then gave him a hard licking when the son failed to do it. There are people in the world who do say that God is unjust in asking us to keep his law, even though we are totally depraved and cannot do it, and then in sending us to hell when we do not do it.

The Arminians say yes to this question; and, so they say, man can keep God's law if he chooses to do so by the choice of his free will. Or, some Arminians say, God no longer demands of us that we keep his law perfectly, but he is satisfied with the best we can do. But there are also people called Antinomians. That name comes from *anti*, which means *against*, and *nomos*, which means *law*. They are "against law." So they say that God does not require of us that we keep the law, because Christ kept the law for us, and we do not have to keep it.

Both views are wrong. We cannot keep the law. We cannot even try to keep it. We cannot even wish we could keep it. Yet, says our teacher, we must keep the law, and God is not unjust when he continues to demand that we keep it, even though we cannot even begin to do this.

This is the lesson we have to learn. It is hard to learn, and we would rather not pay too much attention to it; but, says our teacher, we have to learn this lesson if we truly desire to have our only comfort.

Herman Hanko

---

* Heidelberg Catechism Q 9, in *Confessions and Church Order*, 86.

January 23   **Q&A 9 — It is Our Fault That We Cannot Keep the Law**

Read: Romans 3:1–19; 5:12–21.

Our teacher is now going to tell us why God is not unjust in insisting we keep the law, even though we are unable to do it. The reason is that it is our own fault that we cannot keep the law. We are to be blamed for this inability. Consider the figure of a builder who contracts to build a house for someone, but needs the money before he starts to build. However, when given the money, he squanders it on a round-the-world cruise with his wife. On his return, he is not able to build the house, but the one who gave him the money has the perfect right to demand of him that he do it, even if he cannot.

But why is our sin our own fault? Here too, our teacher has an important lesson for us to learn, taken right from Scripture. Our sin is our fault because God created us good in Adam. We sinned by eating of the tree of the knowledge of good and evil. We committed this act of disobedience, and God punishes us with death for our sin. But how did we eat of the tree when we were not even born? We ate of the tree in Adam, for we were in Adam when Adam sinned, and it is as if we ourselves truly disobeyed.

There are different names given to Adam because we were in him: federal head, legal head, representative head. Whatever name is used, it all means that Adam's sin is the sin of all those who came from Adam—the whole human race. This is the teaching of Scripture. Read Romans 5:12 and 14 once again: "Wherefore, as by one man sin entered into the world, and death by sin; and so death passed upon all men, for that all have sinned… Death reigned from Adam to Moses, even over them that had not sinned after the similitude of Adam's transgression, who is the figure of him that was to come."

This is a difficult doctrine, not to understand, but to confess. Almost no one in our day believes it any more. But we must remember that if we deny that we sinned in Adam, then we deny too that we are saved in Christ. Adam was "the figure of him that was to come" (Rom. 5:14).

Herman Hanko

January 24 — Q&A 10 – God's Just Punishment of Sin

Read: Deuteronomy 27:9–26.

One more lesson is taught by our teacher as necessary to know our comfort. That lesson is that God will surely punish the sins of which we are guilty. He has to punish them. He would not be God if he did not punish them. But let us be sure, first of all, that we understand what the lesson is all about.

There are people in the church, sometimes very conservative people, considered to be evangelicals, who deny this truth. They are afraid of it, because they are of the opinion that an eternity in hell is too big a penalty to be paid for sin. They are like today's liberals who think that capital punishment ought to be abolished, even for the most terrible sins, because it is cruel. They do not like what the Bible says: "Whoso sheddeth man's blood, by man shall his blood be shed: for in the image of God made he man" (Gen. 9:6). They seem to know better than God what is just.

God told Adam that the day he ate of the forbidden tree, he would die. God keeps his word. Death includes, you remember, total depravity (if you find it hard to imagine that total depravity is death, read Ephesians 2:1), physical death, and eternal death in hell. And all the misery, pain, suffering, and trouble in this world is God's punishment for sin, because it is a part of death. Every day we die a bit more physically. We cannot avoid it. It is part of God's curse on man for his sin. And when at last we—man in his unsaved, totally depraved state—do die, and our bodies are carried off to the cemetery, the grave is the door to hell. Our souls go to hell, and our bodies will go when Christ comes back again to judge the living and the dead.

Hell is a terrible place. The wrath of God is totally the experience of those who go there. They can do nothing but suffer, for all their bodies and souls are engulfed by the fierce wrath of God. Read Luke 16:24 and learn how only a drop of water would help ease the pains of hell. Read too how Jesus speaks of hell as the place where the worm does not die and the fire is not quenched (Mark 9:43–44), where is only to be heard weeping and "gnashing of teeth" (Matt. 13:50).

This is what you and I deserve! Let us confess that.

Herman Hanko

January 25 — Q&A 10 – God's Holy Judgment

Read: Deuteronomy 6:1–10; Isaiah 6:1–5.

Many people find it difficult to believe that the punishment of sin could be as severe as the Bible says it is. It is becoming increasingly common, even among evangelicals, to deny the reality of hell. We cannot do that if we want to be faithful to Scripture. Others, and they too are to be found in the Reformed community, deny that the misery that we endure in this life is the result of sin. A minister in the United States,[*] for example, said on TV that the HIV virus was God's punishment for the sin of homosexuality. He was nearly driven out of town and was forced publicly to confess his "error." A classmate of mine during our college days who became professor of philosophy in Yale University, one of the more prestigious universities in the States, lost a son on a mountain-climbing accident on the Lord's Day. The father wrote a book about it in which he denied that God had done this to his son. The questions that come to my mind are: "Who did do it? Or was it an act of Satan? Or blind fate?"

There are two reasons why men do not like the doctrine of temporal and eternal punishment. The first reason is that men do not want to admit how bad their sins really are. They are trying to excuse themselves and charge God with injustice when he punishes them. The second reason is that men do not want as holy a God as he is. He is almost too holy for them. They wish he were not quite as holy as he really is.

Scripture has a difficult time of it to explain to us what holiness really is. This is not because God cannot make his holiness clear, but because we are so thick-headed that it is hard for us to understand spiritual things. Probably the clearest description of God's holiness is in Isaiah 6:1–5, where it is said to be like light that filled the temple, and made the angels cover their faces with their wings and cry out: "Holy, holy, holy is the Lord of hosts: the whole earth is full of his glory" (v. 3). And Isaiah, when he saw it, could only say: "Woe is me! for I am undone, and I dwell in the midst of a people of unclean lips: for mine eyes have seen the King, the Lord of hosts" (v. 5).

Herman Hanko

---

[*] Billy Graham (1918–2018).

January 26 — Q&A 10 — God's Holiness and Our Sin

Read: Job 41:1–6; 1 Samuel 2:2; Leviticus 10:1–7.

God's holiness is very great. It is that great perfection of the triune God that makes God without any trace of sin or imperfection. He is, in fact, the standard of all holiness, and that which is truly holy is like him. He dwells in a light so great that a mere man, even if he were without sin, cannot stand the blazing white light of the holiness of God. God's holiness includes in it all his other communicable attributes: grace, love, mercy, longsuffering, compassion, slowness to wrath, pity, etc.

God's holiness also means that God hates sin with a terrible hatred. He cannot but be revolted at any sin, no matter how small. Sin is detestable to him and must be punished. If God would overlook sin, excuse it, wink at it, or in any other way consider it lightly, he would not be the holy God that he is. He must punish sin, or he is not God.

This is the lesson we have to learn; but we have to learn it in such a way that we believe it as a truth concerning ourselves. We do not often do that. When things go wrong in our lives and we face difficulties or sicknesses, we ask ourselves: Why did God do this to me? That question implies that we do not think we deserve what God sends us. But is this really true? If we truly know our sins and how worthless we are, then we know too that we do not deserve anything good but only God's wrath.

So it will be in the judgment day. The wicked will never say, We did not deserve such punishment. When they see the holiness of God and their own sin, they will say, We deserved what we have received.

But God's people will also see the holiness of God, and they too will see their own sins. They too will say: "We deserve eternity in hell." But they will hear Christ say: "Well done, thou good and faithful servant…enter thou into the joy of thy lord" (Matt. 25:21). And they will understand in a way they cannot understand now that it was only grace that saved them, unmerited favor given through Christ.

So if we do not like the doctrine of temporal and eternal judgment, it is only because we do not understand how holy God is.

Herman Hanko

January 27 — **Q&A 11 — God's Mercy and Justice (1)**

Read: Psalm 103.

In the classroom where we are taught all that is necessary to know in order that we may have comfort, our teacher also informs us that there will be objections brought against those things which we must believe. Does God do injustice when he demands perfection from us who are poor and totally depraved? Is not his punishment much too severe when we do not do what he commands? And now, in question 11, another objection: "You talk of God's justice; but is not God also merciful? Are you not forgetting that mercy?"

The objector—maybe he raises his hand in the classroom to argue with our teacher; maybe he hears what we have been taught and does not like it very well—the objector thinks that the mercy of God is so great that it swallows up God's justice. God could punish sin if he maintained the strict standards of justice; but the Scriptures teach us that God is also merciful; therefore we must emphasize not a vindictive God who makes men pay for every little sin, but rather we must think of a benevolent God who is merciful to us poor sinners.

In other words, this objector wants a God who, when his justice and his mercy clash, puts his justice aside in the interests of being merciful. Or, if we want to put it bluntly, he wants a God in whom the attribute justice is not important.

Our teacher quickly does away with such nonsense. He says, as it were: Of course, God is merciful! All the Scriptures teach this. His mercy is from everlasting to everlasting, and it endures forever. But this does not mean that God is not just. He is just! And to deny his justice is to deny a very important attribute of God. If he is not just, then he is not God. We may not deny his justice, for if we do, we deny him. But our teacher also reminds us of what our sins are like: they are "committed against the most high majesty of God."* So terrible is this that even one little sin is enough to earn for us everlasting hell. And just look at all the sins of which we are guilty!

We sin with body and soul; that is, we sin with our bodies but also with our minds, our wills, and our emotions. We are sinful in everything we do. And we deserve all the punishment God gives us. That is, we deserve extreme punishment. Let us then humble ourselves before God and confess before his great majesty what worthless sinners we really are.

Herman Hanko

---

* Heidelberg Catechism A 11, in *Confessions and Church Order*, 87.

January 28   Q&A 11 — God's Mercy and Justice (2)

Read: Psalm 96.

Question and answer 11 bring to a close the first part of the Catechism. This part deals with the first thing we are to know in order to know our comfort: we must know our sins and miseries.

The teacher who teaches us these lessons is quite insistent we understand fully what miseries our sins are and what terrible consequences come to us because of our sins. Our teacher does not even want to talk about the mercy of God until we have thoroughly mastered the material in the first part.

And we have not learned our lesson properly when we have it all in our heads only; we must have it also in our hearts. If we have it in our hearts, then we will confess that the terrible things our teacher says of us are all true and that all we can do is fall on our faces in the dust before God. This lesson about God's justice and mercy is very important. We may want to find a way to escape the justice we deserve by appealing to God's mercy. But it won't work. Not even we, in our earthly relationships, want to set justice and mercy against each other.

Let us imagine for a few moments a small town in which a vicious murderer breaks into a home, kills the father and mother and drags the children away, where he treats them cruelly. Suppose the man is caught and arrested, tried, and found guilty; but when the judge must sentence him, the judge says to him: "Justice demands that you should be executed. But I am going to be merciful to you and let you go free."

So the man goes free, and after a few weeks, he commits a similar crime and brutally murders five little children. Again, he is apprehended, found guilty, and brought before the judge for sentencing. But the judge once again says to the man: "I know now more than ever you are worthy of death. But I am going to be more merciful yet, and I am going to set you free again."

At that point, the people in the small town would cry out: "This judge must be deposed. We want justice done. If that man continues to be merciful, we will all be dead." And they will cower in their homes behind locked doors until justice is done.

God is merciful, but let us never forget it: God is also just. He has to be just, or he is not God. Let us bow before his justice and confess that we deserve his just judgment. Then the way is open to talk about the wonder of the cross of Christ where justice and mercy met together and kissed each other.

Herman Hanko

THE SECOND PART—OF MAN'S DELIVERANCE

Q. 12. Since then, by the righteous judgment of God, we deserved temporal and eternal punishment, is there no way by which we may escape that punishment, and be again received into favor?

A. God will have his justice satisfied; and therefore we must make this full satisfaction, either by ourselves or by another.

Q. 13. Can we ourselves then make this satisfaction?

A. By no means; but on the contrary we daily increase our debt.

Q. 14. Can there be found anywhere one who is a mere creature, able to satisfy for us?

A. None; for, first, God will not punish any other creature for the sin which man hath committed; and further, no mere creature can sustain the burden of God's eternal wrath against sin, so as to deliver others from it.

Q. 15. What sort of a mediator and deliverer then must we seek for?

A. For one who is very man, and perfectly righteous; and yet more powerful than all creatures; that is, one who is also very God.

January 29 — **Q&A 12 — We Deserve Temporal and Eternal Punishment**

Read: Hebrews 9:27.

As our Catechism turns the page to the great subject of man's deliverance, it does so by reminding us that deliverance must not be separated from the misery of man. Upon careful examination of ourselves in light of the word of God, a conclusion is formed: fallen man is "incapable of doing any good, and inclined to all wickedness."* This bears consequences: God "is terribly displeased with our original as well as actual sins; and will punish them…temporally and eternally."**

If we are going to understand the truth of the gospel, God's great love in giving us his own Son, we must dwell a little bit more on the horrible character of our sin against God. It is ugly in that it comes forth out of a heart that hates God and all he represents. God responds to such action by fallen man in that he places a price on disobedience. In one word, that price is *punishment* for sin. The Catechism describes it as temporal and eternal punishment.

Think upon temporal punishment for a moment. It is God's response to man's daily sin. That response is that he is righteously offended by such conduct and moves to destroy the sinner. It may be that God destroys a man through pride so that he self-destructs; he thinks he can do much more than he can and makes a terrible fiasco of his life. Other times, God may move to bring great sufferings, diseases, wars, and all sorts of calamities. This is not a pleasant thing to consider, but it is real. Look about you and consider the evidence you can see for yourself.

Then there is eternal punishment; that is even worse. This is described as everlasting torment of body and soul in the lake of fire. There is no escape from hell, and there is no relief for those who reside there. The thought is terrifying.

Why must we consider temporal and eternal punishment? It is because of the righteous judgment of God. It is judgment because God examines every fallen man, woman, and child and renders a just verdict of guilt. The guilty sinner must experience the punishment God reserves for such.

"It is appointed unto men once to die [temporal punishment], but after this the judgment [eternal punishment]" (Heb. 9:27). How can such a sinner be saved?

Jason Kortering

---

*   Heidelberg Catechism Q 8, in *Confessions and Church Order*, 86.
** Heidelberg Catechism A 10, in *Confessions and Church Order*, 86.

January 30 — Q&A 12 – Is there Escape from Punishment?

Read: Deuteronomy 27:26.

We now move from temporal and eternal punishment to the possibility of escape in question 12. We must understand the question. Escape is mentioned here, not to belittle the consequence of sin. The word is used that way sometimes, for example, a man escapes from jail. Not here; rather the idea of escape here is the jailor taking the key and unlocking the door. This is important because the question of escape from punishment is before *God!* He has the right to punish the guilty sinner, so if there is any escape from that punishment, it is God who must not only sanction it but also provide it. We can look at this question from two points of view.

From the human point of view, it is most discouraging. May God place the words of Deuteronomy 27:26 upon our hearts: "Cursed be he that confirmeth not all the words of this law to do them." The word *curse* rings with the horror of punishment. The curse is before God; it is his holy response to our guilt for sin. Not only that, the text also includes our response: "And all the people shall say, Amen" (v. 26). We not only hear God say to us, Guilty, and that implies worthy of punishment, but it also means that we agree with that pronouncement of God. Such language carries with it the horrors of God's wrath all our life and for all eternity.

From God's point of view, the question holds forth hope. The question raised by the Catechism helps us hold onto something which may lead to deliverance. "Is there no way by which we may escape that punishment and be again received into favor?"* The answer assures us there is a way of escape. True, it is on God's terms and not ours. Nevertheless, the door begins to open a little bit, and the light of God's favor begins to shine forth, and we begin to see the darkness of wrath dispelled by the light of the gospel. It is in the way of the satisfaction of that justice of God.

It follows from this answer that escape is impossible with man. The hope for salvation must focus on God and God alone. Does this question put hope in your heart?

Jason Kortering

---

* Heidelberg Catechism Q 12, in *Confessions and Church Order*, 87.

January 31 — Q&A 12 — The Need for the Satisfaction of Divine Justice

Read: Exodus 20:5.

The only escape from the punishment for sin is in the way of paying the penalty. We now face the question: why must man die if he is ever to be received into favor with God? The Catechism answers this for us, saying: "God will have his justice satisfied."[*] Justice indicates God means what he says and will act accordingly. This satisfaction includes two things.

First, God must visit "the iniquity of the fathers upon the children" (Ex. 20:5) because their sin is an expression of their hatred of God. This is why our sins offend God. He responds with justice; he rightly and according to his perfect law brings upon the guilty sinner punishment both temporal and eternal. The sinner has to bear this punishment; otherwise, God's word means nothing at all. Reflect on this and tremble before God for your sins.

Second, the guilty sinner must not only deal with the jealous God as he visits his iniquity, but more so, he has to stop hating God. This is the second part of God's sentence of death upon the sinner (it is both legal and spiritual). In his judgment, God gives man over to sin so that he finds sin his pleasure and makes a real mess of his life. Exodus 20:5 refers to God visiting the iniquity of fathers upon their children. God does not punish innocent children for parent's sins. Rather, God carries out his punishment for sin in such a way that the sins of parents become the sins of their children. See the evidence of this in today's world. Natural families do not generally improve spiritually; the children are worse than their parents. This explains why mankind and society become more wicked from generation to generation. It is due to the righteous judgment of God who punishes them.

If the fallen sinner will ever be received into the arms of divine favor, the justice of God requires that he must both pay the penalty for his sin and turn his life around so that he loves God instead of hates him.

Now you begin to understand why salvation is of the Lord; man cannot satisfy such divine justice.

Jason Kortering

---

[*] Heidelberg Catechism A 12, in *Confessions and Church Order*, 87.

February 1 — Q&A 13 — Can We Make this Satisfaction of Divine Justice?

Read: Job 9:2–3.

The Catechism answers this question this way: "By no means; but on the contrary we daily increase our debt."* Do you think you can make yourself right before God? Many people think they can. For example, the Roman Catholics think they can make up for some of their sins by doing good works. There are other churches who teach the same thing. All you have to do is to attend a funeral for some person who claimed he was a Christian and who attended a church that teaches that man earns his own way to heaven by offsetting his bad deeds with good deeds. The family and pastor will give a long list of worthy deeds done by the deceased, and the conclusion will be, he certainly is in heaven.

Is this true? Can we in any way make up for our sins by doing good? The answer here is that God is just, and when he declares that the sinner must pay for his sins by bearing temporal and eternal *punishment*, the conclusion is that man is condemned by his sins, and therefore it is impossible for him to make the payment himself. As far as man is concerned, the door to heaven is forever closed.

When Job was contending with his accusers who said he suffered much pain because God was punishing him for his sins, Job admitted that if the question was whether Job deserved to suffer for his sins, there was no doubt. He could not do anything to make himself just before God, and if the question was to contend with God for any sin, there was no hope for deliverance. With Job, however, the cause of his suffering was not punishment for sin, but God had a different purpose, to show his majesty through suffering.

Can we ever make up for any of our sins? Can we bear the punishment? Can we do some good that would offset the guilt? No, the opposite is true; we increase our debt daily.

Why is this important to God? Is salvation God and man's work, or *only* God's work? God wants us to die unto ourselves that we may live unto him.

Jason Kortering

---

* Heidelberg Catechism Q&A 13, in *Confessions and Church Order*, 87.

February 2 — **Q&A 14 — Is There a Substitute for Us?**

Read: Revelation 5:3.

We can conclude that if God will be satisfied for the sins of man, four things must take place: first, God's wrath must be carried away; second, the one to do this must do it in love for God; third, while doing it, the person must not sin; fourth, in the end the person must change the nature of the sinner so he stops sinning. Obviously, we conclude that the sinner cannot do this. Now the question is raised, what about a substitute?

The possibilities for such a substitute are given in the Catechism. What about some creature? Some animal, since they were sacrificed in the Old Testament? Some fellow human being? Could one of the saints in heaven come down and help out? Or finally, can an angel meet the needs of a substitute?

The impossibility of such a creature is indicated in two ways. Who can substitute or take the place of sinful man? God's justice requires the man who sinned must make payment. He will not transfer such punishment to another creature. The second issue is, who can bear the punishment and deliver the sinner? A mere creature cannot, because it would be destroyed by hellish wrath and be unable to deliver others. The text referenced above asserts these truths.

The vision John saw in Revelation 5 was God sitting on his heavenly throne. The book in his right hand represents the plans he has to save his church and bring the saints to glory. The question is: "Who is worthy to open the book?" (v. 2). Who can bring about the salvation of the sinner and take the church to glory? Silence in heaven is an indictment upon all creation. No one can satisfy justice and complete God's program of salvation. John weeps, for neither man nor any other creature can atone for sin. But look again. The vision focuses upon Jesus: "Weep not: behold the Lion of the tribe of Juda, the Root of David, hath prevailed to open the book" (5:5). And all heaven burst forth into singing.

We look at these verses to keep the right perspective. If there is a substitute, it must come from God alone. Salvation is of the Lord, thank God!

Jason Kortering

February 3 — Q&A 14 – What About a Mediator?

Read: Romans 8:3.

Under the judgment of God, sin brings upon man a storm of wrath and human despair. From God's point of view, we cannot make this storm too black; God instructs us to view our sin as it appears before his holy face. The lightning and thunder of Mount Sinai is real to us as well. The law cannot deliver man from the judgment of God. It can only condemn.

Then there is the question of a mediator. From a biblical point of view, the possibility of a mediator introduces sunshine and favor against the background of hopeless despair. A mediator is more than a substitute, though he is surely that. His function is more than a *human* mediator. We enjoy the function of a mediator in many human situations. For marriage problems, a mediator functions as a counselor, a neutral person who listens to all issues and renders advice that can help solve problems. Countries need mediators to come between warring nations to help solve issues and reconcile offended parties to each other. Here, the mediator takes on a very different function. He does not simply treat God and man as equals, staying neutral, working towards reconciliation for both parties. Rather, his function is to take the side of the sinner and reconcile him to God. God is the offended one, and his holy law has been willingly violated by sinful man.

Even then, to raise the possibility of a mediator is to open the door to hope and reconciliation. Hence the passage referenced above: "For what the law could not do, in that it was weak through the flesh, God sending his own Son in the likeness of sinful flesh, and for sin, condemned sin in the flesh" (Rom. 8:3). God is right in his judgment of the sinner. In justice he sentences the entire fallen human race to everlasting perdition and hell. Only God is able to produce a mediator, one who can come from God's side and meet the requirements of his holy law and bring about reconciliation.

Meditate upon the sweetness of these words. With man it is impossible, but what is impossible with man is possible with God. There is a mediator whom God provides.

Jason Kortering

February 4 — Q&A 15 — The Qualifications of a Mediator

Read: Isaiah 7:14.

We saw how our hope is concentrated in a possible mediator. Sinful man cannot do what it takes to be right with God. We need a mediator. Now the Catechism focuses on what sort of a mediator we need. The answer given is that he must be "one who is very man, and perfectly righteous; and yet more powerful than all creatures; that is, one who is also very God."[*] No wonder, we conclude, that such a mediator can never be produced by the fallen human race; only God can bring forth such a mediator. Let's meditate briefly on the qualifications presented here.

He must be a righteous man. We will not now go into all the reasons why this is so, rather, let's simply look at such a qualification in itself. The mediator must be a righteous man. Where will we ever find such a person? There are plenty of men around. The human race has continued to produce children; one of the most interesting activities is to trace genealogies. You probably do this from time to time. Yes, indeed, we have parents, siblings, grandparents, great-grandparents; some may be able to look back and count five generations. The remarkable thing about all of them is they are all sinners; they were conceived and born in sin. Not one of our immediate relatives, much less our distant past relatives, is qualified to be a mediator, for none are righteous, no, not one.

He must also be powerful, that is, one who is very God. There may be many people who are so proud that they like to think they are as great as a god; some have delusions of imagining themselves to be a god. Sometimes proud man is so delusional, but it can never be factual. Man can only bring forth man, not God and man.

The word of the Lord came through Isaiah when he prophesied the coming of the mediator: "*The Lord* himself shall give you a sign; Behold, a *virgin* shall conceive, and bear a son, and shall call his name Immanuel [God with us]" (Isa. 7:14). These are the qualifications of the needed mediator. Only *the Lord* can give him, not only as a sign, but in reality.

Jason Kortering

---

[*] Heidelberg Catechism A 15, in *Confessions and Church Order*, 88.

Lord's Day 6

Q. 16. Why must he be very man, and also perfectly righteous?

A. Because the justice of God requires that the same human nature which hath sinned should likewise make satisfaction for sin; and one who is himself a sinner cannot satisfy for others.

Q. 17. Why must he in one person be also very God?

A. That he might, by the power of his Godhead, sustain in his human nature the burden of God's wrath; and might obtain for, and restore to us, righteousness and life.

Q. 18. Who then is that Mediator, who is in one person both very God and a real righteous man?

A. Our Lord Jesus Christ, *who of God is made unto us wisdom, and righteousness, and sanctification, and redemption.*

Q. 19. Whence knowest thou this?

A. From the holy gospel, which God himself first revealed in Paradise; and afterwards published by the patriarchs and prophets, and represented by the sacrifices and other ceremonies of the law; and, lastly, has fulfilled it by his only begotten Son.

February 5 — Q&A 16 – The Mediator Must be a Righteous Man

Read: Isaiah 53:11.

The Catechism reiterates here that if someone is going to take the place of sinful man, he has to be not only a man, but even more than a man; he has to be a sinless or righteous man. The Catechism says: "The justice of God requires that the same human nature which hath sinned should likewise make satisfaction for sin."* What does it mean that the same human nature must bear the consequences of sin?

Adam's sin was a willful act on his part. God did not force Adam to sin or trick him into sin. When Eve came to Adam with the fruit of the forbidden tree, it was desirable and something they both wanted. Hence when they disobeyed God, they did it freely; they chose to do this, knowing full well it was against God's clear instruction: "In the day that thou eatest thereof thou shalt surely die" (Gen. 2:17).

If sinful man is going to make payment for this act of disobedience, the sinner in his own human nature must do so as an act of obedience. He must freely desire to do this and take the consequence of his sin willingly. The price for sin is everlasting separation from God's favor and, instead of experiencing favor, to be doomed to the torments of his hellish wrath. To make atonement, man has to say to God, You are right. I deserve this punishment. Now as an act of love I will bear this punishment because I want to return to your fellowship and favor. Nowhere in the human race is there a man qualified to do this for himself or for other sinners. No one *wants* to bear God's hellish wrath, much less is able to. The reason for this is that fallen man is not righteous before God. His will is captured by the power of sin. He is content to revel in his sin, make excuses for it, and even blame God for everything that goes wrong in his life.

The good news of the gospel is that there is a *righteous* man. Isaiah calls him "my righteous servant." That is Jesus; he shall "justify many" and "bear their iniquities" (53:11).

Blessed be God who provides a righteous man for us!

Jason Kortering

---

* Heidelberg Catechism A 16, in *Confessions and Church Order*, 88.

February 6 — Q&A 17 – Only God Can Atone for Sin

Read: 1 Peter 3:18.

The Catechism here asserts that the mediator must in one person be very God. The reason for this is that by his Godhead he sustains his human nature to enable it to bear the wrath of God and, also by that same Godhead, is able to save the sinner and restore him to righteousness and life. The mediator must be personally God for two reasons. Here we consider the first.

He must bear the suffering of the pain of hell and make an end to that by satisfying God. The Bible teaches that the guilty sinner is cast into hell to remain there forever. The penalty for sin is everlasting hell because it is against "the most high majesty of God."* To deliver the sinner from this suffering, the mediator must be able to take the place of the sinner and take that *everlasting* wrath of God upon himself and bring it to a close because God accepts his suffering as payment.

How can anyone bear such terrible suffering? No mere human being can do that. Such a man would succumb to such suffering; he would die of shock. The qualification of our mediator is that he must be both God and man in order that his divinity might strengthen his humanity to bear God's just wrath against sin and satisfy God.

How can such suffering have everlasting value? We know that Jesus suffered the pains of hell while he was on the cross during the three hours of darkness. That suffering had everlasting value because Jesus is truly God.

The text referenced above expresses it well: "Christ also hath once suffered for sins, the just for the unjust, that he might bring us to God, being *put to death in the flesh, but quickened by the Spirit*" (1 Pet. 3:18). To be just, he could not be the product of Adam's human race. He had to come down from the Father, being very God, and take on human flesh. In that flesh, he was able to suffer hellish wrath, bear it, and bring it to an end. Our mediator meets the qualifications; he is a righteous man and personally God. He made atonement for our sins.

Put your trust in him alone.

Jason Kortering

---

* Heidelberg Catechism A 11, in *Confessions and Church Order*, 87.

February 7   Q&A 17 — Only God Can Deliver Man from Sin

Read: 2 Timothy 1:9–10.

I mentioned that there are two reasons why the mediator must be more than a righteous man; he must be very God. The first we considered already, that he must be God in order to bear the punishment God placed on our sins: everlasting wrath and hell. Now we focus on the second reason: he must be very God, as the Catechism says: "That he might obtain for, and restore to us, righteousness and life."* He must make the dead sinner spiritually good and alive.

Those of us who care about the salvation of those who are not Christians can testify to this important qualification of our mediator. Man cannot save himself; neither can fellow man save his neighbor. We may carry in our hearts the *desire* to save, we may put forth the *effort* to save—by this I refer to our effort to share the gospel with them—yet we know in our hearts that only God by the Holy Spirit can convert and change them. That Holy Spirit is given to our mediator who is more than a righteous man, he is very God, and only God can bring forth life out of death.

The words of Timothy explain this. He refers to God who has brought salvation, and he has done this through Jesus Christ. He describes that work of salvation as twofold; first he "abolished death." That he did on the cross. The mediator was very God and bore the punishment of death. But more, he also "brought life and immortality to light through the gospel" (2 Tim. 1:10). Bringing forth that life and immortality is the work of our mediator as his victory over spiritual death right now.

This is most encouraging for us. We have a mediator who not only paid for the sins of his own but also has the power to deliver every one of them from the dominion of sin and the devil. That is his qualification and that is his ministry all through history. He uses the gospel as his means.

Let's celebrate our great God and Mediator who is abundantly qualified to save.

Jason Kortering

---

*   Heidelberg Catechism A 17, in *Confessions and Church Order*, 88.

February 8   **Q&A 18 — Our Lord Jesus Christ is That Mediator**

Read: 1 Peter 3:18.

You may have noticed that as we examined the qualifications for our mediator given by the Bible and summarized by the Catechism, it is impossible to be abstract and theoretical. Each time we examined one of the details, we had to relate it to Jesus. The reason is obvious; our mediator is not a thought or an idea to be set forth like the chapter of a book. He is our life and hope. Hence we could not keep silent as to who he is; we had to make reference to him as the one who alone is qualified to reconcile us to God.

The Catechism now sets him forth in all his glory: "Who then is that Mediator, who is in one person both very God and a real righteous man? *Our Lord Jesus Christ*!"* He meets all the qualifications.

He is a righteous man, as we read in the Matthew account, which quotes Isaiah 7:14, "Behold, a virgin shall be with child, and shall bring forth a son, and they shall call his name, Emmanuel, which being interpreted is, God with us" (Matt. 1:23). The Virgin Mary could not understand how she could become pregnant without a male. The answer was reassuring: "The Holy Ghost shall come upon thee, and the power of the Highest shall overshadow thee: therefore also that holy thing which shall be born of thee shall be called the Son of GInod" (Luke 1:35).

No wonder his name is Immanuel, God with us. He is a real human being who received his human nature from the Virgin Mary. He is also a divine person, as the Holy Spirit fathered him and brought forth the Son of God. Thus, the text referenced above indicates that Christ was the just one who suffered for the unjust. Christ was sinless and thus he was able to offer himself as a substitute for sinners. He was "put to death in the flesh;" this tells us that he accomplished atonement on our behalf. He was "quickened by the Spirit" to make us alive (1 Pet. 3:18).

Children of God say together: "Our Lord Jesus Christ." I trust he is yours as well.

Jason Kortering

---

*   Heidelberg Catechism Q&A 18, in *Confessions and Church Order*, 89 (emphasis added).

February 9 — Q&A 19 — The Knowledge of the Mediator by the Holy Gospel

Read: Romans 1:16.

The gospel is good news, but good news kept secret is not good. The good news of the gospel is that we have a mediator, our Lord Jesus Christ. He is the one who paid the debt of sin and restores us to favor with God. There is nothing more good than such news. The question the Catechism now poses is this: How do you know about the mediator? The answer is: "From the holy gospel."[*] The word *gospel* means good news.

God in his mercy always announces that good news to fallen sinners. The salvation which he provides in our Lord Jesus Christ is in his heart, and from the moment man fell into sin until the present, even unto the end of the world, God is busy heralding forth this good news by which he saves fallen mankind.

The heart of the gospel and its message is salvation through Jesus Christ. This Paul acknowledges: "The gospel of Christ...is the *power* of God unto salvation" (Rom. 1:16). The reason for this is because it is the gospel of Christ. God, through Jesus Christ our mediator, has reconciled the sinner unto himself. Being both God and man, Jesus is qualified to make this reconciliation. As the angel announced to Joseph at his birth: "She shall bring forth a son, and thou shalt call his name JESUS: for he shall save his people from their sins" (Matt. 1:21). It is good news for his people. The apostle Paul defines these people as "everyone that believeth...the Jew first, and also...the Greek" (Rom. 1:16).

God is very honest with us as he communicates to us the holy gospel. He strips us of all pride and self-worth. Only undeserving and unworthy sinners will turn to Jesus by faith and embrace him as their savior. The first work of grace in your heart and mine that prepares us for the good news of Jesus is that we *need* him.

Do you see yourself as a lost sinner, separated from God, worthy of everlasting hell? God sets forth Jesus in the gospel. He calls you to receive him and believe in him as your mediator.

Jason Kortering

---

[*] Heidelberg Catechism Q&A 19, in *Confessions and Church Order*, 89.

February 10 — **Q&A 19 — Christ was the Mediator of the Old Covenant**

Read: Romans 1:1–3.

The old covenant is the name given to the church prior to the birth of Jesus. During that time, God communicated the knowledge of the mediator in different ways. Already in the garden of Eden, God spoke directly to Adam and Eve; this is called a *theophany*. Once when he spoke to Satan, he told Satan that there would be a war between the people whom he would save by the mediator and those who would follow Satan's evil ways. That war would end in the coming of Jesus, who would destroy Satan and all his followers (Gen. 3:15).

During the days of the old covenant, God reminded his people that the mediator would come to cover their sins by instructing them to sacrifice animals. By the shedding of the blood of the substitute (a lamb), God declared to them the gospel of the coming mediator. He held before their eyes a very effective picture of the cross of Jesus, who would come as the mediator in the future. He added to this many ceremonies of the law. The Old Testament Jews had special festivals in which they commemorated the shedding of blood as the covering for sin. One such example is the first feast of the Passover, in which they placed blood on the door posts of their tents to remind them of the night in Egypt when the angel of death passed over them and did not kill their firstborn sons. That blood was a picture of their mediator.

In the reference above, Paul mentions prophets. God also sent prophets to the old covenant people, who told them that their sins would be covered by God's Lamb, upon whom God would lay the iniquity of us all. One such prophet was Isaiah. Read Isaiah 53 for an example of such a prophetic message.

It is good for us to reflect upon this gospel given in the old covenant. There is only *one* mediator and *one* gospel because there is only *one* people of God whom God saves in Jesus Christ. Because of this, we benefit from our reading and study of the Old Testament (the old covenant).

Jason Kortering

February 11 — Q&A 19 — Christ is the Mediator of the New Covenant

Read: Romans 10:4.

Now we can reflect with great thankfulness that Jesus is indeed God's mediator. He is qualified from every point of view; he is personally God, the second person of the Trinity. He is a real man, having been born of Mary. He is a righteous man who is without personal sin, because he was born of the Virgin Mary.

With such qualification, he completed our redemption, he paid for our sins, and God received his suffering and death as a substitute for ours. God raised him from the dead to certify our righteousness in him. One conclusion follows from this: there is only one mediator between God and man, and that is Christ Jesus.

We must make one final point before we leave this Lord's Day of the Catechism. The only way we can be sure that this Jesus is *our* mediator is through faith in him. This is the point of the verse referenced above: "Christ is the *end* of the law for righteousness" (Rom. 10:4). The law refers to the law given by God from Mount Sinai. That law states, Do this and live. Fallen sinful man cannot keep the law in order to be righteous before God. According to the law, there is no hope for man to be received into favor with God. Now we read: "Christ is the end of the law for righteousness." In Jesus Christ there is righteousness because he paid the debt of the law, which is death, and kept the letter of the law, which is righteousness.

This righteousness which is in Christ Jesus is ours by means of faith in him. And this is true for all mankind. There is no righteousness before God for anyone in the world except through faith in the righteousness which Jesus merited for us.

Two things follow from this. First, how important it is that you and I be sure that we believe in Jesus for our righteousness and commit our lives to serve him. Second, how important it is to get the gospel out so that others may learn about Jesus and commit their lives to serve him.

The new covenant is God's gracious covenant; may he be pleased to use preaching and witnessing to gain others for Christ.

Jason Kortering

Lord's Day 7

Q. 20. Are all men then, as they perished in Adam, saved by Christ?

A. No, only those who are ingrafted into him, and receive all his benefits, by a true faith.

Q. 21. What is true faith?

A. True faith is not only a certain knowledge, whereby I hold for truth all that God has revealed to us in his Word, but also an assured confidence, which the Holy Ghost works by the gospel in my heart; that not only to others, but to me also, remission of sin, everlasting righteousness, and salvation are, freely given by God, merely of grace, only for the sake of Christ's merits.

Q. 22. What is then necessary for a Christian to believe?

A. All things promised us in the gospel, which the articles of our catholic undoubted Christian faith briefly teach us.

Q. 23. What are these articles?

A. *1. I believe in God the Father, Almighty, Maker of heaven and earth;*
2. And in Jesus Christ, His only begotten Son, our Lord;
3. Who was conceived by the Holy Ghost, born of the Virgin Mary;
4. Suffered under Pontius Pilate; was crucified, dead, and buried; he descended into hell;
5. The third day he rose again from the dead;
6. He ascended into heaven, and sitteth at the right hand of God the Father Almighty;
7. From thence he shall come to judge the quick and the dead.
8. I believe in the Holy Ghost.
9. I believe an holy catholic church; the communion of saints;
10. The forgiveness of sins;
11. The resurrection of the body;
12. And the life everlasting. Amen.

February 12 — Q&A 20 — Who Then is Saved by the Mediator, Jesus Christ?

Read: Matthew 1:21.

Having set forth the credentials necessary for Jesus to be the mediator, and having set forth the glorious fact that he is not hidden but set forth boldly in the gospel through all ages, the Catechism now addresses the important question: "Whom does this mediator, Jesus, really save?" Many different answers are given to this question. They usually fall into two groups

First, there are those who emphasize that man determines for himself whether he will be saved. You are familiar with them because they are the most vocal and probably the most prolific. They suggest that God has done everything he could to save: he gave his Son, he wrote out a check to atone for every human being to make their salvation possible; now man has to endorse the check, he has to accept Jesus as his savior in order to make it effective. The Catechism asks: "Are all men then, as they perished in Adam, saved by Christ?"* These people answer: all men *could* be saved *if* they desired it. The will of man makes the determination.

Second, there are those who follow the Catechism here and are known as Reformed believers (they are called this because they hold to the truths set forth in the sixteenth century Reformation). Men like Martin Luther and John Calvin were leaders in this work. Reformed believers believe that the Bible teaches that God wills to save a certain people whom he chose in eternity and that he gave Jesus to die for them and sends the gospel to them so that they might believe. An example of such a Bible text is referenced above; Jesus is called Jesus "for he shall save *his people* from their sins" (Matt. 1:21). Jesus was aware of the fact that God, his Father, willed to save only some of the human race when he said in John 17:9, "I pray not for the world, but for them which thou hast given me; for they are thine."

These passages guide the authors of the Catechism to answer the question who is saved by stating: "*Only* those who are ingrafted into [Christ], and receive all his benefits, by a true faith."**

Not man but God determines who is saved.

Jason Kortering

---

* Heidelberg Catechism Q 20, in *Confessions and Church Order*, 90.
** Heidelberg Catechism A 20, in *Confessions and Church Order*, 90 (emphasis added).

February 13   Q&A 20 — Faith Both Ingrafting and Receiving

Read: John 1:12–13.

When the Catechism states that the saved ones are ingrafted into Christ, it emphasizes that salvation begins and ends with God. The writers use the biblical figure of speech as Jesus did in John 15 where he teaches that he is the vine and God the husbandman who joins each branch to him in order to make them alive (John 15:1–2). "Without me," he says, "ye can do nothing" (v. 5). This helps us understand the importance of our union with Christ, for he adds: "Abide in me and I in you. As the branch cannot bear fruit of itself, except it abide in the vine, no more can ye, except ye abide in me" (v. 4). There is an important relationship between ingrafting and receiving.

The sinful and spiritually dead sinner cannot join himself to Jesus, cannot accept him as his personal savior, unless he is first made alive. This sinner is made alive through the ingrafting. Just like the farmer who takes a branch, which is considered dead apart from the vine, and unites it to the vine, God takes the dead sinner and unites him to Christ through the act of ingrafting. The union between vine and branch is completed. The living sap of the vine passes through the graft and causes the branch to live. Life does not go from the branch to the vine but from the vine to the branch. Jesus is the living vine, and God joins each one for whom he shed his blood to him at his appointed time in history. Once that graft takes place, the dead sinner becomes alive.

Proof of the power of spiritual life is that the sinner comes to behold by faith *who* God is, the sovereign and holy one. Before him the sinner is convicted of his sin. He weeps on account of his sins and looks to God with sorrow of heart. Jesus is mediator for *all* who are burdened by their sins (Matt. 11:28–30).

Now such a convicted sinner is ready to receive Jesus as his mediator with thankful heart. By receiving Jesus, he receives power to become a son of God. He admits he is such not by his own will but by the will of God.

Jason Kortering

February 14 — Q&A 21 — Faith Has Conviction of Truth

Read: John 17:3.

Once we are engrafted into Christ Jesus by faith, our hearts are filled with his love. His love for us and our responding love for him affects our minds. Under the influence of that love, we "hold for truth all that God has revealed to us in his Word."*

Knowledge of the universe is exploding around us every day. In our high-tech generation, we pride ourselves in being able to gain access to information. We cannot possibly retain in our human brain all the things that we learn through reading, television, computer research via the internet, on and on. It is not so much what we know but where we can find it. Most of this information we view as formal knowledge, objective truth. As Christians we learn this and process this as any other human being.

But the knowledge of faith is different. From a heart that loves God, we view this information in the light of God's divine revelation, the Bible. The center of this knowledge is God, the creator and sustainer of the universe. Apart from Jesus, the knowledge of God works terror and judgment. But the knowledge of God through Jesus his Son brings purpose and direction to this fallen world. We know that Jesus is savior of his people and is now exalted and reigns over all things to bring them to their conclusion in his kingdom in the new heaven and earth. We learn the truth of history, science, medicine, etc. in the light of the word of God.

More than that, we love God and are thankful that Jesus is *our* Savior and Lord. The truth of the Bible is personally embraced and precious to us. "This is life eternal," we personally know God and his Son, Jesus (John 17:3). This knowledge, which we hold for truth as Christians, sets us at odds with the unbelieving world about us. Those who do not have Christian faith limit their focus upon things seen and do not have the ability to see with the eyes of faith which are illuminated by the word of God. The difference is the knowledge of faith and knowledge limited by unbelief.

As a Christian, do you have conviction of truth, both objective and personal?

Jason Kortering

---

* Heidelberg Catechism A 21, in *Confessions and Church Order*, 90.

February 15 — Q&A 21 — Faith Has Assurance of Personal Salvation

Read: Ephesians 3:12.

Once we are engrafted into Christ Jesus by faith, our hearts are filled with his love. His love for us and our responding love for him affect not only our minds but also our wills. As the Catechism expresses it, faith is "also an assured confidence, which the Holy Ghost works by the gospel in my heart, that not only to others, but to me also, remission of sin, everlasting righteousness, and salvation are, freely given by God, merely of grace, only for the sake of Christ's merits."[*] We are convicted of our personal salvation.

All Christians have conviction of the truth (knowledge); they also possess conviction or assurance of personal salvation. We must not say that it is possible to possess true faith without this conviction. It is inherent in the work of salvation that from hearts filled with God's love we are able to receive our own salvation as a wonder of grace and possess with certainty that we are saved.

Notice with me why we are sure of our own personal salvation. Not because I am good enough for God, and he ought to accept me into his covenant because of who I am or how I have lived. If we truly have the work of grace in our hearts, our sins always cause burden and shame. Even our good works are not reason for acceptance by God because these works are still stained with sin and are never grounds for our acceptance.

Neither are we sure because we have accepted Jesus as our Savior, as if an act of our will makes all the difference with God. If you are in touch with your own spiritual condition, even now as a child of God, you know that your will still vacillates between wanting God and wanting the pleasure of sin. If we look at our own inner desires, we lose all assurance. Rather, our assurance is by way of looking to Jesus by the Holy Spirit. We focus on who we are *in* and *through* Jesus Christ our Savior. He has made us righteous, which is the grounds for our forgiveness of sin. He has made us holy, which is the proof of our union with Christ.

I encourage you not to look to yourself, but to Jesus for your full assurance of salvation. In him we have boldness and can approach God with confidence.

Jason Kortering

---

[*] Heidelberg Catechism A 21, in *Confessions and Church Order*, 90–91.

February 16 — Q&A 21 — Faith Worked by the Holy Spirit Through the Gospel

Read: Romans 10:17.

Now we must focus on one more aspect of faith and salvation. True faith focuses on Jesus as savior; it does that because the word of God explains that Jesus is the only savior. When we are engrafted into him, we are filled with his love so that we gladly embrace all that he says as true and rejoice when he assures us of our personal salvation. The conclusion is that faith is the most important experience. Of more than passing interest is, how do we obtain this faith?

Here too, the Catechism emphasizes that it does not have its roots in man himself. This is no small point when we consider how many in the church world emphasize that faith is the work of man. Oh, yes, they say that it is all of God, even all of grace, but God will not give his grace to anyone who does not of his own will seek it. The tragedy of this emphasis is that man's will is unable to seek after God or to "accept Jesus" as they say. God must work upon the human will and change it in order for man to will and seek after God.

The beautiful point of the Catechism here is that God does this by means of the gospel. Faith is worked by the Holy Spirit through the gospel. To embrace this truth, we must admit our own human depravity and be thankful to God that he enables us to do what we cannot do apart from him.

The apostle Paul expresses it beautifully in Romans 10:17, "So then faith cometh by hearing and hearing by the word of God." In the context, Paul explains that everyone who calls "upon the name of the Lord shall be saved" (v. 13). That is the external evidence of faith that the Holy Spirit works. Remember the jailor: "Sirs, what must I do to be saved?" (Acts 16:30). How does one come to call on the Lord? Paul answers this in Romans 10:17, "So then faith cometh by hearing, and hearing by the word of God." The Spirit works through the preached word.

Have you heard the word? Do you respond by believing? If you do, it is the proof of the Holy Spirit working true faith in you.

Jason Kortering

February 17   Q&A 22 — What is Necessary for a Christian to Believe?

Read: John 20:31.

The Catechism raises a rather rare question here: "What is then necessary for a Christian to believe?"* I suggest it is rare in that it seems that in the ecclesiastical world today, *what* you believe is of little import. We are encountering an ecumenical spirit, that is, one that wants all Christian churches to join together, and if that can't happen, at least to have a common expression of Christianity among all Christians. To get this, many belittle objective faith; they say that statements of belief are of little consequence. It is not important what you believe, simply that you do believe, is their conclusion. The Bible can be interpreted in many ways; doctrine which consists of the teachings of any given church are declared to be important for *that* church but not necessary for every Christian. In the most extreme case, one concludes that some churches would say that it is not necessary that you believe *anything*, simply confess that you need Jesus or some such statement.

Here we have it that there are some things *necessary* for a Christian to believe. These are so important that unless a person believes these things, he or she is not a true Christian. That sounds both strange but also refreshing to hear. What might it be that is necessary for a Christian to believe? The answer is: "All things promised us in the gospel."** The reference above indicates that the heart of the gospel is that Jesus is the Christ (the anointed mediator of the covenant) who himself is the Son of God (truly God), and that in him there is salvation and life through his name (John 20:31). This is necessary because without this faith there is no salvation. Belief in man himself, belief in any human that might seem outstanding, belief in any other god, whether heathen religion or western philosophy, ends in death. There is salvation in no other name than Jesus. God has provided his Son as our savior and in him there *is* salvation. All who confess their sins and acknowledge that the blood of Jesus covers them have the evidence of eternal life.

Once more, do you believe all that the gospel conveys? This is necessary and opens the door to everlasting life.

Jason Kortering

---

*   Heidelberg Catechism Q 22, in *Confessions and Church Order*, 91.
**   Heidelberg Catechism A 22, in *Confessions and Church Order*, 91.

February 18   **Q&A 22-23 — Truth of the Gospel Summarized in the Articles of Faith**

Read: Matthew 28:19–20.

The great commission that our Lord Jesus gave his disciples was to teach and baptize with the assurance that he would be with his people always, even to the end of the world. The Catechism instructs us to believe all things promised us in the gospel. Now it adds: "Which the articles of our catholic undoubted Christian faith briefly teach us."*

A summary of faith is useful. It sounds very pious to say that we believe the Bible and refuse to accept any creed or statement of faith which summarizes what the Bible teaches. In fact, it is impossible to refuse to summarize one's faith; proof is that every church and every group that professes to be Christian has a statement of faith.

The early Christian church also saw the need for such a summary statement. Today we call this summary the Apostles' Creed, not because the apostles wrote it, but rather because it was written in the early centuries of the church to summarize the teachings of the apostles. In our Catechism, it is called "our catholic undoubted Christian faith." It contains twelve articles and has been recited and quoted by the church of all ages, hence it is called catholic. The term is not a reference to the Roman Catholic Church, but *catholic* is used in the proper sense of *universal*, a statement of faith expressed from the days of the apostles until the present. It is also described as Christian faith because it expresses the truth which every Christian has professed. Christians take the Bible very seriously and realize that it is not up to every individual to determine the content of his or her faith, but we are to do it in common together and to involve the church in officially adopting such a statement. It also is undoubted, that is, it is an expression of faith which every Christian holds to be true without any reservation.

It is sad that many churches today pay lip service to these twelve articles but put different meanings into them. The church that apostatizes uses the same terminology but changes the meaning. We are thankful that the Catechism professes that these articles summarize the truth of the gospel, which is essential for faith.

I trust your heart is open to meditate upon these articles and embrace them by faith.

Jason Kortering

---

*   Heidelberg Catechism A 22, in *Confessions and Church Order*, 91.

February 19 — Q&A 21-23 — God Is the Object of Our Faith

Read: 1 Peter 1:21.

You notice that 1 Peter 1:21 makes it plain that our faith is focused upon God. This means two things.

First, it indicates that when we confess our faith to others, we speak about our God. God is the subject of this conversation. The crisis of all world religions is: "Who is God?" The distinguishing thing about the Christian religion is that it openly and without reservation makes known the name of our God. He is the one and only true God of heaven and earth. When we teach our children concerning faith, we speak to them about our God. We tell them the history of his revelation given in the Bible, and we help them focus upon the salvation which God alone has provided for us. When we encourage one another with the comfort so necessary in this life, we share with them the comfort that comes from our God.

Second, when we make this confession about God to others, we do this in the presence of and before the face of this God. We are aware of God's divine involvement in all the affairs of men, most of all in our own affairs. We want God to hear our confession. We want God to pay attention to activities as we relate to other human beings because in this way we praise him and bring glory to him. By faith we give recognition that he is our God.

In one word, God is the *object* of our faith.

There is a reason for this. That reason is that when God bestows upon us true and living faith, we enter into a covenant relationship with him. By faith we realize that we are what we are and we become what we become because of God's wonderful work of salvation in us. It is amazing to us that Almighty God, Creator God, Sovereign God loves us and takes us into his friendship. He raised Jesus from the dead, and now he also raises us from spiritual death (1 Pet. 1:21).

Faith reaches up to him and confesses to him and speaks about him concerning the joy of that fellowship. Our faith and hope is in God alone.

Jason Kortering

Lord's Day 8

Q. 24. How are these articles divided?

A. Into three parts: the first is of God the Father and our creation; the second, of God the Son and our redemption; the third, of God the Holy Ghost and our sanctification.

Q. 25. Since there is but one only divine essence, why speakest thou of Father, Son, and Holy Ghost?

A. Because God hath so revealed himself in his Word, that these three distinct persons are the one only true and eternal God.

February 20 — **Q&A 25 — God Is One Divine Essence**

Read: Deuteronomy 6:4.

The first article of the Apostles' Creed is: "I believe in God."* We noticed already that this God is the object of our faith. We make confession to him and about him in the love of his friendship established with us. Two things have to be said about this God as the object of our faith.

First, we confess that he is the *only* God. This is demonstrated over and over in the Old Covenant. The passage referenced above consists of the words of Moses as he summarized for Israel the instruction given to them in Mount Sinai. One thing is for sure, Jehovah is *one* Jehovah; this means that there *is* only one Jehovah, and he is not a god among many gods; rather, he is the one and *only* God there is. The history which followed demonstrated that Jehovah put down all the supposed gods of Egypt. He killed with a mighty hand the dwellers in the land of Canaan who worshipped other gods. How could he do this? Think about Mount Carmel in the days of the prophet Elijah. Let the living and true God answer by fire. Baal and Ashtoreth remained silent while Jehovah consumed the altar and the land with fire. The people shouted: "The LORD [Jehovah], he is *the* God" (1 Kings 18:39). So through the ages, Jehovah is the same, the one only true God.

Second, he is three persons: Father, Son, and Holy Spirit. We will see later that even though God revealed himself as three persons, he nevertheless is *one* God, not three. The Catechism expresses it this way: "Why speakest thou of Father, Son, and Holy Ghost? Because God hath so revealed himself in his Word, that these three distinct persons are the one only true and eternal God."**

We speak of this one and only true and eternal God as a description of the *essence* of God. God's nature or composition (so to speak) is that he possesses one mind, one will, one heart as he relates to others. We can say this because God made man in his image, and we know the image of God is what distinguishes man from animals or other creatures. Man thinks, man has feeling, man desires, man loves, and these things reflect his creator.

The Lord our God is *one*.

Jason Kortering

---

* Heidelberg Catechism A 23, in *Confessions and Church Order*, 91.
** Heidelberg Catechism Q&A 25, in *Confessions and Church Order*, 92.

February 21 — Q&A 25 – God Is Three Persons

Read: 1 John 5:7.

One of the great mysteries concerning our God is that he is triune. This word is made up of two words; the first can be translated *one* and the other word can be translated *three*. Hence we conclude the confession of the historic Christian faith is that we have one God who has three persons. Three persons subsist in one being. That states briefly what we mean by *triune* or *Trinity*. We considered before what is included in the one being or nature of God.

Now we have to say a brief word about the three persons. A person is an individual who has the ability to think, to will, to talk, to enjoy friendship. Among all the creatures God has made, only human beings, who are created human persons, have this ability. God is three divine persons who function in the one divine nature. To express this somewhat simply, the three persons, Father, Son, and Holy Spirit all function as persons within the one divine nature. They think in the one mind of God but think individually as persons. They desire as persons, they express joy, sorrow, anger as persons. They do all these things in the one heart and will of God.

Each person possesses his own personality and distinct qualities. Thus, each person thinks individually yet is united in the one mind of God. They are divine, co-equal and co-eternal God, yet distinct from each other. They complement each other and contribute to the personal relationship they enjoy within the Godhead.

The Catechism acknowledges this is impossible to comprehend, and it sets God apart from man in his own being and nature. We can at least understand that this allows for God's majesty and power. It is important for us to be humble and accept these truths concerning God. We do this by the simple statement of faith: "God hath so revealed himself in his Word."* Think of the passage referenced above and look at John 14:16, "I will pray the Father, and he shall give you another Comforter, that he may abide with you forever." The Son prays to the Father that he will give the Holy Spirit to his children to comfort them.

The truth of the Trinity is not man-made; it is divinely revealed.

Jason Kortering

---

* Heidelberg Catechism A 25, in *Confessions and Church Order*, 92.

February 22 — Q&A 24 — All That We Believe Involves the Trinity

Read: Matthew 28:19.

The Catechism expressed that it is necessary for us to believe everything that is included in the gospel. The Apostles' Creed summarizes for us this faith and reduces it to twelve short statements of faith. We call these the twelve articles of faith. Now we learn that every one of these articles is an expression of the Trinity. The question is raised: "How are these articles divided?" The answer is: "Into three parts: the first is of God the Father and our creation; the second, of God the Son and our redemption; and the third, of God the Holy Ghost and our sanctification."* The expression of our faith in God the Father is article 1. This is followed by our faith in God the Son which includes articles 2–7. Finally, faith in God the Holy Spirit includes articles 8–12.

No wonder then that Jesus instructed his church to baptize new converts in the name of the Father, of the Son, and of the Holy Ghost. These three persons are the ones who bring about our salvation.

Because our faith is in a personal God, it is expressed as having all three persons as the object of faith. The first is of God the Father and our creation. The Son is involved in creation as John expressed it: "All things were made by him; and without him was not anything made that was made" (1:3). The Holy Spirit was involved in creation: "And the Spirit of God moved upon the face of the waters" (Gen. 1:2). The Father obviously spoke, "Let there be light" (Gen. 1:3); his role is the leading role in creation.

The second is of God the Son and our redemption. Again, the Father is involved: "God [as Father] so loved the world that he gave his only begotten Son" (John 3:16). The Son came into this world (Matt. 1:21), and the Holy Spirit came upon the Virgin Mary (Luke 1:35). The Son assumes the key role in redemption.

The third is of God the Holy Ghost and our sanctification. This Spirit is sent from the Father, by Jesus, into this world (John 14:16–17). The Spirit is the key person in making us holy.

Thus we believe in the Trinity: God, three persons in one divine being.

Jason Kortering

---

* Heidelberg Catechism Q&A 24, in *Confessions and Church Order*, 92.

| February 23 | Q&A 24 — Faith in God the Father |

Read: Luke 3:22.

It is not so easy to quote texts from the Bible that specifically demonstrate the first person of the Trinity. The above reference is an example. God could not say the statement, "Thou art my beloved Son" (Luke 3:22), unless he was the first person speaking to the second person. Nevertheless, on the foreground is not the first and second person but God triune as Father speaking to Jesus as the mediator of the covenant. Behind this statement, nevertheless, is the wonderful truth that God is the first person of the holy Trinity. As we pointed out before, as Father, he assumes the leading role in the creation not only, but also in the sending of his Son and the sending forth of the Holy Spirit. God as Father has an important role in all aspects of creation, redemption, and sanctification. The point is that if he were not the first person as Father, he could not be involved as he is in all aspects of salvation.

There is something important about God the Father. He has made a human analogy within the human family. A father is the one who initiates the formation of a new family by taking the initiative in marriage, by taking a wife. Living with such a wife in love, children are conceived and brought forth. This father nurtures and cares for these children and meets their needs. This is a reflection of God our Father.

Because God is Father, he initiates within the Godhead a covenant of friendship. Love emanates from the Father to the Son and in the Holy Spirit. Already apart from creation, and long before time began, the Father functions in originating (humanly speaking) the divine friendship which is the pattern for covenant friendship with his creatures when time begins. In the creation, he functions as Father, giving origin and persistence to his creation.

Even after the fall, the Father takes on his great role of fathering children out of sin and death, and who by nature are children of the devil, and makes them his dear children. God as Father ultimately takes to himself the perfect family in the perfect creation through Jesus Christ his only begotten Son.

When the Father says to Jesus, "Thou art my *beloved* Son," we embrace our Father with joy.

Jason Kortering

February 24 — Q&A 24 – Faith in God the Son

Read: John 1:1.

In connection with the person of the Son, it is easy to demonstrate that he is a person within the Godhead (a term we use to refer to the one divine being we call God, who lives in covenant friendship as three persons). This is important because there are many within Christianity who claim to teach the Trinity but actually deny it. How do they deny the Trinity? They deny the Trinity by insisting that God is *not* three persons but three modalities, three ways of revelation. God, then, is one person who manifests himself in three ways, as a Father, as a Son, and as a Spirit. Heretics throughout the ages have opposed the doctrine of the Trinity by using such reasoning. They do this because they insist that the idea of three persons subsisting in one divine being is too philosophical and abstract. It is important that our Catechism answered their false reasoning by simply stating: "God has so revealed himself to us in his Word."* That is the key issue: do we let God tell us who he is, or do we make God to be what we want him to be? If we make him to be how we want him, this is idolatry.

I say, God the Son as a divine person can be demonstrated. Psalm 2:7 is a declaration to the Son in eternity: "Thou art my Son; this day have I begotten thee." This is not a reference to Bethlehem, but a reference to his resurrection and ascension. He is a person because the Father could talk to him, personally, and say to him in eternity that he has begotten him in victory. He is a divine person because he could do divine things on earth; he performed miracles which aroused debate as to his true identity. How can he do this if he is only a manifestation of the divine? He could do this because he was personally God the Son. The same was true in the debate that followed Jesus' reference to forgiveness of sins: "Who can forgive sins but God only?" (Mark 2:7). Jesus claimed that power because he was personally God.

What a comfort this affords! All that Jesus did for us while he was on earth, he did for us not as a manifestation of the divine, but as a person who consciously performed redemption. Hence it is genuine for us.

Jason Kortering

---

* Heidelberg Catechism A 25, in *Confessions and Church Order*, 92.

February 25 — Q&A 24 – Faith in God the Holy Spirit

Read: John 14:16–17.

The third person of the holy Trinity is designated God the Holy Spirit or Holy Ghost.

We must exercise some caution and precision when we speak of spirits or ghosts within our culture. These are common terms used within the heathen context. They refer to either humans as spirits or ghosts (the spirits of the deceased ancestors for example) or spirits and ghosts from the realm of the evil spirit world.

It is quite different to speak of our God as being personally the Holy Spirit.

The Bible does speak of our God as "a Spirit, and they that worship him must worship him in spirit and in truth" (John 4:24). Here we reflect upon the person of the Spirit within the Godhead. He is called Spirit, which means literally *breath*. The idea is that the Holy Spirit is the breath of God, the one who enables God to be the living God. He is the one who realizes a relationship of friendship between the Father, Son, and himself as Holy Spirit. When the Father speaks to the Son, he does so through the person of the Holy Spirit. He is called the third person of the Trinity not because he is lower in rank to the Father and Son, but rather because he completes the work of the three persons within the Godhead.

The same thing applies to the work which the triune God does outside of himself. He is the creator God, the savior God, the God who brings all his plans to its consummation, and he does this through the third person of the Holy Spirit. The Spirit breathes the creation into existence. The Spirit comes upon the Virgin Mary to conceive the promised Son. The Spirit gathers the church from all nations. The Spirit ultimately will destroy this present world and create a new one in which righteousness will dwell.

He is a divine person. This explains his efficacy and power. He always gets done what must be done.

Our faith is in him as we think about our salvation. It is sure and steadfast in the Holy Spirit.

Jason Kortering

Lord's Day 9

Q. 26. What believest thou when thou sayest, "I believe in God the Father, Almighty, Maker of heaven and earth"?

A. That the eternal Father of our Lord Jesus Christ (who of nothing made heaven and earth, with all that is in them; who likewise upholds and governs the same by his eternal counsel and providence) is for the sake of Christ his Son, my God and my Father; on whom I rely so entirely, that I have no doubt but he will provide me with all things necessary for soul and body; and further, that he will make whatever evils he sends upon me, in this valley of tears, turn out to my advantage; for he is able to do it, being Almighty God, and willing, being a faithful Father.

February 26 — Q&A 26 — God the Father: The Almighty Creator

Read: Genesis 1; John 1:1–3; Hebrews 11:3.

The Catechism begins in Lord's Day 26 a treatment of the first of the twelve articles of the Apostles' Creed. These articles represent the necessary truths which a Christian *must believe*. True faith holds to these without exception. The twelve articles of the Apostles' Creed are based on the truth of the Trinity. It expounds the truths concerning each of the persons of the Trinity—who exist in oneness of being.

Article 1 of the Apostles' Creed speaks specifically of the first person of the Trinity and specifies his work: creation and providence. The work of the first person of the Trinity is not limited only to him. The Father creates by the Word (John 1:1–3) and through the Holy Spirit (Gen. 1:1–2). One who confesses this acknowledges the infinite power, the infinite wisdom of Father. He created all things on earth and in the heavens *of nothing*! There are no other gods, no other religion, which dare make such a claim.

Yet the Catechism does not treat this great doctrine merely as doctrine. Rather, proceeding from the truth concerning our only comfort in life and death, it reminds the Christian that this Father, the Almighty Maker of the heaven and the earth, is *my* Father for Jesus' sake. He not only wishes to take care of us, but he is both willing and able to do so. And he has promised to do so! His promise cannot fail nor be broken. That's the great wonder of the grace of God for me.

With such a Father, we need never to fear. He is infinite, almighty, the unchangeable Father. He both creates all things without exception and upholds and governs all things that his purpose may be realized. Oh, we oftentimes face troubles and trials of various sorts. At times one may feel absolutely, hopelessly, overwhelmed by this all. Those who have not faith frequently rely on alcohol or drugs of various sorts to deliver them. But such are driven to ever deeper despair. Some have gone so far as to take their own lives in order to escape the trials of this life.

But thanks be to God, our Father can and does provide us all that we need for Jesus' sake.

Gise Van Baren

February 27 — **Q&A 26 — Creation: The Great Work of Our Father**

Read: Genesis 1; Psalm 33.

God, the Father, the first person of the Trinity, is the Almighty Maker of the heavens and the earth. He creates all things by the Word (Son) and through the Spirit: "He spake, and it was done; he commanded, and it stood fast" (Ps. 33:9). Indeed, the testimony of Scripture is that "thy heavens [are] the work of thy fingers, the moon and the stars…thou hast ordained" (Ps. 8:3). He created all things instantly, as Genesis 1 clearly teaches. In verse 3 we read: "And God said, Let there be light: and there was light."

Before this divine action of our Father, there was no time, no space, no matter, no universe. There was nothing of the universe which we now see. There were no people; there were no angels. These first came into being by his word. The Catechism speaks of this not first of all to show the beauty of the creation about us, but rather to show how almighty our Father is. Young lads would often boast, My dad is stronger and bigger than your dad! Perhaps the boast was even true. Yet our confession is far more. Our Father is almighty! Our Father is *all might!* There is no might apart from his. What might exists in creation was fashioned by our Father. He sustains every moment, any being that reveals some measure of might. Could an ant confront the might of an elephant? It is infinitely more impossible for any finite creature to oppose our Father successfully.

Consider today what God the Father has done! He has fashioned as with his fingers the whole of this universe. The fingers seem to be such little digits on the hand. With our fingers we can make small things. We cannot make a tree. We cannot make an animal. Far less can we make stars or planets. Yet it took only the fingers of God to fashion and sustain a universe so vast that man has not succeeded to measure its extent.

It took only the fingers of God to make all of the stars in the universe. We are told that there are as many stars in the universe as there are grains of sand on all of the seashores in the world. In comparison to the sands of the seashore, the earth would be no larger than a fraction of a grain of sand! How almighty indeed is our Father!

Gise Van Baren

February 28 — Q&A 26 – How Great He Is!

Read: 1 Kings 8:22–53; Psalm 8.

The almighty Father, creator and sustainer of the universe, is *our* Father. But our Father has revealed uniquely his might in the planet Earth on which we live. He who beholds that Earth through the spectacles of Scripture cannot but be awed at what is seen there. There is the beauty of the flowers and the entire plant world. One can be struck speechless at lovely fields of flowers. One feels insignificant when he stands by some of the giant redwood trees in California. Our Father forms, colors, and sustains each one as with his fingers (Ps. 8:3). One of the poets has emphasized: "Only God can make a tree."*

Then there is also the beauty of the mountains and canyons. It is an awesome experience to stand on the rim of the Grand Canyon in Arizona and see its great depth and extent. One sees there the rich color of rock—various shades of red—which seems to alter as the sun shines upon it through the day. One is humbled by its vastness and begins to realize how insignificant he is when compared to all of that. One might mention the vast deserts which are found on the earth. One can gaze at the great oceans which cover so much of the earth. God spoke—and these came into being!

But our almighty creator, our Father, shows his greatness and power in smallness as well. There are little creatures, almost too small for the human eye to see; those also he created and directs. Man, for all of his ability to make very small things, is not able to make anything like the many small insects God has made. I marvel when I see one of these almost invisible insects. Legs which are hardly visible, wings which one cannot see carry this insect from point to point. And when one tries to crush that insect under one's thumb, somehow it can sense impending destruction and escape. All of this too is made by our almighty creator and Father.

He is *my Father*. Can the devil have power equal to my Father's power? Can the wisest and most clever human being successfully fight against him? If my Father withdraws his sustaining power from under them, they would cease to exist! And the child of God *believes* in him. He trusts him—for he is able and willing to protect and provide for his own for Jesus' sake.

Gise Van Baren

---

* "Trees," by Alfred Joyce Kilmer (1886–1918).

March 1 — Q&A 26 — Our Father Created All Things in Six Days!

Read: Hebrews 11:3.

Genesis 1 and 2 present the simple, clear testimony of the great work of creation by our almighty Father. In six literal days (each identified as beginning and ending with evening and morning) he fashioned all things within his great universe. It did not take our Father millions or billions of years to finish the work. It was finished in six days. The word *day* almost always refers to a literal day in Scripture. The few exceptions are clearly identified (as in Genesis 2:4). God speaks also of the days of creation in his great law: the ten commandments. God said that we are to rest on the seventh day, for "in six days the Lord made heaven and earth…and rested the seventh day" (Ex. 20:11).

This is an essential truth which can be contradicted only with severe consequences for the interpretation of all of holy Scripture. Scripture is completely infallible, or it is fallible in some or many of its passages. Presbyterian and Reformed churches that began with a denial of the literal creation days soon were led into a pattern of denying or "reinterpreting" many other passages of Scripture. Many heresies have been introduced in this way.

The creation account has in it a simple beauty in describing the great work of creation. The beautiful statement is included with the days of creation: "And God saw every thing that he had made, and, behold, it was very good" (Gen. 1:31). There was no sin, no evidence of the curse or of death in all of that which God had made.

There is clearly presented also an order in that creation: God creates a stage for his work—especially on Earth. He forms the plants needed to sustain life. Then he creates animal life from lower to higher forms. Within each kind there could be and would be changes seen over a period of time. But one kind did not evolve into other kinds.

The climax of this creation was the formation of Adam (whose name means *dust*) from the dust of the earth—and Eve (the first woman) from Adam's rib. Adam was made the head of creation and all mankind. Genesis 2 points out also that the creation was at the same time the establishment of the marriage relationship. From the beginning, God made one man for one woman as long as they both would live. When questioned about divorce, Jesus insisted: "From the beginning it was not so" (Matt. 19:8).

It is humbling to realize that the almighty God who did all this is *my* Father for Jesus' sake.

Gise Van Baren

March 2 — Q&A 26 — One Believes the Father's Work of Creation Only By Faith

Read: Psalm 115.

The creation of all things is a wonder that is properly attributed to God the Father. At the same time, it is the wonder denied by the unbeliever and, in fact, by the devil himself. But the unbeliever, in denying creation by God, must find a substitute to the testimony of Genesis 1 and 2. And a substitute he claims to have found. At first it was presented as a *theory* of origins. Today it is presented as *scientific fact*, generally presented as unquestionably proven. It is the "science" of evolution. In fact, in our day, many churches and denominations have succumbed to the teaching of evolution—except with the disclaimer that God has directed its course.

Some have sought to disprove the purported facts of evolution. The commonly accepted big bang theory of the origin of the universe would seem to be preposterous. Was in fact all the matter of the universe at a point of time billions of years ago all compressed in a very small point? Was that point eternal? If not, what was its origin? What caused its explosion? And how did the sexes evolve with their reproductive organs over millions of years—each at the same time so that conception could take place? The scientist claims today that he has found the proof for evolution in the study of genetics. Darwin's theory of evolution is commonly adopted by most scientists. The scientist today claims that genetics presents proof positive that Darwin was correct.

But what fool the Christian would be to accept the reasoning of unbelieving scientists instead of the testimony of Scripture itself. In fact, God in his word clearly states that one believes the teaching of Scripture concerning origins by faith: "Through faith we understand that the worlds were framed by the word of God" (Heb. 11:3). Hebrews 11:1 states further: "Now faith is the substance of things hoped for, the evidence of things not seen."

Faith, which believes all this, is the fruit of regeneration—being born again. Faith holds to the testimony of God in Scripture. Faith believes that through union with the Savior Jesus Christ, the Father who creates is *my* Father. This is the source of all my comfort in life and death.

Gise Van Baren

March 3 — **Q&A 26 — The Great Question: What Do You Believe?**

Read: Ephesians 1.

The Catechism makes our confession very personal. As in the Apostles' Creed, *I* confess that *I* believe in God the Father Almighty. *I* believe that he upholds and governs all his creation by his eternal counsel and providence. *I* believe and confess that this God is *my* God and *my* Father.

The questions arise: "On what do I make such a great claim? Is it not preposterous? Is it not presumptive to claim all this?" The Catechism earlier states that I learn from the law of God (the ten commandments) that I am so wicked and corrupt that I am "wholly incapable of doing any good, and inclined to all wickedness."* That means that I of myself have nothing to offer to God to earn sonship. I am wholly incapable of doing any good thing in myself. How dare I, then, claim that he is *my* Father?

The claim that God is my Father rests on the completed work of his Son in our flesh, Jesus Christ. I needed one who could represent me before God, who could remove from me all guilt before God. If my guilt for all of my sins were removed, if one could bear the just sentence of death because of those sins, then I can call God my Father. I needed such a mediator between God and myself who is able to represent me as very man, and, as God, who is able to bear the infinite wrath of God for my sins. Jesus is the one. He suffered the agonies of hell for me. He died under God's wrath. He made the payment God required—and the proof is in the fact that he rose again on the third day. He ascended into heaven and sits on the right hand of God. Because of Christ's work, I can call God my Father.

From that, it follows that my Father "will provide me with all things necessary for soul and body."** I can rely on that truth without doubt or question. He provides all that I need for the body—food, clothing, and shelter. He provides care over me and defends me from my enemies. Above all, he provides for my soul—for that spiritual aspect of my being. He will take me to glory when my soul is separated from my body at death. And he will reunite my soul with my resurrected body at Christ's return. What a wonderful confession and assurance!

Gise Van Baren

---

* Heidelberg Catechism Q 8, in *Confessions and Church Order*, 86.
** Heidelberg Catechism A 26, in *Confessions and Church Order*, 93.

March 4 — Q&A 26 – Father Sends to Me All Things in His Great Love!

Read: Matthew 7:7–13.

The Catechism presents all of the essential doctrines of holy Scripture for our instruction. But again, the Catechism now makes the glorious truth of the Trinity and the fatherhood of the first person so very personal. This Father of Jesus Christ, the Almighty Creator is, difficult as it is to believe, *my Father* for Jesus' sake. My Father surely will provide all things necessary for soul and body. Jesus reminds of that fact in Matthew 7:11. Jesus does not promise great wealth or healing of every sickness. He does promise us "all things necessary for soul and body."* In the Lord's prayer Jesus taught us to ask: "Give us this day our daily bread" (Matt. 6:11). We ask for bread for the day—and with that we must be content. If Father is pleased to give much more, we have the added responsibility of using all to the glory of our God.

It is more difficult to understand the care of our heavenly Father when we become sick and soon might die. Why must the Christian endure the terribleness of warfare? Why does the Christian sometimes lose all that he possesses through fire or wind? What about Christian parents who lose a child?

Some have claimed that God sends only health and prosperity to his children. It is the devil who sends the adverse things. Only if one asks his Father in faith will he be healed. If he lacks sufficient faith, he likely will not be healed.

Notice the scriptural truth the Catechism emphasizes: "*He* will make whatever evils *he* sends upon me…turn out to my advantage."** Yes, he also sends to his people poverty, sickness, and death as well. Isaiah 45:7 makes this plain: God makes peace and creates evil. Psalm 119 repeatedly emphasizes that great truth that "affliction has been for my profit."*** And Romans 8:28 teaches that "all things work together for good to them that love God." Therefore, the same chapter points out, there is nothing that can "separate us from the love of God which is in Jesus Christ our Lord" (v. 39).

Is this not a most glorious assurance? The almighty God is able to work all for our good and is willing to do so being "a faithful Father."****

When adversity comes, we do not always understand why. We are tempted to be critical of our Father. Yet we must be content in the knowledge that our understanding of the why is so limited. We are content to leave it to our almighty Father. He knows best what we need—and provides it.

Gise Van Baren

---

* Heidelberg Catechism A 26, in *Confessions and Church Order*, 93.
** Heidelberg Catechism A 26, in *Confessions and Church Order*, 93 (emphasis added).
*** No. 329:4, in *The Psalter.*
****Heidelberg Catechism A 26, in *Confessions and Church Order*, 93.

Lord's Day 10

Q. 27. What dost thou mean by the providence of God?

A. The almighty and everywhere present power of God, whereby, as it were by his hand, he upholds and governs heaven, earth, and all creatures; so that herbs and grass, rain and drought, fruitful and barren years, meat and drink, health and sickness, riches and poverty, yea, and all things come, not by chance, but by his fatherly hand.

Q. 28. What advantage is it to us to know that God has created, and by his providence doth still uphold all things?

A. That we may be patient in adversity; thankful in prosperity; and that in all things which may hereafter befall us, we place our firm trust in our faithful God and Father, that nothing shall separate us from his love; since all creatures are so in his hand, that without his will they cannot so much as move.

March 5 — Q&A 27 – What Is God's Providence?

Read: Hebrews 1; Acts 17:26.

Question and answer 27 presents a definition of "providence of God." Simply put, it is "the almighty and everywhere present power of God whereby" all things without exception are under his direction. He who has created all things must continue to uphold and govern all of this to serve his sovereign purpose: the glory of his name in the way of gathering his people to everlasting glory and life. It is especially comforting to know and believe that this is all done "by his fatherly hand."*

Some who claim to believe that God created all things also claim that God subsequently withdrew from that creation. Creation now continues on its own. Those people, called deists, insist that what now takes place is a matter of chance. The universe and history itself could evolve in a myriad of different ways.

The evolutionist neither recognizes creationism, nor will he acknowledge that there is providence. He scoffs at the idea that there is direction and purpose in all things that exist. He denies that there is necessarily a God who must sustain and govern all things, whether it be the stars in their courses or the smallest of creatures that live on the earth. He would insist that if there were a supreme power directing all things, it would not allow the devastating things which occur on the earth: earthquakes, floods, fires, which destroy vast sections of the land. Surely a supreme power would not allow for wars and diseases.

The Christian confesses that the Almighty Creator also reveals in all things that he sustains and directs everything. He "hath determined the times before appointed, and the bounds of their habitation" (Acts 17:26). He counts the number of stars (Ps. 147:4). And we read in Acts 14:17 that God gives witness of himself in that he gives "rain from heaven, and fruitful seasons."

We see God as both Creator and the God of providence. These two truths are inseparably connected. If this were not true (and then the Bible lies), we would be of all creatures most miserable. But the Christian has confidence and assurance, not merely in some supreme being but in the almighty creator and sustainer of all things who is our Father for Jesus' sake.

Gise Van Baren

---

* Heidelberg Catechism Q&A 27, in *Confessions and Church Order*, 93–94.

March 6   **Q&A 27 — Providence: The Almighty and Everywhere Present Power of God**

Read: Psalm 73.

The Catechism speaks of providence. It is striking that the word only appears once in Scripture (Acts 24:2), and then is not a reference to the work of God. Yet the word is properly used in dogmatics to describe that work of God in preserving and directing all things. Matthew 5:45 speaks of the work of God which sends sunshine and "rain on the just and unjust."

The word *providence* comes from two Latin words: *pro* meaning *before,* and *video* meaning *to see*. The word means more than this according to Scripture. God not only sees beforehand what shall take place and accordingly plans his action, but there is much more. Some claim that the work of God is *only* that he sees before what takes place but has nothing to do with *determining* what happens. He sees beforetime that Adam will fall into sin, so he works out a plan to salvage as much as possible of fallen mankind by sending his Son into our flesh to pay for sin. Rather, Scripture teaches that from eternity God has *determined* everything that takes place.

Some have claimed that those who deny the teaching of common grace in fact embrace the term "providence" to describe the same thing. There is, however, great difference between these two terms. Common grace refers to an undeserved favor of God upon the reprobate unbelievers so that they can do many good things. Because of it man cannot be totally depraved. But this good that he does cannot in any way contribute to his salvation.

Providence includes good gifts of God upon all. The difference is that for God's people, he gives in his favor, while upon the reprobate, he gives in his wrath (see Ps. 73). The Catechism defines it as "the almighty and everywhere present power of God, whereby... he upholds and governs" everything.* The Catechism presents this in contrast to chance. We live in a society where chance is glorified. Gambling finds its allure in its element of chance. Many abuse the good gifts God provides by using them to multiply the chance of obtaining vastly more. God is not in the picture.

The Christian confesses that, without exception, God controls and directs all things within his creation. For those who belong to Christ, "all things work together for [their] good" (Rom. 8:28). We need neither fear nor doubt—for our Father knows what is good for us. For the wicked, however, all works toward their damnation.

Gise Van Baren

---

*   Heidelberg Catechism A 27, in *Confessions and Church Order*, 93–94.

March 7   Q&A 27 — God's Providence Directs All Things!

Read: Job 2.

How inclusive is this work of God's providence? The Catechism emphasizes that it includes everything that takes place: both that which is considered good and that which would seem to be bad. God "upholds and governs heaven, earth, and all creatures." Very specifically, this includes everything on the earth and all events of history on the earth.

Lest there be any doubt concerning the extent of this providence, the Catechism states that "herbs and grass, rain and drought, fruitful and barren years, meat and drink, health and sickness, riches and poverty, yea, and all things come, not by chance, but by his fatherly hand."* That is truly comprehensive!

Most who confess to believe in God would readily agree that all the good things come from our Father (fruitful years, riches, and health). Many insist that we must earnestly pray for these good things. If we do not receive these things, it is because our prayers are not fervent enough or not uttered in the strong faith that God will provide. Did not Jesus teach: "Ask and it *shall* be given to you" (Matt. 7:7–8)?

Others have insisted that the bad things (sickness, poverty) come not from God but from the devil. Is not God a loving God? Does he not earnestly love all his creatures? Would a loving God cause sickness or suffering on any of his creatures? The devastating things that occur fit in with the character of the devil.

Scripture, however, clearly teaches that all things without exception are under the direct control of our Father. Job experienced that truth. He confessed that God sends both the good and evil (Job 2:10). Whether we understand or not, he sends these in his wrath on the reprobate unbeliever; but he sends these also on the believer in his grace.

King David acknowledged this control by God. Concerning Shimei, who was cursing the king as he was fleeing his son Absalom, David said: "Let him alone, and let him curse; for the Lord hath bidden him" (2 Sam. 16:11).

To deny that God sends bad things would be to deny his sovereignty. It would place the devil on a par with God. This would be a devastating view for the Christian who is suffering some serious sickness or terrible adversity. We would be questioning our very faith in God. Rather, our Father is sovereign over all things. Thank God that this is absolutely true.

Gise Van Baren

---

*   Heidelberg Catechism A 27, in *Confessions and Church Order*, 94.

March 8 — Q&A 27 — God's Fatherly Hand Also Sends the Bad

Read: Matthew 10.

One thing often misunderstood is the statement concerning God's "fatherly hand."* The Catechism clearly sets forth what the fatherly hand of God provides. We might state simply that his fatherly hand provides not only the good but also the bad. Many object to the idea that God would send anything bad on his people. Surely the fatherly hand provides that which is good (sunshine, fruitful years, health, and prosperity). Should we not find some other cause for the bad than the fatherly hand of God? Is he not a loving and kind God? Would a loving God send some terrible disease leading to my death? Would he cause dreadful sorrow and grief for dear ones left behind?

But consider the figure well. How did your earthly father deal with you? Did he only give you what you wanted? Were there no occasions that he punished or chastised you in your rebellion? One young lad was heard to cry out as his father spanked him: "Daddy, you don't love me." Yet, upon reflection, one must confess that parents discipline their children *because* they love them.

We see this in God's work. The good things he sends upon the wicked are sent in his wrath. All things he sends upon his people, he sends in his love. The danger is that we think we receive the good things because of what we are or what we have done. But it is not so. The good things the righteous receive are given to be used to God's glory and in mercy for Jesus' sake. In fact, it is a very great responsibility for the Christian to receive much wealth or good health. Why? It is because he deserved none of these things but now has the calling to use all to the glory of Father in heaven.

Are the bad things indeed bad? Not when viewed in the light of Scripture. First, we must never consider them as God's punishment for our sins. The punishment for our sins was borne on the cross by Christ. But second, we must understand that adversity can both instruct and correct the Christian. He can often fall into sin. In the way of adversity (as parents correct their children), God corrects his people. But also, it is God's way of instruction, turning us away from the earthly and temporal, and directing our eyes heavenward.

Many Christians, even in their most difficult trials, state emphatically, God is good. And so he is.

Gise Van Baren

---

* Heidelberg Catechism A 27, in *Confessions and Church Order*, 94.

March 9 — Q&A 28 — Patient in Adversity, Thankful in Prosperity

Read: Job 1.

The Catechism, true to form, again brings the doctrine of providence down to us in a very practical manner. It does not ask, Can prayer change his providence concerning me? It does not claim that I have the right to complain about God's way with me or use this truth of providence to excuse my sin, or that, if God determines all these things, then I could not help but commit certain sins! Rather, the Catechism asks in question 28 about the advantage to me of this doctrine. It is not a question, *will* God work all things to my advantage? The Christian makes the bold assertion that *all* things *will* work out to my advantage. Psalm 119 repeatedly asserts this truth. The psalmist insists that affliction has been for his profit.

One is overwhelmed by this fact. Life can sometimes be so confusing. One may think that everything is against him. All seems hopeless. And, let us face the facts, were it not for the truth of God's providence, there would be no hope—ever. But the Christian confesses that the profound doctrine of providence is of great value and comfort to him. It speaks to him when he receives of God's hand health and prosperity. It speaks to him in a comforting way when he must endure great trial, pain, and adversity. Everything will work out to his advantage.

The emphasis here must be: What does the doctrine of providence mean *for me?* We must not treat this doctrine in the abstract. Were we to ask ourselves, what does this doctrine mean for people, then this study would have no comfort for *me.*

This is not a selfish attitude. It is rather the way to lead us to recognize the great work of our Father. Imagine: from eternity our Father has determined my way. All works for my good only for Jesus' sake.

What a comfort it is for the Christian who knows that God works all things for his good!

Gise Van Baren

March 10 — Q&A 28 – But Must One Be Patient in Adversity?

Read: 1 Corinthians 15; Romans 8.

We have confessed that God has created and by his providence doth still uphold all things. There are spiritual consequences to that confession. We acknowledge thereby that *all things* are in his hands. We confess, further, that all things work together for good to the child of God. This becomes a very personal confession when we state that all things work together for *my* good. That is true for me both in adversity and in prosperity. Whether it is sickness or health, whether it is fruitful or barren years, whether it is riches or poverty—God sends these upon the wicked in his wrath but on his people in his love and grace. How, then, is the Christian to react to all of this?

The Christian is, and must be, "patient in adversity; thankful in prosperity."[*]

One surely would agree that we are to be thankful in prosperity. Of course. We enjoy health, prosperity, fruitful years, etc. Often, however, that is not the case. We can take these good things for granted. We begin to reason that it was our wisdom, our great effort that made us prosperous. We attribute our health to much exercise, to proper diet, to careful supervision over our health by a good doctor. But however much these means are contributing to our welfare, the fact is that God, our Father, directs and governs all of this. We must be thankful to God for it all. Never are we to forget that.

But it might be more difficult to be patient in adversity. This patience surely means that we don't complain about what God has sent upon us. We do not rebel against his way with us. We do not conclude that God is punishing us for some specific sin. Rather, we bear all of this patiently. Have you not heard the Christian who is in great pain and in very difficult circumstances confess that God is good? That's patience!

We ought, however, to go even beyond this. The Christian must also be *thankful* in adversity! Is that too hard for us? Is it not enough simply to grit our teeth and bear it? Yet if affliction is for our profit, if all these things work together for our good (Rom. 8:28), then we can be thankful even through our tears. In ways we do not always understand, affliction "*worketh* for us a far more exceeding and eternal weight of glory" (2 Cor. 4:17).

"In all these things, we are more than conquerors through" Jesus Christ our Lord (Rom. 8:37).

Gise Van Baren

---

[*] Heidelberg Catechism A 28, in *Confessions and Church Order*, 94.

March 11 — Q&A 28 — How Great It Is: I Can Trust My Father!

Read: Acts 7:51–60.

There is a striking confession made by the child of God: he has a "firm trust" in God his Father.* That firm trust remains no matter what my Father determines for me.

That confession is so contrary to much which one hears today. One is told that he must pray—earnestly pray—that his Father will provide with good health or great wealth. If he is very sick, he is to pray for recovery and deliverance. If only his faith is strong enough, his Father will answer with healing. If one seeks many others to pray for and with him, the certainty of healing will be greater.

Lest we misunderstand, we must assert that God hears and answers prayer. That, however, does not mean that God will give whatever we ask him. What is it that we can firmly trust that God will surely do? We confess that there is nothing that can separate us from the love of God. That's the truth of greatest comfort for the Christian. Whether I have serious sickness which may lead to death or I have been given health and strength, neither can separate me from the love of God. Whether I am in abject poverty or have great wealth, neither can separate me from the love of God. Whether I am martyred for my faith's sake or remain relatively free to worship, neither can separate me from the love of God.

Scripture gives remarkable proof of this. Romans 8:35–39 states this explicitly. Stephen was stoned to death (Acts 7:54–60). King Herod killed James, the brother of John, but was unable to kill the apostle Peter because God's angels delivered him from prison (Acts 12). The conclusion is scriptural: God will work whatsoever he sends to his own so that they are preserved in his love.

It is the great truth of God's providence that "all creatures are so in his hand that without his will they cannot so much as move."** That is a profound statement! Fallen angels (including the devil), governments, storms, earthquakes, yes—and all conceivable things in God's creation—are "in his hand." Because that is true, we can believe that nothing can "separate us from the love of God" (Rom. 8:39). If that were not true, we could fear separation from God's love. Then God is not almighty. He himself could not prevent his people from being forever lost. Thank him that he is indeed sovereign and surely preserves his own in love.

Gise Van Baren

---

* Heidelberg Catechism A 28, in *Confessions and Church Order*, 94.
** Heidelberg Catechism A 28, in *Confessions and Church Order*, 94.

Lord's Day 11

Q. 29. Why is the Son of God called Jesus, that is, a Savior?

A. Because he saveth us, and delivereth us from our sins; and likewise, because we ought not to seek, neither can find salvation in any other.

Q. 30. Do such then believe in Jesus the only Savior, who seek their salvation and welfare of saints, of themselves, or anywhere else?

A. They do not; for though they boast of him in words, yet in deeds they deny Jesus the only deliverer and Savior; for one of these two things must be true, either that Jesus is not a complete Savior; or that they who by a true faith receive this Savior must find all things in him necessary to their salvation.

March 12 — Q&A 29-30 – The Savior from Sin

Read: Matthew 1:21.

Lord's Day 11 begins a treatment of God the Son.

We begin by looking at the proper name God gave to his Son. The name Jesus is the personal name given to the Son of God by God himself through an angel. This name reveals to us one of the most important truths of Scripture: there is only one way of salvation. It is striking how the Catechism immediately switches from speaking of the name to speaking of the person of the Son of God. Who he is and what he does are described by his names. The name Jesus teaches us that not man but God determines the way of salvation, and that way is through Jesus Christ alone. The name Jesus says it all! He came to save his people from their sins.

Jesus did not come for political or social reasons. He came for a spiritual reason—to save you from your sins. Your sins are the most serious problem in your life. God demands that every sin be punished by his wrath. No sin will escape that wrath. The soul that sins must die! God has given us a savior from sin in Jesus Christ. Knowing that my sins are forgiven, I can face the trials and sorrows and struggles of today with blessed assurance. I have a savior who did what was necessary to save me from death. He will continue to uphold me and give me all I need as I live my life for him. Confess your sins. Look to Jesus alone today! He is your complete savior.

Allen Brummel

March 13 — Q&A 29-30 — The Only Savior

Read: Acts 4:12.

From the beginning, when God came into the garden of Eden to clothe Adam and Eve's nakedness as sinners, God determined that there could be no remission of sins without the shedding of blood (Lev. 17:11; Heb. 9:22).

Jesus made outstanding claims through his ministry concerning himself: "I am the way, the truth, and the life: no man cometh unto the Father, but by me" (John 14:6). Can you come to the Father by your own works? Can you approach God on the basis of your obedience? There are many who imagine they are Christians because they live according to the golden rule and do the best they can to be good people. In sharp contrast, the Bible teaches that no one will ever be justified by their own works (Rom. 3:20). We must look to Christ. And what a savior God has given us in our Lord Jesus Christ! His name is the only name under heaven by which there is salvation.

Through the years there were many who were required to give their lives for this truth. They insisted with their mouths, Jesus alone, and they were killed because of their confession. May the testimony and blood of the martyrs strengthen our resolve to live our lives with this confession on our lips and in our hearts. Today, may we give thanks to God for the wonderful gift of a savior who is Jesus Christ, our Lord.

Allen Brummel

March 14 — Q&A 29-30 — Glorying in Jesus Alone

Read: 1 Corinthians 1:31.

Out of Lord's Day 11 rises the question that Jesus often posed through his ministry: "Whom do you think I am?" We can hear Jesus himself come and ask us personally: "What do you think of me? Do you love me? Do you know your need for my work, and do you live your life in devotion to me? Or do you actually deny me even though you praise me with your mouth?"

We so easily deny the perfect work of Jesus when we believe that Jesus' work needs to be added to in some way. If there remains something in Jesus' work that needs to be supplemented by our obedience, then the work is not complete, and some glory belongs to man. God sets forth only two possibilities—either Jesus is everything to me, or he is nothing to me. There is no third possibility. From the beginning of God's work of election to the working of new life in me, to the conversion and all the good works I do, I confess that everything is of him. Without him I can do nothing.

Martin Luther said: "When the devil throws your sins in your face and declares that you deserve death and hell, tell him this, 'I admit that I deserve death and hell, what of it? For I know one who suffered and made satisfaction on my behalf. His name is Jesus Christ, Son of God, and where he is there I shall be also!'"* There is no basis for glorying in myself. Today, may all your glorying be in Jesus Christ, the perfect and complete Savior.

Allen Brummel

---

* Martin Luther, *Letters of Spiritual Counsel*, trans. and ed. Theodore G. Tappert (Vancouver, BC: Regent College, 2003), 86–87.

March 15 — Q&A 29-30 — Salvation All of Grace

Read: Galatians 5:4.

A constant temptation is to look to our own works for the worthiness of our salvation. Even though we reject the theology of works righteousness, we look at our lives, and we think we deserve better than we have. We think that we don't deserve the troubles that we are experiencing. It should not be so difficult for us to pay our bills. We should have more joy in our lives. And, if asked why, we point to our own faithfulness. Look at all we have done for our parents and for our church, and look at how godly we've lived. Our sins don't disturb us much, and we don't focus on them. Instead we are as focused as the Pharisees on all the ways in which we are better than others.

That kind of attitude reveals that we don't see a deep need for Jesus. By our walk we deny and show hatred for Jesus. We are guilty of the sin of counting the blood of Jesus of no account—we act like men who could be saved by their own works; therefore Jesus was crucified in vain. Remember, Jesus came to seek and to save that which was lost.

God works the difficult confession that I am a sinner who cannot live in obedience to the law: "The good that I would I do not" (Rom. 7:19). My only hope is the wonder of grace shown me in Jesus Christ. He seeks me as one who is lost, and he gives to me, as one who has strayed and continues to stray each day, the assurance that salvation is not of works but by his wonderful grace alone. Don't return to the bondage of living for yourself—enjoy and live out of the liberty of seeking the glory of God. Look to the wonder of God's unmerited favor in giving to you Jesus, your complete and only Savior.

Allen Brummel

March 16 — Q&A 29-30 — The One Way to the Joy of the Father

Read: John 14:6.

Every other way and every other voice in this world leads to death. The devil and the wicked world are seeking to draw us down the path that leads to destruction. The way of the devil and the way of Jesus Christ stand in sharp antithesis of one another. This sharp distinction will be seen most fully during the time of the antichrist. He will not permit anyone to be honored except himself. He will insist that he is the only way to prosperity, happiness, and salvation. The antichrist will try to force us to submit to him with violence, boycotts, imprisonment, and terrible persecution.

Jesus Christ comes simply to us with a clear command: "Come unto me, all ye that labour and are heavy laden, and I will give you rest" (Matt. 11:28). By the power of his Spirit in our hearts, we respond by faith, and we come to him who alone is able to lift our burdens and give us peace. The fact that we believe Jesus to be the only way of salvation must be evident in our lives. Today, you must be a witness of the power of Jesus Christ by living your life in quiet submission to him. He ordains all things. He is working all things for good to those who love him.

We do not merely confess that Jesus is Savior, but we show by our walk who we are! We are followers of Jesus! Let people see what Jesus has done for you and how important he is to you. Show that you are a different person and that with Jesus, salvation is certain, and the joy is eternal.

Allen Brummel

March 17 — Q&A 29-30 – Living as Faithful Witnesses of Jesus

Read: 1 John 1:3.

It is necessary that we be faithful witnesses of Jesus as we live our lives from day to day. The authors of the Catechism continue the testimony of the disciples that, regardless of the situation they found themselves in, could not neglect speaking about Jesus.

It is shameful that often such open and bold witness embarrasses us. By refusing to witness to those around us, we reveal that we lack the love of God that would move us to love the neighbor by seeking his or her salvation. The fellowship that God has given us in the gospel is rich and blessed. The gospel is the good news of salvation, which good news is summarized in the name Jesus. That name means savior, and that is the whole content of the gospel. Jesus Christ came into this world to save sinners. In the midst of the darkness and despair of life, men and women need encouragement. God will give you opportunities today to lift high the banner of the cross. Don't be ashamed but rather freely boast of Jesus to those around you.

May God cause us more and more to witness to those around us concerning the wonder of Jesus' work in us and for us.

Allen Brummel

March 18 — Q&A 29-30 — Reconciled to God Through Jesus

Read: Colossians 1:19–20.

Reconciliation with God is that which is so desperately needed by man.

We rejoice in the gift of God's Son, by which wonder God accomplished this reconciliation. God and man are brought together through the child that was born, the Son that was given (Isa. 9:6). This work of God takes sinful men and women, forgives them, and brings them into the closest relationship possible with the living God of heaven and earth. We, who were lost and godless, are taken into the family of the living God. The cause of our misery and conflict with God, namely sin, is removed, and we now are able to fellowship with God in Jesus Christ. There is peace with God. The frightening curse is taken out of our lives, and we now realize that God is not a wrathful judge but a loving Father who will judge in mercy and grace.

With this confession on our lips, we are able to pray for the coming of Jesus again on the clouds of heaven. He will come to sever the last tie that joins us to this sinful world and bring us into the fullness of heavenly bliss in the new Jerusalem where God will tabernacle with man. Praise God today for his faithfulness and treasure the glorious and mysterious union that we have with him because of Jesus.

Allen Brummel

Q. 31. Why is he called Christ, that is, anointed?

A. Because he is ordained of God the Father, and anointed with the Holy Ghost, to be our chief Prophet and Teacher, who has fully revealed to us the secret counsel and will of God concerning our redemption; and to be our only High Priest, who by the one sacrifice of his body has redeemed us, and makes continual intercession with the Father for us; and also to be our eternal King, who governs us by his Word and Spirit, and who defends and preserves us in (the enjoyment of) that salvation he has purchased for us.

Q. 32. But why art thou called a Christian?

A. Because I am a member of Christ by faith, and thus am partaker of his anointing; that so I may confess his name, and present myself a living sacrifice of thankfulness to him: and also that with a free and good conscience I may fight against sin and Satan in this life, and afterwards reign with him eternally over all creatures.

March 19 — Q&A 31 — Christ: The Officer of God

Read: Isaiah 61:1.

The official title, similar to that of *Doctor* or *Reverend*, of the Son of God is *Christ*. Christ is the word *Messiah* in the Old Testament, which means anointed one or officebearer. *Christ* points to the office that the Son of God occupies, as he represents God in the midst of this world as prophet, priest, and king.

As we proceed through our devotions this week, we will look at the threefold office of Jesus more fully. It will become evident that Jesus could not be Jesus except he be the Christ. The name Christ explains the way and manner in which Jesus saves us. Jesus was officially ordained, appointed, and called by the Father to perform this important work. The Holy Spirit anointed him at the time of his baptism when a dove descended on him. Anointing always referred to two things in the Old Testament. First, the person was officially chosen by God to occupy a certain office in which he would represent God. Second, the person was qualified by God for that work.

Jesus, in his human nature, needed the sacred anointing of the Holy Spirit to take up this important work. All the prophets, priests, and kings of the Old Testament were but shadows and examples pointing to this representative of God who alone could bring about redemption. He is the one who offered the sacrifice, who perfectly reveals God's will, and who rules and leads us in love. Rejoice that you are in the arms of Christ, the anointed one, who will preserve and keep you to all eternity.

Allen Brummel

March 20 — Q&A 31 — Our Chief Prophet

Read: Deuteronomy 18:18.

Jesus Christ teaches us as prophet through the written and preached word. We usually think of a prophet as one who tells the future, but we may not limit the prophetic office to that. A prophet is a spokesman for God, a teacher. He comes as an official ambassador of the God of heaven and earth with a message from the King. The prophet does not bring his own words, but the words of Jehovah. Who is better qualified for this work than Jesus Christ, who, as the Son of God, designed the plan of salvation? He is the Word of God who comes to us in power and authority in order to set before us God's will. With great clarity and power, Jesus set forth God's will while on earth.

But he died, was resurrected, and, having ascended, he is no longer present to teach us in person. Where in this world will you come into contact with God's prophet? You need to attend church, come under the preaching, and spend time in devotion to the Bible. That is where Christ is present. He now ministers his prophetic office from heaven, and the ministers of the word are but servants, ambassadors of Christ. But it is Christ himself who speaks in every worship service through the faithful preaching, and it is Christ who personally has a message for me every time I open the Bible to study it.

With this in mind, we eagerly attend to and listen to the preaching, and we read our Bibles trusting that by his Spirit, Jesus Christ as our prophet will teach and lead us into the truth (John 14:26).

Allen Brummel

March 21   **Q&A 31 — Our Glorious High Priest**

Read: Psalm 110:4.

Christ is not only teacher, but he is priest. What good would it be for Christ merely to tell us the way to go when we would refuse to listen and obey him? He is "our only High Priest, who by the one sacrifice of his body has redeemed us"![*] He did what no other priest could ever do. He brought the sacrifice, and he offered it up as priest. He is sacrificer and sacrificial lamb at the same time. He paid the price necessary to save us from our sins. He substituted himself for each of his children. Jesus Christ proclaimed the way and paved that way by going through the waves and tumults of God's wrath against his people for their sins.

Now Christ is in heaven as our high priest. He makes constant prayers on our behalf to preserve us and keep us in the faith. He defends us against the wrath of God against sin. He reminds the Father that our sins have been covered, and we are justified by his blood. He is our way to God just as the priest in the Old Testament was the way to God for the people. But we have a victorious, glorified priest, and therefore our prayers will be heard.

Rejoice today in the wonder of Christ's perfect sacrifice on your behalf and in the ability to come to God in prayer with the confidence that those prayers will not be cast off but will be heard. Christ brings those prayers to the Father who has promised to give us all things we desire of him in Christ's name.

Allen Brummel

---

[*] Heidelberg Catechism A 31, in *Confessions and Church Order*, 96.

March 22 — Q&A 31 – Our Conquering King

Read: Zechariah 9:9.

Jesus Christ is our eternal king who "defends us and preserves us" from sin and causes us to enjoy all the wonders of salvation.* The unique nature of Jesus' rule is that he established his kingdom in the way of death. Earthly kings, no matter how powerful, die, and their kingdoms end. Jesus died in order to establish his kingdom in righteousness and purchase his citizens from the bondage of sin. His kingdom, therefore, is unique in that it is not of this world, but it is a spiritual kingdom found in the hearts of God's people and in his church.

Jesus Christ is king of the world by his power. He is king of his church by his grace and love. That sovereign rule over all things is for the purpose of preserving and saving his church. Christ takes us into his kingdom and makes us willing subjects, whose delight is to honor him who has defended us from the devil and continues to defend us against all our enemies. Jesus testified that no one shall pluck his people out of his hand (John 10:28). We have nothing to fear—Jesus Christ is our eternal King!

Allen Brummel

---

* Heidelberg Catechism A 31, in *Confessions and Church Order*, 96.

March 23 — Q&A 32 – Serving God as Prophets

Read: Hebrews 13:15.

The name *Christian* was most likely originally used in a derogatory manner for the followers of Christ. But, according to Acts 11:26, "the disciples were called Christians first in Antioch." As those who confess to be saved by the wonder of Jesus Christ, we count it a great privilege to take the name Christian to ourselves. That name depicts the wonder by which Christ has taken us into his family and makes us partakers of all his blessings, including bringing us into his offices.

We are now made representatives of God in this world, and we who lost the image of God through the fall are by grace restored into the likeness of Jesus Christ. We are made prophet, priest, and king in Jesus Christ.

How are we prophets? We are called to speak the truth, to warn those walking in sin, and to live out of the word. We confess the name of Jesus Christ by spending time with him in prayer and studying the word to grow in our knowledge of God. We teach and train our children to love God and to walk in obedience.

Do you ever feel like you are not worth much? Do others mock you and make you feel small? Remember God's word in 1 Peter 2:9, "But ye are a chosen generation, a royal priesthood, an holy nation, a peculiar people; that ye should shew forth the praises of him who hath called you out of darkness into his marvellous light." What a precious value has been placed on you! You are now a representative of God in this world, called to show forth his praise.

Allen Brummel

March 24 — Q&A 32 – Living for God as Priests

Read: Romans 12:1.

Our priestly calling is set forth very beautifully in the Catechism. We do not merely bring our sacrifices to God, but we are called to sacrifice ourselves! That means that we are to dedicate the whole of our lives in self-sacrificing love to God and to our neighbor. Throughout our lives, we need always to remember that my Christian life is not about me and myself, it is about God and his glory and his will.

This sacrifice is not always easy. There are times we begrudge the fact that we need to make the sacrifices. At times we look at the wicked and become envious for their seeming lack of struggles, as Asaph did in Psalm 73. But God does not only will that we sacrifice, he also wills that we do so willingly.

My comfort is knowing that I am not my own, but I belong to my faithful Savior Jesus Christ. With that spirit, submit your will to his and live as one who seeks to bring glory, not shame, to his name. Don't confess Christ and then allow your behavior to stand in the way of your witness. Rather, confess Christ by your life, and in that way others will see the power of God and his grace in your life. They will be drawn to you for Christ's sake. Remember today that you occupy a special office before God as a Christian priest, called to reflect the spirit of Jesus Christ who gave his all for the sake of the glory of God and the salvation of his people. What a wonderful motivation to live unto him!

Allen Brummel

March 25 — Q&A 32 — Doing Battle as Kings

Read: Ephesians 6:11–12.

God has placed you as his soldier in the midst of a fierce battle. This battle, for the most part, is against ourselves, against our own sinful nature. The fight that is within is that which requires the most effort. Knowing our own weakness and the strength of the devil, we would despair if it were not for the union we have with Christ. "I can do all things through Christ which strengtheneth me" (Phil. 4:13). We go into this battle knowing that the end result is decided. Jesus Christ has crushed the head of the devil, and he has sealed the victory. We may lose individual battles, but the war has been won by Jesus Christ.

As members of the militant church on earth, we take on the full armor of God, knowing and confessing that our strength in battle is not our own but from God. Christ has taken us to be his kings, ruling on his behalf with glory and power. As we do battle against our own nature, against the wickedness in the world, and against the devil, we long more and more for the glorious reign that will take place in glory. We will reign with him eternally! In the midst of the daily fights and discouragements, keep in mind what a glorious future God has given to you and me by grace.

Allen Brummel

Lord's Day 13

Q. 33. Why is Christ called the only begotten Son of God, since we are also the children of God?

A. Because Christ alone is the eternal and natural Son of God; but we are children adopted of God, by grace, for his sake.

Q. 34. Wherefore callest thou him our Lord?

A. Because he hath redeemed us, both soul and body, from all our sins, not with gold or silver, but with his precious blood, and hath delivered us from all the power of the devil; and thus hath made us his own property.

March 26 — Q&A 33 – Only Begotten and Adopted Sons

Read: John 1:12.

Sometimes we are confused by the fact that the Son of God is called the only begotten Son, while we are also children of God. We are taught in Lord's Day 13 an important and beautiful distinction that is lost in many of the modern versions of the Bible, which simply identify Jesus as the Son of God. Not only is that a bad translation, but that teaches bad theology.

There are two kinds of children in the family of God. Jesus is the natural Son, while we are adopted children. The point of this Lord's Day is to set forth the similarity but also the distance that there is between Christ and believers. The difference is as great as that between the creature and the Creator. There is a huge chasm! But at the same time we are made brothers of Jesus Christ by being taken into his family by adoption.

Adoption is a wonderful thing. A child who had nothing, was not wanted by parents, who had an uncertain future, is given a home, security, and legal rights. The one who is adopted should be eternally grateful to God for the parents who took him into their home and gave him their love. We, who are adopted into God's family, likewise have reason for constant joy and thankfulness. God took us, fallen children in Adam who deserved to be destroyed with the devil and his family, and brought us into his household. Our adoption was based in no way on what we were or what we would be. But he adopted us so that we would be his children. Think on that wonder today. Your value is not found in what you have been able to accomplish or what others think of you. Your value is found in the fact that the living God of heaven and earth, the Creator of the universe, has taken you into his family. You are a child of God, and no one can take that wonder from you!

Allen Brummel

March 27 — Q&A 33-34 – A Gracious Election

Read: Ephesians 1:4–5.

God takes us into the family of God by the wonder of predestination. In love, God chose us to himself from before we were born. That decision to choose us was based on nothing other than his good pleasure. He did not choose us because we were more in number or more worthy, but he chose us so that we would praise and glorify him, and so that we would be holy.

In time Jesus Christ takes us into that family by regeneration. He makes us heirs with himself of all the blessings of salvation (1 Pet. 1:2–5). We who are created from dust, who rebel daily against the will of God, are brought into the family of God, and nothing can separate us from that family.

Here the analogy of adoption falls away. Earthly parents can reverse the adoption process if their children show themselves to be rebellious. Earthly parents can't change the moral makeup of their children. God changes his children and makes us look like him spiritually so that we resemble our Father. He makes us partakers even of his divine nature (2 Pet. 1:4)! He pledges his love toward us as a love that is unconditional, not at all dependent on our obedience (Rom. 8:35–39). Rejoice in the wonder of God's everlasting and unfailing love!

Allen Brummel

March 28 — Q&A 34 — Redeemed by Blood

Read: 1 Peter 1:18–19.

As the only begotten Son, Jesus Christ is our Lord. He purchased us to be his own. We by nature forsook God and found ourselves in captivity to sin. We were enslaved and put on the auction block. Christ entered the auction barn and took up the bid to buy us. The language that the Catechism uses in answer 34, as well as in other places, is warm and tender and speaks of the great distress and death from which we were delivered. His was the winning bid because the value of it far outweighed the value that anyone else could provide. Gold and silver fluctuate in value. What he might have paid for us in money thousands of years ago would no longer be worthy. But Jesus Christ laid down his own life. He paid the price of the bid with his own blood.

The result is that we are his servants, and he is our loving Lord. We serve him in love. We belong to him. He has a right to do with us as he pleases. And we know that whatever he does to us is done out of love and for our salvation. He sends trials, afflicts us with cancer and other sicknesses, and brings death into our homes. He does this as our loving Lord to whom we submit in humility, praying for the grace never to forget the wonder of our spiritual adoption and the thankfulness we owe to him.

Allen Brummel

March 29 — Q&A 34 — Redeemed to Glorify God

Read: 1 Corinthians 6:20.

The fact that Jesus is your Lord and you are a servant to him requires a certain attitude in life. Having been "bought with a price," Paul admonishes us to glorify God in our body and in our spirit, which are God's (1 Cor. 6:20).

We were set free from the guilt and power of sin. Sin is such a tremendous power in our lives. We who were captives to sin have been set free. With this redemptive work comes great comfort but also an obligation. We are called to live unto him. Your body belongs to Jesus Christ. What you do with your body must be in accordance with his will. If you pursue the ways of sin in your body, you involve Jesus Christ in those ways of sin. If you unite yourself with a prostitute or commit adultery, you unite Christ with the ways of wickedness (1 Cor. 6:15–17).

Some try to make Christ the Lord of their spirits, but they want to retain the control of their bodies. Christ has redeemed us both soul and body. When his name is Lord, then our name must be servant. And, by his grace, we will serve him and pursue his will. The way of joy and happiness is not found in rebellion but in loving submission to the one who gave his life so that we might live forever.

Allen Brummel

March 30 — Q&A 34 — Our Sonship Proven by Chastisement

Read: Hebrews 12:5–8.

What a remarkable word of God we have in Hebrews 12:5–8 in connection with our sonship! How do we know that we are sons of God? In part, that confirmation comes in the way of trials and afflictions, in the way specifically of chastisement. Our loving heavenly Father corrects the son whom he lovs. He does not look the other way and allow us to walk in all kinds of wicked behaviors. He makes it so that we are caught. We don't get away with our sins.

And the result is troubling for us. We have to suffer the consequences of our sins. Our sorrow for sin is tested. Are we sorrowful because we have offended our heavenly Father, or is our sorrow due to the fact that we got caught? Our sorrow must be a sorrow for the sins we committed in offending our heavenly Father. And we must be thankful to our God who loves us so much that he will not allow us to continue indefinitely down the path of impenitence.

So rather than ask, "Why is God causing these afflictions in my life? Is this because he hates me?" I realize with thankful hearts that my heavenly Father loves me as a child to such a degree that he is willing to stop me from destroying myself, my family, and my life. He causes my sin to be exposed so that I might humble myself before him, repent, and go forward, trusting more fully his strength.

Allen Brummel

March 31 — Q&A 34 – Our Complete Deliverance

Read: Romans 8:1.

Christ has delivered you from all the power of the devil. What a glorious and wonderful truth! The Bible gives us an insight into the power of the devil. He came to Jesus Christ with three compelling, powerful temptations. Again and again he sought to destroy the seed of the woman. The sorrow and pain he caused for the people of God was much. He bruised or crushed the heel of the seed of the woman.

In our lives we see his power repeatedly. Every night as we think on the events of the day, we see how he moved us to pride and to use our tongues wickedly. We see the strife and trouble in our lives. We see how weak we are with regard to the specific pet sins against which we constantly fight. We are tempted to despair. Then we wake up in the morning and immediately see again his power and influence in our lives. Is there no relief? Is there no possibility of victory?

Then we meditate on the wonder that Jesus Christ has delivered us from all the power of the devil. The devil has been conquered! There is therefore now no condemnation for those who are in Christ Jesus! The lordship of Jesus Christ over sin and the devil is reason for great encouragement as we launch again into the fierce battle against sin today. Look to Jesus as your Lord to preserve and keep you faithful!

Allen Brummel

April 1 — Q&A 34 — A Glorious Confession

Read: 1 Corinthians 12:3.

We confess Jesus Christ to be our Lord because of the wonder of God's work in us. By the Holy Spirit, God takes hold of our sinful rebellious natures, which would turn our backs on God altogether, and transforms them. We are given ears to hear and tongues to confess wonders that we would never have confessed on our own.

There are those who will call him Lord merely in fear. At the final judgment, all men will be forced to bow before him in adoration and praise, confessing that he alone is Lord of all. Some will call him Lord with their mouths but not their hearts. Those, Jesus will reject as never having known them. They merely called him by name but never from the heart nor with their lives. Just saying "Lord, Lord" does not do us any good if we refuse to walk according to the "will of [the] Father which is in heaven" (Matt. 7:21). By word and by deed we submit to him. We willingly and joyfully confess Jesus as our Lord and seek to live as his faithful servants, looking forward to the day when our faithfulness will be as that of the angels. And then we will hear too those glorious words: "Thou hast been faithful over a few things, I will make thee ruler over many things: enter thou into the joy of thy lord" (Matt. 25:23)!

Allen Brummel

Lord's Day 14

Q. 35. What is the meaning of these words—"He was conceived by the Holy Ghost, born of the Virgin Mary"?

A. That God's eternal Son, who is and continueth true and eternal God, took upon him the very nature of man, of the flesh and blood of the Virgin Mary, by the operation of the Holy Ghost; that he might also be the true seed of David, like unto his brethren in all things, sin excepted.

Q. 36. What profit dost thou receive by Christ's holy conception and nativity?

A. That he is our Mediator, and, with his innocence and perfect holiness, covers in the sight of God my sins, wherein I was conceived and brought forth.

April 2 — Q&A 35 — The First State of Humiliation

Read: Philippians 2:7.

Lord's Day 14 begins a treatment of the humiliation of Jesus Christ. We talk about five states in Jesus' humiliation: his lowly birth, lifelong suffering, death, burial, and descent into hell.

Jesus' humble birth was an act of marvelous love. Nothing compelled him to become a man. He voluntarily took to himself our flesh and blood. Being born of a woman and lying as a newborn baby in the manger was an equally great and conscious act of love by Jesus as hanging on the cross.

The virgin birth is much more than an important doctrine we must embrace—it was an act of love on the part of Jesus Christ. We will talk of the love of God in sending his own Son. But no less of a wonder is the love of the Son in taking on himself the form of a man. Jesus' birth was an act of love which he himself willed. He who possessed the glory of the Godhead and dwelled in heaven made himself of no reputation for our salvation. He came from life to death so that he could give his people everlasting life.

From the moment of Jesus' birth, a wonderful union came into existence: God and man in one person. This is a divine mystery. Christ never shrank back from coming into our flesh even though he knew that human life would be one of continual suffering. What a humbling truth—Jesus Christ entered this vale of tears for me!

Allen Brummel

April 3 — Q&A 35 — A Real Human Nature

Read: Galatians 4:4.

Jesus took to himself a real human nature which was "of the flesh and blood of…Mary." Although his conception was a wonder, he was born like every other human being, and he was "like unto his brethren in all things."* Jesus took on the flesh and blood of Mary. As a child he had to learn to walk and speak just like we did.

Lord's Day 6 stressed the need for a mediator who would be very God and very man. This Lord's Day underlines the fact that Jesus Christ was that mediator. Jesus united a human and a divine nature into the one divine person of the Son of God. The human nature that he took on himself was a nature with all its infirmities. We never read that Jesus became ill or had any physical problems, but his human nature was susceptible to pain and sorrow. He wept. He suffered hunger and thirst and knew what it was to get tired. He had human feelings and desires. He needed friendship and sympathy, and being forsaken by his disciples caused tremendous pain. The thought of death created exceeding sorrow.

That Jesus was a human being like us is important for at least two reasons. First, he can sympathize with our weaknesses. He knows human life and is our sympathetic high priest. Second, he could take our sins on himself and could be our representative before God. We have a savior like unto us, who knows and sympathizes with our sorrows and struggles and forgives us all our sins!

Allen Brummel

---

* Heidelberg Catechism A 35, in *Confessions and Church Order*, 97.

April 4   Q&A 35 — Born of a Virgin

Read: Luke 1:34–35.

God gave to Mary the distinguished place of being the mother of the Messiah. Mary was a young woman who had kept herself pure for marriage. She was not yet married and could not fathom how she would be able to bring forth a child without knowing a man. God informed Mary through the angel Gabriel that this child would be born without the involvement of a man.

Jesus is the only baby ever born not to have an earthly father. In this regard, Jesus' conception was very different from ordinary conception. While Jesus had an earthly mother, the Holy Spirit took the place of the father. The result of this wonder is that Jesus escaped the original sin and depravity of the human nature. His human nature was without corruption. And, because guilt is imputed to the person, and Jesus had a divine person, he escaped Adam's guilt. He was in all things pure and holy. He who knew no sin was made sin for us.

As white cloth absorbs black ink, Jesus in his perfection absorbed the blackness and filthiness of our sin. Our sin was placed on his account. Even though he had not committed a single sin, he was counted as a sinner before God for you and me. When we understand that wonder, we begin to understand the joy set forth by the Catechism here. He is our mediator! He is the one whom God sent to destroy my sin once and for all.

Allen Brummel

April 5	Q&A 35 — True Seed of David

Read: Romans 1:1–5.

Throughout history God prophesied of the coming of the promised seed. That seed would bruise the head of the seed of the serpent according to Genesis 3:15. The Lord repeated this promise again and again so that his people would not lose courage. Each time the promise was richer, clearer, and more sharply defined. The church knew that the Messiah would be from Abraham, of the tribe of Judah, of the lineage of David.

Mary as a descendant of David is now given the privilege of bringing forth the promised seed. The age-old enmity between the seed of the serpent and the seed of the woman culminated in the birth of Jesus Christ. Satan knew what would happen when the true seed of David was born and tried to do everything in his power to keep Jesus from coming. After Jesus was born, the devil tried to kill him and tempt him to sin. But the seed is victorious. However great the challenge, the sin, the struggle, we know that the victory does not belong to Satan, nor to the world, nor to the antichrist. The victory belongs to the king who rules on the throne of David to all eternity.

Rejoice in the wonder and faithfulness of God's promises! The Bible proves that it is the word of God again and again in that the things prophesied take place precisely as they are prophesied. God is faithful to his promises. Today and every day we lean on his faithfulness for our encouragement and strength.

Allen Brummel

April 6 — Q&A 35 – The Wonder of the Father's Love

Read: John 3:16.

The Son of God coming into the world is a wonder of the love of the Father. As we confess the wonder of the incarnation, we, with the church of all ages, express the cry in John 3:16. What a wondrous love of God for me, a covenant-breaking sinner!

Love is shown in the way of giving. God displayed the fullness of love by giving his Son for the salvation of his church. And, if you ask which world it is that God so loved that he gave his only begotten Son, the answer points to the world of his elect. Not the world for which he refused to pray in John 17:9, but the world of them which God gave him.

The marvel of this love for the world is due to the fact that this world is composed of covenant breakers, adulterers, murderers, publicans, thieves, and rebels. It is a people who have sinned against God. God could well have rejoiced in its total destruction. But he did not! Instead he gave his beloved Son to save that world. Is this not the fullness of love?

God sent Jesus into the world so that we who were in the realm of death could live through him. The life that we live is one of love toward God and the neighbor: "Beloved, if God so loved us, we ought also to love one another" (1 John 4:11).

Allen Brummel

April 7 — Q&A 36 — Covering My Sins

Read: 1 John 4:10.

Notice the application that the Catechism makes to us personally in question and answer 36. This is a confession that we do not make in the abstract, but one which each of us makes personally from the heart by faith. We see the beauty of the Catechism in moving from generalities to a very personal application. Jesus was made "like unto his brethren in all things." But we must get more personal. He was made like unto me, "sin excepted."[*] This was necessary so that he "covers in the sight of God my sins."[**]

We who anxiously and sorrowfully confess our sins, also joyfully confess our savior!

The profit of Christ's conception and birth are tied directly to our personal conception and birth. We were conceived and born in sin. He was born of a virgin and sent by God to cover in God's sight those sins. A propitiation is a covering. Jesus is the complete covering of our sins. There are no sins left uncovered.

Jesus not only had to be conceived and born in this manner for my salvation. But he had to suffer, experience hell, go to the grave, and die. This was the way in which he would deliver you and me from the sin that clings to us. There is no other escape.

Salvation is all of God! In the midst of the reality of my sinfulness, this is my only comfort in life and in death: Jesus covers those sins now and to all eternity!

Allen Brummel

---

[*] Heidelberg Catechism A 35, in *Confessions and Church Order*, 98.
[**] Heidelberg Catechism A 36, in *Confessions and Church Order*, 98.

April 8   **Q&A 36 — A Gracious Gift**

Read: 1 John 4:19.

What is grace? Grace is showing goodness to someone despite that person's unworthiness. Grace does not ask: "What do you deserve?" Grace asks: "What do you need?"

The Father did not ask what his elect deserved or what they had merited. God asked, What do they need? What is necessary to save them? And God gave Jesus Christ to you and me through the miracle of the virgin birth.

Jesus Christ did not come and ask what we deserved. He only was concerned with the Father's will and with what the elect needed. He did not ask, How will they receive me? How will they treat me? He knew they would not receive him. He knew they would rebel against his will. He knew that they would ultimately join those who would cast him out and crucify him. Jesus knew that you and I would deny him, mock him, and be ashamed to be associated with him. But despite that knowledge, he came into human flesh and humbled himself to be our mediator. Is that not the fullest expression of grace? Jesus came to show a love and favor that was completely undeserved by those whom the Father gave him.

We are not saved because of anything of ourselves. We are saved despite ourselves. "We love him, because he first loved us" (1 John 4:19)! Is that not the only response we can have to this gracious gift?

Allen Brummel

Lord's Day 15

Q. 37. What dost thou understand by the words, "He suffered"?

A. That he, all the time that he lived on earth, but especially at the end of his life, sustained in body and soul the wrath of God against the sins of all mankind; that so by his passion, as the only propitiatory sacrifice, he might redeem our body and soul from everlasting damnation, and obtain for us the favor of God, righteousness and eternal life.

Q. 38. Why did he suffer under Pontius Pilate as judge?

A. That he, being innocent, and yet condemned by a temporal judge, might thereby free us from the severe judgment of God to which we were exposed.

Q. 39. Is there anything more in his being crucified than if he had died some other death?

A. Yes [there is]; for thereby I am assured that he took on him the curse which lay upon me; for the death of the cross was accursed of God.

April 9 — Q&A 37 — The Second State of Humiliation

Read: Hebrews 2:9.

Lord's Day 37 introduces the second state of humiliation, Jesus' lifelong suffering. Strikingly, the Catechism notes that suffering as lifelong. There is an interesting question in that regard. How was it possible for Jesus to experience God's wrath all his life and at the same time live in the consciousness of God's favor and love? Jesus was always aware of the love of his Father, but as he came closer and closer to the end of his life, the consciousness of that love faded, and the horror of God's wrath grew. "Especially at the end of his life"* provides us with the solution. The weight of suffering pressed out of him blood and sweat in the garden. At the same time, however, he was aware of God's favor. He still could call upon God as his Father. God loved his perfectly obedient Son in the midst of all the suffering.

God's anger was directed toward the sins which Jesus voluntarily took on himself. Burdened with our sin, he stood before God as the guilty one and was made to taste death. No one before or after him has ever experienced as weighty a burden as the wrath of God against the sins of all the redeemed.

It is hard for us to imagine living in the shadow of the cross as Jesus did his entire life. For us, God gives sad and happy days. Not for Jesus. His suffering was a life sentence. Only one who was very God and man could endure it. What remarkable love!

Allen Brummel

---

* Heidelberg Catechism A 37, in *Confessions and Church Order*, 98.

April 10 — Q&A 37 — Suffering God's Wrath

Read: 1 Peter 2:24.

The intensity and horror of Jesus' suffering provides reason for great joy and encouragement for you and me. There is only one explanation for the terrible suffering that the innocent and perfectly righteous Son of God took on himself. Jesus was being punished for our sin. The purpose was not merely to give us an example of great suffering. Nor was the purpose to merely make salvation possible. Jesus' death was a propitiatory and vicarious sacrifice, that is, it was in the place of his people as a covering of their sins. Every last one of those sins is covered.

We hear the seriousness of sin in the words of the law recorded on Mount Sinai. The hill of Calvary causes us to see the seriousness of sin in the suffering and agony of Jesus. Christ went into hell for his people. He healed our stripes. He covered our sins. There is nothing left to be punished. Every last one for whom Jesus died is dead to sin and now lives unto righteousness by the power of the Holy Spirit.

It becomes evident then that the reference to "all mankind"* and "every man" (for example, Heb. 2:9) in the Catechism and Scriptures cannot mean every human being. If that is the case, they all are saved! Everyone will go to heaven. There is no more sin that needs to be punished in hell. No, Christ set free only those who were given him by his Father. He did so apart from any of their works. The unconditional love of Jesus for his sheep is again evident!

Allen Brummel

---

* Heidelberg Catechism A 37, in *Confessions and Church Order*, 98.

April 11 — **Q&A 37 — God's Everlasting Favor**

Read: Psalm 32:1.

Are you aware of the sins you committed yesterday? How about this morning and today? It is easy for us to minimize and think lightly of sin. But then we are brought to Calvary. We see just how serious our sins are, and we see the wonderful mercy of God in forgiving us all our sins.

At other times some of those sins cause us a lot of grief. We start to think that God is punishing us. It can be hard at times to forgive ourselves of things that we've done, often because of the devastating consequences of our actions. Jesus' suffering and sacrifice have the result, according to the Catechism, of redeeming "our body and soul from everlasting damnation, and [obtaining] for us the favor of God, righteousness and eternal life."[*]

God's favor is his opening of our eyes to see how precious Jesus is and that he is our savior. Righteousness is being right in God's eyes. We are freed from all the guilt and punishment of sin. Eternal life is the crown on the work of Jesus. We are given entrance into the gates of heaven! "Enter into his gates with thanksgiving, and into his courts with praise" (Ps. 100:4). God makes us rejoice in him who wept for us. God makes it such that we are able to live our lives with joy and thanksgiving.

We have many earthly problems, but we are free from sin and eternal punishment. May we, as God's redeemed, never be overly anxious about the suffering of this present time, seeing we have been redeemed from such great distress and death!

Allen Brummel

---

[*] Heidelberg Catechism A 37, in *Confessions and Church Order*, 98.

April 12 — Q&A 38 – Condemned by Pontius Pilate

Read: John 19:4.

Even our children know that Jesus was condemned to death by Pontius Pilate even though Pilate admitted that Jesus was innocent. Pilate tried many ways to get out of having to sentence Jesus. At least seven times the judge declareed Jesus innocent. But at the end of the process, out of fear of the Jews, Pilate confirmed the death sentence. There is no denying Pilate's involvement or guilt, even though he tried to wash his hands of the wicked deed.

What does this have to do with the suffering of Jesus? This establishes not only the time frame of Jesus' death—during the reign of Pontius Pilate—it demonstrates the hatred of the world for the Son of God. Throughout all generations Pilate, the chief officer of the Roman Empire, an empire which prided itself on its pure justice, is known for injustice. God sent his Son into the world. The entire world condemned him: the church world through the Sanhedrin and the world at large through Pilate.

But in this too God's hand was evident. The condemnation of Jesus is our acquittal! God used the judgment of Pilate to declare his death sentence on the one bearing our sins.

Although the wicked world hates Jesus and all who follow him, one day all men must stand before the judgment seat of the living God. The judge of all the earth will judge all men, angels, and devils with perfect judgment. He will free us from the judgment of guilt that we deserve. You who are ransomed in Jesus Christ are acquitted!

Allen Brummel

April 13 — Q&A 39 — The Curse of the Cross

Read: Galatians 3:13.

Many attempts were made to end the life of Jesus. These attempts orchestrated by the devil started early on with the devil trying to destroy Jesus before he was born and then again shortly after his birth. But Jesus could not die in any other way than the way determined by God's counsel. That way was the painful death on the cross.

There is no more painful death than a crucifixion. They tore off Jesus' garments so that his bloody back was against the rough wood of the cross. They drove heavy nails through his hands and feet. Then they set the cross on its end and allowed it to fall into the previously-dug hole. What unbearable pain Jesus must have felt when the weight of his body tore the holes larger in his hands and feet! Then there was the difficulty of breathing, the fever, and the dehydration. This was only the visible, physical suffering.

The cross depicted shame and rejection. The person who was suspended on a tree was rejected by men, and he was rejected by God. He was suspended between earth and the heavens. All who walked past saw the shame of this death, a death reserved for terrible criminals. There hung God's holy Son associated with those criminals. He was publicly defamed but was silent with no words of protest. He bore our shame and guilt so that we could be exalted!

Allen Brummel

April 14 — Q&A 39 – No More Condemnation

Read: Romans 8:1

How terrible it would be to go through life thinking that God is cursing me because of my sins! The superstition that rules in many heathen cultures results in great fear and terror. At each step, one is wondering if he has done enough to please the gods. One's whole life is lived selfishly in an attempt to escape the wrath of the gods and earn favor.

God has delivered us from that superstition. Though we deserve to be punished everlastingly, God put that curse on his own Son so that we could be freed to live not for ourselves, but for him. Jesus Christ died so that the curse of sin would be forever lifted for all those who are found in Christ. The Catechism says that we are redeemed from "everlasting damnation."*

Does this mean that we won't suffer? No, we will suffer, but our suffering is changed into blessing. God turns suffering for the sake of Christ into that which is a blessing for us. We are purified and sanctified through that suffering. God draws us closer to himself as we experience the trials. All kinds of blessings come out of that cup of suffering.

From the suffering of Jesus we learn that no suffering is without purpose, even though at times it may seem to be the case in our lives. Our suffering does not earn us anything. Nothing more is needed! Christ earned it all for us so we can live unto him.

Allen Brummel

---

* Heidelberg Catechism A 37, in *Confessions and Church Order*, 98.

April 15 — Q&A 39 — Glorying in the Cross

Read: Galatians 6:14.

Notice again the personal approach of the Catechism: "I am assured."[*] The more we reflect on the suffering of Christ, the more personal and intimate that assurance becomes. My sin brought Christ to the cross. But there is a blessing for me as well. He went to the cross for me! That is the blessed assurance of the gospel. God promises that the cross is not just for others, but it is for me personally.

I was baptized with Christ. I was crucified with Christ. My old man of sin was nailed to the cross when Christ was nailed to that tree. On Christ alone depends my assurance. Not on myself, my faith, my prayers, or my obedience, but on his perfect work on the cross.

How understandable that this truth brought Paul to make the confession he did in Galatians 6:14. So often we don't even come close to glorying in the cross. We hear about Christ through the preaching. We read about his work in the Bible. But we return to our daily ways. A glorying and rejoicing people are not hesitant to talk with others about their only comfort. A glorying and rejoicing Christian knows what it is to live close to God and to rely on him for everything.

Rejoice and give thanks today for the victory that is yours in Christ! There is nothing worth glorying in but the cross of Christ.

Allen Brummel

---

[*] Heidelberg Catechism A 39, in *Confessions and Church Order*, 99.

Lord's Day 16

Q. 40. Why was it necessary for Christ to humble himself even unto death?

A. Because, with respect to the justice and truth of God, satisfaction for our sins could be made no otherwise than by the death of the Son of God.

Q. 41. Why was he also "buried"?

A. Thereby to prove that he was really dead.

Q. 42. Since then Christ died for us, why must we also die?

A. Our death is not a satisfaction for our sins, but only an abolishing of sin, and a passage into eternal life.

Q. 43. What further benefit do we receive from the sacrifice and death of Christ on the cross?

A. That by virtue thereof our old man is crucified, dead, and buried with him; that so the corrupt inclinations of the flesh may no more reign in us; but that we may offer ourselves unto him a sacrifice of thanksgiving.

Q. 44. Why is there added, "He descended into hell"?

A. That in my greatest temptations, I may be assured, and wholly comfort myself in this, that my Lord Jesus Christ, by his inexpressible anguish, pains, terrors, and hellish agonies, in which he was plunged during all his sufferings, but especially on the cross, hath delivered me from the anguish and torments of hell.

April 16 — Q&A 40 — **The Third State of Humiliation**

Read: Philippians 2:8.

We have here the third state of humiliation, Jesus' death. The Catechism asks why it was necessary for Jesus "to humble himself even unto death."[*] This was the question that Jesus himself faced in the garden. As his disciples fell asleep and wandered away from him, he found himself in anguish of heart. "If it be possible, let this cup pass from me" was his fervent repeated prayer (Matt. 26:39). But it was not possible. And God sent an angel to strengthen Jesus.

If there could have been another way, there would have been. But this was the way God ordained for the salvation of his people. God's justice demanded death for the satisfaction of sin. God demands that justice runs its course. If sin is not punished by death, God's justice would be violated. That may not and could not be.

God's word is truth. God stated in Genesis 2:17 that the one who would eat of the tree of knowledge of good and evil would surely die. The devil tried to encourage doubt about God's word. Adam and Eve gave in to his temptation and fell into the realm of death both spiritually and physically. The second Adam had to enter into that darkness of death and overcome it for his people. God did not make an exception even for his own Son. His truth demanded the death of his beloved Son. This is how important truth is to God! God is bound to his attributes. His justice and truth were satisfied by the death of his righteous Son.

Allen Brummel

---

[*] Heidelberg Catechism Q 40, in *Confessions and Church Order*, 99.

April 17 — Q&A 41 – The Fourth State of Humiliation

Read: Acts 13:29.

The soldiers pierced Jesus' side with a sword. As water and blood gushed out, it was evident that Jesus was dead and there was no need to break his legs. They took the body down from the cross. Would one of his disciples come forward to bury the body? None of the twelve were present, but after Jesus' body was taken down from the cross, Joseph of Arimathaea and Nicodemus requested to have the body so that they could bury it. They took the body, and they buried it in Joseph's new tomb. All of this was according to prophecy.

Not to be buried was viewed as a curse. As Jesus had endured the curse of Golgotha and hell itself, no more curse was necessary.

Yet to have your body buried is not honorable but humiliating. It is difficult for us to lay the bodies of our loved ones in the grave. Man, who was created king over the earth, is laid in the dust of the ground. The act is final. We will never know that person like we did before again. This burial for Jesus, the king of kings, was deep humiliation. Jesus entered into the experience and humiliation of man to such a degree that this too was not omitted.

Christ entered the realm of the dead in order to conquer the power of the grave. The body of Christ had to be buried so that it could rise again and overcome the power of sin and the grave. We bury the bodies of our loved ones by faith, believing that their bodies, with that of Christ's, are "sown in corruption," but "raised in incorruption" (1 Cor. 15:42).

Allen Brummel

April 18 — Q&A 42 – Death Translated to Victory

Read: 1 Corinthians 15:55.

We live in the midst of death. Every day we are reminded of the horror of death by the obituaries in the newspaper. Our loved ones are taken by death. Sometimes death swallows them quickly, at other times more slowly. Where is our comfort in the midst of death? If Jesus died and took away our sins, why must we still face death? Is not the punishment of sin gone?

Christ has transformed death. Death for us is not payment for the penalty of sin. Christ paid that penalty. Death is not satisfaction for the righteousness of the law. Jesus satisfied the demands of righteousness. Death is not the expression of God's wrath. Jesus bore that wrath and cast it away. What then is our death?

Our death is first of all the "abolishing of sin."* God begins the process of sanctification at the moment we are regenerated. That process is slow and difficult. A lifelong battle against sin results in only "a small beginning of [that new] obedience."** God uses many means in our lives to break the power of many besetting sins, but we cannot get rid of them in this life. Death is the servant of God to abolish the sins of his people.

But death is more! It is secondly "a passage into eternal life."*** He that believes in Christ shall never die. God takes our earthly lives so that we may go into the Father's house of many mansions. We sing from Psalm 17:

> When I in righteousness at last
> Thy glorious face shall see,
> When all the weary night is past,
> And I awake with thee
> To view the glories that abide,
> Then, then I shall be satisfied.****

Allen Brummel

---

* Heidelberg Catechism A 42, in *Confessions and Church Order*, 100.
** Heidelberg Catechism A 114, in *Confessions and Church Order*, 133.
*** Heidelberg Catechism A 42, in *Confessions and Church Order*, 100.
****No. 31:7, in *The Psalter*.

April 19 — **Q&A 43 — The Reign of Sin Destroyed**

Read: Romans 6:6–7.

The victory of the cross is not something that we wait to enjoy until we die. Through the power of Jesus Christ both our lives and our deaths are totally changed.

The benefit for our living is that already now the "old man is crucified, dead and buried" with Christ.* We will later deal with the old man in more depth in Lord's Day 33. The old man is that nature we inherited from Adam, which is given over to sin. But Christ gives us something to rejoice in. That old man is in principle crucified and buried with Christ. He still exerts a lot of pressure on us. Daily we do battle against that old man. But already now we have the victory. How is that evident?

Although we give in to the old man and walk according to our sinful desires, there is no pleasure because we experience shame and guilt. God drives us to repent and turn from our sins. Rather than walking in them and enjoying them, we flee from them.

The corrupt inclinations of the flesh no longer rule us. No longer does the devil sit on the saddle of our lives, controlling us and driving us where he pleases. He has been cast off. Christ now sits on the throne of our lives. He rules and governs us. Through the power of his Spirit, we do battle against the power of sin. Our daily question is this: What is it Lord, that thou wilt have me to do?

Allen Brummel

---

* Heidelberg Catechism A 43, in *Confessions and Church Order*, 100.

April 20 — Q&A 43 – The Sacrifice of Thanksgiving

Read: Romans 12:1.

Christ's death was an atonement offering for our sins. Our lives now must be lived as thank offerings to God. As new creatures made after the likeness of Jesus, we both can and must devote our lives to his service.

We must never forget the price that God paid to redeem us. The more we meditate on his suffering and death, the more we must live in praise and thanksgiving for his love and tender mercy. We will praise him forever because he did that which we could never do. We have been taken from the bondage of eternal death.

The will of God is that we be holy, even as he is holy. May you live today in the consciousness of that calling! We who by nature would live for ourselves have been made free from that bondage. We will now live for him! The same Holy Spirit that dwelt in Jesus without measure lives and dwells in us. We really are made new creatures after his likeness.

There is nothing greater we can give than to live our lives for him. It is not enough that our sinful desires were put to death. There also is something new that comes to life as we now live unto him.

Allen Brummel

April 21 — Q&A 44 – The Fifth State of Humiliation

Read: Matthew 27:46.

There is some confusion as a result of the placement of the final state of Christ's humiliation. The Catechism is following the order of the Apostles' Creed. While that order originally may have been due to confusion regarding the understanding of 1 Peter 3:18, we view it as the culmination of Jesus' suffering. Rather than taking a chronological approach, the confession and Catechism approach the humiliation from less to most severe.

Christ suffered the horror of hell while on the cross during the three hours of darkness. God plunged the whole world into darkness as Jesus sank into eternal death for you and me. Christ did not go to a place called hell, but hell came to him. In the midst of his agonies he cried: "My God, my God, why hast thou forsaken me?" (Matt. 27:46). Hell is devoid of God's favor.

It may seem ridiculous to say that Jesus, in a few hours of suffering, could have experienced hell to its fullest for all the sins of his people. But remember that Jesus was very God and very man. The suffering was great, but because he was all powerful it was possible for him to suffer the full measure of God's wrath and curse in a short time.

We recoil in horror to think of the suffering that those who are without Christ will experience. Is there really a hell? Look at the cross of Jesus Christ and you will know the answer. But there is more! Look by faith and believe that Jesus will never let you experience that horror! He took it in its fullness so you can live!

Allen Brummel

April 22   Q&A 44 — Comfort in Temptation

Read: 1 Corinthians 10:13.

Temptations continue to be a part of our lives. We face them every day. The devil comes with all his power and influence and tries to get us to walk in the ways of sin. There are times when those temptations seem so great that there is no way we can overcome them.

Remember the victory that is yours in Jesus Christ! In the midst of the terrible temptations and the horrible guilt and shame, remember that Jesus delivered you!

The devil challenges our faith. The devil tries to convince us that this is an empty comfort. The devil tries to frighten us with God's justice.

We turn to God and his word of comfort. We will not perish, but we will be given everlasting life. There is a way out of the temptations. That way out is through Jesus Christ our Lord and Savior. He will take us to his heavenly home.

He showed mercy to the crucified thief. He shows mercy to you and me in the midst of our temptations. He is in control of all things, turning those temptations into trials, and using them for good. What a great mercy God has shown to us in our distress!

Allen Brummel

Lord's Day 17

Q. 45. What doth the resurrection of Christ profit us?

A. First, by his resurrection he has overcome death, that he might make us partakers of that righteousness which he had purchased for us by his death; secondly, we are also by his power raised up to a new life; and lastly, the resurrection of Christ is a sure pledge of our blessed resurrection.

April 23 — Q&A 45 – Christ Arose

Read: Luke 24:34.

From the point of view of the disciples, tragedy overwhelmed them on every side. The soldiers came late at night and took the bound Jesus to Caiaphas the high priest. As if that was not bad enough, Jesus did not resist them! To add insult to injury, one of their very own, Judas, played the betrayer role, for they all saw him kiss Jesus. Moments later, another one denied him with swearing. None of them raised a finger to help him; rather, they all forsook him and fled. All of this led to the crucifixion, the public display of rejection by God and man. It was obvious from the words he uttered from the cross that his sufferings were indescribable. Then he died, amazingly soon, within a few hours, something unheard of. They took note that he was buried quickly in the unused grave of Joseph of Arimathea.

Now what?

Fear and doubt overwhelmed them. They took refuge in an upper room behind locked doors. No one seemed to remember that Jesus warned them ahead of time that this would all take place. Their hopes were directed to Jesus whom they anticipated would establish some sort of earthly kingdom and triumph over Rome. Rejection and death did not fit into their agenda.

Gradually this changed. They began to realize that Jesus *arose*! Unheard of, beyond human reasoning, the message of the resurrection reached them as they huddled behind those locked doors. The women reported that they saw him as they returned from the grave early that morning. Later, the travelers to Emmaus brought the same message: Jesus arose from the dead, and they had seen him. They in turn were greeted by the disciples shouting: "The Lord is risen indeed, and hath appeared to Simon" (Luke 24:34). That was convincing. Later that day, Jesus appeared to all the disciples in the upper room—only Thomas was absent—and greeted them with the precious words: "Peace be unto you" (John 20:19).

Never before and never after did one arise from the dead. Some were *raised*, but none *arose*. Therein lies the gospel of the resurrection. He gave himself to death that he might arise victoriously. It was *indeed* for the disciples, for it was verified by many witnesses.

The church of all ages confesses: "I believe that Jesus arose from the dead." Do you? Faith in this resurrected Jesus is secure.

Jason Kortering

April 24 — Q&A 45 – The Bodily Resurrection of Jesus

Read: 1 Corinthians 15:20.

As with all teachings of the Christian church, there are those who claim to be Christians but deny all miracles. The bodily resurrection of Jesus from the dead was a miracle. If you cannot accept the miraculous, you cannot be a Christian. It is that basic. It is easy to demonstrate this. Creation is a fundamental teaching of Christianity, and it is from beginning to end a miracle. The very first words of the Bible challenge our faith as Christians: "In the beginning, God" (Gen. 1:1). It is good that we accept by faith this creation (Heb. 11:3). Then we are in a spiritual frame of mind to accept the virgin birth of Jesus, his ministry of miracles, his death, resurrection, and ascension into heaven. It is for this reason that the Catechism treats the resurrection of Jesus as an article of faith: "I believe…the third day he arose again from the dead."*

We do well to emphasize that this confession directs our attention to the body of Jesus. He took on our flesh from the Virgin Mary when the Holy Spirit conceived him within her womb. In this body he was born. In this body he walked on earth and accomplished his public ministry. In this body he suffered and died. In this body he arose from the dead.

Even though no one can explain this scientifically, we believe it by faith because the word of God tells us that this is true. In the preceding verses of the text referenced above, Paul sets forth for us the importance of the resurrection of Christ in order to accomplish his ministry, the reconciliation of the lost sinner with the Father. It is so critical that if it did not take place "your faith is vain; ye are yet in your sins" (1 Cor. 15:17). In addition, those Christians who had already died would have perished (v. 18). In the Holy Spirit Paul asserts: "But now *is* Christ risen from the dead" (v. 20).

Paul clearly refers to Christ's body, which was placed in the grave but now came forth changed. Jesus had to take on our earthly body, weak and humiliated by sin, in order to make satisfaction for our sins. Once that was accomplished, God rewarded him with a body fit for heaven.

Jason Kortering

---

* Heidelberg Catechism A 23, in *Confessions and Church Order*, 91.

April 25 — Q&A 45 — The Risen Lord Appeared Unto Mary

Read: John 20:17.

Once we accept the miracle of the resurrected body, we have to say something yet about the appearances of Jesus in that resurrected body.

The Bible records about ten appearances of Jesus after his resurrection. We call them appearances because when Jesus was present in his resurrected body, no one could see him unless he revealed himself. That body was of the material which marked the new earth. Because of this, we have no record of where Jesus spent his time during the forty days between the resurrection and the ascension. He did not have to eat, nor sleep, nor rest as he did in his former human nature. He could pass through walls and make a sudden appearance in the upper room. If we stop to think of it, many of his appearances were necessary to convince us he was on the other side of the grave. He made sure we understood he was the same Jesus, as when "he shewed unto [the disciples] his hands and his side" (John 20:20). He also made sure we did not view him as a ghost; he asked: "Have ye here any meat?" (Luke 24:41). We know that spirits don't eat food, yet he had a real body (v. 43).

This explains the narrative in John 20. Mary had been delivered from demons, and she rejoiced in her role to minister to the earthly needs of Jesus. When Jesus spoke her name in the garden, she instinctively knew he was Jesus and wanted to embrace him, thinking she could once more have her Lord back. Jesus appeared to her to confirm for her that he was alive, but it was not as it had been in the past. He told her: "Touch me not; for I am not yet ascended to my father" (v. 17). He was on the other side of the grave, and he wanted Mary and us to look towards heaven. Note that a few verses later, Jesus said to doubting Thomas to touch him (v. 27)! I am the same Jesus, put your hands in the nail holes and believe. He ministered to each need by means of the appearance.

The appearances enabled Jesus to take a temporary visual form to confirm his resurrection. May they serve the same purpose to strengthen your faith in his resurrection.

Jason Kortering

| April 26 | Q&A 45 — Jesus Raised for Our Justification |

Read: Romans 4:25.

We turn now to the question: "What doth the resurrection of Christ profit us?"[*] We now want to say something about the first profit mentioned: "First, by his resurrection he has overcome death, that he might make us partakers of that righteousness which he had purchased for us by his death."[**]

Justification is the word used to describe God's response to the death of Christ as the substitute for our sins. Literally it means to make one just or right with God (righteous). When Jesus was on the cross, he prayed: "Father, forgive them; for they know not what they do" (Luke 23:34). That was his high priestly prayer for us and for all those for whom he died. He knew that if God would answer this prayer, he would descend upon the cross and place upon him the guilt of the sins of all those whom the Father gave to him. The Father would deal with him as the guilty sinner. This took place; it explains the hellish wrath and suffering Jesus bore on the cross. At the end, he said: "It is finished" (John 19:30). God did pour out on him his hellish wrath, and he bore it all, even to the end. Hence his atonement for sin was finished. The Father agreed and received him into his presence in heaven that very day.

Nothing proves this so much as the Father's response to raise Jesus from the dead. It was God's answer to Jesus' cry: "It is finished." After his body rested for parts of three days in the grave, God reached down and raised the body of Jesus from the dead. Yes, Jesus arose in power and glory. From God's point of view, he raised his Son. He did that for our justification. God declared in this act of resurrection that he accepted Jesus' suffering and death as the substitute for his people and now declared to all those for whom Jesus died that they are right with him because of what Jesus had done for them.

The resurrection is the legal declaration from God as judge that the debt of sin has been paid. It becomes ours through faith in this God, in Jesus his Son, by which we confess we are right with God only through the perfect work of Jesus.

Is this your faith?

Jason Kortering

---

[*] Heidelberg Catechism Q45, in *Confessions and Church Order*, 100.
[**] Heidelberg Catechism A 45, in *Confessions and Church Order*, 100.

April 27 — **Q&A 45 — Jesus Arose to Make Us Spiritually Alive**

Read: Romans 6:4.

When the Catechism asks what the profit of Christ's resurrection is for us, it mentions three things that are profitable. Now we focus on the second one: "We are also by his power raised up to a new life."* There is an assumption here which is not flattering for us. That is, without Jesus we are spiritually dead. If we are going to become spiritually alive, Jesus had to rise from the dead and make us alive.

We have followed the reasoning of the Catechism, which is opening up to us the reasoning of the Bible. If we are to be happy as Christians, we have to know the reality of our sinfulness. This has been explained to us as God's judgment upon us because of the disobedience of Adam and Eve. He said: "The day that thou eatest thereof [the fruit of the tree] thou shalt surely die" (Gen. 2:17). From this sentence of death no human being can escape. There is only one way out of the prison of death. Jesus came to join us in this prison and made payment for our sins. God accepted his death as our substitute. But we need more than that to make us happy. We need to be delivered from the experience of sin; we need to stop sinning and in holiness enjoy fellowship with God.

Jesus accomplished this by his resurrection from the dead. He must needs die, but death must not consume him. He must overcome death. The resurrection placed him on the other side of death, and, from the vantage point of victor, he comes by his word and Spirit to make us spiritually alive. Referenced above: "Like as Christ was raised from the dead by the glory of the Father, even so we also should walk in newness of life" (Rom. 6:4).

What a blessing this is for us. Sin makes life miserable; holiness makes us free. In the new life of Christ we live and die happily. This life is not perfect nor sinless, no; rather it is the beginning of perfection. As such it is also the beginning of heaven.

May God help us to understand the importance of Christ's resurrection for us.

Jason Kortering

---

* Heidelberg Catechism A 45, in *Confessions and Church Order*, 100.

April 28 — Q&A 45 — Jesus is Able to Open Our Graves

Read: 1 Thessalonians 4:14.

The third profit we have of Christ's resurrection is stated in the Catechism: "The resurrection of Christ is a sure pledge of our blessed resurrection."*

What a beautiful perspective this gives to us of our deaths! We observe death on this side of the grave as horrible defeat. It often takes away a loved one either through prolonged suffering or sudden tragedy. When breathing stops, the body immediately collapses, and decay begins. It is so pervasive that we must put away the body very soon. Accompanying this process of dying are the tears of grief, the pain of separation, and the loneliness of departure. No wonder the Bible speaks of death as the last enemy (1 Cor. 15:26). No one volunteers, no one gives up a loved one, but death must rip them out of our arms.

Here we have affirmed that death is not the end of our loved one who dies in faith. Notice: "If we believe that Jesus died and rose again, even so them also which sleep in Jesus will God bring with him" (1 Thess. 4:14). That is crucial, and believers throughout the world express this in this article of faith: I believe that Jesus died and on the third day rose again from the dead. All who believe this also believe that when we die our bodies go temporarily to the grave, but our souls go into the presence of Jesus. First Thessalonians calls it "sleep in Jesus." Sleep is from the point of view of this world, but awake is from the point of view of the soul's presence with Jesus. Such fellowship with Jesus casts off all tears, pain, suffering, sin, and every evidence of death, and replaces them with conscious deliverance and freedom to enjoy holiness.

Now, because Jesus has risen from the dead, he will come with all the saints who are with him in glory and at the sound of the trumpet raise bodies out of the grave (or wherever the decay remains) and give to every one of us a new body, like unto his own resurrected body. This is necessary because sleeping in Jesus is a temporary condition called the intermediate state of the soul. When Christ comes at the end, he will make a new heaven and earth, and there we will need new bodies fit to dwell there.

May God strengthen our faith in Christ's resurrection.

Jason Kortering

---

* Heidelberg Catechism A 45, in *Confessions and Church Order*, 100.

April 29 — **Q&A 45 — The Resurrection in the Gospel Message**

Read: Acts 3:26.

The message declared by Peter on Resurrection Sunday sets the tone for the apostles' gospel preaching. Already he had said to his adversaries: "The God of Abraham…hath glorified his Son Jesus; whom ye delivered up, and denied" (Acts 3:13). For this they must repent and embrace the living Lord.

This note of victory permeates every message the apostles brought to the people of their day. It was offensive to many because the resurrection of Jesus made things much worse for them than the day of his crucifixion. Now he is not simply a miracle worker; now he is Lord over death, the grave, and sin itself. As you read some of the sermons by the apostles, you will see that it is when they come to the part where they tell the people that Jesus not only suffered, died, but he *arose* from the dead, the audience response becomes vehement and aggressive: "And as they spake unto the people, the priests, and the captain of the temple, and the Sadducees, came upon them, being grieved that they taught the people, and preached through Jesus the resurrection from the dead" (Acts 4:1–2).

For every preacher of the gospel, the message of the resurrection of Jesus from the dead has a key place. It lifts every burdened sinner's soul from despair to forgiveness and life. The Catechism has just explained how the resurrection of Jesus from the dead gives to every believer a threefold profit. No wonder, then, that this resurrection was declared with such enthusiasm by the early church.

We often say that the heart of the gospel is the cross of Jesus, and certainly it is. Yet if we stop to think for a moment, the cross apart from Bethlehem or apart from the empty tomb means very little to us. The good news of the gospel is that Jesus, who was nailed to the cross, was not simply a victim, a human being who was violated by cruel men, but he was very God and very man. Thus, his birth sets forth his qualifications. Also, the cross without the resurrection is a human tragedy. The resurrection is God's mark of approval upon the cross of Jesus. He is a mighty Savior.

Meditate upon the resurrection and embrace it for your soul's salvation.

Jason Kortering

Lord's Day 18

Q. 46. How dost thou understand these words, "He ascended into heaven"?

A. That Christ, in sight of his disciples, was taken up from earth into heaven; and that he continues there for our interest, until he comes again to judge the quick and the dead.

Q. 47. Is not Christ then with us even to the end of the world, as he hath promised?

A. Christ is very man and very God; with respect to his human nature, he is no more on earth; but with respect to his Godhead, majesty, grace, and spirit, he is at no time absent from us.

Q. 48. But if his human nature is not present wherever his Godhead is, are not then these two natures in Christ separated from one another?

A. Not at all, for since the Godhead is illimitable and omnipresent, it must necessarily follow that the same is beyond the limits of the human nature he assumed, and yet is nevertheless in this human nature and remains personally united to it.

Q. 49. Of what advantage to us is Christ's ascension into heaven?

A. First, that he is our advocate in the presence of his Father in heaven; secondly, that we have our flesh in heaven as a sure pledge that he, as the Head, will also take up to himself, us, his members; thirdly, that he sends us his Spirit as an earnest, by whose power we *seek the things which are above, where Christ sitteth on the right hand of God*, and not things on earth.

April 30 — Q&A 46 — Christ Ascended into Heaven

Read: Acts 1:9.

The earthly journey of the Lord Jesus had come to an end. It began in Bethlehem, continued through his ministry as recorded in the gospel narratives, and in a certain sense ended in his crucifixion and resurrection from the dead. During the forty days of his post-resurrection ministry, there was very little interaction with his disciples, at least as recorded in Scripture. He was on earth, but where was he? We have a brief description in Acts 1:3, "To whom also he shewed himself alive after his passion by many infallible proofs, being seen of them forty days, and speaking of the things pertaining to the kingdom of God." He ministered to them through his appearances and through his conversation as he explained to them his kingdom. Little was understood then, for they needed the Spirit to help them.

But now his ascension into heaven had taken place. The passage referenced above states it majestically and yet simply: "He was taken up; and a cloud received him out of their sight" (v. 9). Two things are noteworthy.

First, a cloud received him out of their sight. That cloud is referenced frequently in Scripture; in the old covenant it was the cloud that led Israel through the wilderness, the *shekinah*. It is also called the glory of the Lord, for it shone in fiery power during the night hours. It assumed this form when Jesus was born: "The glory of the Lord shone round about them" (Luke 2:9); the night sky radiated with such light. At Jesus' ascension it took on the form of the cloud. It was not a natural cloud; it was God's cloud, which represented God's presence. In the ascension, it was as if God's arms enfolded his Son as he removed him from the earth and took him to heaven.

Second, take note of the appearance of the angels to the disciples. Acts 1:11 says: "Why stand ye gazing up into heaven? this same Jesus, which is taken up from you into heaven, shall so come in like manner as ye have seen him go into heaven." Jesus left the earth; his earthly ministry was finished. He departed to the place called heaven.

We do not cry; we rejoice. Do you understand why? Would you rather have Jesus here or in heaven?

Jason Kortering

May 1 — Q&A 47 — The Heavenly Christ is Still with Us

Read: John 3:13.

We should take note that the position of the historic Reformed faith concerning the ascension of Jesus into heaven is "that Christ, in sight of his disciples, was taken up from earth into heaven; and that he continues there for our interest, until he comes again to judge the quick [living] and the dead."* The assumption here is that we believe there is a place called heaven and a place called earth, and that in the ascension Jesus traveled from earth to heaven.

"In the beginning God created the heaven and the earth" (Gen. 1:1). Heaven and earth together describe the whole of creation as set forth in Genesis 1. Since there is no mention elsewhere of the creation of the angels, we can include it in the all-comprehensive statement. The account of creation and the whole of Scripture is written with a view to God's redemptive plan for man, and the earth is the home for man. Hence heaven is in the background. Heaven is the created place that manifests God's glory in the realm of the angels and the glorified church. Both await the final revelation of glory in the destruction of this heaven and earth and the creation of a new one.

Notice in John 3:13, Jesus dwelled in that heaven before he was born, and after his earthly ministry returned to that heaven, and is there now until he will return to judge all men.

Does this mean that Jesus is no more with us while we are on earth?

Here the Catechism distinguishes between the human nature of Christ and his Godhead, or divine nature. Because Jesus is both God and man, the Bible teaches that according to his divine nature he does not travel; he makes no changes in location. He is everywhere present as the second person of the Trinity. He is always with us, even now.

Jesus possesses both divinity and humanity, and it was in his humanity that the changes took place. Though Jesus is in heaven, he is with us as he said to his disciples: "Lo, I am with you alway, even unto the end of the world" (Matt. 28:20). His ascension into heaven is for our advantage.

Jason Kortering

---

* Heidelberg Catechism A 46, in *Confessions and Church Order*, 101.

May 2   **Q&A 48 — Can the Ascended Christ Be in Two Places at One Time?**

Read: John 14:2; Matthew 28:20.

These two texts set forth in bold relief the question set forth in the Catechism: if Christ ascended into heaven, "is not Christ then with us even to the end of the world, as he hath promised?" Answer: "Christ is very man and very God; with respect to his human nature, he is no more on earth; but with respect to his Godhead, majesty, grace, and spirit, he is at no time absent from us."*

The Lutherans differ from the Reformed on this answer. They believe that when Christ arose from the dead, divine qualities were transferred to his human nature, for example, omnipresence. This explains their view of the Lord's supper, that Christ is literally present *in* the bread and wine because his human nature is everywhere present. In contrast, the Reformed teach that Christ's human nature was changed in the ascension (glorified) but still retained the limitations common to man. The ascended Christ can be only one place at one time; he was on earth, but through the ascension is now in heaven. Christ said: "I go." He meant, I go away.

At the same time, Jesus assured his disciples that he would remain with them always. The question is, how does he remain with us? The Catechism correctly answers this in two ways; first, according to his divine nature he is everywhere present. This is his Godhead. Being personally God, Jesus also possesses all the virtues of God the Father, Son, and Holy Spirit. One of the great attributes of God is to be everywhere present. This defies our imagination but is taught in the Bible. In the second place, Christ is with us also according to his Spirit, whom he sends to us to abide with us. Through the Holy Spirit, he blesses us with all spiritual blessings including grace.

Even though we may answer the question posed above as yes, the ascended Christ can be in two places at one time, we still need to exercise caution. In the subsequent question and answer we are reminded that these two natures of Christ are never divided or separated. The person and divine nature is greater than the human and yet joined to it.

The ascension helps us understand our wonderful Savior.

Jason Kortering

---

*   Heidelberg Catechism Q&A 47, in *Confessions and Church Order*, 101.

May 3 — Q&A 49 — Christ Ascended for Our Advantage

Read: John 14:1–4.

The final question of this Lord's Day directs our attention to the advantage of Christ's ascension. We need to meditate on this; otherwise Christ's leaving us might bring sorrow and despair. The time of our departure is always filled with tension. This is true in the ordinary everyday experiences of leaving one another for a time. Do you like to say goodbye to your family and friends? If you are going to leave for a pleasant holiday, that is one thing. If you are leaving for an overseas education or a work assignment which is going to be for quite a long time, you feel the tug of separation and the fear of the unknown. I suppose the disciples of Jesus had some of this when they stood looking heavenward after Jesus ascended into heaven. Now they were alone; where did he go? Would they ever see him again?

At such moments, understanding the reason for departure and the advantages which such a departure will bring to your life makes saying goodbye a bit easier.

This pertains to the ascension of Jesus into heaven as well. Jesus explained this to the disciples ahead of time in order to prepare them. This is the message referenced above from John 14. He made it plain he was going to the Father who has a house of many mansions. He left them on earth in order that he might prepare a place for them to dwell in this Father's house. When this place is prepared, he will come to receive them unto himself so they can be with him. Does this not make it a bit easier to accept his departure into heaven? Heaven now becomes the focal point of our pilgrimage through this world.

We look to Jesus who is the author and finisher of our faith. This Jesus is in heaven. He blesses us from heaven; he draws us into heaven.

Jason Kortering

May 4   Q&A 49 — Our Advocate Is in Heaven

Read: Hebrews 9:24.

The Catechism lists three advantages for us by Christ's ascension into heaven. The first one we consider here: "That he is our advocate in the presence of his Father in heaven."*

An *advocate* is the term for a lawyer who has the right to represent clients before the courts. Such a person needs a license to do this and must display qualifications that enable him to pursue such a high position. Jesus as our advocate was qualified through his earthly ministry; he bore our guilt before the law of God. In the resurrection, God certified that Jesus had the right and ability to practice as our advocate before his bar of justice in heaven; he gave him his license to practice. That was no ordinary graduation exercise; it was accompanied by earthquakes, resurrections of the dead, and the tearing of the veil in the temple. Before that divine speech, we look to our representative who is now in heaven and functions as our mouthpiece before the Father.

And what does he say on our behalf?

He prayed before he left: "Father, I will that they also, whom thou hast given me, be with me where I am; that they may behold my glory, which thou has given me: for thou lovedst me before the foundation of the world." These are the sweet words of the high-priestly prayer of Jesus recorded in John 17:24. That legal plea before the Father says it all.

Sorrow turns into joy when we meditate upon this. He is not here. Look heavenward; he is gone away *for us*, on account of our good. Jesus represents us before God's throne and speaks day and night this great petition—Father, I care about my people; take care of them on earth, gather them by my word and Spirit, so conduct the affairs of history that in the end they *all* may be with me in this heavenly glory.

The Father's answer to this plea is all comprehensive. The plan that he has for them, laid down in the foundation of eternity, will be carefully executed and realized. He will do this through the exalted Christ. All things work together for that final good. What an advantage!

Jason Kortering

---

*   Heidelberg Catechism A 49, in *Confessions and Church Order*, 102.

May 5 — Q&A 49 — Our Flesh Is in Heaven

Read: 1 Corinthians 15:20–21.

The second advantage for us of Christ's ascension into heaven is expressed this way: "That we have our flesh in heaven as a sure pledge that he, as the Head, will also take up to himself, us, his members."*

The importance of accepting the bodily resurrection and ascension of Christ is now set forth. It is so down to earth that it affects us as Christians in many ways. We believe there is life after death for us. Even as Christ arose from the dead and ascended into heaven, we also will follow him. We believe that when we die, our bodies are houses without inhabitants. They are not to be discarded or cremated willfully. They are to be laid in graves to testify that a body is an important part of our existence, on earth and ultimately in the new earth.

True, our bodies cannot be taken into heaven without change. Paul in his letter to the Corinthians makes this plain: "Now this I say, brethren, that flesh and blood cannot inherit the kingdom of God; neither doth corruption inherit incorruption" (1 Cor. 15:50). Christ has brought to pass this necessary change in his own body. Through his death and resurrection, he conquered the curse of death upon the body and arose in a glorified body, fit for heavenly glory: "For this corruptible must put on incorruption, and this mortal must put on immortality" (v. 53). And it did when Jesus arose from the dead.

In that glorified body, Jesus ascended into heaven. He did that not simply as an individual, but he did that as the head of the body, his beloved church. Thus the verse referenced above states: "But now is Christ risen from the dead, and become the firstfruits of them that slept" (v. 20). The reference to firstfruits is a reference to harvest time, and the harvesting of the bodies of all the redeemed is connected with Christ who is the first.

You have the guarantee that your body will partake of the glory of perfection. That is quite an advantage that is sealed in the ascension of Jesus into heaven.

Jason Kortering

---

* Heidelberg Catechism A 49, in *Confessions and Church Order*, 102.

May 6 — Q&A 49 — We Seek Heavenly Things

Read: Colossians 3:1–3.

This is now the third advantage for us of Christ's ascension into heaven. It is expressed in the Catechism this way: "That he sends us his Spirit as an earnest by whose power we *seek the things which are above, where Christ sitteth on the right hand of God*, and not the things on earth."[*] There is a close connection between the first advantage and this one. We saw that Christ as our advocate at the right hand of God prays for our complete and final salvation, both personally and as it pertains to the entire church. The answer to that prayer includes the marvelous act of the Father to give to Jesus the Holy Spirit, by whose presence and power we are spiritually changed.

The proof of the presence of the Holy Spirit in our hearts and lives is that we become spiritually active. We turn our backs on the pleasures of sin, repent of our sinful deeds and our sinful nature, and seek after God's way. We desire to walk with God and enjoy fellowship with his people. All of this displays the presence of the Spirit of Christ. Even more than that, it is the earnest, or guaranteed pledge, of perfection.

The direction of this spiritual life is heavenward. We take our burdens to the Father in the name of Jesus; we seek forgiveness for sins and deliverance from the power of sin. Because Jesus is at the right hand of the Father, he takes our prayers and makes intercession for us with the Father. Our Father receives our cries for the sake of Jesus, his Son. "For ye are dead, and your life is hid with Christ in God" (Col. 3:3).

Looking heavenward, we direct our lives to heaven, we "seek those things which are above" (v. 1). What a change in direction. We become heavenly-minded, we measure our spiritual progress by heaven's standard. We act like we belong in heaven. Blessings flow to us from heaven and we direct our lives towards heaven.

Are you thus converted unto God by the resurrected and ascended Lord Jesus?

Jason Kortering

---

[*] Heidelberg Catechism A 49, in *Confessions and Church Order*, 102.

Lord's Day 19

Q. 50. Why is it added, "and sitteth at the right hand of God"?

A. Because Christ is ascended into heaven for this end, that he might appear as Head of his church, by whom the Father governs all things.

Q. 51. What profit is this glory of Christ, our Head, unto us?

A. First, that by his Holy Spirit he pours out heavenly graces upon us his members; and then that by his power he defends and preserves us against all enemies.

Q. 52. What comfort is it to thee that "Christ shall come again to judge the quick and the dead"?

A. That in all my sorrows and persecutions, with uplifted head I look for the very same person who before offered himself for my sake to the tribunal of God, and has removed all curse from me, to come as judge from heaven; who shall cast all his and my enemies into everlasting condemnation, but shall translate me with all his chosen ones to himself, into heavenly joys and glory.

May 7 — Q&A 50 — Christ Sits at the Right Hand of God

Read: Ephesians 1:18–20.

We continue with the confession of our faith in the exaltation of Christ. God raised him from the dead, by that power he ascended into heaven, and now, being in heaven, he sits at the right hand of God. This event was included in prophecy: "The LORD said unto my Lord, Sit thou at my right hand, until I make thine enemies thy footstool" (Ps. 110:1). Jesus also used this language when he spoke to Pilate: "Nevertheless I say unto you, Hereafter shall ye see the Son of man sitting on the right hand of power, and coming in the clouds of heaven" (Matt. 26:64).

The language is figurative, and we immediately think of the days of kings who sat on thrones and had men at their right hands. Each king trusted his right-hand man most and commissioned him to do all his business on his behalf. Now picture the Lord Jesus in this position in heaven. The throne of God is revealed in glory in Revelation 4 and 5. In that vision, God has in his right hand the book, which represents all his counsel for things that must take place in history in order to complete the gathering of the church in glory. Christ takes his place at God's right hand and is qualified to open the book and realize its contents. He is the exalted lamb that had been slain. In Ephesians 1, God wants us to understand that Christ is exalted at his "right hand in the heavenly places" (v. 20).

We express this every time we recite the articles of faith. We do this by faith. We cannot see Christ in heaven, but we know he is there because the Holy Spirit testifies in our hearts that this is true.

What an exaltation that is for Christ! Here on earth, he came under the curse of the law for us; now he carries out the will of God for us, for our final deliverance from sins. May God open the eyes of our understanding.

Jason Kortering

May 8 — Q&A 50 — Christ Is the Exalted Head of the Church

Read: Colossians 1:18.

The Catechism expresses our understanding of Christ sitting at the right hand of God this way: "Christ is ascended into heaven for this end, that he might appear as the Head of his Church, by whom the Father governs all things."* We want to say something about Christ's relationship to his church; he is the *head* of the body and that too, as he sits at God's right hand. The Bible uses this figure of speech in describing the church's relationship to Christ: "And he is the head of the body, the church" (Col. 1:18). This text joins two ideas together: Christ is the head of the body, and he is also the head of the church. The body *is* the church. Ephesians 1:22 speaks the same language: God "gave him [the exalted Christ] to be the head over all things to the church."

Do you appreciate what this means to you as a believer?

The head and the body are joined together by God. He did this in his eternal predestination of love. God gave to Christ a people, his body, and made him to be the head (Eph. 1:3–6). The head controls the body, so Christ earned the right to control his church. He loved us unto death and redeemed us from our sins. God, in response to such faithfulness, rewarded Christ, our head, by setting him at his own right hand. That is honorable and glorious for Christ.

It is blessed for us, for it is also true; the body receives its direction and life from the head. This we do as the church from Christ our head. Our head is not weak, wanting to do something he cannot do. He isn't the kind of head who wants to save everyone but can't accomplish that. No, he is at the right hand of God; he has received the preeminence, the power and glory, so that the Father governs all things through him.

His will is to save his entire church, his body. By faith, we are part of that body. Christ is our head. In such a position of glory, our relationship to Christ is sure and steadfast.

Jason Kortering

---

* Heidelberg Catechism A 50, in *Confessions and Church Order*, 102.

May 9 — Q&A 51 — The Exalted Christ Gives Us Heavenly Graces

Read: John 10:28.

Once more we glance at the Catechism itself. The question is asked: "What profit is the glory of Christ, our Head, unto us?" The answer: "First, that by his Holy Spirit he pours out heavenly graces upon us his members."* Because the head rules the body, the direct benefit we receive from our exalted head in heaven, is that he gives us *heavenly* graces as members of his body. Do take note also that he gives them to us "by his Holy Spirit."

We are reminded of the beauty of this on the first Pentecost. The disciples were afraid, confused, uncertain of their future, and certainly bewildered about what the purpose of Christ's ministry on earth really was. This all changed when Christ poured upon them heavenly graces through the presence of his Holy Spirit. They became clear in their understanding of the truth, the gospel message burned in their hearts; they possessed boldness to speak it; they loved one another and reached out to others to draw them into their fellowship. That very day, three thousand souls were added to the church. The heavenly graces abounded.

It is no less different today. From the text referenced above, the greatest heavenly gift which Christ promised to give to his disciples was "eternal life" (John 10:28). Once they received it, they could not perish because no man could pluck them out of Christ's hand.

Yes, there are many gifts which Christ bestows upon his body, the church. Ephesians 4:8 quotes Psalm 68:18, "Wherefore he saith, When he ascended up on high, he led captivity captive, and gave gifts unto men." The preceding context mentions "lowliness and meekness…longsuffering, forbearing one another in love; endeavoring to keep the unity of the Spirit in the bond of peace" (vv. 2–3). The following verses mention the gifts of office: "He gave some, apostles; and some, prophets; and some, evangelists; and some, pastors and teachers" (v. 11). Central to all of them is the gift of faith and salvation. No man can acquire this for himself; only Christ can give it to him from heaven: "And I give unto them eternal life" (John 10:28).

Christ gives faith in the way of repentance from sin and believing in him as the only way of salvation. It is wonderful to confess such faith.

Jason Kortering

---

* Heidelberg Catechism Q&A 51, in *Confessions and Church Order*, 102.

May 10 — Q&A 50 — The Exalted Christ Defends and Preserves His Church

Read: Matthew 16:18.

There is a second profit given to us from Jesus Christ sitting at the right hand of God. It is stated this way in the Catechism: "That by his power he defends and preserves us against all enemies."* Jesus called these enemies "the gates of hell" in Matthew 16:18. If we look at the church's place in this world through human eyes, we have every reason to call into question the safety and ultimate victory of the church. There are enemies who are capable of destroying the church, of removing it from the face of the earth.

Some of them arise out of hell itself. Think of Satan and the hordes of devils who are at his command—being fallen angels, they are spirits, and as such they lie beyond our ability to see them and acknowledge their presence. They surround us on every side. These same evil spirits have the capacity to influence men, to cause them to become monsters of iniquity and bold in their contempt of that which is holy and true. Some men even do more than boast of their evil ways; they even attack and persecute the righteous.

Of greater concern, these same spirits have access to the heart and life of the church, the body of Christ. Satan attempted to tempt Christ; how much more is he able to tempt us? Sometimes he comes into our lives with a direct frontal attack by infiltrating our thoughts. Other times he comes through fellow mankind by enticing us with the temptations of the flesh to sin against God. This is true because our greatest enemy is our own sinful flesh, which is easily attracted to sin.

The gates of hell come at us from every direction: from the world, from our own flesh, from fellow church members, from society in general, on and on.

This is our comfort: that the gates of hell shall not prevail against us. The exalted Christ shall defend and preserve us as his church. Peter's confession, "Thou art the Christ, the Son of the living God," forms the rock upon which Christ builds his church (Matt. 16:16–18).

Christ is greater than any mortal enemy. He is able to work in our hearts by his Holy Spirit to keep us faithful, even unto death.

Jason Kortering

---

* Heidelberg Catechism A 51, in *Confessions and Church Order*, 102.

May 11 — Q&A 52 – Christ Will Come to Judge

Read: Revelation 20:11–12.

We come now to the ultimate expression of Christ Jesus' exaltation—he is the judge of all rational and moral creatures. Remember this is the same Jesus that the Father gave to cover the sins of the elect. For him to do this required the ultimate humiliation: his lowly birth, his suffering as the substitute for sinners, his willingness to die, his burial, and greatest of all, his bearing on the cross the hellish wrath that the righteous God had against all the sins of all his people.

Now we see this same Jesus, who arose from the dead, ascended into heaven, and sits at the right hand of God, coming at the end of the ages to function as the judge of all creatures. Once condemned by the law, he now sits as judge of the very same law. The Catechism expresses it this way: "That in all my sorrows and persecutions, with uplifted head I look for the very same person who before offered himself for my sake to the tribunal of God, and has removed all curse from me."*

Jesus will be the judge because God rewards him with that position. He alone has the right and the power given to him of his Father to call every creature—past, present, and future, whoever lived on the earth, inhabited the heavens, or dwelled in the deep under the earth—to stand before him in judgment. In the above passage, this is described as "the dead, small and great" (Rev. 20:12).

This is important for us to understand. The purpose of this final judgment of Jesus is not to discover who will go to heaven and who will go to hell. This is well-known to Jesus as judge, for he is Lord of all. It is even known to those who stand in judgment, for they will appear in their resurrected bodies, and their bodies will indicate their destiny, heaven or hell.

The purpose is for Christ to publicly declare that God is just in saving his own and casting the wicked into hell. That is for somber reflection.

Jason Kortering

---

* Heidelberg Catechism A 52, in *Confessions and Church Order*, 103.

May 12 — Q&A 52 — Christ's Judgment Will Be Merciful

Read: Matthew 25:34.

The Catechism expresses it this way: "In my sorrows…I look for the very same person who before offered himself for my sake…to come as judge from heaven, who shall cast all his and my enemies into everlasting condemnation, but shall translate me with all his chosen ones to himself, into heavenly joys and glory."[*] At the end of the ages, Christ will personally come to bring an end to history. There will be an immediate change for the living saints; they will be translated in a moment into their glorified bodies. In those bodies they will appear before the great white throne and stand in judgment before Jesus.

If you are a believer, you have no reason to dread this final judgment. This is because we have no reason to fear the judge. He is the same person who satisfied God's law of righteousness for all those who believe on him. This is amazing because our consciences still accuse us because of our sins. We know the righteousness of God manifests itself in his hostility against both sinners and their sins. We struggle with the question, How can I be sure that God will not punish me in the end for all my sins? I deserve such punishment. Rather than focusing on yourself standing in judgment, focus on the judge; he is Jesus, your savior and my savior who paid the debt for all our sins. He is the one who delivers us from the dominion of sin and makes us willing and ready to live unto him. From this point of view, the text referenced above contains the words of Jesus which he spoke while on earth: "Come, ye blessed of my Father" (Matt. 25:34). When we appear as such, there is no fear of judgment.

Notice, the verdict and final sentence is sure: "Inherit the kingdom prepared for you from the foundation of the world" (v. 34). That is how great our God is. He chose us from eternity, arranged for our redemption from sin in the giving of his Son, and promised to convert us from sin unto life. This he did.

That is pure mercy, love which delivers us from hellish wrath and draws us into sweet fellowship with him. The final judgment opens the way for this to take place.

Jason Kortering

---

[*] Heidelberg Catechism A 52, in *Confessions and Church Order*, 103.

May 13 — **Q&A 52 — Christ's Judgment Will Be Righteous for the Wicked**

Read: Matthew 25:41.

The Catechism expressed judgment for the wicked this way: Jesus "shall cast all his and my enemies into everlasting condemnation."* The Catechism was written during a time of great persecution for the church. Much blood was shed by the enemies of the faith, and the Christians of that day feared and often struggled with God's fairness. How could people who denied the teaching of the Bible and exalted man over God get away with their evil deeds? The answer of the Catechism reminds them that at the end of the world, when Jesus will come again, he will function as their judge at the final judgment. He will say to their enemies: "Depart from me, ye cursed, into everlasting fire, prepared for the devil and his angels" (Matt. 25:14).

At that judgment, the details of men's lives will be revealed to them. All their past conduct will be evaluated in the light of the presence of Jesus. Every evil word spoken in secret, every deed plotted and executed, will be measured by the law of God, the standard of what is right before God. This exposure of evil will be sufficient to silence any complaint against the righteous sentence of Jesus. The testimony will be exhaustive and compelling. The wicked are cursed of God, guilty and worthy of punishment. All will have to hang their heads in shame and admit that they deserve the everlasting fire.

The difference between the people of God and the wicked is not sin or the measure of sin. It is whether sin has been atoned for, the debt paid. Jesus paid it all, and everyone who embraces Jesus as Savior and Lord will stand in judgment free from his personal guilt. The judgment will reveal to him all his sins and make it evident he deserves the everlasting fire as well as the wicked. The difference is between mercy and judgment. God in his mercy covers the guilt of believers in Jesus, while his judgment exposes the guilt of the wicked who reject the gospel. Everlasting fire, because God is everlasting, and sin against him deserves such punishment.

Flee to Jesus as your refuge.

Jason Kortering

---

* Heidelberg Catechism A 52, in *Confessions and Church Order*, 103.

Lord's Day 20

Q. What dost thou believe concerning the Holy Ghost?

A. First, that he is true and co-eternal God with the Father and the Son; secondly, that he is also given me, to make me, by a true faith, partaker of Christ and all his benefits, that he may comfort me and abide with me for ever.

May 14 — Q&A 53 — The Divinity of the Holy Spirit

Read: Romans 8:1–14.

In discussing the Apostles' Creed, our teachers in the classroom of the Catechism divide the twelve articles into three groups. The first group is "Of God the Father" (Lord's Days 9–10); the second, "Of God the Son" (Lord's Days 11–19); and the third "Of God the Holy Ghost" (Lord's Days 20–24). Lord's Day 20 begins a discussion of God the Holy Ghost.

Our teachers are quite insistent on the fact that we understand the truth of the divinity of the Holy Spirit. The Holy Spirit is one of the three persons of the holy Trinity. As one of the three persons, he is equal with the Father, the first person, and the Son, the second person. This means that all three persons are fully and completely divine. The essence of God is not divided into three parts, each person possessing one part. Each person possesses the whole essence as his own.

The one mind of God is not only the mind of the Father and Son but is also the mind of the Holy Spirit. The one will of God is equally the will of the Father, the Son, and the Holy Spirit. God's perfections are equally the possession of all three persons. Each person is omnipresent; each person is omnipotent; each person is eternal; each person is omniscient. This must be true, for there is only one mind in God, one will, and the same perfections belonging equally to all. God's grace, mercy, love, compassion, longsuffering, and holiness belong equally to each person, including the Holy Spirit.

God is a covenant God who dwells in fellowship with himself. His fellowship is perfect, infinitely happy, most blessed, and full of the perfect enjoyment each person has in each other person. The Holy Spirit makes such fellowship possible, for the Holy Spirit joins the Father and the Son by his own procession from the Father and the Son. Just as the Father generates the Son and the Son is generated by the Father, so the Holy Spirit proceeds from Father and Son. The triune God sent Christ, the second person of the Trinity, into this world to take on our human nature. In that nature, he suffered and died, rose again, ascended into heaven, and was exalted as "King of kings, and Lord of lords" (1 Tim. 6:15). The triune God gave the exalted Christ the gift of the Spirit, the third person of the Trinity (Acts 2:33) so that Christ might give his Spirit to the church.

This article and truth concerning the Holy Spirit we must and do believe. Some want to make the Holy Spirit a lesser person of lesser importance than the Father and the Son. We must not do that. Some want to deny the divinity of the Holy Spirit altogether. We must not do that. To deny the Holy Spirit as "true and co-eternal God"[*] is to deny the Trinity and our salvation. We must say: "I believe in the Holy Spirit."

Herman Hanko

---

[*] Heidelberg Catechism A 53, in *Confessions and Church Order*, 103.

May 15 — **Q&A 53 – The Spirit Poured Out on Pentecost**

Read: Acts 2.

When we say with the Apostles' Creed, "I believe in the Holy Spirit," we also say: "I believe that the Holy Spirit was given to the church on Pentecost." When our Lord ascended into heaven and was given the place of highest exaltation at God's right hand, he was also given the Holy Spirit (Acts 2:33). Christ poured out the Spirit given him upon the church. It was on the first day of the week, fifty days after Christ rose from the dead, and ten days from the ascension of Christ into heaven. One hundred twenty disciples were gathered in an upper room for worship. While they were together, the Holy Spirit was given them. Because the Holy Spirit is invisible and because his coming could not be seen, he came with three different signs: the sound of a rushing mighty wind, tongues of fire on the heads of each disciple, and the gift of tongues.

These signs were important, not only because they were visible signs that the Holy Spirit had come to the church, but also because the signs showed how the Holy Spirit was to work in the church. It was a wonderful day for the church, a day to be remembered throughout the whole history of the New Testament church.

The sound of a rushing mighty wind was the means God used to bring a huge crowd together in the street in front of the place where the 120 disciples were gathered. It was the sound of wind only; the day was quiet in Jerusalem. It was a strange sound, for it seemed to be coming from the house where the 120 were worshipping, so that the people who heard it knew where to go.

It was a sign of the work of the Holy Spirit in the hearts of God's people. The Spirit is invisible but unstoppable. He is irresistible in his work and accomplishes Christ's purpose. Jesus had spoken of this already to Nicodemus (John 3:8).

The tongues as of fire are often pictured like a flame of a candle burning on the top of the wick. But the text in Acts 2 leaves quite a different picture in our minds. It is the picture of a column of fire that comes down from heaven, shooting out tongues of fire that swirl around the head of each one of the 120 disciples only to return again to the column of fire. It was a dramatic scene. The fire signified the work of the Holy Spirit, for fire destroys and purifies (1 Pet. 1:7). Fire burns away the dross from ore, the impurities from gold, and the wickedness in us. But in destroying the useless and wicked, it purifies and sanctifies, so that the Spirit, in destroying our old man of sin, creates a new man that is holy and pure.

It was a marvelous sign. It pictures the Holy Spirit in our hearts.

Herman Hanko

May 16 — Q&A 53 — The Sign of Tongues

Read: Acts 2:5–21.

The sign of speaking in foreign languages was also a sign accompanying the pouring out of the Spirit. It was a most powerful sign and spoke of a particular wonderful work of the Holy Spirit. We must abandon the interpretation given this sign by the charismatics, for their interpretation is contrary to Scripture and a distortion of the sign itself. It is clear from Acts 2:8 that the 120 disciples spoke in existing languages, while Charismatics believe that the sign of tongue-speaking is in languages that have never been spoken.

The scene in Jerusalem on that glorious day was in this manner. The crowd that was brought together by the sound of a rushing mighty wind were gathered in the street outside the place where the disciples had met for worship. The crowd, quite obviously, wondered what was happening. The 120 moved through the crowd explaining this great event. They could have spoken in Aramaic, because the people gathered in Jerusalem from all parts of the Mediterranean world understood that language. They were Jews and proselytes (Acts 2:9–11). But the 120 were able to speak the languages of the countries from which these Jews and proselytes came: Parthia, Media, Elam, etc. When one of these 120 met a Parthian, the disciple was able to speak in the Parthian language. When he or she moved on and met someone from Pamphylia, that disciple was able to speak in the language spoken in Pamphylia. So the people were able to say, "How hear we every one in our own tongue, wherein we were born?" (v. 8). And the one thing of which they spoke was "the wonderful works of God" (Acts 2:11). That was an amazing sign! What does it mean?

The Holy Spirit, through this sign, was telling the church and all those who heard the 120 speak that, in the dispensation that now was beginning with the outpouring of the Spirit, the church would be gathered no longer from the nation of Israel but would be gathered from all the nations of the earth. The Holy Spirit of the ascended Christ would gather a truly catholic church. Gentiles were gathered in the Old Testament as well. Consider Rahab, Ruth, the wives of the sons of Jacob, the Gibeonites, etc. But these Gentiles were saved only by being brought into the nation of Israel and becoming Jews by the rite of circumcision.

In the new dispensation, that changed. The Gentiles are saved from every nation, but in such a way that they preserve all their national characteristics. A saved Chinese person does not have to become a Frenchman to be saved, but he remains Chinese. The church in that way is truly catholic and is composed of an almost infinite number of different individuals.

Only in this way can the riches of God's grace be fully revealed. As a diamond with its many facets shows the color of light, so does a catholic church show the splendor of God's grace.

Herman Hanko

May 17   Q&A 54 — The Sign of a Catholic Church

Read: Acts 2:22–36.

Having instructed us in the truth of what happened on Pentecost, our teacher also wants us to know the significance of Pentecost for the believer. Our teacher becomes very personal and suddenly switches to the first personal pronoun: "He [the Holy Ghost] is also given me."* We are told that we must make this truth concerning the Holy Spirit our own personal confession.

There are those who explain Pentecost to mean little else than a revival in the church. Some, usually with charismatic tendencies and beliefs, find nothing more significant in Pentecost than that a much-needed revival took place in the church, the first of many revivals appearing from time to time in the church of the new dispensation. But, as Peter makes clear in his great Pentecostal sermon, this event in the history of the church is as great and important as Christ's resurrection from the dead. Peter does this by pointing to the fact that the prophecy of Joel was fulfilled (Acts 2:16–21).

Part of that prophecy of Joel was: "Your sons and your daughters shall prophesy, and your young men shall see visions, and your old men shall dream dreams: and on my servants and on my handmaidens I will pour out in those days of my Spirit; and they shall prophesy" (Acts 2:17–18). The reference of this prophecy of Joel, quoted by Peter, was to the office of prophet in the old dispensation, an office given to only a very few. That office embraced prophets, priests, and kings, although the offices of priests and kings were kept strictly separate (1 Sam 13:8–14; 2 Chron. 26:16–21). Joel the prophet spoke of the gift of prophecy given to all, and Peter quoted that passage on Pentecost, pointing out that with the gift of the Holy Spirit, all God's people from the least to the greatest and from the youngest to the oldest are now prophets. And that office of prophet given to them includes the office of priests and kings.

God's people no longer need anyone to teach them, for they all are able to know the Lord (Heb. 8:11; 1 John 2:27). They no longer need a priest, for they are able, by the Spirit, to go directly to God in prayer through their intercessor, Jesus Christ. They no longer need a king to rule over them, for they are kings in their own right and able to do the will of God. This anointing was more fully spoken of by our teacher in Lord's Day 12. That Lord's Day, you will recall, speaks of the name given to our savior, Christ. But then it asks of us why we are called Christians, And the answer given is that we partake of Christ's anointing and are, therefore, prophets, priest and kings under Christ.

How great and important an event Pentecost was for us!

Herman Hanko

---

*   Heidelberg Catechism A 53, in *Confessions and Church Order*, 103.

May 18 — Q&A 53 — United to Christ

Read: John 14:1–10.

Our teacher now turns to another element of our faith in the Holy Spirit: "He is also given me, to make me, by a true faith, partaker of Christ and all his benefits."[*] This statement is cast in the form of a very personal confession: he is given to me; he makes me partaker of Christ's benefits. What a confession this is! It seems almost to be too bold on the part of the one making it. And there are those voices that insist that it is too bold a statement to make. Yet our teacher insists that we make it. I possess the Holy Spirit in my heart. By his work I am partaker of all Christ's benefits.

The wonder of making this confession one's own comes from the fact that we make it "by a true faith."[**] According to the definition of faith that our teacher has taught us in Lord's Day 7, faith believes all that God reveals in his word. That faith, therefore, believes that Christ suffered and died, rose again as the eternal Son of God, ascended into heaven, is exalted at God's right hand, and pours out the Holy Spirit on his church.

But then Lord's Day 7 makes this faith a personal faith: It is "an assured confidence, which the Holy Ghost works by the gospel in my heart; that not only to others, but to me also, remission of sin, everlasting righteousness, and salvation are, freely given by God, merely of grace, only for the sake of Christ's merits."[***] Did you notice the personal element that is included in faith? The true faith of the believer always makes it possible for him to make all the truth of Scripture his own personal possession.

First, that faith, so personal, is a gift of God worked in us by the Holy Spirit (Eph. 2:8). Second, that faith is given as a gracious gift. I do not exercise it by my own power. I do not accept Christ as my personal Savior. I do not make my choice to be one with Christ. Faith is given.

Third, that faith unites us to Christ as a branch is united to a tree by grafting. We are, says our teacher in Lord's Day 7, ingrafted into Christ by a true and living faith.[****] That means that we are now one with Christ, members of his body. We become one flesh just as man and woman become one flesh in marriage (Eph. 5:30–32). And finally, that means that all the blessings of salvation Christ earned on the cross become my possession—as they become the possession of every believer.

That faith, a gift of God and worked by the Holy Spirit, becomes active in my life through the preaching of the gospel. The believer reaches out to Christ. He abandons his works as hopeless and useless. He sees himself as the sinner he truly is. Faith drives him to the cross to cling to Christ. That faith is worked by the Holy Spirit.

Herman Hanko

---

[*]   Heidelberg Catechism A 53, in *Confessions and Church Order*, 103.
[**] Heidelberg Catechism A 53, in *Confessions and Church Order*, 103.
[***] Heidelberg Catechism A 21, in *Confessions and Church Order*, 90–91.
[****]Heidelberg Catechism A 20, in *Confessions and Church Order*, 90.

May 19 — Q&A 53 — The Holy Spirit as Comforter

Read: John 14:16–17, 26; 15:26; John 16:13–14.

Our teacher in Lord's Day 20 speaks also of the Holy Spirit as our comforter. He is reminding us of what Jesus said to his disciples, words of our Lord recorded for us in the passages given you to read. John 14–16 record the words of our Savior to his disciples on the eve of his suffering and death on the cross. It was while they were still together at the table where the Lord had celebrated the last Passover with them that he told them in unmistakable words that he was going away from them. This thought filled the hearts of the disciples with a great sorrow, for they had come to love the Lord very much. Jesus explained to them in the words of these three chapters in John's gospel that he had to go away from them, and that, in fact, it was better that he go away from them, for if he would go away on a journey that led to the cross of Calvary and the tomb of Joseph of Arimathea, he would rise again and go to heaven. From heaven he would be with them in a way far, far better than when he walked with them on the dusty roads of Palestine (John 14:1–3).

What was that way in which he would be with them? He would not be with them bodily, for he would be in heaven, and they would be on earth. But he would be with them by his Holy Spirit, whom he would send to them. This is quite startling! Christ would be with them by his Spirit in a better way than he would be with them bodily. But so it is. When we have the Spirit of Christ, whom he poured out on Pentecost, we have Christ himself with us, and Christ's promise is fulfilled: "And, lo, I am with you alway, even unto the end of the world" (Matt. 28:20).

These passages in John 14–16 all speak of the Holy Spirit as our comforter. He comforts us in this world of sin and sorrow. He comforts us while our Savior is absent from us. It is like a bridegroom who, immediately after he and the bride spoke their vows that united them in marriage, went away to be gone for ever so long a time. How sad the bride would be! But the bridegroom assures his weeping bride that he will actually be with her in a very wonderful way and that this will be her comfort.

That comfort that comes through the Holy Spirit to the church in her Lord's absence is a comfort that also has with it a very long letter that the Holy Spirit gives the bride of Christ. That letter is the holy Scriptures. It is a letter from Christ to his bride in which he tells her how much he loves her and how he will come again to take his bride to the place where he is. That is why the comforter is also called the Spirit of truth. It is through the truth in Scripture that we hear our bridegroom's words and are comforted.

Herman Hanko

May 20 — Q&A 53 — The Holy Spirit, The Author of Assurance

Read: Romans 8:1–17.

The teacher, who leads us to learn all these lessons we have to learn to know our only comfort, wants to be sure that they are lessons that lead us to make the truth of Scripture our very own; for if they did not lead us to make these truths our very own, we still would not have comfort. It is possible to read the Scriptures that tell us about the suffering and death of Christ and to conclude: Yes, there was once a man who was also God, who died on the cross in order to pay for the sins of some people whom God gave to him. But I have no idea whether or not I am one of those people.

That kind of speech may sound strange to you, but there are many people in the church, even in so-called Reformed churches, who believe this very thing. They claim to believe in everything Scripture teaches as being factual, but they claim also that they do not know whether that truth of Scripture is true for them. In fact, they rather doubt that it is meant for them. They are born with this doubt; they live all their lives with this doubt; and they die without ever knowing whether they are or are not a true child of God.

This is a terrible way to live; and, as a matter of fact, it is sinful to live this way. God's people may not doubt. They would be like orphans, made a part of the family, showered with all the love all the children receive, given the same food, drink, place to study and sleep, and gifts that all the children receive. They are even mentioned in the father's will as some of the heirs. But all the time they say to themselves and to others: "I do not know whether I really belong to this family or not. Maybe I don't." The parents of such children would have reason to be angry with those children.

The Holy Spirit works assurance in the hearts of the people of God. He works such assurance by the Scriptures themselves when he works faith in our hearts to believe the Scriptures. He works that assurance that we are the children of God when we are surrounded by the tokens of God's love, and his love is shed abroad in our hearts by the Holy Spirit. We are assured of our membership in the family of God when the Spirit testifies with our spirits that we are the children of God. And if we are children, then we are also heirs of salvation and the blessedness of heaven in Father's house when we die.

And so we say with our teacher: "He is also given me, to make me…partaker of Christ…He [comforts] me and [abides] with me for ever."* Even in heaven we will still have the Holy Spirit in us.

Herman Hanko

---

* Heidelberg Catechism A 53, in *Confessions and Church Order*, 103.

Lord's Day 21

Q. 54. What believest thou concerning the "holy catholic church" of Christ?

A. That the Son of God from the beginning to the end of the world, gathers, defends, and preserves to himself by his Spirit and Word, out of the whole human race, a church chosen to everlasting life, agreeing in true faith; and that I am, and for ever shall remain, a living member thereof.

Q. 55. What do you understand by "the communion of saints"?

A. First, that all and every one who believes, being members of Christ, are, in common, partakers of him and of all his riches and gifts; secondly, that every one must know it to be his duty, readily and cheerfully to employ his gifts, for the advantage and salvation of other members.

Q. 56. What believest thou concerning "the forgiveness of sins"?

A. That God, for the sake of Christ's satisfaction, will no more remember my sins, neither my corrupt nature, against which I have to struggle all my life long; but will graciously impute to me the righteousness of Christ, that I may never be condemned before the tribunal of God.

May 21 — Q&A 54 — The Election of the Church

Read: Ephesians 1.

Question and answer 54 of the Catechism is one of the most beautiful lessons in the entire Catechism that our teacher wants us to learn. It is beautiful, partly because of its terse yet complete summary of the teaching of Scripture on the doctrine of the church. But it is also beautiful because it teaches us to make the personal confession: Of that church "I am, and for ever shall remain, a living member thereof." The Lord's Day gives us what amounts to a definition of the church in the words: "A church chosen unto everlasting life."* Thus, the church is the number of the elect who are chosen by God unto everlasting life.

This is a beautiful confession in its own right. God chose his church in his eternal counsel before he created the world (Eph. 1:4). He did not choose an indefinite mass of people; he chose definite people, individuals, whose names are written on the pages of the book of life and whom God knows by name. God chose them in Christ. There is no Christ without the church, just as there is no church without Christ. Christ and his church belong together and form one body (1 Cor. 12:27). God gave his church to Christ so that Christ might die for that church to pay for the sins of its members and thus make his church his own bride (Eph. 5:31–32). All those who are elect are saved and come to Christ. All who come to Christ are those who are elect (John 6:37). No one else comes.

Election is the cause of the salvation of the church in the history of the world. This is clearly stated in our Canons of Dordt head 1, article 7, and the conclusion to the Canons says that "election is the fountain and the cause of faith,"** by which faith we are united to Christ as members of his body. These elect are chosen "unto everlasting life." God's purpose in choosing them is to give them everlasting life in heaven with him. The whole church will be there in a host that is beyond counting. They are more in number, Scripture tells us, than the sand on the seashore and the stars in heaven (Gen. 22:17). They shall be in heaven, without sin, in all the glory of Christ himself who saved them. They shall be there as the bride of Christ, married to him who is their savior. They shall enjoy the blessedness of covenant fellowship with God forever and ever.

Of that church, I believe I am now and forever shall remain a living member.

Herman Hanko

---

* Heidelberg Catechism A 54, in *Confessions and Church Order*, 104.
** Canons of Dordt Conclusion, in *Confessions and the Church Order*, 179.

May 22 — Q&A 54 — The Gathering of the Church

Read: Matthew 16:13–19; Matthew 28:16–20; Acts 13:1–4.

Our teacher wants us to study this lesson very carefully, because many deny its truth in our day. Especially all those who have adopted Arminianism as a correct interpretation of the Bible tell us that the church is gathered by individual people accepting Christ as their personal Savior and letting Jesus come into their hearts. They try to tell us that Jesus wants to save everyone and died for everyone, but only those who accept him will actually be saved. This is a dreadful lie which has affected the church.

There are several truths we have to learn if we are to master this lesson. The first is that "the Son of God…gathers, defends, and preserves to himself by his Spirit and Word, out of the whole human race, a church."* The gathering of the church is the work of the Son of God. In other words, God himself gathers his church, which he has chosen, but he does so through his Son Jesus Christ. But the Son of God not only gathers his church; he also defends and preserves it. The church has many enemies, and they are much stronger than the people of God. It is a miracle, performed by Christ, that the church is not destroyed (Luke 12:32). It is a miracle, performed by Christ, that the church is preserved (John 10:28–30).

The Son of God gathers his church "by his Spirit and Word." Christ uses means to gather his church. He uses the means of the preaching of the gospel (Rom. 10:13–15). But the preaching of the gospel is effective and saves only those in whom the Spirit works, for only those come to Christ whom the Father draws (John 6:44–45).

The Son of God gathers his church from the whole human race. He does not gather them from the nation of Israel alone, as in the old dispensation, but he gathers them from every nation, tribe, and tongue (Rev. 5:9; 7:9; 14:6). It is truly a catholic church that Christ gathers.

Christ gathers his church from the beginning to the end of time. Already God began gathering his church immediately after Adam and Eve fell. My pastor of years ago, Herman Hoeksema, would say, Adam and Eve "fell, but they fell upon Christ who stood behind them."** From that moment on the church was being gathered; even in the darkest days of the history of the church, the Son of God was gathering, defending, and preserving his church. Seven thousand were preserved even through the dark and evil days of Ahab and Jezebel.

The gathering of the church will end with the conversion of the last elect. Christ cannot come again until the last elect is born and saved. But Christ is so eager to come to the rescue of his church that when the last elect is brought to faith and the church is complete, Christ returns.

I am and forever shall remain a living member of that church.

Herman Hanko

---

* Heidelberg Catechism A 54, in *Confessions and Church Order*, 104.
** Herman Hoeksema, *Reformed Dogmatics*, 2nd ed. (Grandville, MI: Reformed Free Publishing Association, 2004), 1:365.

May 23 — Q&A 54 — The Attributes of the Church

Read: 1 Corinthians 12; Ephesians 4:1–14.

Question and answer 54 of the Catechism explains the article in the Apostles' Creed: "I believe an holy catholic church."[*] And so our teacher points us to the attributes of the church. They are three in number.

One attribute is the unity of the church. Our teacher points out that this means that the church agrees "in true faith."[**] There are many churches in the world and many denominations. But this does not mean that all churches are part of the church of Christ and that all denominations belong to Christ's church. Nor does it mean that every member in a given denomination, even if that denomination holds to the truth of Scripture, is a member of the church of Christ. Even in the church that faithfully bears the marks of the true church (the pure preaching of the word, the administration of the sacraments according to the rule of Christ, and the exercise of Christian discipline according to the command of Christ) there are hypocrites who, while outwardly professing faith in Christ, prove not to be members of Christ's body.

We are to learn, however, that the true church of Christ, wherever it is found, is one in faith. Christ is the head of the church, and thus the mind of the church, for the mind is in the head. The mind of Christ is the mind of God himself. And the mind of God is the truth as it is in God and revealed in the sacred Scriptures.

Although the teacher at whose feet we sit does not mention this here, the one great truth upon which all the church agrees is the truth that God is the sovereign Lord who saves his church by his own work and does so through the atoning sacrifice of our Lord Jesus Christ on the cross. One who does not believe this truth with all his heart is not saved.

The unity of the church as an attribute of the church is a fact both now and in heaven. Yet we are admonished by Scripture to seek the unity of the church. This is Paul's earnest exhortation in Ephesians 4:1–3. And we are taught to pray this prayer for the unity of the church in Psalm 122: "Pray for the peace of Jerusalem: they shall prosper that love thee. Peace be within thy walls, and prosperity within thy palaces. For my brethren and companions' sakes, I will now say, Peace be within thee. Because of the house of the Lord our God I will seek thy good" (vv. 6–9).

The peace of the unity of one faith is a priceless gift. It is our calling to do all in our power to preserve it. Of that one church, united in a true faith, I am and forever shall remain a living member.

Herman Hanko

---

[*] Heidelberg Catechism A 20, in *Confessions and Church Order*, 146.
[**] Heidelberg Catechism A 54, in *Confessions and Church Order*, 104.

May 24 — Q&A 54 — The Holiness of the Church

Read: Revelation 21.

The Apostles' Creed puts in our mouths the confession: "I believe an holy, catholic church." It speaks of the church as "catholic." Our teacher in the Catechism explains this to mean that the Son of God gathers his church "out of the whole human race."* The human race was divided into nations, tribes, and languages at Babel (Gen. 11:1–9). While God changed the languages of all the people at Babel to prevent the premature coming of the antichrist, he also had a positive purpose in Babel: to gather a church which is truly catholic. It is a church in which there are no two members alike, for all the many differences between the saints are used by God to reveal the infinite riches of his grace in saving each individual.

But the apostolic confession and our Catechism also speak of the holiness of the church. This comes as something of a surprise, for if we look about us in the church, we see something quite different from a holy church. The individual members of the church are all very sinful as yet and are far from attaining holiness, that is, freedom from all sin. Thus it is not surprising that denominations or individual congregations are not holy either, for they are composed of sinful people. We want to question our teacher: "Are you sure the church is holy? I do not see much evidence of that when I look at the church."

The truth of Scripture, we must remember, is the object of our faith. I believe an holy catholic church. "We walk by faith, not by sight," Paul says in 2 Corinthians 5:7. The fact is that God sees his church in Christ; and he sees it, therefore, as without sin and clothed in Christ's righteousness. He also deals with it as a holy people and promises it that, in fact, he will make it holy so that it is able to dwell with him in glory forever. Scripture is not hesitant to call the church holy. It does so in many places. In 1 Peter 2:9 Peter writes: "But ye are a chosen generation, a royal priesthood, an holy nation, a peculiar people [not an odd people, but a specially chosen people]; that ye should shew forth the praises of him who hath called you out of darkness into his marvellous light." Yet, at the same time, Scripture calls God's people to be holy. In 1 Peter 1:15–16, Peter, under the inspiration of the Holy Spirit, writes: "But as he which hath called you is holy, so be ye holy in all manner of conversation; because it is written, Be ye holy; for I am holy." We must struggle through prayer and faith to become what one day we shall be.

What a blessing that I am and forever shall remain a member of that church!

Herman Hanko

---

* Heidelberg Catechism A 54, in *Confessions and Church Order*, 104.

May 25 — Q&A 55 — The Communion of the Saints

Read: Psalm 133.

We are once again summoned into the classroom in order to learn more about the church of which we are members. The lesson for today is this: In that church in which we live, there is a communion or fellowship of members. This blessing is particularly great and one for which we cannot be thankful enough.

It is a miracle that surprises us if we stop to think about it, for the very essence of sin is that the sinner is totally absorbed in himself; so much so that his own wellbeing, wealth, comfort, honor, and ease are the only things that concern him. He is even willing to step on the heads of his fellow men to climb the ladder of his own ambition. He will sacrifice unborn children and children of the family, wife and friends, fellow employees and neighbors, if some advantage can be gained by doing this. The sinner is totally self-centered and takes the attitude: me first and the devil take the hindmost.

Suddenly, we are told, we come upon a group of people, each one of which never gives one thought to himself or herself, never for a moment worries about "what's in it for me," never is concerned for his own comfort and pleasure but is completely wrapped up and concerned about others. At whatever price has to be paid, everyone else is important, while I am not.

We may very well ask our teacher: How is such a great wonder possible? He is quick with his answer: "All and every one who believes, being members of Christ, are, in common, partakers of him and of all his riches and gifts."* Remember, the Catechism is talking about the work of the Holy Spirit. By the Holy Spirit in our hearts we are united to Christ. The tie that connects us to Christ is faith, for we are grafted into his body by the graft of faith. Through faith everyone grafted into Christ receives the blessings that he merited on the cross for his beloved church. Those blessings destroy the selfishness and sin in every member and make him holy and righteous, as Christ himself is.

In a sense, everyone receives the same gifts and blessings. Jude mentioned in his epistle about "the common salvation" (v. 3), that is, the salvation all God's people have in common. All have the forgiveness of their sins, the righteousness of Christ, the hope of glory, the resurrection of the body, etc. But there is a sense in which each saint has his own unique gifts. Jesus teaches that in the parable of the talents (Matt. 25:14–30; "every man according to his several ability" receives talents, v. 15). Psalm 68 speaks of Christ at his ascension giving gifts to men (vv. 18–19).

God gives to each member of the church gifts that are uniquely his own, for gifts are given that each may serve his own purpose in the body of the church. This gift of God's grace makes the communion of saints possible.

Herman Hanko

---

* Heidelberg Catechism A 54, in *Confessions and Church Order*, 104.

May 26 — Q&A 55 – The Use of Our Gifts

Read: 1 Corinthians 12.

We have learned that the communion of saints means that within the church each member receives the blessings of Christ, but each member also receives gifts and responsibilities unique to him, which make him able to occupy his own unique place. This same truth applies to a congregation. All share in a common salvation, but all also have unique gifts and abilities. There are no two people alike in a congregation, any more than there are two people alike in the whole church.

Each saint lives his own life in the world. Each has his own sins. Each is saved by grace, but in different ways that give him grace for his walk and calling. Each has his or her own responsibilities. Each is important in the church, whether high or low, young or old, brilliant of mind or mediocre, with bodily and mental handicaps or normal in all respects, male or female, employer or employee, etc.

Now then, says our teacher, "Every one [of you] must know it to be [your] duty, readily and cheerfully to employ [your] gifts, for the advantage and salvation of other members."* Away goes all self-seeking and self-centeredness. With a wave of the hand, our teacher tells us, You and what happens to you are not important; what use you are to the congregation of which you are a member—that is the one and only important thing!

The responsibility for the advantage and salvation of your fellow members is and must be your only concern. Are you tired after a day in school? Never mind. It is not important. There is a fellow classmate that is troubled and needs you. Has Christ given you a gift of music? Are you asked to use your gift for worldly entertainment in special programs? That is a waste of your gift. Is it your idea that the church is too small and that you would be wasting your gift if you used it to play the piano on the Lord's day? The teacher says, If you belong to the church, stop thinking about yourself and start thinking about the church and how you are called to serve it.

Are you so busy earning your daily bread that Bible study tonight is too great a burden? Oh selfish person! Why did Christ put you in the church? For your own pleasure? Did Christ seek his own pleasure when he went to the cross for you? For you, a worthless sinner?

There is only one reason why you have, with an unmerited favor of a gracious God, been given a place in that noble and exalted company of saints. That place is to serve others. Maybe that is as a mother in the home, bringing up your children, the children of the covenant, in the ways of God's covenant. Maybe your place is to teach in a school for covenant children. Maybe your place is to be an elder, a deacon, a minister. Maybe your place is to keep the church clean for worship. Maybe your place is to speak a word of good cheer to that lonely fellow saint whose burdens are so great they almost crush her.

The welfare of the church, whatever the cost—that is what it means to believe in the communion of the saints.

Herman Hanko

---

* Heidelberg Catechism A 55, in *Confessions and Church Order*, 104.

May 27 — **Q&A 56 — The Forgiveness of Sins**

Read: Psalm 51; Psalm 32.

There is no greater blessing that we can receive than the forgiveness of sins. If we have this blessing, all is well, no matter what the circumstances of our lives may be. If we have not this blessing, we have nothing, neither in this life nor in the life to come.

The Apostles' Creed makes this confession purely objective: I believe there is such a blessing as the forgiveness of sins. But our teacher makes this confession very personal: "That God, for the sake of Christ's satisfaction, will no more remember my sins, neither my corrupt nature, against which I have to struggle all my life long, but will graciously impute to me the righteousness of Christ, that I may never be condemned."[*] It is necessary and important to make this confession our own. The teacher calls attention to many aspects of this confession. Let us enumerate them.

First, all this blessedness of forgiveness is "for the sake of Christ's satisfaction." We did not earn it, nor even desire it. It is freely given because Christ earned it for us.

Second, we need forgiveness of our sins, but also of our "corrupt nature, against which [we] have to struggle all [our lives] long."

This may come as something of a surprise to us. We are not only to ask for God to forgive our sins, but we are also to ask for forgiveness of our sinful natures, which are the fountains and causes of our sin. In other words, we are responsible and can go to hell for our sinful natures. You ask how this can be when we are born with corrupt natures. The answer is that we are guilty for Adam's sin and therefore deserve the punishment of corrupt and depraved natures. They need to be forgiven also.

Third, when we confess our faith in the forgiveness of our sins and our corrupt natures, we ask God to forget them. This is a bold request. We ask God to put them so completely out of his mind that he does not remember a single one.

Fourth, we ask God that he will impute to us Christ's righteousness. That is, we ask God to declare legally before the heavenly bar of justice that Christ's righteousness is actually our righteousness, and that therefore, God sees us as not only without sin, but being as righteous as he is.

Finally, we confess that we believe we shall never be condemned for any sin: not now in our consciences, not in the judgment day at the end of time, and not ever in heaven.

That is a wonderful confession to make. Even if the world condemns us, or even the devil, or even our own consciences, we say against them all: "I believe in the forgiveness of sins."

Herman Hanko

---

[*] Heidelberg Catechism A 56, in *Confessions and Church Order*, 105.

Lord's Day 22

Q. 57. What comfort doth the "resurrection of the body" afford thee?

A. That not only my soul after this life shall be immediately taken up to Christ its Head; but also, that this my body, being raised by the power of Christ, shall be reunited with my soul, and made like unto the glorious body of Christ.

Q. 58. What comfort takest thou from the article of "life everlasting"?

A. That since I now feel in my heart the beginning of eternal joy, after this life I shall inherit perfect salvation, which *eye hath not seen, nor ear heard, neither hath it entered into the heart of man to conceive*, and that, to praise God therein for ever.

May 28 — Introduction to Lord's Day 22

Read: Psalm 16; Acts 2:29–33.

There are one or two comments that ought to be made about the lesson from our Catechism in Lord's Day 22. The first is that this Lord's Day is remarkably short, especially when we consider how important it is for the Christian faith and how much time Scripture devotes to this subject.

There is, however, a good reason for this. God has so determined that the truth of the Scriptures is developed in the church along the lines of the six main topics in dogmatics: theology (the doctrine of God), anthropology (the doctrine of man), Christology (the doctrine of Christ), soteriology (the doctrine of salvation), ecclesiology (the doctrine of the church), and eschatology (the doctrine of the last things).

In the early church, at the time the three creeds were formulated (the Nicene Creed, the Chalcedonian Creed, and the Athanasian), the doctrine of God was first developed and then the doctrine of Christ. At the time of Augustine, who died in 430 AD, the doctrine of man and the doctrine of salvation were developed. Then followed a long period of a millennium in which the Roman Catholic Church ruled the world, and no doctrine was developed. At the time of the Reformation the doctrine of the church was especially developed, but almost nothing was said about the doctrine of the last things.

And so, you see, the development of the truth followed the six main topics in dogmatics. The Catechism was written in 1563, when the doctrine of the last things was not yet developed. And the resurrection of the body belongs to the doctrine of the last things. It was especially in the last century that the doctrine of the last things was being developed. Nevertheless, the essential ideas that belong to the doctrine of the resurrection of our bodies are all mentioned here.

The second point that needs to be made is the claim of some commentaries that the doctrine of the resurrection of the body was not an object of faith in the Old Testament. This is a flat-out denial of clear scriptural evidence that the Old Testament saints did indeed believe in the resurrection of the body.

Job, who was a contemporary of Abraham, spoke of the resurrection of the body: "And though after my skin worms destroy this body, yet in my flesh shall I see God: whom I shall see for myself, and mine eyes shall behold, and not another" (Job 19:26–27). Hebrews 11:19 tells us that when God spared Isaac at the moment Abraham was ready to plunge his knife into Isaac's heart, Abraham received his son back as a figure of the resurrection of Christ and of our bodies. Psalm 16:10 tells us that David believed in the resurrection of the body: "For thou wilt not leave my soul in hell; neither wilt thou suffer thine Holy One to see corruption." This was quoted, in fact, by Peter in his great Pentecostal sermon (Acts 2:31) as fulfilled in Christ.

The resurrection of the body has always been the faith of the church.

Herman Hanko

May 29 — Q&A 57 — The Intermediate State

Read: 2 Corinthians 5:1–10.

Our teacher, who instructs us in the doctrine of the resurrection of the body, wants us to understand not only what this confession means to us, but also that preceding the resurrection of our bodies is what has been called the intermediate state. This doctrine teaches that at the moment of our deaths, while our bodies go to the grave, our souls go immediately to heaven. These souls live in heaven until Christ comes again at the end of time. This doctrine is taught in this Lord's Day in the words: "My soul after this life shall be immediately taken up to Christ its Head."* This doctrine has been a great blessing to God's people, not only as they look ahead to the time when they must die, but also when they must carry ones they love dearly to the cemetery.

There are many who deny this truth, however. These teach a sort of soul sleep; that is, that when we die, our souls go to sleep and sleep until Christ comes again, when they are awakened to be joined with their bodies. But Scripture is clear that this is not the case.

Solomon describes old age in Ecclesiastes 12:1–7 and ends his picturesque description of old age with the words: "Then shall the dust return to the earth as it was: and the spirit shall return unto God who gave it." Christ tells the thief on the cross when he repented of his sin and asked the Lord to remember him when the Lord came to his kingdom: "To day shalt thou be with me in paradise" (Luke 23:42–43). Christ promised the repentant thief that he would be in heaven with the Lord. Christ's spirit went to God, as he says in his last word on the cross: "Father, into thy hands I commend my spirit" (Luke 23:46). In Revelation 6:9–11, we are told that when the fifth seal is opened, John

9. saw under the altar the souls of them that were slain for the word of God, and for the testimony which they held:
10. And they cried with a loud voice, saying, How long, O Lord, holy and true, dost thou not judge and avenge our blood on them that dwell on the earth?
11. And white robes were given unto every one of them; and it was said unto them, that they should rest yet for a little season, until their fellowservants also and their brethren, that should be killed as they were, should be fulfilled.

Finally, in 2 Corinthians 5:1 we read this: "For we know that if our earthly house of this tabernacle were dissolved, we have a building of God, an house not made with hands, eternal in the heavens." Paul does not say, we will have some day a house not made with hands; he says, at that moment when our earthly house is dissolved, we do have a house not made with hands.

We look forward to heaven at the end of our pathway here in the world.

Herman Hanko

---

* Heidelberg Catechism A 57, in *Confessions and Church Order*, 105.

May 30 — Q&A 57 — The Resurrection of the Body

Read: 1 Corinthians 15:1–11.

Many things will happen when our Lord Jesus Christ comes again at the end of time. Christ will be seen in the heavens coming on the clouds, which he makes his chariot, and coming with the host of angels. He will, at the moment of his coming, be seen by all men. This will indeed be a miracle, for we cannot imagine how, if the Lord is seen in the sky above Singapore, he can also be seen on the other side of the world in the United States. But nevertheless, so it will be. Further, when he comes not only will the bodies of God's people be raised, but the people of God still on the earth will be changed (1 Cor. 15:51–52). The bodies of all the wicked shall also be raised, and those living will also be changed, but their bodies will be united with their souls that have been in hell, and their bodies will be changed to exist in hell. The last judgment will take place at that time. All men who ever lived will be gathered before the great white throne on which Christ sits, and all men will be judged. The righteous will be taken into heaven and the wicked cast into hell. New heavens and a new earth will be created, and we shall inherit this new creation. What a day that will be!

But here in Lord's Day 22 our teacher wants us to think especially about the resurrection of our bodies. Our bodies are important to us, but they are also important to God. When God created man, God formed him body and soul, and so, if for no other reason, our bodies are important because God created them. We are to take care of our bodies, and the mutilation or endangering of our bodies is always a sin. In the Old Testament times, respect for the bodies of those that died was characteristic of all the saints. Abraham bought a parcel of ground in Canaan for a burial place for Sarah; and in that grave, Abraham himself was buried, Isaac and Rebekah his wife were buried, and Jacob and his true wife, Leah, were buried. Burial is the way in which we show respect for our bodies. But believers put the bodies of loved ones in the ground because they bury them in the hope of the resurrection. Paul talks in 1 Corinthians 15:36–38 of a seed that cannot grow into a new plant until it is put into the ground. Our bodies become new only by being planted in the earth.

And so God considers our bodies so important that he saves our bodies as well as our souls. Only the salvation of our bodies does not come about until the resurrection, for they must first be planted in the earth. But God will raise up our bodies at the coming of Christ. Thus we are taught that our only comfort in life and in death, for body and soul, is that we belong to Jesus (see Lord's Day 1).

Herman Hanko

May 31   **Q&A 57 — The Miracle of the Resurrection of the Body**

Read: 1 Corinthians 15:12–23.

There are several considerations that make the resurrection of the body an amazing miracle. Let us mention a few of them. They will help us realize what a great wonder God performs for us when he raises our bodies. Think, first, of the fact that the bodies of every child of God that ever lived will be raised. This includes not only all the saints who lived in both the old and new dispensations, but also all those saints who lived before the flood: Adam, Abel, Seth, Enoch, Methuselah, Noah, and all the rest. The flood was a great catastrophe and tore the earth to pieces. Yet the bodies of the people of God were somehow preserved. Think of all the things that can happen to a human body: it can be and has been burned with fire. The ashes of the pre-reformer John Wycliffe (1328–1384), for example, were strewn on the waters of a river and were carried out to the oceans. Some were drowned; some were eaten by fish; some were eaten by lions in the arenas of Rome—and so became a part of the bodies of fish and animals. Some were buried, turned to dust, and became a part of grass which cows ate and turned into milk, milk that was drunk by others. How impossible it all seems to us!

But we must remember also that the resurrection of our bodies is a truth we believe by faith. No wonder the unbeliever scoffs. With all his science he cannot believe something so scientifically impossible. But we walk by faith, not by sight. We believe in a great God who created all things, is present in every particle of the creation with his whole being, and upholds all things by his word. He can and does preserve every particle of every child of God so that he can raise their bodies at the end of time. This miracle is necessary because our own bodies are raised. We are taught: "This my body, being raised by the power of Christ, shall be reunited to my soul, and made like unto the glorious body of Christ."* The very same body conceived in my mother's womb, grown to adulthood, dead and buried, rotted in the ground, is going to be raised. God does not abandon our earthly bodies and create for us entirely new bodies. No, he preserves our bodies and raises them. They are greatly changed, but they are the same bodies in which we lived on earth.

This is the way it was with the body of Jesus. When our Lord died, he was buried in Joseph's tomb. From that tomb his body arose. After he arose, the body was there no longer. And yet it was changed. It was so changed that our Lord could not be seen unless he took on some form that was visible to the human eye. He could, in his body, enter rooms that were locked and sealed. It was Christ's body that ascended into heaven, is now glorified, and in which body he rules over all.

What an astounding wonder. But what blessedness!

Herman Hanko

---

*   Heidelberg Catechism A 57, in *Confessions and Church Order*, 105.

June 1 — Q&A 57 – The Nature of Our Resurrection Bodies

Read: 1 Corinthians 15:35–49.

Our teacher who is instructing us in the meaning of our faith in the resurrection of our bodies does not have very much to say about the nature of our resurrection bodies. Nor is this so surprising. After all, the Bible does not say very much about heaven. And this too is to be expected, because heaven is the realm of spiritual creatures, while we here on earth are earthly creatures. Even if the Bible would want to tell us about heaven, there is no language that could be used to describe what heaven is like. And even if a language could be found, we would not be able to understand it (see Paul's comments in 2 Cor. 12:1–4).

A few things are told us in the Bible, and our teacher points us to the most important of them: We shall be "fashioned like unto his [Christ's] glorious body" (Phil. 3:21). Christ's body was raised and glorified at the time of our Lord's ascension and exaltation. In his glorified body, he is now in heaven and sits at his Father's right hand, where he is Lord of lords and King of kings. His glorified body is so beautiful, so powerful, so shining with the brightness of his exaltation that God himself in all his glory is revealed through Christ. When we see Christ, we see God himself (John 14:7–11).

Our bodies, raised to be like the body of Christ, shall be just as beautiful, just as glorious, and just as wonderful. The glory of God shining through Christ will also shine through our bodies. If this is the nature of our resurrection bodies, we shall be more glorious than Adam was in paradise. Before he fell, he was a very glorious man. Our bodies now are nothing like Adam's and Eve's bodies. They were beautiful, strong, revealing God's glory. But sin and the curse has filled us with death, made our bodies ugly, and eroded all the powers that Adam and Eve had. But in heaven we will have more beautiful bodies than Adam and Eve had. We cannot even imagine what that will be like. We cannot imagine the beauty of an angel, but we shall be more glorious even than the angels. Somehow, by some great miracle, the beautiful bodies of a newborn baby will be preserved in heaven; the unique glory of man and woman at the peak of their strength will be preserved; the beauty of the grey-haired veteran of the battle of faith will also be preserved. But all traces of sin, the curse and death, will be erased, and every body will be perfect and fully able to serve God in the new creation.

All that will be a miracle, an astounding miracle. We shall be changed. We believe this, for Christ arose; and his resurrection guarantees our resurrection. It is wonderful to contemplate!

Herman Hanko

June 2 — Q&A 57 — Our New Spiritual Bodies

Read: 1 Corinthians 15:50–58.

Paul, by the inspiration of the Holy Spirit, tells us a little bit about our resurrection bodies. He tells us, first, that they will not be flesh and blood such as we have now. He writes: "Now this I say, brethren, that flesh and blood cannot inherit the kingdom of God; neither doth corruption inherit incorruption" (1 Cor. 15:50). Then again in verses 53–54 of the same chapter: "For this corruptible must put on incorruption, and this mortal must put on immortality. So when this corruptible shall have put on incorruption, and this mortal shall have put on immortality, then shall be brought to pass the saying that is written, Death is swallowed up in victory."

Yet, secondly, the apostle tells us a little bit about that resurrection body by contrasting it with our present bodies: "It is sown in corruption; it is raised in incorruption" (v. 42). That is, the body that dies is corrupt. It is corrupt because of sin; it is corrupt because of death that rots it away and finally pulls it down into the grave. But the resurrection body is incorruptible.

"It is sown in dishonour; it is raised in glory" (v. 43). No matter how today's depraved culture worships the human body, our bodies are dishonorable. We hide our bodies beneath clothing. There is nothing beautiful about them. But our resurrection bodies are gloriously beautiful, because they will be without sin and without the rotting power of death.

"It is sown in weakness; it is raised in power" (v. 43). We are now so weak that at the time of our greatest strength, a bacterium, microscopically small, can kill us. Our lives hang by a thread every day. But in heaven we shall be strong.

"It is sown a natural body; it is raised a spiritual body" (1 Cor. 15:44). Our natural bodies can only live in this world. They are subject to all the limitations of our creation. They are bound by the limitations of time and space. If we want to travel by car to Kuala Lumpur, we must travel so many miles, and it will take us so many hours. We are dependent on food grown in this present creation. We are dependent on water for drinking, and if we do not drink any fluids, we will die. All this belongs to our natural life in the world. But our resurrection bodies will be spiritual. They will be like the angels'. They will be so changed that they can live in a heavenly and spiritual creation. What that creation will be like, we do not know. Sometimes we can become very eager to find out, for, above all, we will be without sin. We will see Christ "face to face" (1 Cor. 13:12). And we will be able to see God himself revealed in Christ, in all God's love for us.

That will be glory indeed!

Herman Hanko

Q&A 58 — Eternal Life

Read: Revelation 22:1–9.

The final article in the apostolic confession reads: "I believe in…the life everlasting."[*] And so the teacher, who is showing us what glorious things the Bible says about our future, now teaches us a few things concerning "life everlasting." We must learn, first of all, that we cannot know very much about what everlasting life is like. To drive this home to us, our teacher quotes 1 Corinthians 2:9. That shall have to be enough for us. However, I am sure we will, when finally we open our eyes in glory, say the same thing that the Queen of Sheba said when she saw the glory of Solomon's kingdom: "The one half…was not told me" (2 Chron. 9:6).

Our teacher tells us one surprising thing: we do have the beginnings of heaven in our hearts already while we are here on this earth, struggling along on our pilgrim's journey: "I feel in my heart the beginning of eternal joy."[**] Our happiness is a true happiness, for we know that we belong to Christ, are cared for by him, and will in a very short time see him face to face. There are moments of great joy when, in a flash, the greatness of God's perfections is seen by us, when the blessedness of the forgiveness of sins makes us sing, when our musings on our everlasting destination suddenly bursts upon us in all its splendor.

Our teacher also points us to the fact that we shall inherit perfect salvation. This is a delightful prospect. Here on earth we still sin so much. We confess our sins and find forgiveness with God, but the next day it is the same old story: sin, sin, sin. We weary of sin, of the battle against it, of the times we are overcome by it. But in heaven we will never sin again but will be perfect in loving our God and our neighbor. This is the real blessedness of heaven. Not sunny skies, meadows filled with flowers, cooling breezes, beautiful landscapes, singing birds; but think of it: we will never sin again!

We shall be in heaven with all the saints. We shall meet Adam and Eve, Noah, Abraham, Peter, Athanasius, Augustine, Luther, Calvin, and all the saints. We shall be with the angels who will be our servants. We shall be with Christ, to live with him and see the adoring look in his eyes for us, his bride. And we shall praise God forever. Each will have his own story to tell. It will be a story of a foul sinner saved by grace: Rahab, Ruth, the Philippian jailer, you, me. But the story will be about God's grace in us. Forever and ever. One minister once described everlasting as being like a bird which takes one tiny bit of stone from a huge cliff, carries it a thousand miles, comes back for another, and does this a billion years. Everlasting life is longer than that.

Our home is everlasting.

Herman Hanko

---

[*] Heidelberg Catechism A 23, in *Confessions and Church Order*, 91.
[**] Heidelberg Catechism A 58, in *Confessions and Church Order*, 105.

Lord's Day 23

Q. 59. But what doth it profit thee now that thou believest all this?

A. That I am righteous in Christ, before God, and an heir of eternal life.

Q. 60. How are thou righteous before God?

A. Only by a true faith in Jesus Christ; so that, though my conscience accuse me that I have grossly transgressed all the commandments of God, and kept none of them, and am still inclined to all evil; notwithstanding, God, without any merit of mine, but only of mere grace, grants and imputes to me the perfect satisfaction, righteousness, and holiness of Christ; even so, as if I never had had nor committed any sin: yea, as if I had fully accomplished all that obedience which Christ has accomplished for me; inasmuch as I embrace such benefit with a believing heart.

Q. 61. Why sayest thou that thou art righteous by faith only?

A. Not that I am acceptable to God on account of the worthiness of my faith, but because only the satisfaction, righteousness, and holiness of Christ is my righteousness before God; and that I cannot receive and apply the same to myself any other way than by faith only.

June 4 — Q&A 59 — The Profit of Faith

Read: Romans 4:1–12.

It is quite clear why our teacher, who instructs us in the truth of Scripture, should now ask this important question: What is the profit of your faith? We have been instructed in all the truths that God has revealed in his Word. We have been told that these truths are the objects of our faith. We have repeatedly recited our lessons.

I believe in God the Father.

I believe in his only begotten Son.

I believe in all the work that Christ did from his birth to his exaltation and will do until his second coming.

I believe in the Holy Ghost.

I believe in a holy catholic church.

I believe in the resurrection of the body.

I believe in the forgiveness of sins.

I believe in life eternal.

Now, what profit is there in the fact that we believe all these things? That is a good question.

The answer of the teacher in our classroom is quite surprising. He could have said: Faith makes all these truths our own possession and experience. He could have said: The profit is that God is our Father. Christ is our Savior. Christ died for us. Christ is our Lord in heaven. We are members of the church of Christ. Our sins are forgiven. We shall inherit eternal life. But our teacher does not do that. Rather, he chooses to point us to one truth, which, if true, makes all the other truths ours as well: we are righteous in Christ. If we are righteous, we possess all the other blessings of salvation as well.

It is like a man in prison for an enormous debt, which he cannot pay. He is there until the debt is paid. But someone comes along and pays the entire debt. He can then be released from prison and enjoy all the blessings of freedom with his wife and children, his friends and relatives, and in God's creation. But the important thing is that he is legally declared to have no debt.

And so our teacher points out to us what a wonderful power faith is. Faith believes "that [we are] righteous in Christ, before God."* When faith can and does believe that, then faith can also believe everything else. But to be righteous is first. So our teacher takes great pains to point out several things about this profit of faith. First, we are righteous in Christ. Second, we are righteous before God. Third, we come to the knowledge of our righteousness only by faith. Fourth, this means that we do not come to our righteousness by our works. Fifth, we do not even come to the knowledge of our righteousness because of the worthiness of our faith. Sixth, we become righteous by faith in Christ.**

The only way we possess that righteousness approved of God is to appropriate by faith the righteousness of Christ.

Herman Hanko

---

* Heidelberg Catechism A 59, in *Confessions and Church Order*, 106.
** Heidelberg Catechism A 60, in *Confessions and Church Order*, 106.

June 5 — Q&A 59 — What Is the Righteousness We Have by Faith?

Read: Numbers 23.

We really have to understand what righteousness is, if we are to appreciate this profit of faith. Righteousness is different from holiness. When God created Adam in his own image, he created him in the true knowledge of God, righteousness, and holiness. Holiness has to do with the moral character of one's nature. God is holy, because his divine essence is without the least blemish or moral spot. We are holy when our natures are without the corruption and depravity of sin. Righteousness has to do with our activity.

God is righteous because everything he does is perfectly in harmony with the holiness of his divine nature. We are righteous when everything we do is in keeping with a holy nature we possess. By everything we do, I mean our thoughts, our desires, our emotions, as well as our words and deeds. When all these things reveal a holy nature, then we are righteous. But, as you well know, our natures are not holy. They are not holy in any aspect. They are corrupt, depraved, morally dead, and incapable of doing any good. And because our natures are in no way holy, we cannot do anything right. We are unrighteous. Every thought, desire, word, deed, and emotion is wrong. Each is contrary to God's will. Each deserves the punishment of death.

The righteousness of which the Catechism speaks is the righteousness God gives us by his grace. That is, God declares that all his people have no sin, all that they do is perfectly in harmony with his law and his own divine being, and they are, therefore, heirs of eternal life. We must be clear on what this means. Martin Luther used a Latin expression, *Justus simul peccator.* This Latin expression means that we are found to be just while we are, in our lives, sinners. It is like a judge pronouncing a murderer to have never committed the crime of murder, even though he was found guilty of the crime and even though he confessed it to be true.

The clearest instance of this is found in Numbers 23. You will recall the history. Israel was just east of the Jordan River, on the eastern boundary of Canaan. The nation was camped in a valley. To the south was a high plateau, which was occupied by Moab. Balak was king of Moab, and he was frightened by the nation of Israel. So he hired Balaam, a prophet out of Mesopotamia, to come and curse Israel, for Balak knew that if Balaam cursed Israel, they would never be a threat to him. Balaam tried to curse but could only bless. Finally, Balak, in despair, took Balaam to a place where only the outer fringes of Israel's camp could be seen. It was Israel at its very worst, where the mixed multitude was camped. What did Balaam say? "He hath not beheld iniquity in Jacob, neither hath he seen perverseness in Israel" (v. 21). That was all Balaam could say.

That is what it means to be righteous before God.

Herman Hanko

June 6 — Q&A 59 — Righteous in Christ

Read: Romans 4:13–25.

Yesterday we left Balaam on the heights of Moab blessing Israel when Balak had hired him to curse God's people. Balaam spoke in the same way the donkey spoke when the donkey attempted to prevent him from going to Moab to curse Israel. God caused the donkey to speak words of warning to Balaam. God caused Balaam to speak words of blessing when he wanted to curse. But in the middle of the camp of Israel was the tabernacle and the priests going about their work of sacrificing, and the smoke of their sacrifices rose towards the sky. And so, when Balaam was forced against his will to bless Israel and said, "He hath not beheld iniquity in Jacob, neither hath he seen perverseness in Israel," he added: "The Lord his God is with him, and the shout of a king is among them" (Num. 23:21). God was saying through wicked Balaam, I see no sin in this nation because I am with them, and Christ, their king, is among them. Israel was righteous. And that meant that when Balak and Balaam wanted to curse Israel for Israel's many sins (and they were terrible), God said, as it were, How can I curse them? I do not see any sin in them. All I see is a righteous and holy people. They can only be blessed.

What could be the reason for this? The answer is that, as our teacher points out to us, we are "righteous in Christ."* Christ is righteous because of his death on the cross. All our sins were made the sins of Christ, and all the guilt of all the sins of all the people of God were placed on Christ: "For he hath made him to be sin for us, who knew no sin; that we might be made the righteousness of God in him" (2 Cor. 5:21). Christ was made responsible for all our sins and guilt. For them, he went to the cross on which God poured out all the wrath he had against all the sins of all the elect. Christ suffered what God's people should have suffered. Christ paid the debt that was our debt, and by his perfect obedience he earned for us righteousness. If our debt is paid, we are now righteous.

This was a legal transaction. Legally, Christ stood before God's bar of justice, and God condemned Christ to die for the debt of all the elect. Christ did this willingly and paid that debt by bearing all the guilt of our sins. He therefore became, though guilty for our sins, perfectly righteous. And that righteousness God imputed to us. Not because of what we had done, but because of what Christ had done. He "was delivered for our offences, and was raised again for our justification" (Rom. 4:25).

And so our teacher reminds us that we are righteous before God, in Christ. This great work of God is called justification. The word literally means to make just or righteous. It is God's declaration that he sees no sin in us. What a wonderful blessing that is! We can sing,

> How blest is he whose trespass
> Hath freely been forgiven.**

Herman Hanko

---

* Heidelberg Catechism A 59, in *Confessions and Church Order*, 106.
** No. 83:1, in *The Psalter*.

June 7 — Q&A 59 – The Blessedness of Justification

Read: Romans 8:31–39

Justification is a great work of God in Jesus Christ and a blessing that forms the basis for all the other blessings of salvation. If we are not justified before God, we do not have a right or claim to any of the blessings of salvation, for we are then sinners, worthy only of hell. But if God justifies us, then we have the rightful claim to all the blessings of salvation, for we are found by God to be without sin.

This is a very personal confession on the part of the believer. The teacher in this classroom asks: "What doth it profit thee now that thou believest all this?" And the answer we give to our teacher is this: "I am righteous in Christ, before God, and an heir of eternal life."* This very personal aspect of justification is underscored in the passage of Scripture assigned to us in our lesson: Romans 8:31–39. The scene is a courtroom where God is judge and into which we are brought to be judged. We have many accusers: the devil is there to point out that we really belong to him and have no right to heaven. The world is present to bring accusations against us that we are no better than it is. And our own consciences condemn us so that we are forced by the testimony of our consciences to agree with our accusers and to admit with hanging heads that it is all true.

But then the judge speaks. After examining all the evidence and weighing it carefully in the scales of absolute justice, the judge pronounces us innocent: I have not found iniquity in Jacob, neither transgression in Israel. That is the sentence! It comes to us as a thunderbolt. God, the judge of all the earth, who always judges rightly, finds us to be without sin and cannot find any accusations against us to be true!

At first, we are not sure we have correctly heard it. It seems too good to be true. But then, the sentence of the divine judge sinks into our souls, and we become confident that this amazing wonder is ours. So we turn on our accusers: "Who shall lay anything to the charge of God's elect…Who is he that condemneth?" (Rom. 8:33–34). That means that in our lives when the devil or the world or even our own consciences try to sow the seeds of doubt in our minds by pointing out our sins, we are able to say: Go away devil; get far from me, world; be still, conscience. I know that what you say is true. But I have Christ. He is mine. He bore my sins. He earned for me my innocence. He freely and graciously gives it to me. God imputes it to me for Christ's sake. Whatever you say is a lie. I am righteous in Christ before God.

Herman Hanko

---

*   Heidelberg Catechism Q&A 59, in *Confessions and Church Order*, 106.

June 8 — **Q&A 60 – The Blessings of Justification**

Read: Romans 5.

All the blessings of salvation follow our justification. Our teacher emphasizes in our lesson the greatest of all such blessings: the forgiveness of sins. Here it is:

> I have grossly transgressed all the commandments of God, and kept none of them, and am still inclined to all evil; notwithstanding, God, without any merit of mine, but only of mere grace, grants and imputes to me the perfect satisfaction, righteousness, and holiness of Christ; even so, as if I never had had nor committed any sin: yea, as if I had fully accomplished all the obedience which Christ has accomplished for me.*

How precious is the gift of the forgiveness of sins! I sin against God in thought, word, and deed. I commit sins of omission (by failing to do that which is my duty to do) and sins of commission (I do those things I know are wrong and contrary to the will of God. Knowing what is sin and knowing God disapproves, I do these things anyway). I do not do them once or twice, or even one hundred or two hundred times; I do them over and over again. Yet when the day is finished and I prepare to seek sleep, I bring my sins to the throne of grace to confess them and express my sorrow for them. Every time, the Lord forgives and tells me that he will not hold these sins against me, for he has punished them in his own dear Son. And after rejoicing at the great blessedness of forgiveness, the next day I commit the same sins over again. Again I confess them, and God forgives.

My sins intrude on everything. My confession of sin is not always as sincere as it ought to be. Sometimes I ask the Lord to forgive but not to keep me from that same sin. Sometimes I ask to be delivered from a sin but add, not yet; wait a few days. Our prayers, our singing to God, our thankfulness—all our activities, even the most holy—are sinful. Yet God forgives. I see, God says, no sin in Jacob, neither transgression in Israel.

When we lay our heads on death's pillow, the words of our teacher come to our minds: Death is not the penalty for sin, but the door to glory. What comfort do we have while we live and when we die? Our sins are forgiven us. Hebrews puts it so beautifully: "For we have not an high priest which cannot be touched with the feeling of our infirmities; but was in all points tempted like as we are, yet without sin. Let us therefore come boldly unto the throne of grace, that we may obtain mercy, and find grace to help in time of need" (4:15–16).

> How blessed is he whose trespass
> Hath freely been forgiven,
> Whose sin is wholly covered
> Before the sight of heaven.**

Herman Hanko

---

* Heidelberg Catechism A 60, in *Confessions and Church Order*, 106–7.
** No. 83:1, in *The Psalter*.

June 9 — Q&A 61 — By Faith Alone

Read: Galatians 2:16–21.

The great truth of the Reformation was justification by faith alone. Luther opened the door to reformation in the church with that simple four word statement. The Roman Catholic Church taught differently. This apostate church that held sway over the whole of Europe taught justification by faith and works. One had to do works in addition to believing in order to be saved. Luther had tried that in the monastery. God plagued Luther with the consciousness of his sins. God drove Luther almost frantic, as Luther tried to appease God by all sorts of works. Chief among these works was his confessions of his sins to his superior, Johann von Staupitz. He would spend long periods of time confessing to Staupitz every little sin he could think of; and minutes after leaving Staupitz, he would think of another sin, and hurry back to confess that sin as well. Staupitz got sick of it all and finally said to Luther: "Look here. If you expect Christ to forgive you, come in with something to forgive—parricide, blasphemy, adultery—instead of all these peccadilloes."* Staupitz did not mean that literally, but he tried to show Luther the way to the cross of Christ, a way Luther could not yet see as the way to peace. The blinders of the Roman Catholic church prevented him from seeing the cross.

But God led Luther, through this dark way, to the cross. And when Luther finally saw it, he exclaimed: "I felt that I was altogether born again and had entered paradise itself through open gates."** He saw heaven as a reality for himself through that dark and murky cross of Calvary. The cross revealed heaven because Luther finally turned away from a preoccupation with his own works and saw only the work Christ performed on the cross.

When Luther translated the Bible into German, he translated such texts as Romans 5:1, "Therefore being justified by faith alone, we have peace with God through our Lord Jesus Christ." The Roman Catholics badgered him mercilessly for adding the word *alone*, which they said was not in the original Greek. Luther's reply was: "I knew very well that the word *solum* is not in the Greek or Latin text…At the same time they do not see that it conveys the sense of the text; it belongs there if the translation is to be clear and vigorous."*** It was the word *alone* that infuriated the Roman Catholics. But Luther insisted on it. It was the salvation of the church.

Why do so many leaders in the church and ministers of the gospel want to go back to that awful error of Rome? Why do they want to turn their backs on Luther and his soul-wrenching struggle to come to peace with God? We cannot tell with certainty, but man's pride is a terrible thing, and sinful man wants to preserve some tattered remnants of his pride. So he says, I can do something too. I am justified by faith and my works. We ought to fall on our faces at the foot of the cross and confess that we can do nothing—nothing at all—to be justified.

Herman Hanko

---

* Quoted in Roland H. Bainton, *Here I Stand: A Life of Martin Luther* (Peabody, MA: Hendrickson Publishers, 2015), 36.

** *Luther's Works, Volume 34 Career of the Reformer IV*, eds. Jaroslav Pelikan, Helmut T. Lehmann, Lewis W. Spitz (Philadelphia, PA: Fortress Press, 1960), 337.

*** *Luther's Works, Vol. 35: Word and Sacrament I*, eds. Jaroslav Pelikan, Helmut T. Lehmann, Lewis W. Spitz (Philadelphia: Fortress Press, 1999), 188.

June 10 — Q&A 61 — Justification by Faith Alone

Read: Romans 3:19–31.

The teacher who has assumed responsibility to instruct us in the absolute sovereignty of God in the work of salvation is intent on getting this point, that we are justified by faith alone, across to us. This teacher of ours recognizes that there are also plenty of people around who would quickly say, Yes, we are justified by faith, but who also make faith a work. They make faith a work when they use expressions like, You must accept Christ as your personal Savior; You must let Jesus into your heart; Jesus wants to save you and loves you, but you must accept him. So, after all, they make faith a work and teach, in a sneaky way, that we are saved by faith and works. Here our teacher speaks up: "Why sayest thou that thou art righteous by faith only?" Answer: "Not that I am acceptable to God on account of the worthiness of my faith."*

The point our teacher is making is not a mere doctrinal point; it is our salvation. I, we are reminded, need a comfort in the life I am called to live, but also at the moment of death. If that comfort comes from my works, there is no comfort. The Roman Catholic Church could just as well have hung a sign about its doors, Abandon all comfort, ye who enter here. The Catechism says, your only comfort is that you do not have to save yourself nor contribute one little deed to your salvation. Your salvation is in Christ. That is comfort!

Faith, as we learned earlier from our teacher, is the bond that unites us to Christ. Christ is like a giant reservoir in which all the blessings of salvation for time and eternity are. Faith is the pipeline that connects us to Christ and through which all Christ's blessings flow into us. Or to use another figure, Christ is the dynamo and source of all power. Faith is the electric wire that connects us to the dynamo. If the wire is not there, we give no light. If we are connected to him, we shine in holiness and glory. God gives that faith: "For by grace are ye saved through faith; and that not of yourselves: it is the gift of God" (Eph. 2:8).

It is true that God causes that faith that he gives to come to conscious activity in our lives. We believe. We run to the cross with the load of our sins. We take hold of the savior who hangs there. We make him our savior. And all these things are activities of faith. But let us remember that "it is God which worketh in you both to will and to do of his good pleasure" (Phil. 2:13). God works the will that makes us want to go to Christ. God himself actually works in us "to do of his good pleasure." He makes us do it.

But do not be alarmed by this; that God does it all is "our only comfort."

Herman Hanko

---

* Heidelberg Catechism Q&A 61, in *Confessions and Church Order*, 107.

Lord's Day 24

Q. 62. But why cannot our good works be the whole or part of our righteousness before God?

A. Because, that the righteousness which can be approved of before the tribunal of God must be absolutely perfect, and in all respects conformable to the divine law; and also, that our best works in this life are all imperfect and defiled with sin.

Q. 63. What! do not our good works merit, which yet God will reward in this and in a future life?

A. This reward is not of merit, but of grace.

Q. 64. But doth not this doctrine make men careless and profane?

A. By no means; for it is impossible that those who are implanted into Christ by a true faith should not bring forth fruits of thankfulness.

June 11 — Q&A 62-64 — Objections Made and Answered

Read: Romans 3:1–18.

The Biblical and confessional doctrine of justification by faith alone has been the object of constant attacks. These attacks were already launched against Luther. They were launched especially by the Roman Catholic Church, which hated Luther's doctrine and did all in its power, including terrible persecution, to rid the church of it. Luther stood firm. He called this doctrine the hinge on which hangs the whole church. Or, in another figure, this doctrine determines the standing or falling of the church.

Similar attacks have been made throughout history. They were made wherever the truth of justification by faith alone was preached. They were made in Germany, in Scotland, in the Netherlands, and elsewhere. They are made again in more modern times with particularly fierce attacks that seem to have paralyzed many churches. Following John Wesley and his preaching in England, attacks against justification by faith alone were made on the basis of Wesley's open and radical Arminianism. In the Scottish Church, attacks against this doctrine were made by the Marrow Men, whose objections led to the adoption of the well-meant and gracious offer of the gospel.

Today we face the same attacks. Strangely these attacks come within Reformed and Presbyterian churches. They come from those who claim to be children of the Reformation; and yet they are not hesitant to deny the most fundamental truth of the Reformation. And the fiercest attacks come from those who want to make salvation conditional. These even plead for a conditional covenant. And from such error comes the error of a conditional justification—justification by faith and works. What is worse, such views as are being taught in Reformed and Presbyterian circles today rob the child of God of his only comfort. If your salvation and mine depended on the slightest measure of what we do that is pleasing to God, we are lost. It cannot be any different. To follow these false teachers is to commit the sin of Esau: sell our birthright for a bowl of bean soup.

And so, after teaching us the great truth of justification by faith alone, without any works, our teacher warns us that in the defense of this doctrine we will be under constant and sometimes brutal attacks. We must be prepared for this, for if we know beforehand the nature of the attacks, we can be ready to meet them. We must be ready to meet them and stand our ground, for the battle is not only on the level of our intellects; it is a spiritual battle. Our salvation is at stake. To claim justification is partially or altogether based on works is to lose our salvation.

Our only hope is in justification by faith alone; that is, our only hope for salvation is in the cross of our Savior.

Herman Hanko

June 12 — Q&A 62 — Cannot Our Works Save?

Read: Psalm 53; Psalm 14.

The first objection to which our teacher calls attention is a question that seems to be asked by someone who is surprised by the fact that justification is not based on works: "Why cannot our good works be the whole or part of our righteousness before God?"[*] It is a question that comes from a person who is rather proud of his goodness and is convinced that these works are surely good enough for God to acknowledge their worth. Obviously, the man is proud.

But wait a moment. Do we not often do the same? Is it not true that when God sends us some great affliction, and we writhe beneath the heavy chastisement of God, that we often say, Why me? Why does God do this to me? And what we mean to say is: I do not deserve this, for I have not done anything that makes me worthy of such affliction. That kind of thinking is the same as being of the opinion that our works ought to be the ground for God doing good to us. What makes people think better of themselves than is true?

The only explanation for this is pride. Pride caused Eve to speak with the serpent in paradise and to obey the serpent when he suggested that eating of the forbidden tree would make her as God, knowing good and evil. Pride is the devil behind all our boasting. Pride keeps us from admitting our sin and worthlessness. Pride asks the question: But why cannot our works be the whole or part of our righteousness before God? The two most difficult words in any language to say, because of our pride, are: I'm sorry.

We have a wise teacher to instruct us in the truth. He understands all too well why we like to raise objections to justification by faith alone, without the works of the law. He will point us first to our pride. And then he will tell us what the Bible says about us and our works. All our instruction up to this point is clearly what is taught in the Bible. The Bible also teaches us what to think of our good works. And knowing what the Bible says about our good works, we will never, never think of them as the reason why God ought to justify and save us. And when we stop to think about it all, we will shudder at the thought that our good works would save us. We will cringe with horror that we could ever entertain such an idea.

We will fall on our faces before God, confess our sins, and thank God for Christ.

Herman Hanko

---

[*] Heidelberg Catechism Q 62, in *Confessions and Church Order*, 107.

June 13 — **Q&A 62 – The Uselessness of Our Works**

Read: Psalm 10.

Our teacher is very patient with us and tells us in some detail why it is impossible for our works to be in any way the basis for our justification. The first reason is that if our works must serve as a ground for our justification, they "must be absolutely perfect, and in all respects conformable to the divine law."* This clearly is true. God is in his own divine being a righteous God. He created man in true knowledge and holiness but also righteousness. As all God does is in perfect conformity with his holiness, so he made man able to do all things in perfect conformity with God's holiness. That is the righteousness approved by God.

Where someone is found who is as righteous as God demands, you will find a person whose whole life is in conformity with the law of God. His thoughts and desires, his words and deeds are all perfectly in conformity with the law that God has given for man. But we must not forget that that law is: "Love the Lord thy God." And love him "with all thy heart, and with all thy soul, and with all thy mind, and with all thy strength" (Mark 12:30). An outward conformity with the law will not do. It must be a conformity to the law of God that characterizes our entire nature. But where can such righteousness be found? The answer to that question is the second reason why our good works can never be the ground of our justification: "Our best works in this life are all imperfect and defiled with sin."** That is the indictment of Scripture.

Notice that our teacher is not now talking about wicked people; he is talking about God's people, who, through the power of God's grace, actually do good works. He is talking about our worship of God, our prayers, our instruction of our children, our care for the poor, our refusal to indulge in all the sinful activities of the wicked world in the midst of which we live. Our teacher is talking about our works in this life. Another day is coming for which this life is the preparation. But we live in this life as God's people. Can we claim, in this life, to keep God's law perfectly? We cannot! Worse yet, it is true we do good works, but every good work is imperfect. We sing God's praises, but not from the heart. We pray, but our minds wander during our prayers. We pray for God's grace to escape a particular sin, but we add in our hearts: "Not yet, Lord." I want to enjoy this sin a while first. We help the poor and hope to gain glory for it. We witness to others but do so very imperfectly. Our best works are still imperfect.

In a striking passage, Isaiah calls our "righteousnesses," that is, our very best works, like "filthy rags" (64:6)—that is, like menstrual rags. That certainly does not say much for them. How often we must ask God for forgiveness for our "good" works, for our best works are still corrupted and polluted by sins!

Herman Hanko

---

*   Heidelberg Catechism A 62, in *Confessions and Church Order*, 107.
** Heidelberg Catechism Q 62, in *Confessions and Church Order*, 107.

June 14 — Q&A 63 – The Inability to Merit with God

Read: Matthew 20:1–10.

Our instructor tells us there are other arguments that enemies of the truth will bring. They will try to trap us into agreeing that our works merit with God. And then they will quote some texts: "For we must all appear before the judgment seat of Christ; that every one may receive the things done in his body, according to that he hath done, whether it be good or bad" (2 Cor. 5:10). "See?" they will say, "We will receive something for doing good. The text says so. Here is another verse: 'And, behold, I come quickly; and my reward is with me, to give every man according as his work shall be' (Rev. 22:12). Jesus even calls what he will give us 'a reward' (Matt. 6:4)."

Our teacher tells us that while it is indeed true that Scripture speaks of merit, the reward that we merit is not that we have earned something with God, but it is rather of grace. One of our other confessions puts it very beautifully. Article 24 of the Confession of Faith explains all this:

> Therefore we do good works, but not to merit by them (for what can we merit?), nay, we are beholden [in debt] to God for the good works we do, and not he to us, since it is he *that worketh in us both to will and to do of his good pleasure*. Let us therefore attend to what is written: *When ye shall have done all those things which are commanded you, say, we are unprofitable servants; we have done that which was our duty to do*. In the meantime, we do not deny that God rewards our good works, but it is through his grace that he crowns his gifts.
>
> Moreover, though we do good works, we do not found our salvation upon them; for we can do no work but what is polluted by our flesh, and also punishable; and although we could perform such works, still the remembrance of one sin is sufficient to make God reject them. Thus, then, we would always be in doubt, tossed to and fro without any certainty, and our poor consciences continually vexed, if they relied not on the merits of the suffering and death of our Savior.[*]

There are three things the article says. First, we cannot merit with God even though we do everything he requires of us. For, in that case, we have only done our duty and nothing beyond our duty. The Roman Catholics talk about works of supererogation, by which they mean works we do which go beyond our duty and merit sainthood. In fact, other people less able to perform these works can draw to their account these works, for they are in a bank in heaven and can be drawn on by others. What nonsense!

Second, consider that beautiful expression that the reward of grace is "through his grace that he crowns his gifts." That is, the works are his gift of grace, and so is their reward.

Third, if we had to rely on our good works, our consciences would always plague us. We rely on the merits of Christ and his merits alone.

Herman Hanko

---

[*] Belgic Confession 24, in *Confessions and the Church Order*, 54–55.

June 15 — Q&A 63 – How We Do Good Works

Read: Ephesians 2:1–10.

In the interests of learning fully how it is possible for a child of God to do good works, let us look at how Paul speaks of this very thing in Ephesians 2. We are "dead in trespasses and sins," Paul tells us (v. 1). We are made alive by the power of God (vv. 1, 5). This all is so much God's work that it is rooted in God's love for us and flows to us out of the fountain of his grace, his unmerited favor (vv. 4–5).

The result is that we are saved by grace through faith. That salvation by grace through faith is not of ourselves, but "is the gift of God" (v. 8). Grace is a gift; faith is a gift; and the resulting salvation is a gift. It is never our work. By making all these his gifts, God shuts the door to all boasting (v. 9). If our works entered in, we would boast of our contributions. But we can hear some objector, off to the side, shouting, But what about works? You are forgetting our works. You are right, the apostle says, we do good works. But let me tell you about those good works. And then see once whether you can still boast in them.

First of all, we must remember that we are God's workmanship (v. 10). Now, a workmanship is a work of stunningly beautiful art that shows by its beauty the skill of the artist and demonstrates why he is to be praised. That is what we, as God's saints, are. We are a work of the divine artist who makes us his divine work so that we show forth his praise.

Second, we are a divine work of art "in Christ Jesus" (v. 10). Christ Jesus and his people are one work of art, planned in eternity, prepared in the cross of Christ, painted throughout history, finished in all its glory in heaven.

Third, the purpose God has in mind in preparing this masterpiece of the church in Christ is so that the church can do good works: "Created in Christ Jesus unto good works." These good works are "before ordained" (v. 10). That is, every good work each saint does is determined for him by God in his eternal counsel before the creation of the world. This is possible because Christ merited them. Our good works are God's gifts, merited by Christ, graciously given. Good works are part of our salvation.

Finally, even the fact that we do these good works is ordained by God from all eternity. He gives us the privilege, the blessings, the power to do that which Christ merited for us. And these good works, part of God's masterpiece, are to the praise and the glory of the divine artist. God is praised for our good works, because God gave them to us to show his power and grace.

Do you want to talk about works? says Paul; These are our good works. Where is the merit? We ought to thank God for the good works we do.

Herman Hanko

June 16 — Q&A 63 — Good Works, the Fruit of Justification

Read: Romans 6.

Never, never ought we to make our good works the ground or reason for our justification. Many may do that very thing, as they have done it throughout the new dispensation. But to make our works in any way a contributing factor to our salvation is to lose our salvation. Put yourself once as standing before the judgment seat of Christ at the end of the world, where Christ sits blazing with all the holiness of God himself, in dazzling garments of white. It is your turn to be judged as worthy or unworthy of heaven. You are commanded to produce your works, which would then be judged to determine whether you ought to go to heaven or hell. You pull a book from your pocket and say to Christ: "On February 10, 1989, I prayed three times during the day. On June 5, 1997, I took care of one of the sick members of my church. In November 2000, I brought a cake over to a friend in the block next to ours." Do you think that Christ will order the angels to escort you into heaven?

Our best works are corrupted and polluted by sin. What then can we say about the myriads of our other works? We will, I am sure, try to hide our best works behind our backs so that Christ cannot see them.

But what about these good works? We surely do them. And we are admonished in Scripture, again and again, to do them. We do pray. We do sing praise to God. We do visit the sick. We do hate sin and struggle to walk in obedience. Yes, we do these things, and many more. But we do them not to be justified; we do them because we are already justified. They are the fruits of justification, not the grounds.

Consider a prisoner who is put in prison for the crime of theft. He is sentenced to prison, for he is guilty. So the sinner is sentenced to the prison of spiritual depravity and death because of his sin. But someone pays the debt for the thief. He is then innocent of his crime. Can a just judge, nevertheless, keep him in prison for that crime? No, he must let the prisoner go free. So Christ paid our debt, and we are justified; that is, we are declared by the judge of all the earth to be innocent. Can God then keep us in the prison of depravity and death? No! He who has justified us now delivers us from the slavery of sin and death. That is, he sanctifies us. We are made holy as he is holy.

It takes us a long time to be made holy—all our lives. Our souls are made holy when we die and our bodies in the resurrection from the dead. But we are holy in principle. And because we are holy in principle, we do good works. They too are of God.

Herman Hanko

June 17 — Q&A 64 – A Careless and Profane Christian Is Impossible

Read: Matthew 25:31–46.

What about "careless and profane"* Christians? Are there such people? Do you know of such a person? Are you such a person? Does the doctrine of justification by faith alone make you want to sin as much as you like because you are going to heaven in any case? No matter how much you sin? I know people who do say this as an excuse for their sins. Young people are sometimes tempted to say this. They go to shows, drink too much alcohol, go to wild parties where ungodly music is played, and live as the world. When they are reprimanded for their sins, they fall back on the excuse: "I am justified without my works. I am going to heaven because my sins are forgiven."

What can be said to these people? This can and must be said: "If you excuse your sin because of the doctrine of justification alone, you are not a Christian, for a Christian would never say anything like that. You may claim to be a Christian. You may have been baptized. You may have gone to a Christian school. You may go to church every Lord's day. But you are not a Christian." Paul says the same thing in Romans 6. He has developed beyond any fear of contradiction the truth of justification by faith alone. He receives an objection: "What shall we say then? Shall we continue in sin, that grace may abound?" (v. 1). To which he responds: "God forbid" (v. 2).

Some in Paul's day carried the whole matter to that extreme. They said: "It is better to sin wildly, for the greater sinner we show ourselves to be, the more wonderful is our justification." There was a woman who claimed to be a prophetess in the church of Thyatira who taught the same thing (Rev. 2:20–23). But one who is a true Christian does not say these things. The reasons for this are as follows.

First, the sinner who is justified is also sanctified, that is, made holy. A just judge does not declare a prisoner innocent and then let him stay in jail. If a man is innocent, the judge orders his release. So God, the righteous judge, does not declare us to be without sin and then leave us in the prison of our sins; he delivers us from our sins. Depravity was the punishment for our sins; if our sins exist no longer, the punishment is taken away. We are sanctified. This is Paul's argument in Romans 6.

But there is more. The justified sinner, in his own consciousness, never can and never will, say: "Now I can sin as much as I like." I have attained justification; I can now eat and drink and be merry. That is a spiritual impossibility. The justified sinner is so overwhelmed by the wonder of God's grace in Christ that all he wants to do is please his Savior. And when he sins, he does not say, I'm justified; it doesn't matter. He says: "God be merciful to me a sinner" (Luke 18:13).

Herman Hanko

---

* Heidelberg Catechism Q 64, in *Confessions and Church Order*, 107.

Lord's Day 25

Q. 65. Since then we are made partakers of Christ and all his benefits by faith only, whence doth this faith proceed?

A. From the Holy Ghost, who works faith in our hearts by the preaching of the gospel, and confirms it by the use of the sacraments.

Q. 66. What are the sacraments?

A. The sacraments are holy, visible signs and seals, appointed of God for this end, that by the use thereof, he may the more fully declare and seal to us the promise of the gospel, namely, that he grants us freely the remission of sin and life eternal, for the sake of that one sacrifice of Christ accomplished on the cross.

Q. 67. Are both Word and sacraments, then, ordained and appointed for this end, that they may direct our faith to the sacrifice of Jesus Christ on the cross as the only ground of our salvation?

A. Yes, indeed; for the Holy Ghost teaches us in the gospel, and assures us by the sacraments, that the whole of our salvation depends upon that one sacrifice of Christ which he offered for us on the cross.

Q. 68. How many sacraments has Christ instituted in the new covenant, or testament?

A. Two, namely, holy baptism and the holy supper.

June 18 — Q&A 65 – The Means of Grace

Read: Ephesians 2:1–8.

The subject of Lord's Day 25 is what has been called the means of grace. Part of the reason why there is such an unusually long section in the Catechism on this subject is the historical fact that the truth of the sacraments was a greatly debated subject at the time of the Reformation. This debate engaged not only the church of Rome and Protestantism, but it was also between the two major branches of Protestantism, one more or less following the teachings of Martin Luther, the other those of John Calvin.

We can, however, learn much from the biblical teaching of this section of the Catechism. The whole of the Catechism teaches us the wonderful truth that we are saved only by the grace of God in Jesus Christ. The grace of God comes to us through faith in Jesus Christ. We must know him, trust in him, and glory in him alone as our Savior. Even our faith is a gift of God's grace (see Eph. 2:8). It is not of ourselves, that we should have something to boast in ourselves. We give thanks to God for the faith he gives us!

God uses means to work faith in our hearts. These are called means of grace. These means God himself also has given and ordained in his church. Being saved by Jesus Christ is a great spiritual mystery and wonder. It is a mistake of some Christians, however, to imagine that being a Christian is merely a matter of a mystical personal experience or some vague personal relationship with him. Faith in Jesus Christ involves knowing the truth of God revealed in Jesus Christ. Faith is knowing the fullness of the treasures of salvation, which are in him alone. We must grow in our faith by growing in the spiritual understanding of this truth and embracing it with our hearts. Faith involves growing up unto the fullness of the treasures of wisdom and knowledge as they are in Christ. We must grow up unto the stature of the full measure of the knowledge of Jesus Christ "unto a perfect man," or in other words, a mature Christian (Eph. 4:13). This faith God works in us by the means he has himself ordained and appointed in the church (Eph. 4:11–16).

As Christians, we are called to confess this truth and to live by it for the glory of Jesus Christ. We do not come to know Christ Jesus through a personal quest of our own great knowledge and intellectual powers. God gives us the wisdom and knowledge of faith. He also works the conviction and assurance and comfort of faith in our hearts.

When the Bible teaches us that our faith is the gift of God, it means more than faith being given to us as merely an external gift, somewhat like a package or present that we then take with our hands and make our own. That faith is a gift of God's grace means that God actually works faith in our hearts. He does this by the mysterious and wonderful operation of his Spirit in our hearts. God works both the power to believe in our hearts and also our actual believing by the means of grace of which Lord's Day 25 speaks.

When we experience lively and true faith in our hearts, we should thank him for this wonderful gift. By this gift, we are spiritually united to Christ, rely on him completely, and glory in him alone.

Arie den Hartog

June 19 — Q&A 65 – How God Works Faith

Read: Ephesians 4:11–16.

We first believe when we are regenerated by the Spirit of God. In our regeneration, God gives us the power to believe. He wonderfully changes our hearts from being unbelieving and rebellious to being repentant and believing. God works in our hearts by the Holy Spirit, renewing our minds and giving us new understanding so that we can receive his truth. The heart is the spiritual center of man. When God regenerates us, he gives us new hearts. He makes us willing and active in our own faith. All of these are wonderful aspects of God's work when he gives us the gift of true faith.

When we are born again, we are babes in Christ who must be fed and nourished by the word of God. We must grow to maturity in the faith. We must be made strong and steadfast in the faith, able to face opposition and to distinguish the truth from the many false teachings that are in the world. We need to be edified, to be built up in the faith. Ephesians 4:13 speaks of growing up in "the stature of the fulness of Christ."

Faith is not a mere passing emotion or momentary exciting experience. Our faith must be founded on the knowledge of the truth of God. If this is not the case with us, then according to the words of the apostle in Ephesians 4:14, we will always be children, "tossed to and fro, and carried about with every wind of doctrine, by the sleight of men, and cunning craftiness, whereby they lie in wait to deceive." To avoid this tragic end, so common in the lives of many professing Christians, we must be made strong in the faith.

The preaching of the word is not only the means whereby we are first called to faith, it is also the means God continually uses to build us up and make us strong in our faith. We must be strong in our faith so that we might be able to endure the temptations of sins, the trials that God sends us in our lives, and the doubts and fears common to the Christian life. We must be strong in the knowledge of the truth of the word of God so that we are not deceived and led away again from the Lord. The way of the devil is to deceive and thereby to lead astray those who once believed by leading them away from faith in God and Jesus Christ.

Our faith in God and the knowledge of his truth must equip us for lives of good works whereby we serve our Lord and glorify him in every part of our lives. The means of grace are therefore very important for the Christian. He or she must not despise them in his or her life. If anyone does this, he or she will inevitably become weak, unstable, and vulnerable to the work of the devil to destroy him or her.

In Ephesians 4, we are told that the exalted Lord of his church gave to her apostles, prophets, evangelists, pastors, and teachers (v. 1). All of these men were given the solemn duty of preaching the word of God in order to strengthen the faith of the saints of God, to equip them fully for their Christian lives and for their calling in turn to edify one another in the love of Christ, building each other up in the knowledge and love of the truth of the word of God.

We are greatly in need of the means of grace and should attend to them faithfully, especially by going to church every Lord's day.

Arie den Hartog

June 20 — **Q&A 65 — The Preaching of the Word as the Chief Means of Grace**

Read: Romans 10:14–21.

There is little understanding today of what the preaching of the word in the church is. The preaching has been replaced in the worship services by all kinds of other things: movies, shows, artistic dance, entertainment programs enlisting popular so-called Christian rock groups, discussion forums where everyone shares his or her own opinion about things, or simply Bible studies instead of listening to the preaching. Today, there is heavy use of modern-day electronic media and things like PowerPoint presentations. When these new ways of worshipping God are used, there are usually much larger audiences. There is greater interest. The opinion is out there that the very fact that there is so much greater interest in these new methods itself proves that these ways of doing things are much more effective and bring more results. This may make us wonder, if we are still using the old and tried way of preaching, whether we should change our ways to be more effective in our modern day and time.

The new ways of worshipping God reflect little understanding of a truth that is very obvious from Scripture, if one pays some attention to what Scripture says. God calls his people through the preaching of the word. The preaching is a divine institution. It is the means that God himself uses to call his people to salvation in Jesus Christ. The very fact that the prophets in the Old Testament, Jesus in the New Testament, and the apostles all preached ought to make us take notice. Why was this? This was the practice over thousands of years. In the great commission, the Lord sent his apostles to preach unto all sorts of nations and peoples (Matt 28:19–20). Each of the countries that the apostles were sent to had its own culture. But the preaching of the gospel transcended all of these cultures. God used the preaching in all of them to call his people unto salvation. Never from age to age did the Lord change his own ordained way to save his people, nor did he change the means whereby he accomplishes this salvation.

In Romans 10 we read:

> For whosoever shall call upon the name of the Lord shall be saved. How then shall they call on him in whom they have not believed? and how shall they believe in him of whom they have not heard? and how shall they hear without a preacher? and how shall they preach, except they be sent? as it is written, How beautiful are the feet of them that preach the gospel of peace, and bring glad tidings of good things! (vv. 13–15)

Paul says in 1 Corinthians 1:23–25, "But we preach Christ crucified, unto the Jews a stumblingblock, and unto the Greeks foolishness; but unto them which are called, both Jews and Greeks, Christ the power of God, and the wisdom of God. Because the foolishness of God is wiser than men; and the weakness of God is stronger than men."

Let us trust in God's own way to call us to faith and build us up in the faith. But in order to do that, we must seek out the church where there is true preaching of the gospel. And we must also understand what true preaching really is. This I will address in our next meditation.

Arie den Hartog

June 21 — Q&A 65 — What is the Preaching?

Read: 1 Corinthians 1:23–31.

We are saved by the power of God. We are saved through faith in Jesus Christ. Throughout all ages, God has sent out preachers of the gospel in order that men everywhere might be saved. The church has the great commission of Christ to preach the gospel. And we are saved through coming under this preaching and receiving it by a true and living faith in humility before God. This does not mean that the mere words of a mere man can save anyone—not even the words of a popular, eloquent, or very persuasive preacher, no matter how large the audience he is able to gather. There are many popular false teachers who have large followings, sometimes all over the world, who are not God's instruments of salvation at all. These deceive many and lead many astray. Against these we must also be warned. Jesus warned many times about the many false prophets that would arise in the last days.

A true preacher is the minister of God. He stands in the service of the word of God. He does not bring his own word. The word of a mere man does not have the power to save. The meaning of this is actually in a sense very simple. The infallible word of God is contained in the Bible. The complete revelation of all that we need to know about God and Jesus Christ for our salvation is recorded in the Bible. The solemn duty and obligation of the preacher is simply to bring the word of God and the word of Christ, nothing else. Anyone called to be a preacher must devote his life to this. He must earnestly and prayerfully search what the word of God has to say and what it truly means. The preacher must compare Scripture with Scripture to be sure he is bringing to the people of God only the word of God. This alone will build them up in the faith.

True preaching is the simple, clear, and authoritative exposition and declaration of the word of God. The preacher is called of God to his office through the faithful church of Jesus Christ. God has appointed and qualified elders in his church. One of the most important duties of these elders is to judge and guard the preaching. Even the ordinary child of God, one who is not an elder, has the Spirit of God and is able to judge the preaching. John tells Christians: "But ye have an unction from the Holy One, and ye know all things…But the anointing which ye have received of him abideth in you, and ye need not that any man teach you: but as the same anointing teacheth you of all things, and is truth, and is no lie, and even as it hath taught you, ye shall abide in him" (1 John 2:20, 27).

The Christians in Berea in the days of the apostle Paul did this. They were able to judge the preaching of the greatest missionary and preacher that ever lived save Jesus Christ himself. We read about them in Acts 17:11, "These were more noble than those in Thessalonica, in that they received the word with all readiness of mind, and searched the scriptures daily, whether those things were so." We all must follow this amazing example. The Christian must place himself under the true preaching of the gospel. The apostle Paul gives thanks to God for such true and faithful Christians: "For this cause also thank we God without ceasing, because, when ye received the word of God which ye heard of us, ye received it not as the word of men, but as it is in truth, the word of God, which effectually worketh also in you that believe" (1 Thess. 2:13).

Arie den Hartog

June 22 — Q&A 66 – The Sacraments as the Secondary Means of Grace

Read: Romans 4:1–11.

The preaching of the word is the chief means of grace. God has added to the preaching a secondary means of grace, the two sacraments of baptism and the Lord's supper. There is a reason why they are properly called the secondary means of grace. The sacraments do not have any magical power in themselves to work faith. They can only strengthen the faith that by the grace of God is already in the hearts of those who receive the sacraments.

One lesson we can learn about the history of the Protestant Reformation is that God used this mighty movement to teach us the right understanding and use of the sacraments. The proper administration of the sacraments is one of the marks of the true church of Jesus Christ. The church of Rome before the days of the Reformation had corrupted the sacraments. It also wrongly added five additional sacraments by its own imaginary authority. The church of Rome, especially during the Middle Ages, gave the sacraments a place in the church that corrupted their use in the church. Because of Rome's false and superstitious teaching regarding the sacraments, they were given a position independent of and above the preaching in the church. It was and is maintained even today by the church of Rome that the sacraments in themselves have the power to save. Preaching in the church of Rome was virtually eliminated or reduced to mere moral homilies.

Scripture teaches that the sacraments are of benefit only to believers. So true is this that wrongful use of the sacraments adds to the condemnation of those who partake of them without repentance and faith in their hearts. Read 1 Corinthians 11:18–34. The church must forbid unbelieving and unworthy people from receiving the sacraments. The sacraments must be kept holy in the church. The honor and glory of Christ is maintained when the church is faithful in this regard. And when the holy sacraments are properly received with faith and reverence for their intended meaning, they are a great blessing to the church and great encouragement and comfort to the believer.

We limit the sacraments strictly to the two which Christ instituted in the church. Sacraments are not human inventions. They are not even mere traditions that originated from the church herself. They were given by Christ to his church. Christ Jesus himself operates in connection with the sacraments which he himself has ordained in the church and through which he works in the hearts of believers. We only need the two sacraments which Christ has instituted in the church because they signify and seal to us all the blessings of salvation. Baptism signifies and seals to us the washing away of all our sins. The Lord's supper is a spiritual sign of our daily communion with Christ and of our being partakers with Christ of all the benefits which he has merited for us by his sacrifice on the cross.

If the sacraments are to be of spiritual benefit to us, we must be very careful that we do not have any superstitious ideas regarding their power and significance in our lives. We need to have a good spiritual understanding of the meaning of the sacraments. This is the reason why there was so much debate about this at the time of the Reformation and why the Catechism has such a lengthy section on the sacraments.

Arie den Hartog

June 23 — Q&A 66 – The Meaning of the Sacraments

Read: Acts 2:37–47.

The sacraments have often been misunderstood and misused. One of the reasons why the Reformation of the church was necessary was because of the abuse of the sacraments by the church of Rome. It is easy to use the sacraments out of mere custom or superstition or without the proper attitude of faith and spiritual understanding. In New Testament times, this was being done by the church of Corinth. The apostle Paul wrote his first letter to the church of Corinth to correct the serious abuse especially of the sacrament of the Lord's supper. We can read about this in 1 Corinthians 11:18–34. Because of the abuse of the Lord's supper, the members of the church of Corinth who ate and drank unworthily were eating and drinking "damnation to [themselves], not discerning the Lord's body" (v. 29). The judgment of God even came upon the whole church. The name of Christ was being dishonored.

One of the greatest evils with regards to receiving and observing the sacraments is to treat them as though they have some inherent mystical power in themselves. This leads to superstition and idolatrous use of the holy sacraments. Christ has given the sacraments for the worship of the one only true God in a spirit of trusting in Christ, not in mere outward ceremony.

We must properly distinguish between the outward sign of the sacraments and the blessed reality they were intended to signify. These two must not be confused. When Christ gave the sacraments to the church, he chose simple outward signs. In the case of baptism, the sign is water. In the case of the Lord's supper, the sign is the broken bread and the poured-out wine. The water in baptism signifies the precious reality of the atoning blood of Jesus Christ as the only ground of our righteousness before God. The bread in the Lord's supper signifies our Lord's broken body sacrificed for us on the cross, and the wine signifies his precious blood which was poured out in his suffering and sacrifice for us on the cross. Only the blood of Christ could atone for our sins.

The mystery of the meaning of the sacraments is that they are visible signs of invisible spiritual realities. By these outward signs, Christ intends to strengthen our faith in him and in his suffering and death on the cross and all the riches of salvation that we have through his perfect sacrifice.

The Lord accommodates the weakness of our faith with regards to the hearing of the preaching of the word. The preaching of the word appeals to our ears. We receive the preaching through faith, the faith that God gives us. This faith is able to receive those things that we cannot see, but things that God has nevertheless given to us in his word. Peter tells us in 1 Peter 1:8–9 that we have not seen Christ in his bodily appearance. We will not see him until he appears again in glory at the end of the world. Yet already now, we rejoice in Christ. We cannot see the spiritual realities of salvation that we have in Christ. However, we know and glory in these blessings as we receive them by faith according as we are told of them in his word.

In the sacraments, God gives us visible signs and seals of his grace in Christ. He appeals to our sight, our taste, our touch to strengthen our faith in Jesus Christ. This the Lord does with the sacraments and through the work of his grace and Holy Spirit in our hearts.

Arie den Hartog

June 24 — Q&A 67-68 — The Lord's Purpose in the Sacraments

Read: Hebrews 9:23–28.

The Catechism teaches us that both the preaching of the word and the sacraments are ordained and appointed of God for the purpose of directing our faith "to the sacrifice of Jesus Christ on the cross as the only ground of our salvation."* By his once and for all sacrifice on the cross, Jesus fully and perfectly accomplished all of our salvation. Nothing else need be or even can be added to the perfect sacrifice of Jesus Christ. To suggest that something needs to be added to the perfect sacrifice on the cross is really blasphemy, for this suggests that somehow the sacrifice of Christ was not sufficient; something else was needed.

One of the ways in which the sufficiency of Christ's sacrifice has been denied in the church is through the misuse of the sacraments—a strange thing indeed. When we have a false understanding of the sacraments, especially in imagining that the sacraments have somehow in themselves the power to save us, we begin to trust in the sacraments themselves rather than Christ Jesus, the only hope of our salvation.

When God gave the two sacraments to the church, he himself intended to direct our faith and trust in the one sacrifice of his own dear and eternal Son on the cross, and to remind us of the absolute sufficiency of this amazing and wonderful sacrifice. The whole of our salvation was accomplished by the sacrifice of Jesus Christ on the cross. This truth must be maintained in the church. God then gave the sacraments in order that by the proper use of them, we might glory in Christ Jesus alone and find all our hope and assurance of salvation in his cross alone. The apostle Paul wrote about the great importance of this in the book of Galatians. He makes his own confession to be our example when he writes in the concluding chapter of this book: "But God forbid that I should glory, save in the cross of our Lord Jesus Christ, by whom the world is crucified unto me, and I unto the world" (Gal. 6:14).

The proper use of the sacraments involves then the important issue of glorying in Christ alone and trusting in none other than in the cross of Christ for our salvation. No wonder the great men through whom God brought about the Reformation of the church were so earnest and zealous about the proper use of the sacraments and why there was such a lengthy debate regarding the proper administration of the sacraments. As I wrote in an earlier meditation, this explains why there is such a lengthy section in the Catechism on the sacraments.

Let me offer one closing thought. The proper use of the sacraments is maintained in the church when the proper relationship between the preaching of the word and the observance of the sacraments is maintained. The sacraments should not be administered independently from the church and the preaching of the word. Whenever the sacraments are being administered, the preaching of the word continually explains to the church the true meaning of the sacraments. The church must never be confused about this.

Arie den Hartog

---

* Heidelberg Catechism Q 67, in *Confessions and Church Order*, 108.

Lord's Day 26

Q. 69. How art thou admonished and assured by holy baptism that the one sacrifice of Christ upon the cross is of real advantage to thee?

A. Thus: That Christ appointed this external washing with water, adding thereto this promise, that I am as certainly washed by his blood and Spirit from all the pollution of my soul, that is, from all my sins, as I am washed externally with water, by which the filthiness of the body is commonly washed away.

Q. 70. What is it to be washed with the blood and Spirit of Christ?

A. It is to receive of God the remission of sins freely, for the sake of Christ's blood, which he shed for us by his sacrifice upon the cross; and also to be renewed by the Holy Ghost, and sanctified to be members of Christ, that so we may more and more die unto sin and lead holy and unblamable lives.

Q. 71. Where has Christ promised us that he will as certainly wash us by his blood and Spirit as we are washed with the water of baptism?

A. In the institution of baptism, which is thus expressed: *Go ye, therefore, and teach all nations, baptizing them in the name of the Father, and of the Son, and of the Holy Ghost. He that believeth, and is baptized, shall be saved; but he that believeth not, shall be damned.* This promise is also repeated where the scripture calls baptism the washing of regeneration and the washing away of sins.

June 25 — Q&A 69 — Baptism Instituted by the Lord

Read: Matthew 28:16–20.

The sacraments are the precious gifts of Christ to his church. They are to be used with understanding of what they mean for the confirmation and assurance of believers and members of the church. The very fact that our Lord himself gave the sacraments to the church is of great significance. They were not mere inventions of men or even traditions begun in history by the church. Exactly for this reason, they are so significant. Even today, Christ by his grace and Spirit blesses his beloved church and her believers through the sacraments.

The first of the sacraments that Christ gave to the church is the sacrament of baptism. Baptism in its simple meaning is the sign and seal of the washing away of our sins through the precious blood of Jesus Christ offered on the cross for us. Already in the Old Testament, there were many ceremonies that involved cleansing. Some of these involved washing with water and others the sprinkling of the blood of bulls and goats. All these ceremonies testified to believing Israel that there could be no approach to the holy God except that first of all our sins are dealt with, atoned for and washed away. We are always sinning, and every time we approach God to worship him, we must be cleansed of our sins.

John the Baptist, under the direction of the Lord, took the Old Testament ceremonies of cleansing and made them the sign of his preaching. John the Baptist preached that the kingdom of God was now at hand, because Jesus the Son of God was come into the world. John was appointed of God to be the forerunner of Jesus. Jesus, through all of his ministry, his cross and resurrection, exaltation and return, would bring in the kingdom of God. Entrance into that kingdom is only by repentance and the forgiveness of sins. John preached the great urgency of repentance. Those who did repent and believed the message concerning the kingdom preached by John were baptized in the river Jordan as the blessed sign of the forgiveness of their sins. The ministry of John the Baptist came to its climax when on a certain day, Jesus stood in the audience of John while John was preaching. John then declared to the people: "Behold, the Lamb of God, which taketh away the sin of the world" (John 1:29).

The next time Jesus was in the audience of John, Jesus came forward to be baptized of John. This was a great surprise for John. But Jesus told John: "Suffer it to be so now: for thus it becometh us to fulfill all righteousness" (Matt. 3:15). The amazing fact that Jesus came forward to be baptized was a sign of the truth that Jesus accepted from God the Father the fearful reality that only he could make atonement for the sins of his people through the shedding of his own blood on the cross. There was no other way that we could become the citizens of the kingdom of God except through the washing away of our sins. The ceremonies of the Old Testament, no matter how many times they were repeated over and over again, could not themselves cleanse God's people from their sins. These ceremonies were only types and pictures of a greater sacrifice which needed to be made. There was the need for a greater sacrifice. Jesus, the Lamb of God, alone could make that sacrifice.

Our baptism is a sign of this amazing truth!

Arie den Hartog

June 26 — Q&A 69 – The Baptism of Jesus and the Institution of Baptism

Read: John 1:29–34.

It is amazing that Jesus himself was also baptized. The reason for this was due to the fact that Jesus could enter into his kingdom only through the sacrifice of himself on the cross for the sins of his people. When Jesus was baptized by John in the Jordan River, God gave two wonderful signs. There was a voice from God the Father, which said: "This is my beloved Son, in whom I am well pleased" (Matt. 3:17). The second amazing thing that took place was the descending of the Spirit of God upon the Lord Jesus under the visible sign of a dove (v. 16). Both of these signs had great meaning. The baptism of Jesus marked the beginning of his public ministry. From the very beginning of his public ministry, Jesus had the testimony of God that he is the beloved Son of God. Jesus, the Son of God in our human nature, performed all of his work by the Spirit of God that came upon him.

Jesus himself made baptism a sacrament when he gave the great commission to his disciples after his resurrection and just before his ascension into heaven. The Lord commanded his disciples to preach the gospel to all nations of the world after his ascension. The disciples were commanded to teach men all the things which he had taught them during the whole of his earthly ministry. By learning the truth of the Lord, men and women from all nations would themselves become disciples, followers of Jesus. Then he commanded his disciples to baptize whoever believed (Matt 28:19–20).

No one could be baptized until he first had heard the gospel preached. The Lord sent his disciples to preach. He continues to command the church today to preach the gospel. The preaching of the gospel is the power of God unto salvation. Through instruction in the truth, the elect of God become the disciples of Jesus. The preaching of the gospel continues to equip God's people for Christian living. The preaching of the gospel equips God's people to be the disciples of the Lord Jesus Christ. The word of God must be their guide and encouragement in their lives. So the church must preach extensively and continually all that Christ commanded. We must hear the word of Christ over and over again and learn it more and more deeply. We are also to be encouraged in our faith by our baptism. Our baptism is a sign that we belong to the Lord Jesus Christ and that he will be with us to the end of the world (v. 20).

It is clear from the book of Acts that the apostles of Jesus clearly understood the Lord's commission to preach and to baptize. On the day of Pentecost, three thousand came to the knowledge of the truth of Jesus Christ and were baptized and then were added to the church. In the book of Acts, there are numerous examples of baptism following the preaching. When the gospel was explained to the Ethiopian eunuch by Philip the Evangelist, God worked faith in his heart. When Philip and the Ethiopian came to a body of water, this man earnestly asked: "See, here is water; what doth hinder me to be baptized? And Philip said, If thou believest with all thine heart, thou mayest" (Acts 8:36–37). See the amazing account of this in Acts 8. More such amazing accounts followed in the book of Acts.

Arie den Hartog

June 27 — Q&A 71 — Baptism in the Name of the Blessed Triune God

Read: Matthew 28:16–20.

We are struck by the fact that our Lord commanded that baptism should be done in the name of the blessed triune God: Father, Son, and Holy Spirit. The only true baptism is the baptism that is performed in the name of the Trinity. We also read in the word of God that at times, baptism is done in the name of the Lord Jesus Christ. On the day of Pentecost, Peter commanded believers to "be baptized…in the name of Jesus Christ for the remission of sins" (Acts 2: 38). The meaning of "in the name of Jesus Christ" is that baptism must be done by the authority of the Lord Jesus. Our baptism means that we become members of Christ and receive all spiritual blessings from him.

In time, however, the formula that has commonly been used for baptism was the one Jesus gave to us in the great commission. Baptism in the name of the triune God puts on the foreground the greatest mystery of the Godhead. The one only true and living God, who is absolutely one in his being, is at the same time three in his persons, Father, Son, and Holy Spirit. From the beginning, we must know and confess this truth about God's triune being, even though this truth is at once also a mystery far beyond our comprehension. We should not be troubled by this if we know that God in his infinite being is so much greater than we can fully know. If this were not true, we would be equal with God, and God would not be God.

It is clear that this three-person God is one God only and not three gods. For this reason, the baptism formula uses the word *name* in the singular. All three persons are involved in all of God's works of creation, providence, and redemption. Without a God who is the eternal Father, there could never have been the great demonstration of the love of God by which our salvation was accomplished. This love was revealed in the highest sense when God gave us his own dear Son "to be the propitiation for our sins" (1 John 4:8–10). Jesus, the Son of God, saves us by sending into our hearts the Spirit of God, the third person of the triune God.

Baptism is a sign that we are incorporated into the covenant fellowship of the blessed triune God. The liturgy commonly used for baptism in Reformed churches has a beautiful statement regarding the Trinity in connection with our baptism. Let me quote this in the conclusion of today's meditation:

> When we are baptized in the name of the Father, God the Father witnesseth and sealeth unto us, that he doth make an eternal covenant of grace with us, and adopts us for his children and heirs, and therefore will provide us with every good thing, and avert all evil or turn it to our profit. And when we are baptized in the name of the Son, the Son sealeth unto us that he doth wash us in his blood from all our sins, incorporating us into the fellowship of his death and resurrection, so that we are freed from all our sins and accounted righteous before God. In like manner, when we are baptized in the name of the Holy Ghost, the Holy Ghost assures us, by this holy sacrament, that he will dwell in us and sanctify us to be members of Christ, applying unto us that which we have in Christ, namely, the washing away of our sins and the daily renewing of our lives.[*]

You are encouraged to look up several passages of Scripture which are the basis of the truth of this statement in the liturgy, such as Romans 6:1–11 and Colossians 2:10–13.

Arie den Hartog

---

[*] Form for the Administration of Baptism, in *Confessions and Church Order*, 258.

June 28 — Q&A 69-70 — Baptism with the Spirit of Jesus Christ

Read: Matthew 3:1–11.

During his ministry, John the Baptist made this prophecy concerning Jesus: "I indeed baptize you with water unto repentance: but he that cometh after me is mightier than I, whose shoes I am not worthy to bear: he shall baptize you with the Holy Ghost, and with fire" (Matt. 3:11). This prophecy was fulfilled on the day of Pentecost. Pentecost was actually the work of the exalted Lord Jesus Christ. He poured out his Spirit on his church. Jesus received the Spirit from the Father, and then Jesus from his throne in the heavens "shed forth" his Spirit on his church (Acts 2:33). This was a once and for all, never to be repeated, event. This is how Peter in Acts 2 explains the wonder of Pentecost to the multitudes gathered in Jerusalem.

Pentecost was the baptism of the church by the Spirit of Jesus Christ. This was the beginning of the New Testament age. It was a very dramatic and wonderful event! It happened not only according to the prophecy of John the Baptist, but also according to the promise of Jesus. Jesus gave his disciples the power to preach by sending them his Spirit. By the Spirit of Jesus Christ, the disciples could understand the wonderful works of God and the mysteries of salvation in Jesus Christ. They could then understand, as never before, what it meant that Jesus is the Son of God, why he had to die on the cross, and why he also arose again after his crucifixion. They could understand the prophecies of Scripture about the exaltation of Christ and his glorious return at the end of the ages. With understanding of these things, they could then preach with boldness and power.

The Spirit of Jesus Christ was also poured out on those who believed at the preaching of the apostle Peter on the day of Pentecost. When they were deeply moved by the truth of Christ and brought to repentance, they asked Peter what they must do. And "Peter said unto them, Repent, and be baptized every one of you in the name of Jesus Christ for the remission of sins, and ye shall receive the gift of the Holy Ghost" (Acts 2:38). On the day of Pentecost, when the Spirit was given, three thousand were added to the church.

From this history in the book of Acts, we can conclude that water baptism is a sign of being baptized with the Spirit. This is further explained by several passages later in the letters of the apostles. Every believer receives the baptism of the Spirit when he or she is born again of the Spirit of God. Water baptism and Spirit baptism are not to be wrongly separated. The right understanding of the relationship of these two is that water baptism is the outward sign of having received the Spirit of Jesus Christ. This is one of the beautiful meanings of baptism. It is a sign of having received the Spirit of Christ.

Every believer receives the fullness of the Spirit when he or she is regenerated. They need not tarry for a so-called second baptism. All the blessings of salvation in Jesus Christ are given by the Spirit of Christ to believers. Our water baptism is a wonderful outward sign and seal of this.

Arie den Hartog

June 29 — Q&A 70 – The Meaning of Our Baptism

Read: Acts 22:1–16.

The simple but wonderful meaning of our baptism is that it signifies and seals unto us the washing away of our sins by the blood of Jesus Christ. The expression "blood of Jesus" does not mean that we must be literally washed by the blood of Jesus. Rather, the blood of Jesus signifies the suffering and atonement of Christ by his precious sacrifice on the cross. It calls to mind the obedience and love of this sacrifice and all the shame, agony, and suffering involved in this sacrifice of Jesus for us. As earthly water washes away the filth of the body, so the blood of Jesus washes away the guilt and corruption of our sins.

When Jesus gave us the sacraments, he gave very simple and plain signs, easy to understand. No one, not even the church, should add to the simple sacraments any ritual or ceremony of their own devising. Such additions to the sacraments that Christ gave us simply obscure their simple and beautiful meaning. The Catechism has one of the best statements of any confession explaining the meaning of baptism. To the question, "What is it to be washed with the blood and Spirit of Christ?" the Catechism gives the answer: "It is to receive of God the remission of sins freely, for the sake of Christ's blood, which he shed for us by his sacrifice upon the cross; and also to be renewed by the Holy Ghost, and sanctified to be members of Christ, that so we may more and more die unto sin and lead holy and unblamable lives."*

The simple meaning of baptism is that it signifies and seals to us that all our sins have been washed away by the sacrifice of Jesus Christ on the cross. Our sins have two aspects. The guilt of our sins that make us worthy of condemnation has been atoned for by the satisfaction of Christ. Also, the corruption or spiritual defilement of our sins is washed away by the Spirit of Christ. We are made holy before God.

All our sins are washed away by the blood of Jesus Christ, both our original sin, which we inherited from our fallen parents, and sins that we commit personally every day. Every sin that we commit all our lives long is washed away by the blood and Spirit of Jesus Christ. The church of Rome teaches that only original sin and sins committed before baptism are washed away by baptism. The church of Rome has a very wrong understanding of baptism. Because of what she believes, she had to invent other sacraments, which the Lord himself never instituted in the church, to deal with sins committed after baptism. Because of this false idea, the church of Rome teaches her members that they still have to satisfy for sins not washed away by the blood of Christ. After death, they will be tormented for a time in purgatory before they can go to heaven. By this doctrine, the church of Rome held the saints of God captive in terror and at the same time compelled them to give money to the church to escape the torments of purgatory.

The Reformed church restored the gospel truth concerning the meaning of baptism. This truth is that baptism signifies that all our sins are forever washed away by the blood of Jesus Christ. We therefore have peace with God and can die in great and blessed comfort. No additional sacrament is needed as a sign of atonement for sins committed after our baptism, for baptism is the sign of Christ that he has washed away all our sins.

Arie den Hartog

---

* Heidelberg Catechism Q&A 70, in *Confessions and Church Order*, 109.

June 30 — Q&A 70 – Baptism Has an Even Richer Meaning

Read: Romans 6:1–6.

From question and answer 70 of the Catechism we can learn what Scripture teaches about the rich meaning of our baptism. It would be good if you could read this question and answer again before you read this meditation.

There are several beautiful aspects of the meaning of baptism, all clearly taught in the word of God. First, baptism is a sign of our new birth. Our baptism is a sign that we have received the Spirit of Christ, and by his power we are made alive from the dead and made new creatures in Christ (Matt. 3:11; Rom. 6:4). Water baptism is a sign of our spiritual baptism. We disagree with the teaching of the charismatics who claim that a born-again Christian is in need of a second baptism. According to this teaching, there is a need to be baptized a second time by the Spirit. We do not believe Scripture teaches two baptisms. Rather, water baptism is a sign of having been baptized by the Spirit. Our one baptism is a sign that when we were born again, we received the fullness of the Spirit. There is no need for another baptism. All the blessings of Christ have been given to us by his Spirit, of which our water baptism is a sign. Baptism is a sign that the fullness of the Spirit of Christ was given to us.

Second, baptism is a sign of our being members of Christ and of our mystical spiritual union with him. Romans 6 speaks of our being "baptized into Christ Jesus" (v. 3). Baptism is a sign that we belong to him. We were purchased by his precious blood to be his own. We are mystically united to Christ.

Third, and related to what was said above, our baptism is a sign that our old sinful nature was crucified with Christ, so that now we no longer serve sin. The dominion of sin over us has been destroyed by the power of the cross of Jesus Christ. According to Romans 6, we are therefore also raised with Christ unto "newness of life" (v. 4). Our baptism is a sign of the new life we have in Christ.

Fourth, water baptism is a sign of our being baptized by the Spirit of Christ into the membership of his body, called the church. First Corinthians 12:13 speaks of this. So, our baptism is a sign that we belong to the church of Jesus Christ, which is spiritually the body of Christ. We must also serve her, as members of the body serve the whole body. We are living members of the church whom Christ himself has saved and gathers and keeps in the world. Each of us has a place and calling in this church. The one same Spirit of Christ has given to every member of the church his or her particular calling.

Finally, our baptism is a sign that we have an obligation to live as Christians. The life of the Christian is called a new and holy life. The Christian life is one lived by the power of the Spirit, which we have received from Christ. This means that we are to love God with all our heart, soul, mind, and strength. We are called to deny ourselves, take up our cross, and follow Christ in our lives. We deny the meaning of our baptism when we fail to do this. On the other hand, we are not to despair at the difficulty of Christian living. Christ has given us his Spirit. We are called to walk in the Spirit and to live by the Spirit and so bring forth the fruits of true Christian living. See Galatians 5:22–26, which speaks of the fruit of the Spirit that we must bring forth.

Arie den Hartog

July 1 — Q&A 70 – Baptism Unto a New, Holy, and Unblameable Life

Read: Romans 6:1–13.

One of the many facets of the meaning of our baptism is that we are by the grace and Spirit of Christ baptized unto a new and holy life. This is the teaching of the passage from God's Word which you were asked to read from Romans 6. Our baptism is a sign of our mystical union with Christ. Christ is our legal and representative head. This in part is the meaning of the truth that he is our Lord. God laid upon Christ the guilt of our sins according to which we stand condemned before the just and holy God of heaven and earth. Jesus satisfied for all of the guilt of our sins through his death on the cross. We are also made spiritually one with Christ. Christ has given to us his Spirit when we are born again. Of this, baptism is the sign. The power of the Spirit of Christ is the power of Christian living.

By the Spirit of Christ, we are made new creatures. Our old man of sin, representing the old sinful nature that we all inherited from our fallen parents, was crucified with Christ. It was put to death at the cross of Christ. We still have the remnants of our old sinful nature. Our old sinful nature is our corrupt nature out of which arises all kinds of sinful, corrupt thoughts, lusts, and evil passions, such as unclean thoughts, thoughts of pride, hatred and envy, covetousness and worldliness. As long as we are still in the body of sin, we still struggle with these evil inclinations. We must resist these sinful inclinations and strive to overcome them and put them entirely away. Christian living involves an ongoing spiritual battle. This battle is not only with the devil and the temptations of the ungodly world we live in, but also with the remnants of our own sinful nature.

However, thanks be to God, we have been delivered from the bondage of sin because our old sinful nature was crucified with Christ! Therefore, sin can no longer have dominion over us. We have been freed from the slavery of sin. We could never have conquered sin in our own strength. Christ has given to us the victory over sin. Our baptism is also a sign that we have the new life of Christ in us. The new life of Christ is the principle in us of love for God and desire after holiness. Because of the new man in Christ, we delight in the law of God in our inner man, desiring to do that which is pleasing to God in obedience and service to God. Christ himself gives us this new life. He works that new life in us more and more. For this, we are continually thankful to God. The Christian life is one of complete reliance on Christ, trusting in him and seeking daily his grace and Spirit, and glorying in him as our Lord.

That Christ gives us the new life does not exclude our own will and efforts. The Reformed believer confesses that his or her life is in Christ Jesus. This does not mean that we are passive in the new life. The new life of Christ makes us ready and willing to serve Christ and live unto him. Read again Lord's Day 1 of the Catechism, where we are told that the comfort of belonging to Christ is also that he makes us ready and willing to live unto him.

In every area of our lives, our personal lives, our lives in society, and our lives in the church of Christ, which is his body, we are called to serve and glorify him.

Arie den Hartog

Lord's Day 27

Q. 72. Is then the external baptism with water the washing away of sin itself?
A. Not at all; for the blood of Jesus Christ only, and the Holy Ghost, cleanse us from all sin.

Q. 73. Why then doth the Holy Ghost call baptism "the washing of regeneration," and "the washing away of sins"?
A. God speaks thus not without great cause, to wit, not only thereby to teach us that, as the filth of the body is purged away by water, so our sins are removed by the blood and Spirit of Jesus Christ; but especially that by this divine pledge and sign he may assure us that we are spiritually cleansed from our sins as really as we are externally washed with water.

Q. 74. Are infants also to be baptized?
A. Yes; for since they, as well as the adult, are included in the covenant and church of God; and since redemption from sin by the blood of Christ, and the Holy Ghost, the author of faith, is promised to them no less than to the adult; they must therefore by baptism, as a sign of the covenant, be also admitted into the Christian church, and be distinguished from the children of unbelievers as was done in the old covenant or testament by circumcision, instead of which baptism is instituted in the new covenant.

July 2 — **Q&A 72 – The Sign and Reality of Baptism**

Read: Romans 4:1–12.

The sacraments are visible signs and seals of the invisible grace of God to us in Christ Jesus. The sign does not by some mysterious change become the reality. It always remains only a sign. However, those who receive this God-ordained sign by faith are also blessed by the reality to which it points. The sign of baptism, which is the water of baptism, does not at any stage become the reality of the blood of Christ.

During the time of Jesus, some of the false teachers of the Jews committed the error of boasting in the mere sign of circumcision. The scribes and the Pharisees, as they were called, boasted in the Old Testament covenant sign of circumcision. Because they were circumcised, they imagined themselves to have a special standing with God. They boasted among themselves: "We be the circumcised." They imagined that those who were not circumcised could not be in the same spiritual class as they were. In fact, many of them thought that without circumcision no one could be saved.

Against this error, the word of God teaches that circumcision is nothing, neither is uncircumcision, but a new heart is everything: "For he is not a Jew, which is one outwardly; neither is that circumcision, which is outward in the flesh: but he is a Jew, which is one inwardly; and circumcision is that of the heart, in the spirit, and not in the letter; whose praise is not of men, but of God" (Rom. 2:28–29). In the next chapter of Romans, the same apostle speaks these words: "It is one God, which shall justify the circumcision by faith, and the uncircumcision through faith" (3:30).

The Bible does indeed sometimes speak of the reality of baptism using the wording of the sign. So people in the New Testament time, when they came to repentance and faith in Jesus Christ, were exhorted to be baptized and washed of their sins (Acts 22:16). There is a resemblance between the sign and the thing which it signifies. As water washes away the filth of our bodies, so the blood of Christ washes away our sins. However, this does not mean that the mere rite of baptism itself could wash away sins.

When believers receive baptism by faith, they may be assured of its blessed reality of the washing away of all their sins, of being incorporated into the body of Christ and receiving all the blessings of salvation in him. There have also been those who wrongly place their confidence in their outward baptism and afterwards are careless about Christian living. Some even go so far as to falsely imagine that because they were baptized, they will be saved even though they live lives of impenitent ungodliness. Somehow, they imagine that they have standing with God just because they were baptized at some point in their lives. There will indeed be those who received the sign of baptism but nevertheless go eternally lost. Our concern must be that we have the spiritual reality that baptism signifies, namely the forgiveness of sins through the cross of Jesus Christ, and the new heart that the Spirit of Jesus Christ alone can and does give us.

When we know that we have these spiritual realities through lively faith in our hearts, we have continual comfort and assurance in our baptism. Furthermore, the spiritual reality of our baptism will be both the power and the incentive for serious Christian living. The spiritual reality of baptism requires daily repentance. Then, our boasting will not be in ourselves but in God only.

Arie den Hartog

July 3 — Q&A 73 – The Blood of Jesus Christ Alone Cleanses Us from All Sin

Read: 1 John 1.

The opening question and answer of Lord's Day 27 addresses the main error of the church of Rome with regard to its teaching about baptism. It also teaches us how serious this error really is. And finally, it teaches us the blessed positive truth that the blood of Christ alone cleanses us from all sin.* When one believes that the external water of baptism itself cleanses us from sin, this means that there is another power besides the blood of Christ that cleanses us from sin. This is a denial of the perfection of the wonderful sacrifice of Christ on the cross.

We are all subject to falling into this kind of error. How easy it is for us to imagine that the mere going through a religious ritual and ceremony has some kind of spiritual value. We can also be superstitious about the external power of the sacraments. There are those who believe that somehow they have been saved simply because they were baptized. The purpose of the sacrament of baptism is to teach us that nothing else but the blood of Jesus alone can wash away our sins. The term "blood of Jesus Christ" is used often in Scripture. For example, 1 Peter 1:19 speaks of our being redeemed by "the precious blood of Christ, as of a lamb without blemish and without spot."

We must remember that the Scriptures are using figurative language. The blood of Jesus Christ refers to the sacrifice of obedience and suffering which Jesus endured in order to atone for all of our sins and to merit for us perfect righteousness before God. This sacrifice was the demonstration of the amazing greatness of God's love for us. The reason why this blood is by Peter called precious is because it was the blood of the Son of God in our flesh, who is in himself infinitely precious, not only to us; even more significantly, he is infinitely precious before God, his Father. The preciousness of the blood of Christ indicates further that his sacrifice on the cross involved the deepest misery, agony, shame, and humiliation on the part of our Savior. The preciousness of the blood of Christ is also in that he offered himself for us to God in perfect obedience and love. The sacrifice of Christ on the cross is therefore of infinite worth in the sight of God, abundantly sufficient to cover the guilt of the sins of all the people for whom he died. Because of the infinite worth of the sacrifice of Christ, he was able to merit perfect and everlasting righteousness and life for his people.

Our baptism must lead us to trust and glory in none other than the precious blood of Jesus Christ. Receiving baptism with proper understanding involves a great exercise of our faith. Whenever we remember our own baptism, we must do so by meditating on the cross of Jesus Christ and all that it means for our salvation. All our sins were atoned for at the cross because of the infinite worth of the once and for all sacrifice of Christ. We therefore must not add any work of our own, nor trust in and glory in any mere ritual or ceremony, not even in the power of the sacraments themselves. The whole meaning of our baptism is Christ alone, all sufficient and all glorious, the only hope of our righteousness before God, and all our hope for favor and blessing and life eternal in the presence of God.

Arie den Hartog

---

* Heidelberg Catechism Q&A 72, in *Confessions and Church Order*, 110.

July 4 — **Q&A 74 — Infant Baptism**

Read: Acts 2:39–47.

The Reformed church practices infant baptism. Since the time of the Reformation, there has been considerable dispute concerning this practice. At the time of the Reformation, a group arose called the Anabaptists who denied baptism for all infants. They insisted that baptism should only be administered to confessing adult believers. They argued that it is impossible for infants to confess faith. Some even argued that God could not be said to work in the hearts of infants at all. All children were to be considered ungodly until they could show evidence of faith and repentance.

Some Protestants who do not go so far maintain that even if God does work in the hearts of little infants, they should not be baptized until they are old enough to show evidence of repentance and faith in their lives. These insist that there are no examples of the baptism of infants in the New Testament. They maintain that this practice is based on nothing more than human sentiment, perhaps the sentimental affection of parents for their own children.

Indeed, most of the examples of baptism given in Scripture are those of adults. The Scripture records for the most part only the history of the preaching of the gospel to first generation Christians, and these must indeed first confess their faith in the Lord Jesus and repent of their sins before they are baptized. It is true that in Scripture, there is no specific example of the baptism of infants. The question is a bit more involved than this, however.

The Catechism sets forth what the Reformed churches believe about infant baptism. Infants, "as well as adults, are included in the covenant and church of God…Redemption from sin through the blood of Christ, and the Holy Ghost, the author of faith, is promised to them as well as to adults."*

The basis for the baptism of infants is the truth of God's covenant. According to the truth of the covenant, God gathers his church in the line of continued generations with believers and their children. According to the promise of God's covenant, the blessings of salvation belong to covenant children (Gen. 17:7). While we cannot determine this for certain from Scripture, we believe that covenant infants are usually regenerated in infancy. There is mention of covenant infants being known of God from birth in Jeremiah 1:5, Psalm 71:6, Luke 1:15, and Galatians 1:15. Significantly, the Catechism says that the gift of faith is given by the Holy Spirit, who is the author of this gift also to covenant infants.

In the Old Testament, children were circumcised eight days after they were born. Circumcision, according to Romans 4:11 was "a seal of the righteousness of the faith.'" It was not merely an outward sign of belonging to the nation of Israel. If infants were included in the covenant in the Old Testament, they surely were not excluded when the promises of the covenant were all fulfilled in the coming of Jesus Christ. In the New Testament the truth of the covenant was revealed in richer and broader realization. It would hardly follow then that children would be excluded after they had been included in God's covenant before. The day of Pentecost marks the opening of the New Testament age. Peter, preaching the gospel on the day of Pentecost, proclaimed: "For the promise is unto you, and to your children, and to all that are afar off, even as many as the Lord our God shall call" (Acts 2:39).

Arie den Hartog

---

* Heidelberg Catechism A 74, in *Confessions and Church Order*, 111.

July 5 — **Q&A 74 — The Baptism of Covenant Infants**

Read: Acts 10:34–48

Our Lord Jesus considered covenant children to be the children of God. Therefore, he took them into his arms and blessed them. He even made them examples of the childlike faith that is necessary for entrance into the kingdom (Matt. 18:2–3). He warned everyone of the severe judgment of God should they hurt one of these little ones (v. 6). He said concerning these little ones: "Of such is the kingdom of heaven" (19:14). The truth of God's covenant way of saving his people in families, including believers and their children, is the reason why after Pentecost, whole families were at once brought to faith in Jesus Christ and saved. Properly, whole families were then baptized. Whether or not the family baptisms mentioned in the Scripture included infant children cannot be proven either way. We would expect that, of the several examples of family baptisms mentioned in Scripture, at least some of them included infants.

Infant baptism does not mean that the grace of salvation is somehow inherited by the children through the genes of their parents, somewhat like physical characteristics. The truth of the covenant means that God, by his sovereign grace, according to the promise he makes throughout Scripture in both the Old and New Testament, is pleased to bestow his grace upon the children of believers (Acts 2:39). Church history abundantly proves that God continues his church with believers and their children. This is simply the wonderful way of the working of God's grace. No Christian ought to ignore or refuse to acknowledge this wonder of God in his church.

Covenant children are to be brought for baptism by their parents. At the time of the baptism of these children in the Reformed church, parents are required to solemnly vow to raise their children in the knowledge and fear of the Lord. They are made to promise that they will do this to their utmost power. There are many admonitions in the letters of the apostles instructing parents to bring up their children in the fear and nurture of the Lord. When covenant children come to mature adulthood, they are admonished to make public confession of their faith in the Lord before his church. Covenant children are all the days of their lives exhorted to faith and repentance in Jesus Christ, without which there is no salvation.

In the Old Testament, not all those who were circumcised in infancy later showed themselves to be children of God. Scripture has the example of the twin sons of Isaac and Rebecca. Both Jacob and Esau were circumcised, as God commanded for all children of believers, but God said: "Jacob have I loved, but Esau have I hated" (Rom. 9:13).

In the New Testament times, all children of believing parents are to be brought to church for baptism. Parents must believe the promise of God's covenant concerning these children. It is in the hope of the promise of the covenant that godly parents are to raise their covenant children in the fear and admonition of the Lord, always depending completely on the grace and Spirit of the Lord to make the instruction of their children effective unto their salvation. In fact, if God does not work in the hearts of children, they cannot receive and benefit from the godly instruction of their parents.

Arie den Hartog

July 6 — **Q&A 74 — Understanding the Unity of the Covenant**

Read: Ephesians 2:11–22.

Some reject the practice of infant baptism. They say that Scripture speaks of two covenants, one in the days of the Old Testament with the Jews, and another in the New Testament age with the Gentiles. So they would maintain that even though children in the Old Testament were circumcised, it does not follow that children of covenant parents in the New Testament should be baptized. The Reformed church maintains that the covenant in the Old and New Testament is one. God has one covenant people. There is only one way of salvation, and that is through faith in Jesus Christ. God established an everlasting covenant with Abraham, who is the father of all the faithful from both the Jews and the Gentiles. Ephesians 2, as well as other passages of Scripture, speaks of Jews and Gentiles being made one in Christ. The middle wall of partition has been broken down. The Gentiles who were once aliens and strangers to the covenant of God are now one with the Jews in the household of faith. The same promises that were made in the Old Testament to the Jews are in the New Testament given to the Gentiles, who are now gathered from all the nations of the world.

Baptism is a sign of God's one everlasting covenant with believers and their children, even as many as the Lord would call. It therefore follows that if children of believers in the Old Testament were distinguished from children of the heathen by the covenant sign of circumcision, this ought also to be done in the New Testament by the covenant sign of baptism. For this reason, when the Spirit of Christ was poured out upon the church on the day of Pentecost the apostle Peter declared to those who repented and believed that they should be baptized because of God's covenant promise to them and, amazingly, to their children (Acts 2:39). Children were not suddenly for some strange reason excluded from the covenant. In the book of Acts, we find a number of examples of the baptism of whole families at once. The important thing about these examples is not whether or not at the time of baptism there were infant children in these families. The important thing is that whole families were baptized at once because of the truth of God's covenant, which is with believers and their children.

The practice of infant baptism does not imply that all the children of believers are God's elect. History has indeed shown that this is not the case. In the Old Testament times, Esau and Jacob had the same covenant parents. Jacob was loved of God. He was a child of the covenant, but Esau was a reprobate. Both of these sons of Isaac and Rebecca were circumcised. So are all children of believers to be baptized. God's election of grace alone determines whether one belongs truly and spiritually to the covenant of God. Exactly because salvation is by grace alone, covenant children can and ought to be baptized on the basis of the covenant promise of God. Even though some of these children might in later life show that they are not truly children of God, it was not wrong to baptize them. All children born of covenant parents must be instructed in the truth of the promises of the covenant and be exhorted and admonished to repent and turn to the Lord who is the only hope of salvation. God will realize his covenant purposes in the lives of children of believers by his Spirit of grace according to his purposes of election.

Arie den Hartog

July 7 — **Q&A 74 — Covenant Children Are Included in the Church**

Read: Ephesians 6:1–9.

The Reformed church believes that children of covenant parents belong to the Christian church. This is one of the reasons for the practice of infant baptism in the Reformed church. The meaning of this is not merely that their names are found on the rolls of the Reformed church but that they are really and spiritually part of the church of Jesus Christ. No one is ever included in the church except by God himself. God includes covenant children in his church. They must be given special instruction by the church, and they must be recognized and treated by the church as true members of God's church. That children are part of the church is evident from the fact that children are at times even directly mentioned. They are pointed to their Christian calling. The passage from Paul's letter to the church of Ephesus that I asked you to read before reading this meditation is an example of this. When the letters of the apostles were read in the apostolic churches, children were there as part of the worship services.

So the Reformed church does not exclude children. She does not treat them as though they are not, and even cannot be, truly children of God, because they are not yet old enough to understand the truth and confess faith in Jesus Christ. In most cases, children of covenant parents are regenerated in their infancy. The psalms speak of God knowing his people from their mothers' wombs (Ps. 71:6; 139:14–16). There are examples of the same teaching in the Old Testament prophets (Isa. 46:3; Jer. 1:5). This same truth was spoken of in connection with the announcement of the birth of John the Baptist (Luke 1:15).

Covenant children is the name which Reformed believers love to call their children. Because these children are covenant children, they are distinguished from the world. They are regarded as being very precious in the church. They are not little devils, as one theologian characterized them, or even unregenerate unbelievers, as others assume.

One of God's purposes for Christian marriage is the purpose of bringing forth covenant children. This is one of the many reasons why marrying in the Lord is so very important. In the Old Testament days, the patriarchs were very concerned that their children married God-fearing partners and fellow members of the covenant nation. They would even go to great lengths to see that this would happen, such as when Abraham went to great lengths to find a God-fearing wife for his son Isaac. The prophet Malachi admonished men in Israel not to deal treacherously with the wives of their youth, whom the Lord had given to them (Mal. 2:15). They must not put away their covenant wives. It is the Lord's purpose in marriage that a godly seed should be brought forth. In 1 Corinthians 7:14 Paul states that a godly woman is not to put away her unbelieving husband, for the unbelieving husband is sanctified by the believing wife, and even if only one of the partners in marriage is a believer, yet the children are holy.

The truth that is the basis for the practice of infant baptism is a very significant one. It impresses on a believing and God-fearing couple the urgency of devoting themselves to the important task of raising their covenant children in the fear of the Lord. An important part of this task is raising our covenant children to know their place in the church and to have proper love for the church. When the word of God is being preached in the church, it is also addressed to them, and they must be taught to listen carefully to it.

Arie den Hartog

July 8 — **Q&A 74 — The Covenant Responsibility of Parents**

Read: Colossians 3:16–21.

No doubt not all who read the meditation today are married and have children. Even the unmarried and those to whom God has not given covenant children by God's grace should still be interested in the subject of this meditation. As members of the church, even if we are single or married without children, we should be concerned about the proper nurture of covenant children. In one of our meditations, we emphasized that these children are members of the church. They must be so regarded by all members of the church. Parents in particular should be given support and encouragement to raise their children in the fear of the Lord. The practice of infant baptism in the sphere of the church does not at all eliminate or minimize the need for the serious instruction of children in the church. It does not mean that repentance and faith are not necessary for these children. In the case of adult baptism, none ought to be baptized by the church except those who demonstrate repentance in their lives and who confess faith in Jesus Christ. In the case of covenant infants, this repentance and faith will not evidence itself until later in their lives. God uses covenant parents and the church to work and develop this faith in the hearts of children.

The Reformed church teaches that we conceive and bring forth our children in sin. These children are born in spiritual depravity. This depravity is passed down from parents to their children. Grace is not inherited by covenant children through the genes of their parents. The grace of God alone can and will deliver these children from this depravity. When covenant parents bring their children to be baptized in the Reformed church, they are admonished and exhorted to do their utmost in raising their children in the fear of the Lord. Parents of covenant children must teach them the knowledge of the true God and the reality that there is no hope of salvation except through faith in Jesus Christ and his death on the cross. Parents are bound by their covenantal responsibility to admonish their children, to call them to repentance and faith, even daily.

This is a mighty responsibility for those to whom the Lord gives children. The true church of God takes a great interest in this as well. The children of the covenant are the hope of the church of the future. The task of raising children is a very difficult one and takes a lot of sacrifice, diligence, and steadfastness on the part of parents. No amount of labor on the part of parents, however, can make any of their children God-fearing. God himself must do this. He must give his Holy Spirit to the hearts of these children to work faith and repentance in their hearts. Covenant parents are wholly dependent on the Lord. In all their labors, they must pray for grace to be able to properly train their children. They must pray most earnestly, clinging to the promises of God's covenant.

Those who oppose the practice of infant baptism in the Reformed churches, falsely imagining that it implies that covenant children do not need to repent and believe in the Lord Jesus, simply have a wrong understanding of the practice of infant baptism. In fact, the practice of infant baptism and its covenantal basis should be the strongest imaginable motive for parents to labor earnestly and prayerfully in the raising of their children.

Arie den Hartog

Lord's Day 28

Q. 75. How are thou admonished and assured in the Lord's Supper that thou art a partaker of that one sacrifice of Christ, accomplished on the cross, and of all his benefits?

A. Thus: That Christ has commanded me and all believers to eat of this broken bread and to drink of this cup in remembrance of him, adding these promises: first, that his body was offered and broken on the cross for me, and his blood shed for me, as certainly as I see with my eyes the bread of the Lord broken for me and the cup communicated to me; and further, that he feeds and nourishes my soul to everlasting life, with his crucified body and shed blood, as assuredly as I receive from the hands of the minister, and taste with my mouth the bread and cup of the Lord, as certain signs of the body and blood of Christ.

Q. 76. What is it then to eat the crucified body and drink the shed blood of Christ?

A. It is only to embrace with a believing heart all the sufferings and death of Christ, and thereby to obtain the pardon of sin and life eternal; but also, besides that, to become more and more united to his sacred body by the Holy Ghost, who dwells both in Christ and in us; so that we, though Christ is in heaven and we on earth, are notwithstanding *flesh of his flesh, and bone of his bone*; and that we live and are governed forever by one Spirit, as members of the same body are by one soul.

Q. 77. Where has Christ promised that he will as certainly feed and nourish believers with his body and blood, as they eat of this broken bread and drink of this cup?

A. In the institution of the supper, which is thus expressed: *The Lord Jesus, the same night in which he was betrayed, took bread, and when he had given thanks, he brake it, and said: Take, eat, this is my body, which is broken for you; this do in remembrance of me. After the same manner also he took the cup, when he had supped, saying: this cup is the new testament in my blood; this do ye, as often as ye drink it, in remembrance of me. For, as often as ye eat this bread, and drink this cup, ye do show the Lord's death till he come.*

This promise is repeated by the holy apostle Paul, where he says: *The cup of blessing which we bless, is it not the communion of the blood of Christ? The bread which we break, is it not the communion of the body of Christ? For we, being many, are one bread and one body; for we are all partakers of that one bread.*

July 9 — Q&A 75, 77 — The Institution of the Lord's Supper by the Lord Himself

Read: 1 Corinthians 11:18–34.

Lord's Day 28 of the Catechism begins a very extensive discussion of the Lord's supper. The Lord's supper is the second sacrament which the Lord gave to his church for her comfort and the strengthening of her faith. In our first meditation on this Lord's Day, let us think about the truth that this sacrament was given to us by the Lord Jesus Christ himself. The Lord's supper is not a mere invention of man. It is not even a mere tradition begun by the church many years ago. This is the Lord's own sacrament. It was given to us in the greatness of his love to help us to remember his greatest work accomplished for our salvation, namely, his sacrifice on the cross.

We should be deeply impressed by the fact that our Lord instituted this sacrament on the very night in which he would be betrayed into the hands of his enemies. The next day he would be condemned to be crucified. This would be the most wicked deed that man has ever committed. But all this would happen according to God's sovereign plan for our salvation. By means of his suffering and death on the cross, amazing as this truth is, Christ redeemed his people and fully accomplished their salvation. Through the death of the cross, our Lord would show us his own great love for us.

Christ Jesus himself was gathered with his disciples in the upper room in intimate fellowship with them to celebrate the last Passover with them. Concerning this fact, Jesus was deeply conscious. So Jesus said to his disciples in words recorded in Luke 22: "With desire I have desired to eat this Passover with you before I suffer" (v. 15). The reason why this Passover would be the last is because Jesus on this night would fulfill the Passover. Jesus would be the Passover lamb. Jesus would not only be the high priest who would offer this sacrifice, but he would also offer himself as the sacrifice. At the time of this intimate profound meeting with his beloved disciples, he gave the sacrament of the Lord's supper. Our Lord desired that his suffering and death on the cross would be constantly remembered by them and meditated on again and again. This remembrance must be the source of comfort, hope, and joy for all those who believe in Jesus. Jesus intended that the holy ordinance of the Lord's supper be continually observed in the church. For that reason, at the time of his institution of the supper, Jesus said: "This do in remembrance of me" (v. 19).

That the Lord Jesus intended this ceremony to be continually observed by the church is clear also from the words of the inspired apostle Paul in 1 Corinthians 11. There, Paul speaks of having received special instruction regarding the Lord's supper directly from the Lord himself: "For I have received of the Lord that which also I delivered unto you" (v. 23). We believe that Paul received this special instruction while in Arabia being prepared by the Lord for the work that the Lord had called Paul to do as an apostle.

Paul states in 1 Corinthians 11 that by celebrating the Lord's supper, the church of Jesus Christ proclaims the Lord's death until the final and blessed return of the Lord (v. 26). So, the celebration of the Lord's supper must cause us to look more and more earnestly for the return of the Lord who so loved us that he gave himself for us. Whenever you celebrate the Lord's supper, think of the fact that this sacrament was given to his church by the Lord, and think also of the circumstance in which it was given.

Arie den Hartog

July 10 — **Q&A 75 — The Lord's Supper and the Passover**

Read: Luke 22:7–20.

Jesus purposely instituted the Lord's supper at the time when he was celebrating the last Passover with his disciples. Jesus knew that he would fulfill the Passover. He would sacrifice himself as the great Passover lamb. It is significant that the Passover was a meal. It was a covenantal meal in which God was spiritually present with his people. There were other ceremonies like that in the Old Testament, combining a sacrifice and a meal. The main part of the Passover was the eating of the Passover lamb, which in the days of Jesus had first been slain and offered in the temple. It then was brought to the upper room where Jesus and his disciples were gathered. The sacrificed lamb was a type of the sacrifice of the Lord Jesus Christ. Without the sacrifice of the lamb, which testified of the necessity of atonement for sin, God's people could not have fellowship with God. God is holy, and his people are sinners. In order for the people of God to have fellowship with God, first of all their sins must be removed by the death of the lamb. God is the absolutely holy one. No sinner can have fellowship with this God without being consumed because of his sins.

After the lamb had been sacrificed, it was eaten by a family or a group of God's people together. That this ceremony was a meal was a sign of the blessed reality of God's covenant fellowship with his people. The lamb of the Passover was not merely to be looked at but also to be eaten by those who were celebrating together. In this celebration, there was also bread and wine. This whole ceremony depicted the beautiful truth that we have covenant fellowship with God through the sacrifice of the lamb. This covenant fellowship involved partaking of the spiritual blessings of the covenant, symbolized by eating the lamb, eating the bread, and drinking the wine.

At the time of Jesus, the Passover was an elaborate and solemn ceremony. Every part of this ceremony also had great spiritual meaning. There was expressing of thanksgiving to God. It included the singing of a hymn or a psalm. This hymn was one of the Old Testament psalms which ends with the words: "Hallelujah, praise ye Jehovah." Psalms 113 or 118 may have been sung during the ceremony.

At the end of the last Passover meal, Jesus took the bread that was commonly part of this meal, broke some of it, passed it to his disciples, and commanded them to eat of it. He also took the cup of wine, which was passed around several times during this celebration, blessed it, passed it to his disciples, and commanded them to drink of it. Jesus commanded that this simple ceremony be repeated over and over again in the church until the day when he would come again at the end of the world. The broken bread of this ceremony was a simple sign of the body of Christ, which would be broken on the cross. Even though Scripture prophesied that not a bone of Jesus would be broken in sacrificing himself on the cross, Jesus suffered the agony of the piercing of his hands and feet. Later, after his death, one of the soldiers attending the crucifixion pierced his side with a sword. The wine symbolized the precious blood of Jesus' great and precious sacrifice, and all the agony and suffering this involved for Jesus. In the Lord's supper, we are to remember by the broken body and shed blood of Christ all of this suffering and agony of Christ and the great salvation which it accomplished for us. By the suffering of Jesus Christ, all the benefits of salvation become ours through our faith in him.

Arie den Hartog

July 11

Q&A 75 — Remembering the Suffering and Death of Our Savior

Read: Isaiah 53.

The chief purpose of the celebration of the Lord's supper is in order that the church might remember the suffering and death of our beloved Savior. This should be the most prominent of all the aspects of our celebration of the Lord's supper. There are so many dimensions to this remembrance. So much of Scripture speaks of it.

The suffering and death of our Savior on the cross was absolutely necessary. The justice of God required it. Our sins were so dreadful in the sight of God that they could not be atoned for in any other way than by the death of the Son of God on the cross. Rather than allowing our sin to go unpunished, God punished our sins by offering up his own dear Son to the death of the cross. The cross speaks of the awful reality of our sin and the justice of God in punishing that sin. Jesus bore the punishment that our sins deserved on the cross. He died in our place and for us.

Jesus gave himself as an offering and perfect sacrifice to make atonement for our sins: "Surely he hath borne our griefs, and carried our sorrows: yet we did esteem him stricken, smitten of God, and afflicted. But he was wounded for our transgressions, he was bruised for our iniquities: the chastisement of our peace was upon him; and with his stripes we are healed" (Isa. 53:4–5). The death of Jesus on the cross involved suffering far greater than we can ever understand. It caused Jesus, in the darkness of that suffering, to cry out in bitter anguish: "My God, my God, why hast thou forsaken me?" (Matt. 27:46). By his death on the cross our Lord Jesus fulfilled all obedience to the law of God for us when we were wholly incapable of doing this ourselves. By his active obedience and willing sacrifice on the cross Jesus fulfilled all righteousness for us. This righteousness is not imputed to us freely by the grace of God. It becomes ours through faith in Jesus Christ and his sacrifice. The celebration of the Lord's supper must be an act of faith.

The death of Jesus Christ on the cross was the most amazing demonstration of the love of God. For when Christ died, we were yet the enemies of God. We are hopelessly guilty and depraved sinners. We all deserve the judgment of hell. We can do nothing of ourselves to make atonement for sin. We have no strength in ourselves to deliver ourselves from the power and destruction of sin. "Herein is love, not that we loved God, but that he loved us, and sent his Son to be the propitiation for our sins" (1 John 4:10); no one can ever measure the breadth, length, depth, and height of the love of Christ who gave himself for us to the suffering and death of the cross. Every time we stand before the cross of the Son of God we are filled with awe and amazement.

The Lord's supper was given to us in order that we might remember the suffering and death of our Savior. There is no greater power to sanctify us and inspire in our Christian life to love God and give him humble thanksgiving, than the remembrance of his love in Jesus Christ. The celebration of the Lord's supper must again and again engage us to meditate on the wonder of the sacrifice of Christ. Never should we forget it!

Arie den Hartog

July 12 — Q&A 76 — Eating the Flesh and Drinking the Blood of Jesus

Read: John 6:51–59.

Jesus does not in John 6 speak directly about the Lord's supper. He does, however, definitely speak about the meaning of the Lord's supper. In partaking of the Lord's supper, we eat the flesh and drink the blood of Jesus (John 6:54)—a very striking expression. However, this is not to be understood literally. Jesus himself makes this plain when the multitudes that were listening to him were offended by his words. He says in verses 61–63: "Doth this offend you? What and if ye shall see the Son of man ascend up where he was before? It is the spirit that quickeneth; the flesh profiteth nothing: the words that I speak unto you, they are spirit, and they are life." This explanation of Jesus very definitely excludes the false idea that in the Lord's supper, when we eat the bread and drink the wine, we are literally eating the body of Christ and drinking the blood of Christ. The very thought of this is a gross abomination. This would not profit at all. We say this reverently, and because Jesus himself said it.

There are several aspects of the meaning of the discourse of Jesus in John 6. First of all, Jesus emphasizes the necessity of his incarnation. It was necessary for Jesus to take on himself our flesh and blood, that which composes our human nature. Jesus had to take on our flesh and blood in order that he could sacrifice himself on our behalf on the cross.

It is not wrong to say that the Son of God died on the cross. But it would be wrong to say that Jesus suffered and died in his divine nature. The divine nature of God cannot suffer and die. Jesus suffered and died very really in his human nature. But at the same time, because of the amazing greatness of this suffering, Jesus was sustained by his divine nature. Only the Son of God could bear the wrath of God that our sins deserved.

Jesus had to give his flesh and blood, his own life for us, by sacrificing himself on the cross. Many are offended at the cross. They cannot imagine that the suffering and death of Christ on behalf of his people are necessary. They consider the cross to be foolishness. They also cannot imagine that our sins are so serious in the sight of God that they could only be atoned for by the suffering and death of the Son of God.

Eating and drinking Christ means that we must by faith appropriate the suffering and death of Christ. This begins with the humble realization and confession that the suffering and death of Christ on the cross was made necessary by the awful reality of our sins. In the Lord's supper, Jesus commanded his disciples and us to eat his flesh and drink his blood. As I said in an earlier meditation, the sacrament of the Lord's supper is in the form of a meal. At this meal, Jesus provides for us all the blessings of salvation, which he has merited for us and for our salvation. We appropriate these blessings through faith in him. We do not merely look at the bread and wine in the Lord's supper; we eat the bread and drink the wine.

When we eat the bread and drink the wine, Jesus feeds and nourishes our souls unto life eternal. Jesus is the living bread that is from heaven. In the Lord's supper, we acknowledge that Jesus is the bread of life. By receiving through faith the benefits of Christ's cross, we have the blessings of life eternal already now. We have the hope that he will raise us up also in the last day and give us eternal life in heavenly glory.

Arie den Hartog

July 13 — **Q&A 76 — Communion with Christ**

Read: John 6:47–56.

The Lord's supper is indeed rich in its meaning. One of the names given by Scripture to this sacrament, and commonly used in the Reformed church, is the name *communion*. In the Lord's supper, we have communion with Christ and are made partakers of all of his benefits. It is exactly because of this truth that the Lord made this sacrament in the form of a meal around a table. This truth of the Lord's supper should be preserved when the church celebrates this sacrament. In the Lord's supper, Christ is present with his church. He is the host at the table, and we who join the Lord's table receive by faith the spiritual food which he provides.

The Reformed church believes that Christ is truly present in the Lord's supper. He is not bodily present. After his ascension, Christ is now bodily present in heaven, sitting at the right hand of the majesty of his heavenly Father. The human nature of Christ, like our human nature, can only be present in one place at one time. Until the Lord returns bodily at the end of the ages, he remains bodily present in heaven and not on earth. However, following the teaching of God's word, the great reformers, especially John Calvin, and the Reformed church, restored through this great reformer, believe that Christ is really spiritually present in the church. The Lord himself promised that where two or three are gathered together in his name, there he is in the midst of them. He also promised that he would be with his church to the end of the world.

Jesus is not only spiritually present with his church when she celebrates the Lord's supper. He is at all times present with his beloved church through his word and Spirit. The Lord's supper is a sign and seal of the presence of Christ with his church. In the Lord's supper, Jesus reminds us of all the blessings of salvation, which he merited for us through his suffering and death on the cross. That we have communion with Christ means that he is invisibly, though really and spiritually, present with us. God's people through faith in Christ have living fellowship with Christ. Christ is truly with us, and we know that by faith. He is with us to bless us with all spiritual blessings of salvation. In this sense, Christ feeds and nourishes our souls with his body and blood. He is to our souls the bread of life. Those who eat only earthly bread shall finally die. Jesus is the bread of life. Whosoever eats of this spiritual bread by faith will live forever. Read John 6:47–56 again.

If we have a right understanding of the Lord's supper, we realize that our fellowship with Christ is not limited to the few times in which the Lord's supper is celebrated in the church. Rather, by the Lord's supper, we are assured of the blessed reality of our communion with Christ, and this communion is more and more strengthened. It is enjoyed throughout our Christian life. It can be rightly said that the heart of true Christian living is fellowship with Christ. In this fellowship, we have a living, personal, experiential knowledge of Christ with us, and we with him. In this communion with Christ, we have the hope and joy of everlasting and perfect salvation which is yet to come. In heaven, there will be an everlasting and blessed feast of communion with God and with his Son Jesus Christ.

Arie den Hartog

July 14 — Q&A 76 — United to the Sacred Body of Christ

Read: Acts 2:41–47.

The church is the living spiritual body of Christ. The members of the church are the members of his body. The true church of Jesus Christ is united together by the Spirit of Christ through faith as one body, having one Lord and Savior, one God and Father (Eph. 4:1–3). This is also celebrated in the Lord's supper. The Catechism speaks of this in Lord's Day 28 when discussing the meaning of the Lord's supper. Our spiritual union with Christ's body is often called a mystical union. It is called by this name because the reality of this is a great mystery. It cannot be understood by those who have no faith and are not partakers of the body of Christ. The reality of this truth is known only by the child of God through the work of the Spirit of Christ in his heart and by his indwelling Spirit in his church, uniting the members of the body to one another. The apostle John speaks of this spiritual mystery in 1 John 3:24, "And he that keepeth his commandments dwelleth in him, and he in him."

The blessed spiritual reality of this is strengthened through the proper understanding of and observance of the Lord's supper in the church. The Lord's supper is a supper of fellowship with Christ and with one another. In New Testament times, a love feast was often celebrated in connection with the Lord's supper. At this feast, the members of the church expressed their love for one another when those who had an abundance of earthly things brought food for the poor and hungry, especially during times of famine. Widows were also taken care of through this practice. Out of this practice arose the office of deacons in the church.

So close is our spiritual union with Christ that in Ephesians 5 it is said that we are "members of his body, of his flesh, and of his bones" (v. 30). Christian marriage is a picture of this blessed mystical union. The love of Christ for his church is the bond of this fellowship. This love was demonstrated in the highest imaginable way in the cross of Jesus Christ. There, Christ gave himself for the church, that he might sanctify and cleanse her by his word and Spirit. This reality is signified and sealed in the Lord's supper. Christ is spiritually present in the church when his Spirit dwells among her members. They are built up into Christ through the hearing of the preaching of the word and through the celebration of the sacraments.

We have a beautiful picture of the church as the body of Christ, living in communion with Christ, and the members with each other, in the description of the church in Acts 2:42, "And they continued steadfastly in the apostles' doctrine and fellowship, and in breaking of bread, and in prayers." The "breaking of bread together" spoken of in this passage was most likely the celebration of the Lord's supper. This description is continued in verse 46 of Acts 2: "And they, continuing daily with one accord in the temple, and breaking bread from house to house, did eat their meat with gladness and singleness of heart." These blessed spiritual realities are seen in the true church of Jesus Christ even today, when, with proper understanding and unity of faith, she celebrates the Lord's supper together.

Arie den Hartog

July 15   Q&A 76 — Governed by One Mind and One Spirit

Read: Ephesians 4:11–16.

For our last meditation on Lord's Day 28, we consider one more phrase in its beautiful discussion of the meaning of the Lord's supper: "We live and are governed forever by one Spirit, as members of the same body are by one soul."* The whole of the first part of Ephesians 4 speaks of this truth. No doubt, Paul is not speaking in this passage about the Lord's supper directly. Yet the Catechism is correct when it makes reference to what Paul says in this passage, in explaining the rich and blessed meaning of the Lord's supper. The church as the body of Christ is united by the Spirit of Christ "in the bond of peace" and unity. In that bond, she confesses together "one Lord, one faith, one baptism, one God and Father of all, who is above all, and through all, and in" all the saints who are members of the church (vv. 3–6). The reality of this is celebrated in the Lord's supper.

The church is and must be united together in the truth. She may not tolerate heresies and divisions among her members. Paul admonished the church of Corinth concerning this in 1 Corinthians 11:18–19, "For first of all, when ye come together in the church, I hear that there be divisions among you; and I partly believe it. For there must be also heresies among you, that they which are approved may be made manifest among you." Paul admonished the church of Corinth because of this situation. The sacrament of the Lord's supper is a celebration of the unity of the members of the church. In 1 Corinthians 10, Paul speaks of the unity that must characterize the church, with explicit reference to the celebration of the sacrament of communion: "The cup of blessing which we bless, is it not the communion of the blood of Christ? The bread which we break, is it not the communion of the body of Christ? For we being many are one bread, and one body: for we are all partakers of that one bread" (vv. 16–17).

The church grows up into this unity through the preaching of the word in her midst, and this unity is also strengthened by the proper celebration of the supper. In Ephesians 4, Paul speaks further about this: "But speaking the truth in love, may grow up into him in all things, which is the head, even Christ: from whom the whole body fitly joined together and compacted by that which every joint supplieth, according to the effectual working of the measure of every part, maketh increase of the body unto the edifying of itself in love" (vv. 15–16).

The application of the truth of the Lord's supper in the lives of the members of the church is that they must live together in the unity of faith and love in Jesus Christ. When this is not the case because of sin and division among the members of the church, the Lord's supper is desecrated, and the name of the Lord is greatly dishonored.

In the church and in connection with the celebration of the Lord's supper, the members of the church must endeavor to keep the unity of the Spirit in the bond of peace. The members of the church must live together in humility with one another and in unity in the love of Christ for one another.

Arie den Hartog

---

*   Heidelberg Catechism A 76, in *Confessions and Church Order*, 113.

Lord's Day 29

Q. 78. Do then the bread and wine become the very body and blood of Christ?

A. Not at all; but as the water in baptism is not changed into the blood of Christ, neither is the washing away of sin itself, being only the sign and confirmation thereof appointed of God; so the bread in the Lord's Supper is not changed into the very body of Christ; though agreeably to the nature and properties of sacraments, it is called the body of Christ Jesus.

Q. 79. Why then doth Christ call the bread his body, and the cup his blood, or the new covenant in his blood; and Paul, the communion of the body and blood of Christ?

A. Christ speaks thus, not without great reason, namely, not only thereby to teach us that as bread and wine support this temporal life, so his crucified body and shed blood are the true meat and drink whereby our souls are fed to eternal life; but more especially by these visible signs and pledges to assure us that we are as really partakers of his true body and blood (by the operation of the Holy Ghost) as we receive by the mouths of our bodies these holy signs in remembrance of him; and that all his sufferings and obedience are as certainly ours as if we had in our own persons suffered and made satisfaction for our sins to God.

Lord's Day 30

Q&A 80

Q. 80. What difference is there between the Lord's Supper and the popish mass?

A. The Lord's Supper testifies to us that we have a full pardon of all sin by the only sacrifice of Jesus Christ, which he himself has once accomplished on the cross; and that we by the Holy Ghost are ingrafted into Christ, who according to his human nature is now not on earth, but in heaven at the right hand of God his Father, and will there be worshipped by us—but the mass teaches that the living and dead have not the pardon of sins though the sufferings of Christ, unless Christ is also daily offered for them by the priests; and further, that Christ is bodily under the form of bread and wine, and therefore is to be worshipped in them; so that the mass, at bottom, is nothing else than a denial of the one sacrifice and sufferings of Jesus Christ, and an accursed idolatry.

July 16 — **LD 29 – Truth Versus Error in Understanding the Lord's Supper**

Read: Galatians 1.

It is tragic that false teaching soon appeared in the church regarding the meaning of the Lord's supper. This false teaching soon corrupted the observance of the Lord's supper. One of the reasons why the church had to be reformed (formed anew or formed again) was because the Roman Catholic Church had corrupted the Lord's supper. This corruption was so serious because it led to all sorts of superstition and even idolatrous ideas of the sacred ordinance of the Lord's supper.

It is never a pleasant thing in itself to have to condemn error. However, when the great truths of God are involved and the glory of the name of Jesus Christ is involved, the church must be faithful to condemn errors, and, if necessary, even separate herself from them. The prophets of the Old Testament had to condemn error, and they did this courageously. Our Lord Jesus condemned the false teachings of the scribes and Pharisees of his time. He even pronounced woes on these false teachers for their hypocrisies and their self-righteous attitude. Paul, the apostle of our Lord Jesus Christ, felt compelled to condemn errors. In the book of Galatians, for example, he condemned the teachers of salvation through the works of the law who insisted on the necessity of circumcision for salvation. So serious did the inspired apostle consider the errors of these false teachers that he called them another gospel, which is no gospel. He went so far as to pronounce the curse of God on the teachers of this false doctrine in the church of Galatia (1:8).

So, believing the truth of the Lord's supper as being of greatest importance for the proper worship of the church, the leaders of the Reformation condemned the false teaching of the church of Rome. The name that is given to the corrupted celebration of the Lord's supper in the church of Rome is the name *the mass*. Over time, the observance of the mass became central to the worship service. The celebration of the mass was exalted wrongly above the preaching of the word. In many churches of Rome, there is hardly any preaching at all. The members of this church are admonished to attend the mass regularly. Simply by the superstitious partaking of the mass, the members of the church of Rome are wrongly assured that they can receive Christ. The errors concerning the mass (called by the Reformers "the popish mass"*) continue to our modern times. It is called the popish mass because of the regulation of the Pope with respect to the administration of the mass. The church has not turned from its false teaching but only confirmed its erroneous teachings at several church councils over time. The church at Rome also officially pronounces the curse on anyone who disagrees with it, whereby it really condemns all of Protestantism.

For all of these reasons, the Reformed church in the Catechism takes great pains to distinguish truth from error with regards to the proper understanding of the sacrament of the Lord's supper. We should not be offended by this. If we love the Lord, we should be concerned about maintaining the truth of the sacraments which he himself ordained in the church. Only then can this sacrament serve for the encouragement of the faith of the church and the glory of the name of the Lord presented in this sacrament.

Arie den Hartog

---

* Heidelberg Catechism Q 80, in *Confessions and Church Order*, 116.

July 17 — **Q&A 78 — The Bread and Wine Do Not Become the Literal Body and Blood of Christ**

Read: Matthew 26:26–29.

The church of Rome teaches that during the Lord's supper the bread and wine are changed into the literal body and blood of Christ. This change is termed *transubstantiation*, literally "change of one substance into another." In the language of the debate about the meaning of transubstantiation, the church of Rome states that even though the bread and wine continue to look like, feel like, and taste like bread and wine, they are in fact really the body and blood of Christ. The change of the elements takes place when the priest in the mass repeats the words of consecration. The church of Rome teaches that the word *is* used by Jesus when he said concerning the broken bread in the Lord's supper: "This is my body," and concerning the wine, "This is the new testament in my blood," must be taken literally (Luke 22:19–20).

The errors that followed from these teachings of the church of Rome are that in the mass, communicants must imagine that Christ is literally present and being consumed. Rome teaches that the transubstantiated elements are even worthy of being worshiped as though they are Christ himself. Furthermore, the elements of the sacrament have in themselves the power to save and bless those who receive them. Christ can be taken and received by the physical hand and mouth of the communicants.

Also in the church of Rome, the cup of wine was taken away from the ordinary members of the church. It was feared that there was a danger of sacrilege should a drop of wine, which had been transubstantiated into the blood of Christ, accidentally fall to the ground from the lips of a communicant. So, in the church of Rome, only the priest drinks the wine, and he is said to do this on behalf of the whole church. Also, a debate was held that led to the teaching that the whole Christ is in each one of the elements and even in every single consecrated wafer of the Lord's supper.

The Reformed church maintains the truth that the bread and wine in the Lord's supper always remain ordinary bread and wine, even though in a sacramental way these elements are signs and pledges of the sacrifice of the body and blood of Jesus on the cross. It is quite obvious that when Jesus first instituted the Lord's supper, he could not have meant by the words of consecration that the bread and wine were changed into his body and blood. In fact, at the time of the institution of the supper, the Lord was present with his disciples in the wholeness of his body. He did not pluck off his flesh and give it to the disciples nor drain some of his blood to give to them. Jesus did not say concerning the elements of the supper that they change into something which they quite obviously do not appear to be. Such a gross misunderstanding and superstitious ideas of the Lord's supper confuse the simplicity of its teaching as intended by the Lord.

The meaning of the word *is* in Scripture often is "this signifies." This is true also in common language today. Jesus himself used the language: "I am the way" (John 14:6); "I am the door" (10:7); "I am the bread of life" (6:35). In none of these expressions did Jesus mean that there is the change of substance of the sign into reality.

Communion with Christ is nowhere in Scripture presented as a matter of mere physical and carnal contact with him. Our communion with Christ is definitely a spiritual act and not a carnal one. We receive the blessings which Christ has merited for us by his sacrifice on the cross only in the spiritual way of faith.

Arie den Hartog

July 18 — Q&A 79 – The Language of Scripture Regarding the Lord's Supper

Read: 1 Corinthians 11:23–29.

The church of Rome tries to argue from the language of Scripture to support its false teaching of transubstantiation. According to this teaching, the elements of the Lord's supper turn into the literal body and blood of the Lord and are literally and physically consumed by those who receive the sacrament. The language the Catholic Church cites is used in several places in Scripture, including 1 Corinthians 11. Also, in 1 Corinthians 10, Paul speaks of "the cup of blessing" which is received in the Lord's supper as "the communion of the blood of Christ" (v. 16).

The Catechism answers that the Bible uses sacramental language in which the sign is said to be the reality for good reasons. The first reason is that sign and reality of the sacrament bear a definite resemblance to each other, otherwise it could hardly be a sacrament. As earthly bread and wine support this temporal life, so the "crucified body and shed blood" of Christ are the "true [spiritual] meat and drink whereby our souls are fed to eternal life."* This is a simple comparison and by no means implies a change of substance of the elements. According to the word of God, the physical creation is full of signs and symbols of spiritual truths of God. The sacrament is simple in its meaning, using the simple signs of bread and wine to impress upon us more clearly the truths of the cross of Christ.

Jesus intends that by these visible signs and seals we can in a better way understand the invisible mysteries of our salvation. The purpose of the sacrament is the confirmation and strengthening of our faith. The Spirit of Christ in the sacraments uses these signs and pledges for this purpose. So, as surely as we by faith receive the outward signs and pledge with our physical hands and mouths, so certainly by the Spirit of Christ, the spiritual realities of the sacrifice of Christ become ours. We appropriate the spiritual verities of the sacrifice of Christ through faith in Jesus Christ. We have through faith the assurance of the forgiveness of our sins, and the righteousness of Christ is imputed to us as certainly as if we had in our own persons suffered and made satisfaction for our sins to God.

In John 6, Jesus uses the kind of language referred to in the above-mentioned debate. He speaks of the necessity of eating his flesh and drinking his blood. But when he has declared this, he immediately excludes any false carnal understanding when he says that the words he speaks are spirit and life: "The flesh profiteth nothing" (v. 63). The right understanding of the presence of Christ's body and blood in the sacrament of the Lord's supper will maintain the right understanding of the spiritual relation we have with Christ and the spiritual way in which we receive from him the blessings of salvation. It is therefore very important to maintain the truth with respect to the Lord's supper. The false teaching of Rome has led to all sorts of superstition, which leads away from true faith in Christ.

Arie den Hartog

---

* Heidelberg Catechism A 79, in *Confessions and Church Order*, 115.

July 19 — Q&A 79 — The Spiritual Presence of Christ in the Lord's Supper

Read: John 14:15–26.

John 14–17 record the discourses Jesus had with his disciples at the time when he was in the upper room and at the time when he instituted the Lord's supper among them. These chapters therefore also give rich instructions concerning the meaning of the Lord's supper. The Reformers, especially John Calvin, taught the truth that Christ is indeed present with his church in the Lord's supper. The church of Rome insists that Jesus is bodily present in the elements of the Lord's supper. According to this teaching, Christ is present only where he is both in his human and divine nature. Even the great reformer Martin Luther, who restored to the church the most glorious and blessed truths of the gospel, was confused in his teaching about the Lord's supper. He taught that Jesus is bodily present in, with, and under the elements of the Lord's supper, though in a mysterious and invisible way.

The confusion of Luther with regards to the presence of Christ in the Lord's supper caused Luther to defend a teaching that confused the human and divine natures of Christ. We believe that Jesus as the Son of God has both a divine and a human nature after his incarnation. The human nature of Christ is like ours, limited and confined to one place. After his ascension, Jesus Christ is now bodily in heaven and no longer on earth. It is therefore wrong to teach that Christ is in any way bodily present with the church when she celebrates the Lord's supper. Christ, according to his human nature, cannot be present everywhere on earth where the Lord's supper is being celebrated.

Though Christ is now bodily in heaven, according to his divine nature and by his Spirit, he is present with his church. This presence is not limited to the times when the church celebrates the Lord's supper. Jesus promised always to be with us even to the end of the world. This is a great comfort for the church while she is still on earth.

The Lord's supper in its true meaning is a sign and pledge of the real abiding spiritual presence of Christ with his church. When the Lord's supper is celebrated by the church, Christ is present. He is the divine host at the table of the Lord's supper. He imparts his heavenly and spiritual blessings to those who partake of the Lord's supper by faith. The Lord's supper is not merely an outward memorial feast. The blessed reality of celebrating the Lord's supper is the reality of communion and fellowship with Christ. In the celebration of the supper, we rejoice in the blessings he gives as the living Lord in the midst of his church.

When we celebrate the supper, we should think of Christ being both in heaven and on earth. Jesus is in heaven according to his human nature, now as the exalted glorious Lord; and according to his everywhere-present divine nature, Jesus is now both in heaven and earth. According to his ever-present divine nature, he is never absent from us. What a blessed mystery!

Arie den Hartog

July 20

Q&A 80 — Celebrating the One Sacrifice of Christ in the Lord's Supper

Read: Hebrews 9:22–28.

I am going to consider question and answer 80 of the Catechism with Lord's Day 29. This question and answer was added later to the Catechism to distinguish the serious errors of the church of Rome from true understanding of the Lord's supper. We have in an earlier meditation already made mention of this. In the sovereign providence of the Lord, when the church must defend the truth of God's word against error, she often enriches her understanding of the positive truth of God's word at the same time. Question and answer 80 of the Catechism summarizes the serious errors of the church of Rome with regards to her doctrine on the Lord's supper. Be sure to read this question and answer before you continue with this meditation.

The most serious error of the church of Rome is her belief that in the mass, the priest must offer Christ again under the elements of the transubstantiated bread and wine. The communion table in the church of Rome has been changed to an altar. This re-offering of Christ under the elements of the bread and wine is being performed daily in the church of Rome by the priest in the ceremonies of the mass when he places the bread and wine on the altar. Further, it is maintained that the sacrifice of Christ will not benefit those who come to the mass unless it is offered again by a human priest in the mass. The church of Rome pronounces a curse on all those who do not agree with this false teaching.

The Reformed church considers this to be a very serious error. It maintains that this re-offering of Christ by the priest is a denial of the once and for all perfect sacrifice on the cross. What an affront that is to our Lord! In the Reformed church, the Lord's supper is a celebration of the once and for all perfect sacrifice of Christ on the cross. This sacrifice was made by the Lord Jesus himself, who is God's own Son. This sacrifice involved the sacrifice of his own blessed body. It was perfect and therefore never again needed to be repeated. How can a repeated offering by a mere human priest, who is a sinner just like all of us are, add anything to the perfect sacrifice of Christ himself?

The sacrifice of Jesus was absolutely perfect. It was infinitely precious in the sight of God. It made atonement for all the sins of all of God's people. It merited perfect and everlasting righteousness for all of the elect of God. It obtained for all those who belong to Christ and believe in him all the blessings of salvation and the hope of life eternal. In Hebrews 9:12 we read: "Neither by the blood of goats and calves, but by his own blood he entered in once into the holy place, having obtained eternal redemption for us." In verse 28 of the same chapter we read: "So Christ was once offered to bear the sins of many; and unto them that look for him shall he appear the second time without sin unto salvation." We look for no repetition of this offering. To repeat this offering is to imply that the sacrifice of Christ was not perfect, that there is a need for another offering.

As Reformed believers, we say with the inspired apostle Paul: "God forbid that I should glory, save in the cross of our Lord Jesus Christ" (Gal. 6:14).

Arie den Hartog

July 21 — Q&A 79-80 — Worshiping Christ in Heaven and Not on Earth

Read: Colossians 3:1–11.

The church of Rome believes that in the Lord's supper, the bread and wine are changed into the literal body and blood of Christ. Because of this imagination, it is the practice of the church of Rome to worship Christ in the elements. When a person comes to the communion rail and receives the wafer from the hands of the Roman Catholic priest, he or she is taught to bow before the consecrated wafer. Wherever the remains of the consecrated elements of the mass are kept in the church, the members of the church are taught to bow in worship. There have been times in church history when the transubstantiated elements of the Lord's supper have been paraded through the streets, and Roman Catholic devotees lining the streets have bowed before them in adoration. There were also times when the consecrated elements were kept under glass somewhere in the church, and people came to worship before them. There are statements in the decrees of the council of Trent that emphatically declare that the consecrated elements of the Lord's supper are supposed to be worthy of the same honor and worship as Christ Jesus himself.

The Reformed church declares the practices of the church of Rome to be accursed idolatry. Idolatry is giving honor to someone or something other than God. The honor of worship is only due to God. It is idolatry to worship the elements of the Lord's supper, for they are in fact ordinary bread and wine, and they are in no sense God or Jesus. Christ Jesus is now not bodily on earth. The church of Rome is wrong in its teaching to insist that Christ's literal body and blood are present in the consecrated elements of the Lord's supper and there to be worshipped.

We know from God's word that Christ is now in heaven. He is there as the glorified Lord sitting at the right hand of the Majesty on high, even God the Father. When we celebrate the Lord's supper, we do not worship the bread and wine, nor do we have any superstitious regard for them. They are but ordinary bread and wine. They have no power in themselves to bless. Rather, when we celebrate the Lord's supper, we lift up our hearts through his Spirit in our hearts. We lift up our hearts to worship Christ who is now enthroned in glory in heaven. He alone is worthy of our worship. He appears now in heaven as the lamb of God who by his sacrifice atoned for all of our sins. We worship and adore him, giving him all the thanks of all our hearts for his loving sacrifice and perfect obedience, whereby we have the forgiveness of sins and righteousness and eternal life. We look by faith to Christ as he is now in heaven, as the source and fountain of all the blessings of salvation. No one else, nothing else beside the blessed triune God, is worthy of worship. Jesus, along with the Father and the Holy Spirit, is worthy of our worship because he is the Son of God in our human nature.

Think about these great truths every time you celebrate the Lord's supper!

Arie den Hartog

July 22 — Q&A 79 — Christ in Heaven, His Church on Earth

Read: Luke 22:14–20.

There is one more beautiful truth concerning the Lord's supper referred to in the Catechism that I want to meditate on. Christ gave the Lord's supper to his church to celebrate on earth knowing that he himself would soon go to heaven. Ever since his ascension, Christ is now bodily in heaven, and his church is on earth. In Luke 22:15–16, we find one of the records of the institution of the Lord's supper. Jesus said to his disciples: "With desire I have desired to eat this Passover with you before I suffer: for I say unto you, I will not any more eat thereof, until it be fulfilled in the kingdom of God."

If the church imagines that Christ is still bodily on earth when she celebrates the Lord's supper, she becomes confused as to why she must still look for his coming again in glory. The true understanding of the Lord's supper teaches that Christ is in heaven, and his church is on earth. The church is comforted by the spiritual presence of Christ in the Lord's supper and the continual remembrance of the blessings of salvation he merited on the cross and continues to pour out on his church. However, the joy of the church is not yet perfect. The church looks with eager expectation and longing for the glorious and blessed return of the Lord. Only then will she have perfect fellowship with her Lord. Only then will her joy be made perfect in the presence of her Lord in heaven.

The apostle Paul states in 1 Corinthians 11 that in celebrating the Lord's supper, the church must "shew the Lord's death till he come" (v. 26). As long as the church is on earth, she must preach the gospel. The truth of the suffering and death of Christ on the cross is to be central to this preaching. The church also preaches the truth of the resurrection and ascension of Christ and the blessed hope of his coming again, all of which follow from what Christ accomplished on the cross. The proper celebration of the Lord's supper also includes an earnest longing for his coming again. The church celebrates the Lord's supper with the view to his coming again. She is as a bride waiting for the coming of her bridegroom.

The Catechism speaks of the fact that Christ is not now on earth but in heaven (question and answer 47). We are however ingrafted into Christ. We are members of his body. Christ is our head. The body of Christ, which is the church, longs to be finally with Christ, her head in heaven. This longing is worked in the hearts of the members of the church by the Spirit of the exalted Christ. Only when the church is in heaven with Christ will she be able to have perfect communion and fellowship with him. Philippians 3:20 speaks of the truth that even presently "our conversation is in heaven; from whence also we look for the Saviour, the Lord Jesus Christ." Properly, the celebration of the Lord's supper encourages us to look to Jesus in heaven and stirs up the hope that we have in our hearts by the Spirit of Christ.

Interestingly, according to the prophecy of Revelation 19, we look for another feast, which is even more wonderful than the Lord's supper, which we will celebrate together with all the saints in heavenly glory. This feast will be the great heavenly marriage feast of the Lamb: "Let us be glad and rejoice, and give honour unto him: for the marriage of the Lamb is come, and his wife hath made herself ready." (Rev.19:7).

Arie den Hartog

Lord's Day 30

Q&A 81-82

Q. 81. For whom is the Lord's supper instituted?

A. For those who are truly sorrowful for their sins, and yet trust that these are forgiven them for the sake of Christ, and that their remaining infirmities are covered by his passion and death; and who also earnestly desire to have their faith more and more strengthened, and their lives more holy; but hypocrites, and such as turn not to God with sincere hearts, eat and drink judgment to themselves.

Q. 82. Are they also to be admitted to this supper, who, by confession and life, declare themselves unbelieving and ungodly?

A. No; for by this the covenant of God would be profaned, and his wrath kindled against the whole congregation; therefore it is the duty of the Christian church, according to the appointment of Christ and his apostles, to exclude such persons, by the keys of the kingdom of heaven, till they show amendment of life.

July 23 — Q&A 81 – Careful Observance of the Lord's Supper

Read: 1 Corinthians 11:17–34.

In the last few meditations on the truth of the Lord's supper, we shall focus on the question of who may come to the table of the Lord. The Lord's supper must be carefully observed. This follows from its holy meaning and significance. In this sacrament, we remember the amazing wonder of the suffering of our Savior in his death on the cross and what this sacrifice accomplished for us. We believe that our Lord Jesus Christ is spiritually present with his church when the Lord's supper is properly observed. We have communion and fellowship with him, and through faith we partake of the blessings he has merited for us on the cross. This requires a certain sincere spiritual attitude and worship of Christ.

Lord's Day 30 of the Catechism gives us very significant instruction. This instruction can be divided into two parts. Question and answer 81 deals with the personal question of examining ourselves and impresses on us the importance of coming in humble repentance and faith to the Lord's supper. Question and answer 82 deals with the responsibility of the church, through her elders, to supervise the administration of the supper so that no ungodly person is allowed to come to the supper. The passage I asked you to read from 1 Corinthians 11 gives us important instruction. This passage is part of the special revelation concerning the Lord's supper that Jesus personally gave to the apostle Paul while Paul was being prepared for his office and work as an apostle of the Lord. In the next few meditations, I will refer often to this passage.

In the Reformed church, it is common that two important activities are practiced whenever the Lord's supper is administered. First, there is a week of spiritual preparation before the Lord's supper is celebrated. During this week, the members of the church who are going to celebrate the Lord's supper together are admonished to examine themselves. Self-examination is a personal and spiritual exercise.

Secondly, the Reformed church believes that the church must supervise those who come to the table of the Lord. Those who are members of the church are under the regular supervision of the elders of the church who are appointed by Christ, we believe, to take spiritual oversight over the lives of the members of the church. Members in good standing are exhorted to join the celebrations of the Lord's supper. Visitors from other denominations who have not been under the oversight of the elders are interviewed and questioned concerning their confession of the truth and their lives as Christians. This practice is given various names in the church, such as close communion, supervised communion, or restricted communion. There are some differences regarding this practice among Reformed churches. Some do not allow anyone who is not a member of the particular local church to join the communion table. Others allow visitors who express agreement in faith and testify of a sincere godly walk to join the table.

Those who do not understand this practice might be offended if they are questioned with regards to their faith and Christian living before they are allowed to come to the Lord's table. What everyone must understand, however, is that the holiness of the Lord's supper must be regarded. The glory of our Lord, and proper regard for the sacredness of his sacrifice for us on the cross, is most important.

Arie den Hartog

July 24 — Q&A 81 — For Whom Was the Lord's Supper Instituted?

Read: 1 John 1.

The question, "For whom is the Lord's Supper instituted,"* is beautifully answered by the Catechism. Be sure to read Lord's Day 30 again if you have not already done so. Before anyone comes to the Lord's supper, he should carefully examine himself. This requirement is spoken of in 1 Corinthians 11. The Lord's supper was instituted for those who are truly sorrowful over their sins. This sacrament is not for those who imagine that they are righteous in themselves. We do not come to this sacrament to boast that we are without sin. If we indeed were without sin, there would be no need for us to come to the Lord's supper. The Lord's supper presents to us the amazing sacrifice Jesus made on our behalf to atone for our sins. The whole reason for all the shame, agony, and suffering of Jesus on the cross was the greatness of our sins—your sins and my sins. We certainly cannot have proper regard for the Lord's supper if we are not conscious of the seriousness of our own sins. The Lord's supper was instituted for those who sincerely and heartily repent of their sins.

We do not come to the Lord's supper to testify that we have arrived at some high spiritual state of holiness above the other members of the church. Every true child of God will confess concerning himself that he is still a great sinner. John says in 1 John 1 that "if we say that we have no sin," we lie "and the truth is not in us" (v. 8). We must know our own sins and the seriousness of these sins against God. The seriousness of our sin is not merely that we have done evil against our fellow men or because we are in trouble and distress in our lives as a result of our sin. Our sins are so very serious because they were committed against the most high majesty of God. When David confessed the grievous sins of his adultery with Bathsheba and his murdering of Uriah, he confessed before God in deep sorrow of heart: "Against thee, thee only, have I sinned, and done this evil in thy sight: that thou mightest be justified when thou speakest, and be clear when thou judgest" (Ps. 51:4).

To be sorry for our sins, we must understand that our sins are very many, and they have grievously offended the holy majesty of God. In order to understand the reality of this, we need to remember that according to the word of God, our sins are not merely a matter of the words we have spoken and the evil deeds we have done. Our sins involve the secret thoughts, desires, and purposes of our hearts as well. God knows all of these. He judges our heart. He requires perfection in our inward being as well as in our outward walk. Every unclean thought, every inclination to pride and self-centeredness, every impulse of anger and hatred against God and the neighbor, is sin. The worldliness of our purposes, the adultery of our hearts, the hatred we might harbor against our brother even for a moment, even all these are known to God, and they are sinful. Even weakness of faith, doubt and worry, is sin. We are sinful Christians because we are not really devoted to God with our whole hearts. The Catechism speaks of the fact that "even the holiest men, while in this life, have only a small beginning of this [new] obedience."** Our shortcomings and our failures are part of the reality of our sins before God. When we come to the Lord's supper, we must be truly sorry for all of these. We must examine ourselves in the light of God's word, the absolutely perfect standard for Christian living.

Arie den Hartog

---

* Heidelberg Catechism Q 81, in *Confessions and Church Order*, 117.
** Heidelberg Catechism A 114, in *Confessions and Church Order*, 133.

July 25 — **Q&A 81 – Those Who Come to the Lord's Supper**

Read: Isaiah 53.

Be sure to read question and answer 81 of the Catechism again before you read this meditation. Those who come to the Lord's supper must desire that their sins be forgiven them. We sin daily. Our sins are grievous in God's sight. We must be truly sorry for them and repent of them. We long for the assurance that all our sins are forgiven us for the sake of Christ Jesus and because of his great sacrifice on the cross. To come to the supper of the Lord, we must of course have a true and saving knowledge of the Lord Jesus Christ. We must know and believe that he is God's own Son. We must understand why Jesus Christ died on the cross and what he accomplished through his death. New Christians should receive instruction in the great truths of the gospel, especially in the truths of what it means that Jesus, in the greatness of his love, offered himself for us on the cross. His sacrifice was absolutely necessary to pay for our sins. In our coming to the Lord's supper, we should be consciously thinking about and meditating on the truths of Christ and of his cross and the amazing wonder of his love for us. Our sins incur the just and holy wrath of God. They separate us from God. They make us worthy of his judgment. We deserve to be condemned because of our sins. So serious are our sins against the holy God that we deserve to be forever cast away from his presence into the everlasting torment of hell.

Jesus died the awful death of the cross to pay for our sins. He suffered the wrath of God on our behalf. He bore the judgment of God that our sins deserved. By his death on the cross, he paid the awful penalty of our sins. He satisfied the justice of God. He even bore the agony of hell that our sins deserved. In the deepest hour of his suffering, the dreadful darkness that came over the cross, Jesus cried out with a loud voice: "My God, my God, why hast thou forsaken me?" (Matt. 27:46).

When we come to the Lord's supper, we must desire to have our faith more and more strengthened. The Lord's supper is for those who are weak in faith. We are all weak in faith. The Lord gave us this sacrament to encourage us and to strengthen our weak faith.

When we come to the Lord's supper, we must desire to have our lives made more and more holy. Holiness is love and consecration to God. There is no greater power to motivate us to holy living than the true spiritual remembrance of the suffering and death of Jesus on the cross. This is the purpose of the Lord's supper.

We are helpless against the power of sin. We cannot overcome the power of sin ourselves, as it continues to operate in our sinful nature and heart. Only God, by the power of his grace and Holy Spirit, can and will deliver us from the destruction of sin in our lives. He is pleased to do this through the preaching of his word and through our observing the Lord's supper. True Christian living is holiness before God. Holiness is separation from sin. It is love for God. Holiness is spiritual perfection and devotion to God. Only when we are made holy by the grace and Spirit of God can we have fellowship with God and with his Son Jesus Christ. Of this, the Lord's supper is a sign and pledge.

Arie den Hartog

July 26   **Q&A 81 – Eating and Drinking Judgment to Themselves**

Read: Psalm 50:16–23.

The apostle Paul in 1 Corinthians 11 speaks of how serious it is when a person comes to the table of the Lord and does not truly repent of sin. He becomes "guilty of the body and blood" of Christ (v. 27). He eats and drinks judgment to himself (v. 30). The Lord intended that the Lord's supper should be the source of great blessing and encouragement for his people. But when one comes with a sinful attitude to the Lord's supper, he eats and drinks judgment to himself. How awful this is! God's word warns us about this, and we must take this warning seriously. When one partakes of the Lord's supper with an evil heart of unbelief and sin, he makes himself guilty of the body and blood of the Lord. What could be more serious than this! Who would deserve a more severe judgment than one who is guilty of crucifying the Son of God afresh?

The Catechism warns us about hypocrisy in answer 81. In Jeremiah 17:9–10, we read: "The heart is deceitful above all things, and desperately wicked: who can know it? I the LORD search the heart, I try the reins, even to give every man according to his ways, and according to the fruit of his doings." A hypocrite is a sham. He pretends to be what he is not. Before the world, he tries to show himself as some great saint, while in his heart and life, he is really evil and refuses to repent at all. God exposes the hypocrite. He cannot hide before God. God knows the heart when it is evil. Man cannot escape his condemnation. God searches the heart of man through his word, which is "quick, and powerful, and sharper than any twoedged sword, piercing even to the dividing asunder of soul and spirit, and of the joints and marrow, and is a discerner of the thoughts and intents of the heart" (Heb. 4:12).

The ungodly must be warned not to come to the holy supper of the Lord lest he be condemned. The Lord's supper is a sacrament of holy fellowship with God and with Jesus Christ. The impenitent man who does not turn to God, as we all should, will be judged by God. Many professing Christians today do not want to hear anything negative, but serious warnings from God's own word must be sounded forth and listened to. These warnings are not intended to frighten us or to discourage us from coming to the Lord's supper. We must examine our own hearts, repent, and turn again unto the Lord. In the spiritual activity of examining ourselves we must earnestly pray that God will help us. A proper prayer in preparing ourselves to come to the Lord's supper is the humble prayer of Psalm 139:23–24, "Search me, O God, and know my heart: try me, and know my thoughts: and see if there be any wicked way in me, and lead me in the way everlasting."

As fearful and necessary as these warnings are, no sincere Christian should be terrified by them. God will receive in mercy all those who come in humble and sincere repentance to him. Those who come to the Lord with humble and sincere hearts, genuinely repenting of their sins, will be blessed by partaking of the Lord's supper. After all, the Lord gave us this sacrament not to turn us from him in fear and dread, but to assure us that all our sins are forgiven us for the sake of Jesus Christ and his sacrifice on the cross. We receive this assurance with humble faith and thankfulness to God.

Arie den Hartog

July 27 — Q&A 82 – The Need for Supervision of the Lord's Table

Read: Hebrews 13:7, 17–21.

We have been considering the need of every believer who comes to the Lord's supper to prepare himself through self-examination. This is a deeply personal calling and responsibility. Additionally, the elders of the church have the calling to supervise the administration of the Lord's supper. First Corinthians 4:1 speaks of the fact that the ministers of Christ are "stewards of the mysteries of God." In 1 Corinthians 11, where Paul gives extensive instruction about the proper observance of the Lord's supper, he in fact admonishes the whole church concerning this serious matter. Because the church of Corinth was careless about the celebration of the Lord's supper, and was tolerating heresies and divisions among her members, therefore the judgment of God came upon the whole church. Many were sick in the church and many were asleep. The reference to falling asleep is to death. So serious was the judgment of God on this church!

Elders, properly elected and ordained in the church, receive their authority from Christ and his apostles. The members of the church must submit to the oversight of the elders. The matter of who may come to the supper of the Lord must not be left entirely to the discretion of the members of the church. It is common in many churches that the only thing that is done to fulfill the calling of the elders to supervise the Lord's supper is to make a very general announcement before the celebration of the supper that sincere Christians who have repented of their sins and confessed faith in Jesus Christ may come to the table of the Lord. More is involved than this in the oversight of the elders.

The Lord's supper was given to be celebrated by the church spiritually. The Lord's supper is not a public ceremony. It is not one to which the whole world is invited. When Jesus instituted the Lord's supper, he was in the upper room in intimate fellowship with his disciples who by his grace were one with him, believing in him and keeping his commandments. It is wonderful that true people of God join together to celebrate the Lord's supper in close fellowship with the Lord and with each other.

Evil men and false teachers do not belong to this communion. We believe that the right reading of the gospel accounts suggests that Judas was dismissed before the Lord instituted the supper. There are often those who join the worship services but do not know and acknowledge their sins. Some are ignorant concerning the truth. Some, even though they know their sins, will not acknowledge and confess their sins, and wrongly imagine that their sins need not be confessed and repented of. There are hypocrites mixed with the true members of the church. This is Satan's work, as the parable of the wheat and tares teaches us.

Christ, through his apostles, has appointed elders to have spiritual oversight of the church. No one who will be a member of the church may despise this oversight and refuse to submit to it for his own spiritual benefit and correction. The Lord has given to the elders the calling to watch over the celebration of the Lord's supper, to guard the honor and glory of the name of the Lord every time this sacrament is administered in the midst of his church.

Arie den Hartog

July 28 — **Q&A 82 – Supervising Our Confession and Life**

Read: Ephesians 4:11–16.

In celebrating the Lord's supper, the church must be united together in the blessed truth of the Lord Jesus Christ. Her members must also be committed to live by this truth in all godliness and sincerity. There is freedom and space for differences on minor issues, but the church must be truly one in knowing, loving, and confessing the great doctrines of Jesus Christ and of salvation in him.

Paul admonished the church of Corinth because when she celebrated the Lord's supper, there were divisions and heresies among her (1 Cor. 11:18–19).

There are many churches where it does not matter what a person believes. Everyone has the right, these churches say, to his own opinions and private interpretations of Scripture. There is no absolute truth. There are many different interpretations of Scripture. One is not more right than the other. The members of such churches come to the table of the Lord in some sort of vague spirit of brotherhood and human friendliness. Everyone claiming in a very shallow and general way to be a Christian is allowed to come to the table of the Lord. Differences with official positions of the church are allowed. Often, in these churches, even grossly ungodly living is tolerated in a false spirit of so-called Christian love.

The truth of God can and must be known from the infallible Scriptures, which are the word of God, and by the enlightening of the Spirit of Christ in the church. The elders must be constantly engaged in teaching and preaching the truth of the Lord and admonishing the members of the church to live by this truth. They must be courageous to defend the truth and resist false teachers and evil works. By so doing, the church is built upon the truth and is able to stand strong in a world of confusion and ungodliness.

Members of the church must walk humbly with one another, putting down every inclination of pride and self-exaltation, which can so easily arise from our sinful nature. The elders must labor among members of the church when divisions threaten her blessed and glorious unity in Christ. Heresies divide the church. Knowledge and love for the truth unite her. False teachers must be identified and corrected, and if they do not repent, they must be rejected (Titus 1:9–11; 3:10). Impenitent wickedness must be properly dealt with by the elders of the church through the use of the keys of the kingdom, which is Christian discipline.

By the Lord's supper, we show our unity in Christ in doctrine and life. We read of the church of Pentecost that her members

42. continued steadfastly in the apostles' doctrine and fellowship, and in breaking of bread, and in prayers…
46. And they, continuing daily with one accord in the temple, and breaking of bread from house to house, did eat their meat with gladness and singleness of heart,
47. Praising God, and having favour with all the people. And the Lord added to the church daily such as should be saved. (Acts 2:42, 46–47)

Sinful divisions in the church may not be ignored when she celebrates the Lord's supper. They must be resolved, and peace and love must prevail among the members of the church before the Lord's supper can properly be administered. The name of our Lord Jesus Christ is exalted when we know and love and maintain his truth in his church. The elders of the church are appointed to guard the church from errors and preserve her blessed unity.

Arie den Hartog

July 29 — Q&A 82 — Kept From the Table of the Lord

Read: Isaiah 1:11–20.

The Catechism uses strong words: those "who, by confession and life, declare themselves to be unbelieving and ungodly" must be kept from the table.* There are churches that boast of tolerating everyone, no matter what they believe or how they live. They maintain that such tolerance shows the love and friendliness of the church. If, however, error and ungodly living are tolerated, and there is no admonition and no discipline in the church, the end result will be that the name of Christ will be dishonored in the church, and it will be impossible to properly observe the Lord's supper in a God-glorifying way. The concern of the church must rise higher than merely pleasing certain individuals who are her members for fear of offending them.

So serious is this matter of keeping ungodly men from the table of the Lord that the Catechism states that if such sinful tolerance is permitted in the church, "the covenant of God will be profaned" and the wrath of God "kindled against the whole congregation."** The Lord's supper celebrates the covenant of God. The highest purpose for which the church celebrates the Lord's supper is the worship of God and glorifying him.

The apostle Paul had to admonish the church of Corinth because divisions and heresies were tolerated in her midst. Paul says emphatically that he does not praise the church for this. He points out in 1 Corinthians 11 that the wrath of God came upon the whole church so that many were sick and many fell asleep, they died (v. 30). Therefore, the church of Corinth was called to repentance. The implication, as can be gathered from the rest of Paul's letter to the church of Corinth, was that the elders had to rectify this matter. Only when heresy and ungodliness were removed from the church did she again experience the blessing of the Lord upon her.

One of the famous actions of the great reformer John Calvin, recorded by church historians that loved the truth of the Reformation, was an incident that took place in Geneva where Calvin was the pastor at the time. He was convinced that certain evil men called the libertarians should not be allowed to come to the table of the Lord. When these men insisted on coming to the table regardless of what they were told, Calvin placed himself bodily in front of the communion table and refused to allow them to come to the table of the Lord.

It takes great courage and strength to stand for the truth in our day. It takes great zeal and love for the honor and glory of the Lord to insist on maintaining the truth and opposing error and wickedness that can, and does, at times even come into the church. There is little of this kind of zeal in our day in many churches. Tolerance for all sorts of evils and for false teachers in the church has caused the church to be overrun by heretics and corrupted by the false teaching of ungodly men. When this happens, the name of God is blasphemed. That is how serious this is. May God give us men of courage who stand for the truth. And may we, as members of the church, know and love the truth, instruct one another, and build one another up in the truth. May we also be an example and encouragement to our fellow saints to maintain true godliness, not only for our own personal lives but also in the midst of his church. When faithful elders maintain the truth and peace, and unity prevails, the church will be greatly blessed of God in her celebration of the sacrament of the Lord's supper, and his glory will shine in her midst.

Arie den Hartog

---

* Heidelberg Catechism Q&A 82, in *Confessions and Church Order*, 117.
** Heidelberg Catechism Q&A 82, in *Confessions and Church Order*, 117.

Lord's Day 31

Q. 83. What are the keys of the kingdom of heaven?

A. The preaching of the holy gospel, and Christian discipline, or excommunication out of the Christian church; by these two, the kingdom of heaven is opened to believers, and shut against unbelievers.

Q. 84. How is the kingdom of heaven opened and shut by the preaching of the holy gospel?

A. Thus: when according to the command of Christ it is declared and publicly testified to all and every believer, that, whenever they receive the promise of the gospel by a true faith, all their sins are really forgiven them of God, for the sake of Christ's merits; and on the contrary, when it is declared and testified to all unbelievers, and such as do not sincerely repent, that they stand exposed to the wrath of God and eternal condemnation, so long as they are unconverted; according to which testimony of the gospel God will judge them both in this and in the life to come.

Q. 85. How is the kingdom of heaven shut and opened by Christian discipline?

A. Thus: when according to the command of Christ, those who under the name of Christians maintain doctrines, or practices inconsistent therewith, and will not, after having been often brotherly admonished, renounce their errors and wicked course of life, are complained of to the church, or to those who are thereunto appointed by the church; and if they despise their admonition, are by them forbidden the use of the sacraments; whereby they are excluded from the Christian church, and by God himself from the kingdom of Christ; and when they promise and show real amendment, are again received as members of Christ and his church.

July 30 — Q&A 83 — The Keys of the Kingdom

Read: Matthew 16:13–20.

Lord's Day 31 speaks about the authority and discipline of the church. In describing this authority, the Catechism uses a biblical figure of "the keys of the kingdom of heaven."* This figure does not have its origin with the Catechism but with God's own word. The figure is used in several places in Scripture, including in Matthew 16:13–20. The same idea is also spoken of in John 20:23 and also Revelation 3:7.

The kingdom of God is pictured as though it is a high-walled fortress. Cities in the Old Testament time had such walls to protect them from being overrun and destroyed by enemies. Access in and out of the city was only through a gate. The key is the power to open and close this gate for those going in and out.

Jesus spoke very often during his ministry about the kingdom of God. The entire sermon on the mount recorded in Matthew 5–7 has the truth of the kingdom as its main theme. Jesus also called this kingdom the kingdom of heaven and the kingdom of righteousness and glory. It is also referred to as the kingdom of Christ.

When we are saved by the wonder of the grace of God, we are made citizens of this kingdom.

The kingdom of God is the spiritual realm where God rules in absolute sovereignty and power. God is known and acknowledged by the subjects of this kingdom. The authority of this kingdom was given to the hands of Jesus when he was exalted to the right hand of God (John 5:22–23). The king in God's kingdom is, and must be, obeyed and served by these subjects. The citizens of the kingdom know and do the word of Christ their king. Within the walls of the kingdom, the citizens are protected by God and by King Jesus from their greatest enemies. Being a citizen of this kingdom is exceedingly blessed and glorious. This kingdom will be finally realized in all of its perfection and glory in the new heavens and earth when Jesus comes again at the end of time. King Jesus will come to establish his kingdom of righteousness after overthrowing the wicked kingdoms of this world. In the everlasting heavenly kingdom, Jesus will reveal his glory and power among the subjects of his kingdom, whom he has redeemed by his sacrifice on the cross.

The concepts of kingdom and church in the figure of the keys of the kingdom refer to the same blessed reality. King Jesus is Lord and king both of his church and kingdom. The true members of the church of Jesus Christ are now, and will be in heaven, the citizens of this kingdom. Christ has given authority to his church to rule in his kingdom while this church is still on earth.

Today, the power of the keys is given by the Lord himself, especially to the pastors and elders of the church. These elders have a very serious responsibility to properly exercise their power and authority for the benefit of the citizens of the kingdom and the glory of Christ the king.

The power of the keys is a very great power. Imagine what Jesus says in Matthew 16:19, "And I will give unto thee the keys of the kingdom of heaven: and whatsoever thou shalt bind on earth shall be bound in heaven: and whatsoever thou shalt loose on earth shall be loosed in heaven." In our meditations on Lord's Day 31 of the Catechism this week, I want you to consider something about what all of this means. I hope that you will take a great interest in this subject and meditate on it.

Arie den Hartog

---

* Heidelberg Catechism Q 83, in *Confessions and Church Order*, 118.

July 31 — Q&A 83 – The Spiritual Nature of the Keys of the Kingdom

Read: John 20:19–23.

The power of the keys of the kingdom is spiritual in nature. This is very important to understand. The same thing can be said in another way. The authority that Christ has given to his church on earth is spiritual in nature, not physical. God has given physical earthly power to the state. This power is called in Scripture the power of the sword (see Rom. 13:1–3). Kings and princes, governors, prime ministers, and other rulers of the nations of this world are given by God the power of the sword. The power of the sword is the power to maintain law and order in the state. It is the power to administer physical punishment to evildoers and the power to reward those who do well. As Christians, we are to honor all those in authority over us. This honor is especially shown by submission and obedience. The Bible teaches that the government does not bear the sword in vain, so we ought to have a proper fear of those whom God has appointed to rule in the state. Those who do evil should fear being punished by the state for their evil doing, for the state even has the power to put those who do great evil to death. The power of the sword given to the state is also the right to defend itself against aggressors and to wage war against them.

The power of the keys which Christ has given to the church, however, is spiritual. The church does great wrong when she imagines that she also has the sword's power. She does wrong when she threatens physical punishment to those whom she judges, even rightly, to be wrong. She does wrong when she takes up the sword and engages in war to advance the cause of the kingdom of Christ and his truth. God has not given this power to the church. Throughout history there have been churches who have imagined that the church has the power of the sword. They have engaged themselves in worldly politics. They have been the leaders to stir up revolt against governments perceived to be unjust. They have at times even encouraged civil disobedience. Any church who does this does not have the blessing of God. She will herself be punished by the state, and God will judge her through this punishment.

The key power given to the church is spiritual. It has to do with declaring the forgiveness of sin and the salvation of God's people.

That the power of the keys is spiritual does not mean that it is really nothing, or that it need not be feared because such spiritual power really cannot do anything. That would be a very grave mistake. The spiritual power of the keys of the kingdom is the power to open and shut the kingdom of God. It is the wonderful power to declare to the penitent sinner that his sins are forgiven for the sake of Christ Jesus. Believers are declared righteous before the sovereign of heaven and earth. God's people are promised a place in the glorious kingdom of Jesus Christ. The key power is certainly a great and wonderful power.

The power of the keys is also the fearful power to declare to impenitent sinners that, as long as they continue in their wicked sin and impenitent lives, they are in danger of being cast out of the kingdom unto everlasting judgment in hell by the just and holy God.

The power of the keys is ultimately that of Christ, the king of his kingdom. In the book of Revelation, it is said that Christ has "the keys of hell and of death" (Rev. 1:18). It is also said, with reference to the kingdom of God, that Christ is the one who opens, and no man shuts, and shuts, and no man opens (3:7).

Arie den Hartog

August 1 — **Q&A 83 — The Wonderful Power of the Preaching**

Read: John 3:16–18, 36.

How wonderful from a positive point of view is the power of the gospel! The power of the gospel is the power of Jesus Christ. It is not the power of a mere man, not even that of a preacher of the gospel. The statement "according to the command of Christ" is mentioned twice this Lord's Day.[*] The key power of the kingdom is the power of the declaration and preaching of the word of Christ, the sovereign king of his kingdom. The wonderful positive power of the keys of the kingdom is this: "When according to the command of Christ it is declared and publicly testified to all and every believer [by the preaching], that, whenever they receive the promise of the gospel by a true faith, all their sins are really forgiven them of God, for the sake of Christ's merits."[**]

All men are by nature born as sinners. (Rom. 3:10). Because of this awful reality, all men stand condemned before the just and holy God, the sovereign of heaven and earth. They have no part in the kingdom of God. Any man who does not repent—no matter who he might be, no matter how great he might imagine himself to be, no matter how popular and honorable he might be before the men of this world—before God he stands condemned. For this reason, he has no place in God's kingdom. When we are living according to the word of God, it matters not what men may say of us. But what does matter, what should be the absolutely most important concern of our lives, is what God says concerning us.

The gospel is God's good news that declares that all those who repent and believe in Christ by a true faith will be saved. They will be saved because their sins are forgiven them through the sacrifice of Jesus Christ on the cross. As long as a person is an impenitent sinner, he stands condemned. He is in danger of being thrown into everlasting hell. The gospel promises that all those who truly believe in Jesus Christ will immediately receive life from God in Jesus Christ. The gospel declares that those who truly believe in Jesus Christ the Son of God, the Savior who sacrificed himself on the cross for the sins of his people, will become heirs of his everlasting and glorious kingdom. This is what it means that the preaching of the gospel is the key power of the kingdom!

The duty of the church through her ministers is to preach the gospel of Christ in all its truth, power, and glory. She may not ever compromise the truth of the gospel. The church may not say something to men that Christ has not said. The church has the solemn obligation through her ministers to be faithful ministers of Christ and official heralds of his truth, bringing nothing but the word of Christ in all its power, beauty, and holiness. The church must declare the truth of God and also the perfect demands of his holy law. Whenever the church preaches the gospel, she must sound forth the serious call to repentance and faith in Jesus Christ. Without repentance, there can be no salvation. But to the penitent sinner, the gospel declares the hope of salvation and the inheritance of the glorious kingdom of Christ.

The preaching of the gospel is the power of the Spirit of God to bring about repentance in the hearts of God's people and to give them hope, assurance, and comfort with regard to their citizenship and blessing in the glorious kingdom of Christ, in spite of the shame, persecution, and suffering they experience in this present world.

Arie den Hartog

---

[*]   Heidelberg Catechism A 84 and 85, in *Confessions and Church Order*, 118–19.
[**] Heidelberg Catechism A 84, in *Confessions and Church Order*, 118.

August 2   Q&A 84 – The Discriminating Power of the Preaching of the Gospel

Read: 2 Thessalonians 1:1–9.

The preaching of the word of Christ must sound a note of warning to those who refuse to turn from their wicked ways. According to the words of the Catechism, the sounding of the word of warning is the exercise of the keys of the kingdom. The Catechism has this to say: "When it is declared and testified to all unbelievers, and to such as do not sincerely repent, that they stand exposed to the wrath of God and eternal condemnation, so long as they are unconverted; according to which testimony of the gospel God will judge them, both in this life and in the life to come."*

It is especially this aspect of the power of the keys of the kingdom that many churches neglect. They teach that God loves all men. They teach that God has a wonderful plan for everyone. Many minimize the seriousness of sin. Recently, there has been a lot of public media attention in the United States on a famous preacher who declares that there is no hell. All men in the end are going to be saved. This he deduces from his false understanding of the love of God for all men. A God who loves all men certainly will not cast the majority of the human race into everlasting hell. According to this preacher, all talk about the future of man is mere speculation. This preacher has a large following, and no wonder. Foolish and sinful men want to expel from their thinking any fear of the judgment of God upon their worldliness, ungodliness, and gross wickedness.

God is indeed a God of mercy and love, according to which he saves his people in spite of their unworthiness and sin. But God is also a God of severe justice. Holiness and righteousness are absolute perfections of God. Because of the holiness of God, he pours out his wrath on the wicked ungodly. He will in the last day judge them by his own standard of perfect righteousness and give them the judgment which they justly deserve.

In fact, the Bible warns in Luke 12 that servants who knew the word of their lord and did not listen and obey it shall be beaten with double punishment (vv. 47–48). The meaning is that those who have heard the preaching of the gospel and the call to repentance and have hardened their hearts to it will have an even more severe judgment than the millions who die without ever hearing the preaching of the gospel.

It is the solemn duty of the church to be very serious about sin. God hates not only those sins of word and deed, but all evil thoughts and desires of men's hearts when they are not repented of. Our modern times are ones of great apostasy. One of the main characteristics of this apostasy is the minimization of sin. Churches that do not warn men about God's judgment on sin are not the ministers of salvation for men, but they are in fact deceivers of men. The blood of the men that they have failed to warn will be on them.

The faithful preacher of the gospel of Christ, in obedience to his word, must sound a clear warning about the seriousness of sin. He must clearly set forth exactly what sin is. He must show how sin is absolutely contrary to the word of God. He must warn of the severe judgment of God that will come on the impenitent. It is a fearful thing to fall into the hands of an angry God. And we who also hear this word of God must repent and turn to Christ in whom alone is deliverance from judgment and salvation.

Arie den Hartog

---

*   Heidelberg Catechism A 84, in *Confessions and Church Order*, 118.

August 3 — Q&A 85 – Christian Discipline

Read: 1 Corinthians 5:1–12.

There are two keys of the kingdom. In our last meditations, I have written about the preaching of the word, which is the first and primary key of the kingdom. The second key is Christian discipline administered by the church. The church must also use this key in obedience to and in honor of Christ. Several of the letters to the seven churches of Asia Minor recorded in the first three chapters of the book of Revelation contain strong warnings to churches who were not dealing with evil persons in their midst through the use of Christian discipline.

Christian discipline is an official work that the church must perform through her elders. It involves admonishing sinners who are members of the church to repent. When, after repeated admonition, those continuing to live in sin do not repent, they must be excommunicated from the Christian church. Excommunication is a public declaration concerning an impenitent sinner that he is no longer a member of the church and that he is barred from the privileges and blessings of church membership, such as partaking of the Lord's supper. When a person who has been disciplined in a biblical way is finally excommunicated, he or she is to be shunned. The members of the church are exhorted not to have any fellowship with that person in the hope that he or she will be ashamed and turn from his or her wicked course of life. Christian discipline is a fearful work. But it has positive purposes. The primary purpose is that the sinner might repent and be saved by the mercy of God. For this, the church must continually pray while the process of discipline is being performed. There is need of discipline in order to maintain the holiness and purity of the church. There must be concern that the name of Christ be not blasphemed by the world when gross public sinners are allowed to continue as members of the church.

Christian discipline must also deal with those who are false teachers in the church. If false teachers are allowed to continue in the church, the truth of Christ will be corrupted, and there is great danger that other members of the church will be led astray from the truth by these false teachers. Paul warned the elders of the church of Ephesus that the time would come, after his departure, that evil men would arise from among the membership of the church. How shocking! Paul calls these "grievous wolves," who do not spare the flock of Jesus Christ whom he purchased with his precious blood. He goes on to say that these evil men will speak "perverse things," and "draw away [many] disciples after them" (Acts 20:28–30).

The elders of the church are exhorted to watch carefully against evil men. These must be identified and publicly admonished. Members of the church are to be warned concerning them. If these evil men do not repent, they must be excluded from the church. Even the ordinary members of the church must be involved in and concerned about the work of discipline. We must submit ourselves to those whom God has appointed in the church as overseers to watch for the spiritual welfare of our souls. If we are disrespectful of the elders, we make their work grievous to them. When the elders admonish us about our sins, we must not be offended but turn from our sins for the saving of our own souls. If we belong to a church that is faithful in the exercise of discipline, we should be thankful to God. Finally, the exercise of discipline is a labor of love, love to bring the sinner to repentance and also love for the honor and glory of the name of the Lord.

Arie den Hartog

August 4 — Q&A 85 — The Biblical Order for Doing Christian Discipline

Read: Matthew 18:15–20.

Because the work of discipline by the church is a very serious matter, the Lord himself has given us a detailed description of how discipline should be done. This order is found in the passage of Matthew 18. Be sure to read this passage carefully before reading this meditation. The order given by the Lord himself is of course characterized by his perfect wisdom. The church should always follow this order carefully. If she does not follow this order, there will often be great confusion in the church. When members of the church bring complaint against other members, they must be told to follow this order.

Offenses that arise between brethren should be dealt with personally. They need not be told to the church. If these offenses can be resolved in a personal way by brother speaking to brother, the result will be the reconciliation of brethren in the Lord. It is a blessed thing when this takes place, even with the involvement of the elders of the church.

Before an accusation against a brother is brought to the church, two witnesses should be sought. The word of one person is hard to believe. When there is only one who accuses another, the matter is often reduced to the word of one brother or sister against another brother or sister, and it is often difficult, if not impossible, to establish the truth.

When the offending person refuses to repent or even acknowledge his or her sin, then it must be told to the church. "Tell it unto the church" in Matthew 18:17 cannot possibly mean to tell it to all in the church, to every member or to a public assembly of the congregation. Discipline is properly the work of God's appointed elders. They are charged with this work, usually endowed with wisdom from the Lord, and best qualified to deal with this difficult work. Over time, a discipline case can become very involved and complicated.

Not every sin committed by church members should be made the object of discipline. We all sin repeatedly and must repent of our sin daily. Everyone must confess his faults to his brother in Christ, and everyone should be ready to forgive the lesser sins, even though these sins are still serious in themselves. Everyone must constantly remember that we are all sinners. Confession and forgiving in the love of Christ covers a multitude of sins in the communion of the saints of the church.

Usually, only gross public sins that create great offences in the church are the object of church discipline. There are two types of such sins. The Catechism speaks of "those who, under the name of Christians maintain doctrines" that are not in harmony with the truth that by God's grace the church must maintain and confess together.[*] Members of the church should be placed under discipline when they are promoting false teachings in the church, and when they are living in gross public sins.

The above being said, it is also really the case that only one sin is the object of discipline. This is the sin of hardened impenitence after having been repeatedly admonished by the church. Even the most dreadful sins are forgiven by the mercy of Christ when they are repented of. And then there is no need to proceed with discipline. If at any point in the process of discipline, the one under discipline makes sincere repentance, the discipline of this person should be lifted. This is announced to the church, and there is great joy in the church because of the repentance and salvation of a sinner.

Arie den Hartog

---

[*] Heidelberg Catechism A 85, in *Confessions and Church Order*, 119.

August 5 — Q&A 85— A Few Additional Comments About Discipline

Read: 2 Thessalonians 3:6–15.

Christian discipline is, and must be, a work of the love of Christ. It is a work of love because its first objective is the restoration of a brother to the church. Christian love must also control the manner and attitude in which the work of discipline is done. The erring brother must be repeatedly admonished in a brotherly way. This can easily be violated. As the exercise of discipline involves admonishing a person about his or her sins, it can become very emotional. Sometimes, rash accusations are thrown back and forth. Sometimes even those appointed to perform this difficult work can grow weary and become impatient. This can lead to harshness and lack of compassion.

Discipline is not a work that can be done in a hasty matter. Those who walk in sin must be repeatedly admonished. All lawful means must be tried to bring the sinner to repentance. The church must be exhorted to pray earnestly to God for the repentance of the sinner and the labors of the elders with such a person. Only when a person shows clearly that his heart is hardened, and he absolutely refuses to listen to the church, does the church proceed to the extreme remedy of excommunication.

On the other hand, the church should not extend discipline beyond a reasonable time frame. Ultimately, the impenitent sinner must not be tolerated in the church; otherwise, great damage will be done to the whole church.

When discipline is performed by the church according to the word of Christ, it has great authority and power. No one should imagine that he can be careless and flippant when, after long careful labors of the representatives of Christ in the church, he has been excommunicated from the church of Jesus Christ. Excommunication means that the impenitent sinner has indeed been excluded from the kingdom of Christ by God himself and is in very serious danger of being cast away from God into hell forever. Simply going to another church in order to escape discipline will not change the matter. When a person has been admonished by the church on the basis of the word of God, and he remains impenitent, he must realize that he will be judged by and punished by the Lord himself. So Jesus told the disciples: "Whatsoever ye shall bind on earth shall be bound in heaven: and whatsoever ye shall loose on earth shall be loosed in heaven" (Matt. 18:18).

After a person has been excommunicated, the members of the church must have no fellowship with that person. When they do meet with that person, they have the solemn duty to call him repeatedly to repentance. If we do not do this, we ourselves become responsible for the sins of the excommunicated person. Even after a person has been properly excommunicated by the church, there must still be earnest prayer made for the repentance and salvation of such a person. And when an excommunicated person returns to the church by the grace of God, he must make confession of his or her sins against God and against the church. When the sinner does sincerely repent, that person should be restored to the church. This occasion should always be one of great joy in the church and thankfulness to God. There is joy among the angels of heaven, before the presence of God, when even one sinner repents.

Pray for the church of which you are a member, that she might be faithful in doing the work of discipline and not be ashamed, knowing that this is the will of Christ.

Arie den Hartog

THE THIRD PART—OF THANKFULNESS

Lord's Day 32

Q. 86. Since then we are delivered from our misery merely of grace, through Christ, without any merit of ours, why must we still do good works?

A. Because Christ, having redeemed and delivered us by his blood, also renews us by his Holy Spirit after his own image; that so we may testify by the whole of our conduct our gratitude to God for his blessings, and that he may be praised by us; also, that every one may be assured in himself of his faith by the fruits thereof; and that by our godly conversation others may be gained to Christ.

Q. 87. Cannot they then be saved, who, continuing in their wicked and ungrateful lives, are not converted to God?

A. By no means; for the Holy Scripture declares that no unchaste person, idolater, adulterer, thief, covetous man, drunkard, slanderer, robber, or any such like, shall inherit the kingdom of God.

August 6 — LD 32 — A Knowledgeable Faith and Gratitude

Read: John 17:3.

The Christian faith is a knowledgeable faith. Christ expressed this truth in John 17:3 when he declared that the purpose of his bestowal of eternal life to us is exactly for true knowledge!

Little wonder then, that Lord's Day 1, question and answer 2 reminds us that true comfort is enjoyed in the way of a triple knowledge—knowing our misery, knowing how we are delivered from all our sins and miseries, and knowing how to show gratitude to God for his salvation of us.*

Lord's Day 32 is the first Lord's Day of the third part of that triple knowledge.

We have learned that the knowledge of our misery is the knowledge of our sin, captured by the term total depravity. Knowing that we are totally depraved, we then know that *all* our salvation comes from God to us through faith in Christ. Against the idea that the Christian faith is simple and has little content, our Reformed fathers rightly maintain that "true faith is…a certain knowledge, whereby I hold for truth all that God has revealed to us in his Word,"** and included an exposition of the historic Apostles' Creed as a summary of the content of faith.

True gratitude is also a knowledgeable gratitude. God himself reveals to us how we are to show thanks to him. Gratitude is expressed by a life of good works arising out of a life of daily conversion (Lord's Days 32–33). It is further expressed by a loving obedience to God's law (Lord's Days 34–44) and engaging in covenant speech with God through prayer (Lord's Days 45–52).

By spelling out these truths, our Catechism helps us to relate to God rightly and properly by steering us clear from sin.

Many do not value precise knowledge in Christianity today. Yet in other spheres of life, we have little use for one who wants to be a surgeon, engineer, or lawyer if he has no desire to have good and precise knowledge in his field of study. Give thanks to God for guiding our Reformed fathers to this precise summary of God's word and pray that we may daily desire to grow in this knowledge of God.

Dennis Lee

---

*   Heidelberg Catechism Q&A2 , in *Confessions and Church Order*, 84.
** Heidelberg Catechism A 21, in *Confessions and Church Order*, 90.

August 7 — **LD 32 – The Place of Good Works in the Christian Life**

Read: Ephesians 2:8–10.

There is not a single religion on the face of this earth that I know of that does not set forth the importance of its followers doing good works.

But when we consider the question, "Where do good works belong in salvation," we get different answers. Virtually all religions teach that good works need to be performed in order to earn or merit salvation. And although the Roman Catholics say they believe in the work of the cross of Christ and grace, they also say that nobody is going to heaven except that he build on top of the work and grace of Christ by his own good works: attending mass, etc. This deadly error of one's good works being partly the ground, cause, or means of obtaining our salvation has now come upon the scene of conservative Presbyterian and Reformed churches in a new way in our day: through the federal vision movement. Its basic error is that it teaches that God's covenant is conditional, that is, in some way dependent on the believer. Accordingly, the believer's justification and salvation are dependent on his own good works.

But how radically different the sound of grace in Scripture is! Twice, and within a short space of two verses, we are reminded that salvation is "not of yourselves: it is the gift of God" and "not of works, lest any man should boast" (Eph. 2:8–9). God knows our sinful nature will want to keep extolling itself if we had a part to play in obtaining our salvation and so added these two negative statements after setting forth the wonderful truth that we are saved only by his wonderful grace!

Where then does God's word and the Reformed faith place good works in the Christian life? Not in the second part of our triple knowledge, but in the third part: gratitude to God following salvation (see Eph. 2:10; Lord's Day 32). For of ourselves and prior to salvation, we are "wholly incapable of doing any good" and "inclined to all wickedness"* (see Rom. 3:10–12; Eph. 2:1–3). Is that your confession, and do you diligently live it out?

Dennis Lee

---

* Heidelberg Catechism Q 8, in *Confessions and Church Order*, 86.

August 8 — LD 32 – What Good Works Are (1)

Read: Romans 14:23; Hebrews 11:6.

Because Lord's Day 32 sets forth the place of good works and the necessity of good works, it is certainly not out of order to spell out what good works are. Although the biblical definition of good works is not set forth in Lord's Day 32, it is set forth in Lord's Day 33, question and answer 91.

Today and over the next few days, we will treat this very important idea of what good works are.

Suppose a terrorist gunman breaks into a house with a mother and her children at home. This gunman threatens to and is now about to gun down the children of the home with his AK-47. The mother pleads with the gunman not to. But the gunman is adamant. He is going to go ahead and finish off her children. Now she flings herself in front of her children to shield them from the shots he fires, protecting them and dying as a result. Is that act of the woman truly a good work? The answer is, it depends. It depends on what? It depends on whether the mother is truly a believer, and whether she does that act in true faith. The reason is because faith in Jesus Christ is one of the very necessary ingredients for a deed done by us to be considered as a good work by God. Romans 14:23 declares plainly that "whatsoever that is not of faith is sin." Hebrews 11:6 is just as comprehensive: "Without faith it is *impossible* to please" God.

Accordingly, we find our Reformed fathers beginning their answer to question 91: "But what are good works?" Answer: "Only those which proceed from a true faith."*

The answer given by the word of God and our Catechism to this question and subject of good works is a very unpopular answer. Do you believe it, and do you work the works of service to God by a true faith from your heart?

Dennis Lee

---

* Heidelberg Catechism Q&A 91, in *Confessions and Church Order*, 122.

| August 9 | LD 32 — What Good Works Are (2) |

Read: 1 Samuel 15:22.

Suppose a man is admitted to the hospital. His daughter, a young Christian lady, finds out from the doctor that her father has only several days to live and will therefore remain in hospital and subsequently be transferred to hospice care, where he will die. In order to give her father peace of mind during his last days of life, she tells the doctor and nurses not to disclose to him his medical condition. She herself tells him that all is well, and that he is being kept at hospital until he regains his health.

Is she doing a good work?

Continuing to understand what good works are, our Reformed fathers inform us that first, they "proceed from a true faith," and second, they "are performed according to the law of God."*

As proof of this second aspect of what good works are, our Reformed fathers point us to the rash sacrifice of King Saul, who disobeyed God and did not wait as God had told him to wait for priest Samuel to perform the sacrifice (1 Sam. 15:22). Saul's sacrifice, done against God's clear instruction, far from being a good work, was displeasing to the Lord.

Accordingly, what the young lady did was not at all a good work! While the world might consider it to be a good work, she lied to her father, and her concern of having her father die with peace of mind was misplaced. The calling of this lady was to bring her father God's word of comfort if he is a Christian, or else to bring him the gospel of repentance and faith in Christ and words of warning in that connection if he isn't.

The world's idea of good works is radically different from what God himself considers to be good works. Often, the argument used by the world is the end justifies the means. So, a white lie leading to a good end is acceptable, even good. What is your response to that?

Dennis Lee

---

* Heidelberg Catechism A 91, in *Confessions and Church Order*, 122.

August 10   LD 32 — What Good Works Are (3)

Read: 1 Corinthians 10:31.

Suppose a wealthy man finds out he is soon going to die. Among the many things he does before his death, he donates most of his estate to charitable organizations. He did so because he wants his name to be remembered.

Does this dying rich man do a good work by giving his estate to the poor?

The answer is no. The dying rich man, in all his giving to charity, does not do a good work. The reason for this is because his motive for all that giving is for his name and glory and not for the glory of God.

And that is the third and final aspect of what constitutes a good work in the sight of God: that work, besides its proceeding from a true faith and its being done according to his law, must have the glory of God as its motive.[*] And for proof of this, we have 1 Corinthians 10:31, "Whether therefore ye eat, or drink, or whatsoever ye do, do all to the glory of God."

We have covered the threefold biblical, Reformed definition of what constitutes a good work. So let us ask ourselves: Are we thankful to God for his salvation? If so, we will show it by a life abounding in good works. The just shall live by faith, and so by faith, let us do good. Let us live according to his word. And let us live for his glory and not ours.

Unbelievers often shame us believers with what have been called glittering bad works. At the same time, the good works that a believer does in his or her calling or station in life may seem trivial and mundane and are even despised by the world (for example, a Christian man who gives a good witness by his quiet, diligent labor; or a covenant mother being a keeper of the home, caring for and nurturing her young children). Keeping in mind the proper understanding of what good works are, let us be undeterred in being faithful to Christ, calling to mind that we are not our own but belong to him. Let us perform what he calls us to do in true faith and for divine glory. It is in this way that we enjoy our one and only comfort in Christ.

Dennis Lee

---

[*] Heidelberg Catechism A 91, in *Confessions and Church Order*, 122.

August 11 — LD 32 – Why Must We Still Do Good Works (1)?

Read: Romans 6:1–2.

When question 86 is worded, "why must we *still* do good works?",[*] understand that our Reformed fathers are answering an objection, a classic, wicked objection raised by the Roman Catholic Church against those who teach salvation by grace. That objection is this: if salvation is entirely by the grace of God, to the exclusion of good works on the part of the believer, then why is there any need for, why must we *still* do good works?

But that objection is not originally with the Roman Catholics. The apostle Paul encountered that objection from the enemies in his day of the same gospel of grace which he preached and which we share with him. How does the inspired apostle answer that objection? The answer is found in Romans 6:1–2, "What shall we say then? Shall we continue in sin, that grace may abound? God forbid. How shall we, that are dead to sin, live any longer therein?"

Question and answer 87 only affirms the answer of Romans 6:1–2, for it declares plainly that one who does not do good works, but on the other hand abides in evil works, cannot possibly have been saved by God (see 1 Cor. 6:9–10).

Why then, positively, must we still do good works?

The main reason is that good works are the purpose of God's salvation (Eph. 2:10). Christ "redeemed and delivered us by his blood."[**] That means that Jesus Christ has rescued us out of the bondage and prison of sin. But he does not stop there. The Catechism says that he also "renews us by his Holy Spirit after his own image; so that we may testify by the whole of our conduct our gratitude to God for his blessings."[***] This means that Christ continues to cause us to live in him after he rescues us out of prison.

The bottom line is, he freed us from sin not for us to live in sin again, but for us to abound in good works! By abounding in good works, we show gratitude to God. This is the purpose of God's salvation of us in and through Jesus Christ.

Good works are the purpose of God in our salvation. Are good works personally purposed by you this day in your life?

Dennis Lee

---

[*] Heidelberg Catechism Q 86, in *Confessions and Church Order*, 120 (emphasis added).
[**] Heidelberg Catechism A 86, in *Confessions and Church Order*, 120.
[***] Heidelberg Catechism A 86, in *Confessions and Church Order*, 120.

August 12 — **LD 32 — Why Must We Still Do Good Works (2)?**

Read: Matthew 5:16.

Why must we *still* do good works? The Catechism reminds us that we, whose only comfort is that we belong to our faithful Savior Jesus Christ and who hold to God's glorious gospel of grace, have many, many reasons to do good works after experiencing God's salvation in our lives.

First, by doing good works, God is praised by us. For our good works are the works of God to begin with. Philippians 2:12–13, Ephesians 2:10, and Matthew 5:16 remind us of this. God is praised and glorified when we do good works because those works come from the God of those people who perform them.

Second, by doing good works, others are gained to Christ. That also is the thought of Matthew 5:16. Our Reformed fathers also cite 1 Peter 3:1–2 on this point, and there we are reminded that believing wives are called to submit themselves also to their unbelieving husbands, one reason being that "they also may without the word be won by the conversation of the wives; while they behold your chaste conversation coupled with fear."

Third, by doing good works we are assured of our own faith. The Catechism says that good works are "the fruits thereof [of faith]."* In John 15, where Jesus speaks of himself as the vine and all those joined to him by faith as the branches, he says in verse 8: "Herein is my Father glorified, that ye bear much fruit; so shall ye be my disciples." Now, if we don't do good works, then we have no faith. And if we continue not to do any good works, then we are most certainly not going to heaven (1 Cor. 6:9–10). Good works do not, in any way, earn our way into heaven. But God's people do not live this kind of unthankful life. Theirs are lives of good works! When we see our good works, we know that God is working in us; we know that we are disciples of Christ.

We have many reasons to do good works. Let us abound in them and in that way abound in showing thanks to the God of our salvation.

Dennis Lee

---

* Heidelberg Catechism A 86, in *Confessions and Church Order*, 120.

Lord's Day 33

Q. 88. Of how many parts doth the true conversion of man consist?

A. Of two parts: of the mortification of the old, and the quickening of the new man.

Q. 89. What is the mortification of the old man?

A. It is a sincere sorrow of heart that we have provoked God by our sins, and more and more to hate and flee from them.

Q. 90. What is the quickening of the new man?

A. It is a sincere joy of heart in God, through Christ, and with love and delight to live according to the will of God in all good works.

Q. 91. But what are good works?

A. Only those which proceed from a true faith, are performed according to the law of God, and to his glory; and not such as are founded on our imaginations or the institutions of men.

August 13   **LD 33 — The Idea of Conversion**

Read: Isaiah 6:10; Isaiah 59:20.

To convert is to turn. Conversion involves a turning *from* something *to* something else. It refers to a change of disposition. Basically, we turn from sin ("more and more to hate and flee from them"*) to a life of gratitude unto God ("live according to the will of God in all good works"**).

The word and idea of conversion is found in the New Testament (see Luke 1:16-17) and Old Testament.

First, consider Isaiah 6:10. Here, God makes it clear that he has more than one purpose to the gospel that he calls prophet Isaiah to preach to Old Testament Israel. It is not just to comfort, save, and convert his people, but it is also to harden the hearts of the reprobate wicked, to blind them. Contrary to those who teach that God sincerely desires the salvation of all (the well-meant gospel offer), according to this word of God, it is God's desire and purpose that a certain group of people *not* be saved but rather be hardened through the good word brought by his servant Isaiah.

Second, consider Isaiah 59:20. This verse makes clear exactly unto whom the redeemer, Jesus Christ, comes in Zion. Because not all Israel is Israel (Rom. 9:6–8), he redeemed not everyone at the cross and comes not to everyone. But he comes "unto them that turn from transgression in Jacob" (Isa. 59:20), that is, he comes unto them who are converted by him.

Marvel that God chose to convert you, a hell-deserving sinner, from your sins. But don't stop there. Do you daily flee and turn from your sins, and turn unto God by the power of Christ's cross (see Rom. 7:18–25)? Because our old man will be with us till the day we die, we need daily and constantly to mortify him and be quickened unto love, joy, and obedience in the Lord to do his word and will. We need to be converted daily.

Dennis Lee

---

*   Heidelberg Catechism A 89, in *Confessions and Church Order*, 121.
**   Heidelberg Catechism A 90, in *Confessions and Church Order*, 122.

August 14 — **LD 33 — The Character of True Conversion**

Read: Luke 1:16–17.

We consider the character of true conversion today. True conversion is something radical. It takes place right in the core of our being. It is something that is *of the heart*. It is a *turning* that is from deep within our soul.

It is not something skin-deep. It does not only say, I am sorry. And we know, from the tone of those words, when someone is not truly sorry, don't we? Still more, true conversion is not something that changes and turns around on something only because of the consequences or results that will happen if we don't. For example, medical documentaries may tell us about the harmful results of taking drugs. But true conversion working in us does not only make us stay away from drugs because of that. We do so because our bodies are temples of the Holy Spirit.

God reveals in his word the true and deep nature of true conversion—he works his work of conversion in our hearts. Besides Luke 1:16–17, in Colossians 3:15, we read: "And let the peace of God rule in your hearts, to the which also ye are called in one body; and be ye thankful." We are called unto salvation and called into the body of Christ by a wondrous and radical change. Peter reminds us in 1 Peter 2:9 that we are called "out of darkness into his marvellous light." We are graciously given a new, radically different identity in Jesus Christ by this calling: we are "a chosen generation, a royal priesthood, an holy nation, a peculiar people."

True conversion, being a work of God, is radical and deep. But it has to take place constantly in us, so that we "more and more…hate and flee from"* our sins and turn to God. We need to daily "work out [our] own salvation with fear and trembling. For it is God which worketh in [us] both to will and to do of his good pleasure" (Phil. 2:12–13).

Dennis Lee

---

* Heidelberg Catechism A 89, in *Confessions and Church Order*, 121.

August 15 — **LD 33 — The Power of True Conversion**

Read: Acts 26:18.

Consider these beautiful words that describe not only the radical character but also the power of true conversion: "From darkness to light…from the power of Satan unto God" (Acts 26:18). As Paul himself experienced this power of conversion, he was now going to be used by Jesus to work mighty conversion in the hearts and lives of God's elect.

First, true conversion takes us away from the darkness and power of Satan. What was darkness like in the life of Paul prior to true conversion? He tells us: "I verily thought with myself, that I ought to do many things contrary to the name of Jesus of Nazareth" (Acts 26:9). How Paul hated and persecuted Christians!

What can we say about this power of darkness? It is a power that makes us fulfill the lusts of our flesh and of the mind. It is a power that makes us by nature the children of wrath and disobedience, and in that disobedience, dead in sin (Eph. 2:1–3). From that power, Paul was converted unto light and life with God.

Light is the complete contrast to darkness, so that if one lives contrary to the name of Jesus in darkness, one does not live in obedience, submission, and service to the name of Jesus in light. In Jesus is found light and life with God (John 8:12). Just as earthly light from the sun gives earthly life to plants and animals, so also spiritual light from Jesus Christ gives life to God's people. Light also dispels darkness, and by it gives us sight and direction in life. It is none other than the word of God that is a light to our feet, guiding us on the path of life.

This life that we have been given is a holy life of communion and friendship with God by his word and Spirit. Because it is driven by the almighty power of God it is an indestructible life, so that nothing shall be able to separate us from the love of Christ (Rom. 8:35–39). Praise God from whom all blessings flow!

Dennis Lee

August 16 — LD 33 – True Conversion Distinguished

Read: Philippians 2:12–13.

The reason why true conversion is radical, powerful, and breaks with sin is because it is God's work. It is a wonderful work of God!

Yet we must take care in distinguishing it from other wonderful works of God in our salvation. True conversion is not the work of redemption performed by Jesus Christ. That work took place at the cross some two thousand years ago. Redemption took place once and for all at the cross—outside of us. Redemption was the once-for-all payment of the purchase price for all our sins and for all other benefits of God's salvation. And neither is true conversion regeneration, a work which, like true conversion, takes place inside of us. How do we distinguish the two?

First, true conversion follows from regeneration. God first puts the seed of new life inside of us—that's regeneration. Then comes conversion as a result of that new life in us, translating us from darkness to light, from the power of Satan to God.

Second, in regeneration we are passive, but in conversion we are active (Phil. 2:12–13). Just as we have nothing to do with our physical birth (we are passive at the time of our birth), so also we have nothing to do with our spiritual birth (we are passive in our being born again). But in the work of conversion which God works, we are active. We consciously reject the way of sin and darkness, and we consciously turn to light and life with God.

Third and finally, regeneration is a one-time thing, but conversion is a lifelong process. We are born once but converted many times thereafter.

Take time to consider all the wonderful works that God performs in order to save us from our sins. Especially consider that it cost God nothing less than the suffering and death of his beloved, only begotten Son, so that all these works might be applied to us. Give thanks to God for your salvation so rich, full and free!

Dennis Lee

August 17 — **LD 33 — An Example of True Conversion**

Read: 1 Peter 5:1–2.

The doctrine of true conversion becomes real to us when we consider the example of Peter. As a result of his great confidence in himself, Peter experienced a terrible fall, but he was reinstated by Jesus, showing to us later on in his life his true conversion from his proud confidence in his flesh to humility and dependence upon God.

Peter's fall is well known to us. Peter denied his Lord three times, as Jesus said he would. But we know that Peter repented from his sin because Jesus reinstated him before his ascension into heaven, telling Peter three times to show his love for him by feeding his flock (John 21:15–17).

We also know that Peter experienced true conversion in other ways. First, whereas he denied Jesus at Gethsemane, Peter preached Christ crucified boldly in Acts 2. Second, so dearly did he hold to the words of his Lord when he was reinstated that he admonished the elders of the scattered churches in 1 Peter 5:1–2, "Feed the flock of God"! Third, our Canons affirm Peter's true conversion by pointing out Peter's "lamentable fall" in the best of all places: the fifth head of doctrine, "The Perseverance of the Saints," article 4—reminding us of God's work of grace in causing Peter to be recovered spiritually, to be truly converted, to persevere unto the end of his salvation.[*]

Those who are truly converted can fall into grievous sin. If Peter could, if David—described to be "a man after [God's] own heart" (Acts 13:22)—could, then we can. Calvinists, who confess the P of TULIP, understand that they can fall into grievous sin. Do you? And do you therefore take great care daily to mortify your old man (Col. 3:5)? And what if we fall into a lamentable state of sin? Don't deny it, don't hide it, don't wait for time to pass by! Repent and live! Be converted and healed!

Dennis Lee

---

[*] Canons 5.4, in *Confessions and Church Order*, 174.

August 18   **Q&A 88-89 — What True Conversion Consists Of**

Read: Colossians 3:5, 8, 12.

True conversion consists "of two parts: the mortification of the old, and the quickening of the new man."* That means that the Christian life is one of constant struggle between the new man and the old man. It implies, therefore, that the Christian will never be perfect in holiness and obedience before God in this life. Those who teach that we can achieve perfection in this life are wrong. The Christian life is a constant struggle as a result of the existence of the old nature of sin in him, and there is a constant need to mortify him.

Answer 88 of this Lord's Day maintains that both natures will be there in the believer. In doing so, it gives an understanding of conversion that is thoroughly biblical (see Col. 3:5, 8, 12).

Questions and answers 89 and 90 point out the two godly affections of true conversion: the "sincere sorrow of heart" on account of our sins against God, associated with the mortifying of the old man, as well as the "sincere joy of heart in God" when living in holiness associated with the quickening of the new man.

We conclude today's devotion on the note of the joy of true conversion. This, like "godly sorrow" (2 Cor. 7:10), is a thoroughly biblical idea. For Paul, when he speaks of the quickening of the new man in Colossians 3:12, brings up love in verse 14 and peace in verse 15. Where there is true love and peace, there is also true joy!

True joy is a vital ingredient to the Christian life. In the midst of trials and afflictions that we experience, let us not forget that we are abundantly blessed by God and experience the great riches and comfort of his word and gospel. "Rejoice in the Lord alway: and again, I say, Rejoice" (Phil. 4:4). For we are "more than conquerors through him that loved us" (Rom. 8:37).

Dennis Lee

---

*   Heidelberg Catechism A 88, in *Confessions and Church Order*, 121.

August 19 — Q&A 90-91 — What True Conversion Produces

Read: Colossians 3:18–22.

True conversion will produce a life of good works. And good works, as you will recall, were explained in last week's meditations. Recall briefly that, firstly, they proceed from a true faith; secondly, they are done according to the law of God; thirdly and finally, they are done with the motive of glorifying God.

The life of true conversion is such that the true convert abounds in good works not only in some areas of his or her life (areas which he or she might find it easier to do good works in for whatever reason), but in every area of life.

Colossians 3:18–25 concludes with a series of good works in the area of married life (for both husband and wife), family life, and also our life at work. Peter tells us in 1 Peter 2:11–25 very much the same thing—how we should abound in good works in our relationships with all kinds of people around us. Would you say that you live a zealous life abounding in good works?

People who are truly converted are thankful to God for his wondrous salvation of them and will always show that thankfulness to him with a life of good works. This is true for all of God's people. Yes, even for those of us who have experienced grievous falls in our lives and have been brought back by him and restored unto a living fellowship with him. May Peter's fall and then his recovery by the Lord in the way of true conversion encourage us to live fervently the life of true conversion and to abound in good works!

Let good works abound in all areas of our lives. Let us do good works at home, at work, at school, and with one another in church, with a heart and mind ready to serve, to forgive, to receive, and ready for active and committed service unto the Lord.

Dennis Lee

Lord's Day 34

Q. 92. What is the law of God?

A. God spake all these words, Exodus 20, Deuteronomy 5, saying:

I am the Lord thy God, which hath brought thee out of the land of Egypt, out of the house of bondage.

1. *Thou shalt have no other gods before me.*
2. *Thou shalt not make unto thee any graven image, or any likeness of any thing that is in heaven above, or that is in the earth beneath, or that is in the water under the earth: thou shalt not bow down thyself to them, nor serve them: for I the Lord thy God, am a jealous God, visiting the iniquity of the fathers upon the children unto the third and fourth generation of them that hate me; and showing mercy unto thousands of them that love me, and keep my commandments.*
3. *Thou shalt not take the name of the Lord thy God in vain: for the Lord will not hold him guiltless that taketh his name in vain.*
4. *Remember the sabbath day, to keep it holy. Six days shalt thou labor, and do all thy work: but the seventh day is the sabbath of the Lord thy God: in it thou shalt not do any, thou, nor thy son, nor thy daughter, thy manservant, nor thy maidservant, nor thy cattle, nor thy stranger that is within thy gates: for in six days the Lord made heaven and earth, the sea, and all that in them is, and rested the seventh day: wherefore the Lord blessed the sabbath day, and hallowed it.*
5. *Honor thy father and thy mother: that thy days may be long upon the land which the Lord thy God giveth thee.*
6. *Thou shalt not kill.*
7. *Thou shalt not commit adultery.*
8. *Thou shalt not steal.*
9. *Thou shalt not bear false witness against thy neighbor.*
10. *Thou shalt not covet thy neighbor's house, thou shalt not covet thy neighbor's wife, nor his manservant, nor his maid-servant, nor his ox, nor his ass, nor any thing that is thy neighbor's.*

Q. 93. How are these commandments divided?

A. Into two tables: the first of which teaches us how we must behave towards God; the second, what duties we owe to our neighbor.

Q. 94. What doth God enjoin in the first commandment?

A. That I, as sincerely as I desire the salvation of my own soul, avoid and flee from all idolatry, sorcery, soothsaying, superstition, invocation of saints, or any other creatures; and learn rightly to know the only true God; trust in him alone, with humility and patience submit to him; expect all good things from him only; love, fear, and glorify him with my whole heart; so that I renounce and forsake all creatures, rather than commit even the least thing contrary to his will.

Q. 95. What is idolatry?

A. Idolatry is, instead of, or besides that one true God who has manifested himself in his Word, to contrive or have any other object in which men place their trust.

August 20 — Q&A 92 – The Law of God

Read: Exodus 20:1–17.

How do we express gratitude to God for salvation from sin? Lord's Day 34 gives part of the answer to that important question. The first section of the Catechism showed our great need for salvation, explaining that by nature we are incapable of obeying God's law and are on the path to eternal destruction. The second part of the Catechism taught that we are delivered through faith by Christ, who made satisfaction for our sins and purifies us within by his Spirit. Now we are in the third section of the Catechism, which reveals how to live in thankfulness to God for this great salvation; and that is by doing good works. Those good works include prayer (Lord's Days 45–52) and obedience to God's law (Lord's Days 34–44).

The Catechism teaches that obedience is the way we express gratitude to God for salvation based on Scripture passages like Exodus 20. That chapter begins with God saying: "I am the Lord thy God, which have brought thee out of the land of Egypt, out of the house of bondage" (v. 1). Then God's ten commandments follow. Jehovah did not give Israel these commands before he delivered them from Egypt with the goal that they would earn deliverance by their obedience. Instead, the idea expressed at the beginning of Exodus 20 is this: "I am the Lord who saved you! Now here are my commandments that teach you how to live as my saved people. Keep them in thankfulness to me."

Israel's deliverance out of Egypt is a type of our salvation from slavery to sin. In the law, God is saying to us today, I am the Lord thy God, which hath delivered you from sin. Now obey my commands in gratitude. So the law is not given to us either to show us what things we must do to save ourselves. Instead, it shows us our sins as the first part of the Catechism explains, reveals our need for Christ, and tells us how to live in gratitude for salvation. We do not obey to be saved but are saved to obey.

Are you thankful for Christ's deliverance of you? You show that by following God's commandments. That is what Christians do by Christ's gracious work in their hearts.

Matt De Boer

August 21 — Q&A 93 – The Completeness of the Law

Read: Psalm 19:7–14.

The law of God is divided into two parts, according to question and answer 93. The first table, which is the first four commandments, reveals how we must act in relation to God. The second table, which is the last six commandments, shows how we must live towards our neighbor.

The implication of answer 93 is that the law of God is perfect, or complete. The number ten, the number of completeness in Scripture, further emphasizes this. In ten simple, basic commandments, the law of God shows what kind of life pleases him. There are many other commandments in Scripture, but all the other commandments fit under these ten commandments. These ten commandments are even a summary of everything else that comes later in the law given to Moses, the civil and ceremonial laws. The ten commandments show us how to live to God's glory in every area of life, including in how we worship, how we treat those in authority, how we work, and how we relate to our spouses and neighbors.

Not only does the law of God then show us how to live in thankfulness, but the law is also something for which we believers are thankful. Sometimes, we want to please people we love, but we do not know what will please them. God gives us his law, his complete will, showing us exactly how to please him each day. This is why believers saved in Christ "love…the law" (Ps. 119:97) and why we want the law to be read every Sunday in church.

God's law is precious. Thank him for it today!

Matt De Boer

August 22 — Q&A 94 — The Only God

Read: Isaiah 44.

Lying behind the first commandment, "Thou shalt have no other gods before me" (Ex. 20:3), is the truth that Jehovah is the only God.

The name *God* in the original language, Hebrew, most likely stems from a verb that means to be strong or mighty. The one who is God is strong of himself. He has controlling power over all things in heaven and on earth. Since the one who is God has power over everything, including men, he is deserving of worship.

In Scripture, Jehovah teaches that he is God alone. Isaiah 44:6 states: "Thus saith the Lord the King of Israel, and his redeemer the Lord of hosts; I am the first, and I am the last; and beside me there is no God."

Jehovah further indicates that he alone is mighty God with his descriptions of himself in Isaiah 44. In verse 24, he says: "I am the Lord that maketh all things; that stretcheth forth the heavens alone; that spreadeth abroad the earth by myself." If you look outside today, you may see the sun. Jehovah made it! Consider your bodies, the many muscles, bones, your brain, and nerves, and how it all works together so you can move. Jehovah is the almighty one who made your body and all things.

God indicates in Isaiah 44:28 that he is also the sovereign ruler of all he made, saying he is the one "that saith of Cyrus, He is my shepherd, and shall perform all my pleasure." Jehovah governs even the great political rulers so that they do his will.

Isaiah 44 shows that God is also the mighty judge of all men. In verse 11, the Lord speaks about idol worshippers, saying: "Behold, all his fellows shall be ashamed: and the workmen, they are of men: let them all be gathered together, let them stand up; yet they shall fear, and they shall be ashamed together." Jehovah saw the people's sins, and he had power to bring them to shame.

He is the great judge, but verse 6 reveals that he is also the powerful savior: he is "the Lord the King of Israel, and [the] redeemer the Lord of hosts." The one who is creator, ruler, judge, and savior is the mighty God, and that is Jehovah alone.

Let us meditate on God's almighty power today and humble ourselves before him.

Matt De Boer

August 23 — Q&A 94-95 – The Worship of Idols

Read: Psalm 115.

John Calvin wrote, "The human mind is, so to speak, a perpetual forge of idols."[*] Since every man has a sinful nature, men worship idols instead of the one true God.

Question and answer 95 describes idolatry as placing your trust in any other object besides Jehovah. Trusting in something is a major part of worship, but only part. Most basically, to worship idols is to place anything above Jehovah. An idol is anything that matters to you more than the Lord and his praise.

Psalm 115 references the kind of idolatry that is most prevalent today, and that is the idolatry of self. Verse 1 says: "Not unto us, O Lord, not unto us, but unto thy name give glory, for thy mercy, and for thy truth's sake." The Israelites were tempted to seek victory over their enemies so that people glorified them, ascribing value to them instead of Jehovah. Today, we might seek to get videos of fun or great things we do and then work to attach the right caption on social media so we get "likes," our popularity grows, and we are glorified. Or we might work hard at our jobs, at school, or in a sport, so that others praise us with their words. With our actions and in our hearts, we sometimes say, Not to you, Lord, but unto *my* name give glory. In addition to seeking glory for ourselves, it is easy to trust in ourselves. We can trust in ourselves for life, thinking, I am going to keep myself healthy with this diet and by being active. We think all about what we can do for our health and say nothing, or very little, to God.

Related to the worship of self is the worship of other men and of material things. We can so easily fall into the fear of man. We worry about how they view us, and we do all we can to get their approval. We can become so concerned about what others think of us, and how to fit in, that other people become our idols, and we even do wrong things to try to please them. Material things can become much too important to us as well. It can happen that our motivation to work each day is not to obtain gifts that we can use to serve God's kingdom, but to procure more things for ourselves. We can start wanting things of the earth so badly that we work and work at the expense of truly teaching our children God's word, truly helping at church, and truly resting on the Sabbath.

Do you have idols in your life now? If so, what are they? Let us repent.

Matt De Boer

---

[*] John Calvin, *Institutes of the Christian Religion*, trans. Henry Beveridge (Peabody, MA: Hendrickson, 2008), 1.11.8, 55.

August 24 — Q&A 94 – Fleeing Foolish Idolatry

Read: Isaiah 46.

Are you running from idolatry? God demands that we do so "as sincerely as [we] desire the salvation of [our] own [souls]."*

When giving this command in Scripture, God often shows how foolish idolatry is. He does so throughout the book of Isaiah, including in Isaiah 46.

In Isaiah 46:1–2, Jehovah teaches that the gods of other nations cannot carry their people to safety, but these idols are actually carried away captive by enemies: "Bel boweth down, Nebo stoopeth, their idols were upon the beasts, and upon the cattle: your carriages were heavy loaden; they are a burden to the weary beast. They stoop, they bow down together; they could not deliver the burden, but themselves are gone into captivity." Instead of these Babylonian idols helping the Babylonians, these idols would be carried away as luggage by the Medes and Persians. God is basically saying here: "Why would anyone worship something that can be captured and carried away as baggage instead of me, one who carries his people and cares for them? Idolatry is foolish!"

Then, in verses 6–7, God shows that idols cannot create anything and are powerless to save:

6. They lavish gold out of the bag, and weigh silver in the balance, and hire a goldsmith; and he maketh it a god: they fall down, yea, they worship.
7. They bear him upon the shoulder, they carry him, and set him in his place, and he standeth; from his place shall he not remove: yea, one shall cry unto him, yet can he not answer, nor save him out of his trouble.

God is asking: "Why would you worship something that you make yourself and who cannot help you instead of me, who sets kings in their places and hears the cries of his people?"

Idolatry today is just as ridiculous. Missionaries have stories about idol worship in the countries where they serve. When a natural disaster strikes, the families grab their idols, little statues, off the shelves to try to save them from destruction. Their god should be helping them, but instead they try to save their god. Foolish! But it is just as ridiculous to trust in yourself or in other men as we sometimes do. Men are creatures made by God. Neither you nor any other man can save people from sin and the consequences for it. No man can send the rain for the crops, and no man can make medicine heal your body. The only power that you or any man has is from God, who created all things and rules all things.

Pray for strength to flee foolish idolatry today.

Matt De Boer

---

* Heidelberg Catechism A 94, in *Confessions and Church Order*, 124.

August 25 — Q&A 94 — The Worship of God Alone

Read: Deuteronomy 6:1–15.

When God says in the first commandment, "Thou shalt have no other gods before me," the implication is that we must worship Jehovah alone. Not merely sometimes, or only on Sundays, but we must do this every day, just as we must obey all the other commandments every day.

But what does it mean to worship God alone? Question and answer 94 explains.

First, worshipping God is to know him rightly. This means that we understand rightly who he is as creator, ruler, judge, and savior, but even more, we know him personally and experientially. We know he is our God for Jesus' sake, who cares for us. We have a personal relationship with him, hearing what he says to us in his word and speaking back to him in prayer and song. Knowing the truth about God and engaging in this personal relationship with him is worship.

Second, worshipping God is to "trust in him alone." This means that we lean not on our own understanding, but we look to God's word for guidance. We rely on him to provide all we need physically and spiritually, expecting "all good things from him only."*

Third, worshipping God is to submit to him "with humility and patience."** This involves bowing before his rule even during hardships and trials. We trust that our Father knows best and say along with Job: "The LORD gave, and the LORD hath taken away; blessed be the name of the LORD" (Job 1:21).

Fourth, to worship God is to love him (Deut. 6:4–5). Loving God means we delight in him so much that we seek his glory and fellowship. What we want in our hearts, souls, and minds is to be near him, serving him. We must be consumed with God!

Fifth, to worship God is to fear him (Deut. 6:13). Fearing God is standing in awe of him, of his holiness, power, love, mercy, and grace, with the result that we live in the constant awareness of him and obey him.

Last, worshipping God according to answer 94 means that we glorify him. We ascribe worth to him, giving him recognition in what we say, do, and accomplish.

Let us pray today that God would make us concerned with bringing recognition to him and not ourselves.

Matt De Boer

---

* Heidelberg Catechism A 94, in *Confessions and Church Order*, 124.
** Heidelberg Catechism A 94, in *Confessions and Church Order*, 124.

August 26 — Q&A 94 — The Only Savior

Read: Exodus 34:1–17.

While examining this first commandment, have you seen your failure to worship God perfectly as the perfect God demands? By God's grace, you have. The answer to our problem of sin is God alone.

The first commandment itself implies that Jehovah is the only one who can deliver anyone from sin and the penalty for it. He is the only God. He is the only one powerful enough to save from sin, the devil, and corruption.

The gospel truth is that God sent his only begotten Son to pay for all the idolatry and sin his people have ever committed. The gospel truth is that Jesus now works in his people to put away idolatry and worship him.

Our calling is to trust in Christ for deliverance. Those who look to him alone are forgiven and are being cleansed within. This is why the Catechism says I must flee idolatry "as sincerely as I desire the salvation of my own soul."* Those who continue in idolatry are not placing their trust in Jesus alone. They have no salvation from sin and death.

Do you trust in Jesus alone for salvation? Or do you trust in yourself, thinking you have salvation because you mostly try to do the right thing and have always gone to church? Let us trust in Jesus, the sacrificial lamb, for our acceptance with God. Today, pray to God the words of Moses after Israel fell into idolatry: "Pardon our iniquity and our sin, and take us for thine inheritance" (Ex. 34:9).

Matt De Boer

---

* Heidelberg Catechism A 94, in *Confessions and Church Order*, 124.

Lord's Day 35

Q. 96. What doth God require in the second commandment?

A. That we in no wise represent God by images, nor worship him in any other way than he has commanded in his Word.

Q. 97. Are images then not at all to be made?

A. God neither can nor may be represented by any means. But as to creatures, though they may be represented, yet God forbids to make or have any resemblance of them either in order to worship them or to serve God by them.

Q. 98. But may not images be tolerated in the churches as books to the laity?

A. No; for we must not pretend to be wiser than God, who will have his people taught, not by dumb images, but by the lively preaching of his Word.

August 27 — LD 35 — God's Forbidding of Images

Read: Exodus 32:1–19.

Maybe when you hear the law read you cannot tell much of a difference between the first and second commandments, but there is one. The first commandment concerns whom we are to worship. The second commandment states how we are to worship.

Exodus 20:4–5 teaches that we may not bow down to or serve an image of anything "in heaven above" or "in the earth beneath." With this commandment, God is not forbidding the making of images altogether. It is not necessarily wrong, for instance, to depict a lion. The idea is that we may not make an image in order to worship and serve that image. Additionally, concerning what is being prohibited here, since the first commandment already forbade making an image of a creature for the purpose of worshipping it, the emphasis of the second commandment is that we may not make an image and use it for the worship of God.

Part of the reason this command is in the negative is that worshipping God with images is something into which men easily fall, and so we must be warned. Proud man always wants to bring God to his level, to a position where God can be seen, touched, and fully understood with the mind. By nature, men want to decide who God is and what he is like.

It is a temptation to attempt to worship God using images, and Israel fell into this temptation according to Exodus 32. They had heard God's voice thundering from the mountain and had seen the mountain covered in smoke and quaking. God showed himself to be glorious. Israel responded by trying to bring God down to their level. They made an image of a calf and said it was Jehovah.

Making images of Jehovah is something into which the Roman Catholic Church has also fallen. They have images of Jesus, who is God in the flesh, arguing that we need these pictures to teach people about him. Men need to be able to visualize God and Christ.

It is a temptation for the rest of the church world today, including us, to do something similar. Some, for instance, think, It is too hard to listen to God's word preached. Our attention spans are short. We need something better, especially for kids, that will help them understand. Thus, there is a demand for less preaching in the worship service and more skits that depict what Christ did on this earth.

However, answer 98 says: "We must not pretend to be wiser than God, who will have his people taught, not by dumb images, but by the lively preaching of his Word."* The perfectly wise God knows best how his people are to learn about him. Let us submit to him!

Matt De Boer

---

* Heidelberg Catechism A 98 in *Confessions and Church Order*, 126.

August 28 — LD 35 — God is a Spirit

Read: John 4:1–26.

God forbids that we worship him using images because he is a spirit. John 4:24 says: "God is a Spirit: and they that worship him must worship him in spirit and in truth." You and I have physical bodies and can be seen. That God is a spirit means that God does not have a physical body. He cannot be seen.

One who makes an image of God is trying to make a physical likeness or depiction of him. However, Jehovah cannot be viewed and has not been viewed, so an image of him cannot be made and used for worship. That image would be inaccurate.

That God is a spirit means that we may not worship him using images, and it indicates that we must worship him in a spiritual manner. To worship God "in spirit," as we are commanded in John 4:24, is to worship him from the heart. We must do this in our everyday worship but also in our worship in the official services on the Lord's day, which is what the second commandment is especially addressing.

Are you worshipping God from the heart? It is easy for us not to. It can happen that we go to church, but we do not know what we are singing, praying, reading in the Scripture, or what is being preached, because our minds are somewhere else, or we are dozing off.

We must ask ourselves often: "Where is my heart during the worship services, and where are my children's hearts?" Let us be fully engaged and praise our great God and Savior joyfully from the heart.

Matt De Boer

August 29 — **LD 35 — God is Glorious**

Read: Isaiah 40:12–31.

An image of God may not be used in worship because God is a spirit and because God is glorious.

God's glory is the sum total of his attributes shining forth. He is eternal, everywhere present, all-powerful, all-knowing, holy, righteous, loving, gracious, and merciful. God and his glory are described in Isaiah 40:12, "Who hath measured the waters in the hollow of his hand, and meted out heaven with the span, and comprehended the dust of the earth in a measure, and weighed the mountains in scales, and the hills in a balance?" God is the omnipresent one that powerfully controls the entire earth and all the molecules of water and knows everything about them. Verse 13 says: "Who hath directed the Spirit of the Lord, or being his counsellor hath taught him?" *Directed* means *measured*. No man can measure God in any way, for he is infinite and beyond our full comprehension. Verse 17 continues: "All nations before him are as nothing"! Jehovah is mightier than the United States, Russia, and China combined. Verse 22 says that he "sitteth upon the circle of the earth, and the inhabitants thereof are as grasshoppers."

As Isaiah speaks of God's glory and majesty, he says in verse 18: "To whom then will ye liken God? or what likeness will ye compare unto him?" The idea is that we cannot make a likeness of him. It would not be great enough and would dishonor him. We can make an image of a human greater than what that human is, causing him to look stronger or more handsome. But whatever image is made of God will be infinitely less than what God is. The holy, eternal, and almighty creator and ruler of all is too glorious to be depicted.

Since Jehovah is so glorious, he has the right to determine exactly how he will be worshipped. Certainly, no creature has the right to decide. Let us stand in awe of him and follow his way.

Matt De Boer

August 30 — LD 35 — God is Jealous

Read: Deuteronomy 4:1–24.

We may not worship God using images because he is a spirit, he is glorious, and he is a jealous God. The second commandment says: "Thou shalt not bow down thyself to them, nor serve them: for I the Lord thy God am a jealous God" (Ex. 20:5).

Jealousy is not always sinful. It is sinful when we are jealous of someone who gets to go on a trip or who has a skill we do not. That is envy and covetousness. But jealousy is sometimes spoken of in a different way than envy or covetousness. The proper form of jealousy is guarding that which rightly belongs to you. For example, it is not wrong for a husband to be jealous over his wife's love. Her love rightly belongs to him. He does not share her with another.

God is properly jealous over his own honor. He guards his honor as something that rightly belongs to him. He will not tolerate it being given to another. This also applies to us. We are Jehovah's bride, whom he has purchased in Jesus Christ. He is jealous over our love and honor of him. If we worship him using an image, we take away from the honor and love that rightly belongs to him. We give it to something that is supposedly him but is not him. He hates this!

As believers who have been made Christ's bride, we ought to be jealous for his honor and worship as he commands.

Matt De Boer

August 31 — LD 35 — The Regulative Principle

Read: Nehemiah 8:1–18.

We may not worship God using images, but, positively, we must worship as Jehovah demands in his word.

This positive requirement is implied in Nehemiah 8. The Jews at this time did not know what God demanded for their worship of him. Hosea 4:6 indicates that the people had little knowledge of how to worship God before captivity. After being in captivity far away from the temple for over one hundred years, many of the families had even less knowledge of God's law concerning worship. In Nehemiah 8:1–3, we read that the Jews gathered in Jerusalem and asked Ezra "to bring the book of the law of Moses." They wanted Ezra to read them the law so that they might see what God demanded for worship. Ezra did so, and even had helpers go among the crowd and further explain the law, so that they understood (v. 8). Verse 13 tells us that the chief rulers and fathers gathered again later to hear more of what God commanded regarding worship, specifically what he demanded for the feast of booths. Ezra, Nehemiah, and the Jews clearly saw that they must worship as God commands in his word.

This is the explicit teaching of John 4:24, "God is a Spirit: and they that worship him must worship him in spirit and in truth." Worshipping God "in truth" means that we worship him in the way of truth. The truth is God's word, the Bible.

Based on passages like Nehemiah 8 and John 4:24, the Reformers taught what is called the regulative principle of worship. This principle is basically stated in answer 96, which says we are not to worship God "in any other way than he has commanded in his Word."[*]

Because we are to worship God only as he commands in his word, Reformed churches include the following elements at the worship service: prayer, singing, giving, reading, and hearing of the word.

The preaching of the word is central, and that is a beautiful thing. Worship is God speaking to us first, and then we get to speak back to him. The holy and glorious God speaks to us believers about Christ and his love, and then we respond in praise and adoration.

Matt De Boer

---

[*] Heidelberg Catechism A 96, in *Confessions and Church Order*, 125.

September 1 — **LD 35 – The Threat Attached**

Read: Psalm 81.

God attaches a threat to the second commandment. Exodus 20:5 says: "Thou shalt not bow down thyself to them, nor serve them: for I the Lord thy God am a jealous God, visiting the iniquity of the fathers upon the children unto the third and fourth generation of them that hate me."

That God visits the iniquity of the fathers upon the children does not mean that God punishes a child for his father's sin, but it does show that part of God's judgment for sin on parents is that their polluted children often follow in their footsteps. When parents ignore the second commandment, the result is often that their children do the same. Several times in Israel's history parents fell into wrong worship, and then their children and grandchildren followed suit (Ps. 81:11). There were times of revival in the land, especially when Israel had godly leaders, but there were quite a few long periods of wrong worship.

Psalm 81 shows that wrong worship has dreadful consequences. In Israel, parents that bowed to images led their children away from the Messiah and the sacrifices that pointed to him. Not being directed to Christ, they walked in more and more sin. God gave many "over unto their own hearts' lust" (v. 12), and he allowed enemies to triumph over them so that they did not enjoy rest in the land (vs. 13–14).

There are similar consequences today for wrong worship. Imagine parents that abandon a church with true preaching, seeking entertainment. They and their children are not hearing the true preaching every week that reveals God and Christ. The parents weaken in their knowledge of Jehovah. The children and grandchildren will likely know very little at all of the truth concerning God, will not rightly know Christ, and will walk in unrepentant unbelief. Or imagine what happens when parents do not worship joyfully at the services. Maybe the dad often sleeps or looks really bored during the sermon. Maybe the parents grumble about going to God's house because an event or game is at the same time. If parents have a wrong attitude towards worship, often their children's attitudes will be worse, and their grandchildren's worse yet. And God tells us that those who continue in unrepentant disobedience to the second commandment are destroyed forever.

It is notable that the second commandment is the only commandment that speaks about the effects of parents' disobedience on children, showing how serious the demand to worship rightly is for moms and dads.

Pray today for forgiveness for your failures and strength to have the proper attitude towards worship.

Matt De Boer

September 2 **LD 35 — The Promise Attached**

Read: Deuteronomy 7:1–16.

God attaches a threat to the second commandment, but also a promise. Exodus 20:6 says: "Shewing mercy unto thousands of them that love me and keep my commandments."

Wonderfully, God forgives us believers for our failures to keep the second commandment, and he works in us to turn and gratefully obey it. We do not perfectly obey, of course. Yet Christ, who always worshipped God exactly as he demands, lives in us! By his powerful mercy, we do obey in thankfulness for salvation.

As we obey by Christ's power, we experience great mercy. God's mercy is his tender affection and pity by which he lifts us out of the depths of despair and unto joyful life with himself. This mercy is enjoyed by us as we follow his second commandment. For example, when we include the proper elements in our worship services, like the preaching of the gospel, we are directed to Christ. In this way, we come to know our Savior more and are lifted to the enjoyment of his friendship!

Our children get to experience this mercy too. By God's powerful work in us, we teach them how to worship God as he commands in his word, and we give them a good example to follow. Through this instruction, Christ moves them to worship properly. As they then come to his house and hear the preaching about Christ, they are lifted to joyful life with him too.

Thank God for his mercy today. Then, pray that you and your children might enjoy that mercy further in the way of right worship.

Matt De Boer

Lord's Day 36

Q. 99. What is required in the third commandment?

A. That we, not only by cursing or perjury, but also by rash swearing, must not profane or abuse the name of God; nor by silence or connivance be partakers of these horrible sins in others; and, briefly, that we use the holy name of God no otherwise than with fear and reverence; so that he may be rightly confessed and worshiped by us, and be glorified in all our words and works.

Q. 100. Is then the profaning of God's name, by swearing and cursing so heinous a sin that his wrath is kindled against those who do not endeavor, as much as in them lies, to prevent and forbid such cursing and swearing?

A. It undoubtedly is, for there is no sin greater or more provoking to God, than the profaning of his name; and therefore he has commanded this sin to be punished with death.

September 3 — **LD 36 — The Greatness of God's Name**

Read: Ezekiel 36:16–28.

"Thou shalt not take the name of the Lord thy God in vain; for the Lord will not hold him guiltless that taketh his name in vain" (Ex. 20:7). Such is the greatness of the name of the one only true God that it must always be held in highest honor. The third commandment does not only forbid the profane abuse of God's holy name; it condemns the vain use of God's name. As we must understand, that makes the prohibition of the third commandment very broad!

Ezekiel 36 confirms that, especially in verses 20–23. God's sinful people were rebuked sharply for their sinful walk of life, which God condemned by saying they profaned his holy name. As those who bore the name of the children of God, the people of Jehovah, they profaned his name by their sinful walk. The Lord told his people that he would sanctify his great name by cleansing them, with the consequence being this: "Then shall ye remember your own evil ways, and your doings that were not good, and shall lothe yourselves in your own sight for your iniquities and for your abominations" (v. 31). That is how they had profaned God's name.

That means positively that our calling is to use the holy name of God with fear and reverence always. That is a calling that reaches into every aspect of our lives and everything that we do and say.

Remember, this commandment comes to us as the redeemed of Jehovah, those who have been delivered from the bondage of sin and death, and who therefore desire to serve God in thankfulness for who he is and what he has done for us in Christ Jesus. Do you know him in that way? That must be our perspective as we consider the calling of the third commandment.

Steven Key

September 4   **LD 36 — The Revelation of God**

Read: Psalm 8:1.

At the foundation of the third commandment is the truth that the great God has revealed himself to us by his name. Frequently in Scripture, emphasis is given to the name of God. To sing Psalm 8:1 is to express: How excellent is Jehovah, our Lord, as he has revealed himself in all the works of his hands.

We read in Psalm 75:1, "Unto thee, O God, do we give thanks, unto thee do we give thanks: for that thy name is near thy wondrous works declare." There again the *name* of God denotes him and his presence. It is the revelation of his divine being.

To mention yet another text from the psalms, Psalm 115:1, "Not unto us, O Lord, not unto us, but unto thy name give glory, for thy mercy, and for thy truth's sake." Again, we who are the children of God acknowledge that all glory belongs to God alone.

That God's name reveals himself is also evident in the New Testament with the name Jesus Christ. Think, for example, of John 1:12, which speaks of those elect whose spiritual birth would be seen not of men, but of God: "But as many as received him, to them gave he power to become the sons of God, even to them that believe on his name." Clearly, the reference to believing on his name is a reference to believing on him. God's name Jesus Christ is the only name "under heaven given among men, whereby we must be saved" (Acts 4:12).

By his names God reveals himself to us as the one only true God. He makes himself known as the creator. He alone is the sustainer and preserver of all his creation. To his people in particular, he reveals himself in his name Jehovah or Yahweh, the I Am. Malachi explains that name so beautifully in Malachi 3:6, "For I am the Lord [I am Jehovah], I change not; therefore ye sons of Jacob are not consumed." God reveals himself in the name Jehovah as the God who is unchangeably faithful to his covenant people. He will never fail us who are his. God is God alone.

Steven Key

September 5   **LD 36 — The Majesty of God**

Read: Psalm 111:9.

Repeatedly God reveals himself in the Bible as the Holy One. He is the one set apart. Because he is the almighty, the Lord who as the creator rules over all, he is also totally consecrated to himself. He sovereignly governs all things to accomplish the purpose of his own will and the glory of his own name.

The Lord is "clothed with honour and majesty" (Ps. 104:1). His own perfections or attributes are also his name. They belong to his own being. Some of those attributes are so strongly tied to his own being, as it were, that no other creature can even bear them. For example, his eternity (Ps. 90:2) and his unchangeableness (Mal. 3:6) are so powerfully intertwined with him that they belong to no created being. They are exclusively God's attributes.

God reveals himself also by other perfections that are communicable. That is, God has been pleased to have some of the light rays, as it were, of those attributes shine forth from his creatures as a reflection of how good he is. Even though his people may be said to be holy or just or merciful or loving or good by virtue of the work of the Holy Spirit in them, yet none of them is that way in himself or herself, and not one bears any of those attributes perfectly and infinitely. Only the name of God himself is revealed by those perfections of his own being. He is love. He is mercy. He is holy. He is good. Those are his names.

So, with just this brief reminder of the significance of his name, and of every single revelation of himself in the various names by which he has revealed himself, we remember that God's name is so great that there is no other name to be compared to it. For that reason, the use of his name requires deepest reverence and honor.

Steven Key

September 6 — LD 36 – Profanity

Read: Leviticus 19:12.

Any one who is not completely sheltered from the world knows how common the sin of profaning God's name is today. The prevalence of this sin is in fact one of the signs which tell us that Christ is coming quickly. Revelation 17—that chapter that tells about the great beast the antichrist, particularly in its religious aspect—speaks of the beast being "full of names of blasphemy" (v. 3). That tells us of the direct attacks upon the name of God that are prevalent in the kingdom of antichrist. The prevalence of such blasphemy in our day indicates the nearness of Christ's coming in judgment.

Still more, this sin is not limited to any age group or class of men. Profanity is heard in the corporate boardrooms as much as among the drunkards. What was once referred to as the language of sailors has now become just as much the language of women. That is the development of sin.

Men think that there is no consequence to this sin. They take God's names on their lips without any thought whatsoever. If not using God's proper names as fillers or in expressions of anger, they use God's attributes in profanity. The latter has even affected Christians. How quickly we can use expressions like, "mercy," or "goodness," or "holy," or "gracious," without even realizing that we are taking the very attributes of God upon our lips and making them common. That is what profanity is. It is *to make common*. It is to take that which reveals God and his glory and to drag it down to the level of nothingness. It is to take the name that is so full of glory and majesty that it ought never to be spoken but with fear and reverence, and to make it something light and frivolous.

We must understand that swearing is not merely, as it is sometimes described, the effort of a feeble mind to express itself forcefully. Oh no. Cursing and swearing is the effort of the carnal mind to drag God from his throne! That is why God "will not hold him guiltless that taketh his name in vain" (Ex. 20:7).

Steven Key

September 7 — **LD 36 — Mindless Worship**

Read: Matthew 15:8.

It isn't just coarse profanity that grievously violates this third commandment, but also the sinful silence that fails to give to God the glory that is his due. Positively, we are called to use God's name only with fear and reverence. It is only by taking his name upon our lips in that way that we rightly confess him and worship him and that he is glorified in our words and works.

That means that whenever we use the name of God without thought or without due consideration and reverence, we violate the third commandment. Whenever we use God's name without gratitude of heart for who he is and what he has done, we profane his name. That is a piercing thought. Then we might well ask the question: "Who has been more guilty of profaning the name of God—the man who sits in the tavern, making a ruckus with his friends, or we who take that name so often upon our lips in the worship service?"

What do we do to God's name when, after arguing and bickering at home, we rush off to church—not having prepared at all for worship, not having prayed for God's blessing—and we sing,

> O Lord of Hosts, how lovely
> Thy tabernacles are...
> My soul is longing, fainting
> Thy sacred courts to see;
> My heart and flesh are crying,
> O living God, for thee?*

Aren't we the guilty ones, who take his name repeatedly upon our lips without thought, who let our minds wander at his word? Are not we the guilty ones, who voice our prayers without thought to him whose majesty causes the angels to hide their faces before him?

Is our talk, as those who represent God's name, directed to the advancement of his glory? The name of God is profaned, when it is used without due consideration and reverence, or when it is misrepresented by us who bear his name, being known as Christians. How we need a savior! How blessed are we when, as members of Christ by faith, we may worship God in joyful thoughtfulness!

Steven Key

---

* No. 227:1, in *The Psalter*.

September 8 — **LD 36 — Sinful Silence**

Read: Leviticus 5:1.

The Catechism reminds us that even our silence can involve us in profaning God's name. "By silence or connivance" we become "partakers of these horrible sins in others."* Connivance is faking ignorance of a sin, acting as if nothing is wrong when God's name is under attack.

The issue in sinful silence is the question of neutrality. Can we be neutral toward God? The Bible says, Impossible! The words of our Lord are unmistakably clear: "Whosoever therefore shall confess me before men, him will I confess also before my Father which is in heaven. But whosoever shall deny me before men, him will I also deny before my Father which is in heaven" (Matt. 10:32–33). We are called to confess the holy name of God with fear and reverence.

Obedience to the third commandment is not merely a matter of obligation to say something to the one who openly abuses God's name in our hearing. Yes, we must tell such a person that we are offended because of our love for God whose name he profanes. But we must also understand that the third commandment requires that we glorify God in all that we do and say! To ignore God and his word is simply intolerable wickedness. If we have any spiritual life within us, how can we possibly ignore the God of our salvation or pay him less attention than a common pet? How can we possibly declare his name in the church, but ignore him when it comes to school or job or home or life in general?

To walk in such neutrality toward the great name of God is sin that proves that love is lacking. And, don't forget, love is the fulfillment of the law! To the church, to us, comes the call of Isaiah 40:9, "O Zion, that bringest good tidings, get thee up into the high mountain; O Jerusalem, that bringest good tidings, lift up thy voice with strength; lift it up, be not afraid; say unto the cities of Judah, Behold your God!" We shall not be silent.

Steven Key

---

* Heidelberg Catechism A 99, in *Confessions and Church Order*, 126.

September 9 — LD 36 — The Blessed Privilege of Confessing God's Name

Read: Psalm 116:13.

Let us not forget, we are viewing the third commandment, and all the commandments, in the light of what we are *by grace*. We are those whom God has delivered out of the house of bondage, whom he has freed from sin and death and hell.

Because we have so often taken God's name in vain, failing to honor him with fear and reverence, failing even to worship him with the attention due to his name, failing to confess him as we ought in the midst of the world, Jesus stood before God to bear the wrath that had to be borne for the violation of this precept. God would not hold him guiltless. Though Jesus was perfectly innocent and without sin in himself, yet he took our sins upon him. For our sins he experienced in his own body and soul what it meant when God commanded that such profanity of his name be punished by death.

By Christ's perfect satisfaction of God's justice we have been reconciled unto God, received by him into the very fellowship of his covenant life of perfect love. In that light, we rejoice in the name of the God of our salvation. When the Spirit of this great God, the Spirit of Christ, dwells in us, we view these commandments with a love that motivates us to walk in them out of thankfulness to God. God's name is glorious, and rich blessings accumulate with the right confession and worship of him.

"Out of the abundance of the heart [the] mouth speaketh," says the Scripture in Luke 6:45. When our hearts are the dwelling places of the Spirit, we cannot be silent bystanders but must glorify God in all our words and works. We bear his name and have been formed to show forth his praise. Thus the third commandment lays the greatest calling upon us and gives us the most blessed privilege. Let us live in thankfulness to him. Let us be aware of the name that we bear, and of him whom we are called always to reverence. For in his name is also our strength and our salvation.

Steven Key

Lord's Day 37

Q. 101. May we then swear religiously by the name of God?

A. Yes; either when the magistrates demand it of the subjects, or when necessity requires us thereby to confirm fidelity and truth to the glory of God and the safety of our neighbor; for such an oath is founded on God's Word, and therefore was justly used by the saints both in the Old and New Testament.

Q. 102. May we also swear by saints or any other creatures?

A. No; for a lawful oath is calling upon God, as the only one who knows the heart, that he will bear witness to the truth, and punish me if I swear falsely; which honor is due to no creature.

September 10   **LD 37 — God's Name and the Oath**

Read: Deuteronomy 6:13.

The Catechism devotes one Lord's Day to each of the ten commandments, with this exception. A whole Lord's Day is given to the matter of the oath. That indicates the significance of the oath historically. But today, when the oath is taken so frivolously and violated so brazenly, we must understand how it must be used aright.

Historically, the reformers insisted on developing the biblical teaching of the oath because many Anabaptists laid hold of one thing concerning the oath, and that was the biblical injunction: "Swear not at all" (Matt. 5:34). They connected that position with their view of an absolute separation between the sacred and the secular. The Christian must live a life of absolute separation—not just spiritual separation, as is certainly true; but absolute separation. And therefore, the Anabaptists insisted that they must not be subject to the magistrates and their requirements of the oath to confirm truth in the public realm. Some of the descendants of the Anabaptists still hold that idea today.

But we see the same idea today from a very different perspective. While the Anabaptists at least based their ideas on Scripture, albeit a misinterpretation of Matthew 5:34–35 and James 5:12, the prevalent idea today is not based upon Scripture at all. Today, from the highest office of the land to the lowest citizen, the idea is simply that we may each exercise a personal religion but must not come with the Scripture to any area outside the church. The Bible does not belong at all to the public sphere of labor or politics or education. Religion, even professed Christianity, is put into a little box to be opened up only on Sunday, and that only if a person feels like it on Sunday.

Lord's Day 37 takes up the sword of God's word against all such unbiblical and unchristian thinking and develops the biblical truth concerning the oath as a world-and-life view. For a Christian, the oath may be sworn on select occasions as a fruit of grace, out of a life of thankfulness. It is taken properly only by those who live in the consciousness of belonging to their only Savior in life and death.

Steven Key

September 11 — LD 37 — Fidelity and Truth

Read: 1 Peter 2:13–14.

The occasion for the oath is found not in the church but in the public realm, where the Christian lives in the midst of the world of unbelief and sin. We may swear an oath by the name of God "when the magistrates demand it" of us their citizens, or "when necessity requires us thereby to confirm fidelity and truth to the glory of God and the safety of our neighbor."* Other circumstances can be eliminated. It is on very limited occasions, therefore, that the oath may be used.

The fundamental calling of the magistrate (1 Pet. 2:14; Rom. 13) is to punish the evildoers and praise those who do well. The magistrate, therefore, must make judgments of the actions of men in the public realm. Justice and just judgment can only be exercised on the basis of truth. But Scripture exposes the sinfulness of man, telling us in Jeremiah 17:9, "The heart is deceitful above all things, and desperately wicked: who can know it?"

Because of man's depravity the oath is necessary in the public realm. The magistrate cannot know men as anything but liars. Therefore, to uphold truth, the magistrate must call everyone before God's face as occasion requires it. It is as God's servant that the government official may summon a man before the highest tribunal and ask: "Do you promise before God to perform the discharge of your office faithfully?" It is as God's servant that the officer of the court must summon me before the face of God and ask me to declare God as my witness that I will speak the truth.

By swearing such an oath, we who are the children of God honor him. We do so by honoring those whom God has appointed to govern, confirming before God's face fidelity and truth. *Fidelity* is the promise faithfully to execute one's calling. *Truth* is confirmed by taking God as our witness in a court of law. These two—fidelity and truth—are the very pillars of society.

Steven Key

---

* Heidelberg Catechism A 101, in *Confessions and Church Order*, 127.

September 12 **LD 37 — The Biblical Use of the Oath**

Read: Hebrews 6:16.

When a government is characterized by corruption and when citizens are wrongfully charged with crimes and convicted by lies, the result can only be moral decline and chaos in society. God will not and cannot tolerate the profaning of his holy name by false oath-taking. But we must examine our use of the oath as Christians. "May we then swear religiously by the name of God?"* The answer, for these limited occasions, is yes, for we will do so to the glory of God, expressing our conviction that God is the God of truth before whom we stand.

The oath is biblical. The Catechism points out that "such an oath is founded on God's Word, and therefore was justly used by the saints both in the Old and New Testaments."** Notice that we don't just follow the examples of believers in Bible times. We sometimes have to tell our children, You may not do this or that just because so-and-so does it. But the oath itself is scriptural. It is "founded upon God's Word, and therefore was justly used by the saints." God himself commanded the oath to be sworn in his fear (Deut. 6:13).

That compels us to face more carefully the charge of the Anabaptist, who appeals to the words of Jesus and of James: "Swear not at all." To them, those words settle the matter completely. All oaths are forbidden by Scripture, rather than sustained and approved by Scripture as our Catechism maintains. Both appeal to Scripture. It seems that we have a contradiction in the Bible. We see Deuteronomy 6:13 instructing the church to swear by God's name; and we see in Hebrews 6:16 that men swear by God's name, even following his example. But when we come to Matthew 5:34–35 and James 5:12 we find the exhortation: "Swear not."

Whenever we stand before Scripture and find texts which apparently are at odds with each other, it is time to stop and examine more carefully the truth set forth. For all Scripture is in harmony and never contradicts itself.

Steven Key

---

*   Heidelberg Catechism Q 101, in *Confessions and Church Order*, 127.
** Heidelberg Catechism A 101, in *Confessions and Church Order*, 127.

September 13 — LD 37 — No Contradiction

Read: Matthew 5:34.

Jesus does not contradict the biblical use of the oath. The Lord was confronting and exposing as grievous sin the frequent use of oaths in everyday conversation. The Jews had become accustomed to making strong expressions, often without thought. It had become common to emphasize statements with expressions such as I swear, or, as truly as the Lord lives, and such like statements. That, Jesus said, is the taking of God's name in vain. Still more, in the church such oath-taking ought not to even have a place. For us who are in Christ Jesus, our statements must be true. Our yes must mean exactly that, and our no must mean just that. An oath is out of place among those who are brothers in Christ. That is the emphasis.

But that the Lord—and the same holds true with James—did not mean to totally forbid the oath is evident from the fact that the oath continued to be used with approval in the New Testament age. Even Christ himself, when standing before the judgment seat of the Jews, did not refuse the oath, declaring that he was the Son of God. And as we read in Hebrews 6:17, the great God, who has no cause to add emphasis to his words, accommodated himself to the weakness of men and swore an oath by himself. He whose word is truth itself, confirmed by an oath "the immutability of his counsel." When we, therefore, might be required to swear an oath, our thought and our prayer must immediately be: "Let me, O Lord, be an imitator of thee, that my words, as words of truth, might be a reflection of my conscious standing before thy face."

Even while living in a world that does not fear God and that repeatedly takes his name in vain by ungodly violations of the oath, we are called to use the oath to confirm fidelity and truth to the glory of God. The oath must be taken seriously. The oath must be kept. Therefore the oath must be understood by us.

Steven Key

September 14   LD 37 — God's All-Seeing Eyes

Read: Psalm 11:4.

To swear an oath is a tremendous event. It is an amazing thing that God allows his name to be used in confirmation of truth. To take an oath in God's name is to say, I stand here in the presence of God whose eyes are as flames of fires, penetrating even to the deepest thoughts and intents of the heart; I recognize that the day is coming when I shall appear before him in final judgment, when he shall reveal all that is true. That is what swearing an oath means.

Still more, because we call upon God as the God of truth, to swear an oath in God's name is to call all his punishments upon us if we swear falsely. How great the sacrilege, how gross the dishonor, to take the name of him who is eternal and unchangeable truth and use it to cover a lie! To swear falsely is to pervert the name of the only true God. To swear in his name without regard to the greatness of that name is to dishonor him, and he sees it: "His eyes behold" (Ps. 11:4).

That is why, as you can well understand, God's name is not to be introduced thoughtlessly in an oath, and the oath is not to be taken without necessity. When we who swear by his name know his greatness and glory and that all must stand before his tribunal and answer to him who is the protector of his own holy name, then we will view the oath most seriously. Then we understand that swearing an oath is a kind of divine worship, where honor must be given to God, even the God of our salvation. Let's not forget that! As we take his name, his majesty is brought before us, his glory. The God of our salvation stands before us to know and uncover the hidden things and to maintain the truth. When truth and faithfulness are extinguished or covered by the lie and unfaithfulness, God's name is blasphemed. His name is glorified when faithfulness and truth shine brightly.

Steven Key

September 15   **LD 37 — The Infinitely Glorious God**

Read: Isaiah 45:22–23.

The oath reminds us that we are but creatures, finite and of dust. Men boast in their accomplishments, but the oath declares that not even the wisest man is able to penetrate the deepest recesses of man's heart. Who of men knows what a man is made of? Which judge can know precisely if the witness speaks the truth? Who knows whether those taking office will be faithful to that office? God alone knows! And that is why finite man, and particularly the magistrate, must invoke the assistance of the infinitely glorious God who alone knows all things. That is why men are put under oath: to invoke the presence of the great God, who will punish him who swears falsely, who will eventually reveal justice and cause the truth to triumph. It is the name of God that is extolled and magnified by the oath.

But the necessity of the oath also reminds us that we are sinners. The God before whom we stand and from whose perfect righteousness we cannot escape is the one who says: "Look unto me, and be ye saved" (Isa. 45:22). From him alone comes salvation. From his mouth comes the word in righteousness. To him alone belongs all glory and honor. Especially was his righteousness and truth revealed in his only begotten Son, our Lord Jesus Christ. As those redeemed by Christ, we desire to express our love for God and for our neighbor, also in the proper use of the oath.

Part of our expression of glorifying God is seeking the welfare of the neighbor. Seeking the neighbor's good or safety is an extension of our glorifying our redeemer. When truth and fidelity are maintained by the proper oath, not only is God glorified thereby, but the welfare of our neighbor and all of society is promoted.

Steven Key

September 16 — LD 37 — Speaking the Truth in Love

Read: Ephesians 4:25.

We stand before the oath as those who are in Christ Jesus, who himself said of his calling and office: "I come to do thy will, O God" (Heb. 10:9). Our view of the oath, therefore, is a view through special eyes and from a special place. We are the redeemed. We have our citizenship in heaven. That governs what we say and do, and what we don't say and do. That is true in public life, where the oath is necessary because of the power of Satan's influence. We, of all people, are able to take an oath in God's name, for we are his. But in the church, it is because we are in Christ Jesus that the oath ought to have no place. We are called always to speak the truth in love.

As Christians, our whole life is an oath. Each word and each action as a child of God is just as weighty as an oath. When at marriage a husband promises to love and to honor, or wife promises to submit and assist, and both to live faithfully according to God's word, that is just as weighty as an oath. We represent God's name in those callings. We represent God's name in everything we do and in every station of life. Our lives, therefore, are to be lives which faithfully represent the glory of our God in truth.

Then we are reminded too that the only way we speak the truth in love is by the Holy Spirit of Christ our Savior living in our hearts. After all, we have failed, too many times to count, to live before God's face in holiness and truth. While the holiness of God demands the death of all those who violate even in the least degree one of his commandments, the weight of his wrath falls upon his Son, our Lord Jesus Christ, who took our punishment upon himself. Let us, then, who have failed faithfully to perform our vows, come and reverently bow before him who caused all our unrighteousness to be borne by Christ. Then we shall express our gratitude to God and live to his glory.

Steven Key

Lord's Day 38

Q. 103. What doth God require in the fourth commandment?

A. First, that the ministry of the gospel and the schools be maintained; and that I, especially on the sabbath, that is, on the day of rest, diligently frequent the church of God, to hear his word, to use the sacraments, publicly to call upon the Lord, and contribute to the relief of the poor, as becomes a Christian. Secondly, that all the days of my life I cease from my evil works, and yield myself to the Lord, to work by his Holy Spirit in me; and thus begin in this life the eternal sabbath.

September 17 | **Q&A 103 — Busy on the Lord's Day**

Read: Deuteronomy 5:12.

Do you live with a fervent desire for the sabbath rest? If our obedience to the law of God is to be honest obedience, true obedience, the reflection of a spiritual life in Christ, that is the question we must face. We may not think that we have obeyed God's law in the fourth commandment if only we have gone to church on Sunday. As children of our heavenly Father, as those delivered from the bondage of sin and death, we stand before the law. That law, therefore, is a light upon our pathway, a guide to the life that we want to live in thankfulness to God who has so loved us. So also do we view this fourth commandment. The sabbath rest, for us, is far more than an obligatory appearance in church on Sunday. Worship in God's house, even if it is true worship, is only the beginning of the sabbath rest. That is evident from our Catechism's exposition of the fourth commandment.

It is striking that the Catechism in its consideration of this commandment doesn't even mention the negative part which forbids Sunday labor. Exodus 20:10 emphasizes that on the sabbath day, we shall not do any work: "Six days shalt thou labour" (v. 9)—another positive Christian calling; but not on this day. In fact, you may not even have employees doing work for you on the sabbath day. So says the fourth commandment. But the Catechism does not even mention that. That does not mean that the negative part of the law no longer applies. There is no approval given to working on Sunday. Not at all. But the approach is entirely different. The approach is positive. It is not to say: "Do not." Rather, it tells us that we are to be so busy in other things on the Lord's day that we don't have time for work. We don't have time even for earthly pleasures.

What could keep us so busy on the Lord's day? This: enjoying fellowship with our God through Jesus Christ and laboring to enter into the spiritual rest which he has given us on the sabbath day, which, since the resurrection of Christ, is now the first day of the week.

Steven Key

September 18 — Q&A 103 — True Rest

Read: Exodus 31:12–17.

"Six days may work be done; but in the seventh is the sabbath of rest, holy to the Lord" (Ex. 31:15). What is the idea of the rest to which we are called on the Sabbath? When we think of rest, we probably think of some form of relaxation, perhaps even sleep. But that certainly is not the idea of the sabbath rest. It cannot be, for we are told in Scripture that God never slumbers and never sleeps. His rest does not take on that form. Furthermore, we are told in Hebrews 4 that there "remaineth…a rest to the people of God" (v. 9), to which we look forward and for which we long.

The sabbath rest points to a perfect work into which we may enter with all the enjoyment of body and soul. God himself is the prototype of this rest. He is the one who instituted the sabbath day and revealed his own life as the example for us entering its rest. What is his prototype? The fourth commandment itself explains: "For in six days the Lord made heaven and earth, the sea, and all that in them is, and rested the seventh day: wherefore the Lord blessed the sabbath day, and hallowed it" (Ex. 20:11).

The Bible teaches us that God constantly upholds and governs everything. There is nothing that takes place in this creation that is outside God's sovereign control. That means that he is never idle. He never ceases to work. He is always accomplishing his purpose, moving all things toward the end that he has in mind. But at the same time, God always rests. Everything he does, he does for his own glory and enjoyment. Therefore, he constantly enters into the enjoyment of his own perfect work.

We must not think that God needed to take one day for the enjoyment of his perfect work. But he revealed himself in such a way for our sake, that we also may enter the rest which he has ordained for us his redeemed people, and that we might do so in a special way during a day set apart for that purpose.

Steven Key

September 19 — **Q&A 103 — God's Perfect Work**

Read: Deuteronomy 5:15.

The Sabbath, now observed on the first day of the week in the Christian church, was set apart by God for our sake. It was set apart that we might enter his perfect work, the enjoyment of his covenant fellowship with us in Christ Jesus.

What is that perfect work? It is not a work of our own. Our works are all corrupted with sin. The perfect work into which God calls us to enter is his work. Deuteronomy 5 explains. After telling us that the Sabbath is the Sabbath of Jehovah our God, God gives the command that in it we shall not do any work, in order that we, our families, and any who are our servants, may rest (vv. 12–14). He then explains that rest in verse 15: "And remember that thou wast a servant in the land of Egypt, and that the Lord thy God brought thee out thence through a mighty hand and by a stretched out arm: therefore the Lord thy God commanded thee to keep the sabbath day."

The purpose of the entire sabbath day, therefore, is to enter the enjoyment of the salvation that God has given us. It is very important that we understand this: the purpose of the Sabbath and the meaning of the sabbath rest is to enter the enjoyment of the salvation that God has given us.

The history of Israel's deliverance from bondage represented their deliverance from the bondage of sin and death by the wonderful work of God's grace. The salvation, which we God's people enjoy, is God's mighty work of sovereign grace, by which he has delivered us from the bondage of sin and death and has given us new life in Christ. By that new life in Christ, we are not only delivered from death and hell, which is "the wages of sin" (Rom. 6:23), but we are taken into the very fellowship of God himself! That is the rest God gives us to enjoy especially on the Sabbath.

Steven Key

September 20 — **Q&A 103 — A Lasting Rest**

Read: Isaiah 57:19–20.

That we Christians may enter the rest which is fellowship with God is truly something special. We believe in the triune God—Father, Son and Holy Spirit. That isn't just an abstract doctrinal truth to us, but a truth of very practical and personal implications. The triune God, being three distinct persons in one divine being, lives a perfect life of fellowship and love within himself. He doesn't need us. The unity of the Godhead is characterized by perfect fellowship and love, self-sufficiency, and independence. But when God saves us, he takes us into his own life! He takes us into the enjoyment of his own covenant life of fellowship and love, his family life, as it were.

To enter his rest on the sabbath day is to enter into the enjoyment of his love and fellowship in a special way and to receive a taste of the riches that are ours in Christ. Do you know that rest to which God calls his people? Do you desire it? Do you enjoy it?

The Sabbath is not for everyone. The last verses of Isaiah 57 tell us that "the wicked are like the troubled sea, when it cannot rest, whose waters cast up mire and dirt" (v. 20). There is no rest for those who are outside of Christ. Where there is no personal relationship with God through Jesus Christ, there is no desire for the sabbath rest. There is no desire for the house of God, no longing to hear Christ in the preaching of the gospel, no urgency for fellowship with those who are members of the body of Christ. Then one would rather work and make money or seek entertainment and pleasure.

That we may enter the rest of the Sabbath, and that we desire it, is something special. It is, in fact, the beginning of the eternal Sabbath. There is more to this rest than what we enjoy here and now on the first day of the week.

Steven Key

September 21   Q&A 103 — A Day Set Apart

Read: Hebrews 4:9.

We sometimes speak of the Sabbath as the foretaste of everlasting glory. That's what it is when we are truly entering into that rest. We experience in a special way the fellowship of our God and enjoy his conversation with us, his instruction, his gospel. We gather with his people to remember his mighty work of grace with us and to glorify him as the body of the redeemed. When we focus our wholehearted attention upon him, to the praise of the glory of his grace, then we are enjoying a foretaste of heaven. That is the Sabbath. That is the day of rest.

In order for the Sabbath to be a day of rest, however, it must also be a day for holiness. That is why it is a day set apart for the people of God: "The Lord blessed the sabbath day, and hallowed it" (Ex. 20:11). There are those who like to quote a passage like Mark 2:27, "The sabbath was made for man, and not man for the sabbath," as if Jesus meant to say that we now have the freedom to do what we wish on the Sabbath. But let us not forget, our freedom is not in self-seeking but in serving God. So they should also continue to quote: "Therefore the Son of man is Lord also of the sabbath" (v. 28). We keep the Lord's day holy by using it unto the Lord.

The Catechism emphasizes from a positive point of view how we set apart the sabbath day and make it holy. We do so as members of the church on this earth. We do so particularly by gathering for worship on the Lord's day. If the character of the sabbath day is that of entering into fellowship with God by contemplating the revelation of himself in holy Scripture, then the heart of this day is found pulsating through the ministry of the word. Preaching must always receive the primary emphasis in the Church's worship. To keep the sabbath day holy we must hear faithful preaching. Living in obedience to the fourth commandment means that we "diligently frequent the church of God," fellowship with our brothers and sisters in Christ, and join in the worship of Jehovah our God.* He alone gives rest.

Steven Key

---

*   Heidelberg Catechism A 103, in *Confessions and Church Order*, 128.

September 22 — **Q&A 103 — God's Wonderful Provision**

Read: Matthew 11:28–29.

The Sabbath is sorely needed by us. We need this rest because we are weary and heavy laden (Matt. 11:28). Christians are not those who are better than everyone else. Christians are those who realize their need for Christ. The burdens that we must bear cannot be carried by us alone. Sometimes in our pride, we like to think that we are able to get along quite well with our own ability and strength. That pride will be crushed. We stand always before death. Do you live in that consciousness?

Some say that this commandment doesn't apply anymore. We have seen that the law of God embodied in the ten commandments is unchangeable. The fourth commandment is part of that unchangeable law of God. Yet in our day, there are multitudes who act as if this commandment does not apply to them. Why is that? Would we be those who pick and choose the commandments that we would obey?

More pertinent is the question: Are we thankful Christians who live in the joy that only comes through fellowship with the living God? Are we those who have seen the wonder of that salvation which is ours only by the grace of God in Christ Jesus? Then we also recognize that we are completely dependent upon his grace for our whole lives and our entire Christian walk. We are sinners. There is not a moment that goes by that we can be without Christ, lest we perish. This is the day, the one day of every week, the first day, in which we may enjoy the fellowship of our God in such a way that it carries us through the week and through all our trials and sorrows. This is the day in which we may receive strength from on high, strength that comes in knowing that our Savior walks with us and talks with us. This is what makes this day such a precious gift of God to us. Would we act as if we don't need this day?

Steven Key

September 23   **Q&A 103 — Calling the Sabbath a Delight**

Read: Isaiah 58:13–14.

Our Lord Jesus Christ laid down his life on the cross of Calvary to enter God's rest on our behalf. He now says: "Come unto me and rest." That is our need.

If we recognize that need, some of us may have to reevaluate our lives with respect to the Sabbath. This day isn't made for our earthly pleasure. This day isn't given us for earthly labor. For the sake of devoting our entire focus to our spiritual labor of entering into the sabbath rest, we are to set aside our normal daily labors. We are to be too busy in spiritual things to have time for the earthly. Yes, we recognize that there are some labors necessary on the Lord's day—but not as a normal practice that robs us of our necessary fellowship with God. We don't take jobs that regularly rob us of fellowship with our Redeemer. So important is the continual nourishment of our spiritual lives and our fellowship with God that we would allow nothing to rob us of that fellowship! We long for the rest which only he can provide through his appointed means of grace.

So we begin already in this life the eternal Sabbath. "He that keepeth the commandment keepeth his own soul" (Prov. 19:16); he keeps his soul in fellowship with his Redeemer, and therefore in the rest which shall finally find its culmination in everlasting glory. In that comfort we live in hope. We are Christ's! To him we come in repentance. In him we find forgiveness. Through him we enjoy rest in the fellowship of God's covenant. May God give us grace, so that in our celebration of our Sabbath today, we receive a foretaste of the everlasting Sabbath that awaits us.

Steven Key

Lord's Day 39

Q. 104. What doth God require in the fifth commandment?

A. That I show all honor, love and fidelity to my father and mother and all in authority over me, and submit myself to their good instruction and correction with due obedience; and also patiently bear with their weaknesses and infirmities, since it pleases God to govern us by their hand.

September 24 — **Q&A 104 — Father and Mother and All in Authority**

Read: Exodus 20:12.

As we continue our study of the ten commandments as the rule of our life of gratitude to God, we enter now the second table of the law and those commandments which treat specifically our relationship to our neighbor. The law begins with our closest neighbor and those relationships that develop from that nearest bond, that of the family. So we are told: "Honour thy father and thy mother" (Ex. 20:12). The fifth commandment, therefore, calls our attention to the significance of authority and the requirement of honor and due obedience.

As the Catechism points out, the truth set forth in the fifth commandment is not only a matter of how children must behave themselves toward their parents, but also how we must act with respect to all who are placed in positions of authority over us. That becomes very clear when you put the law in the light of the whole Bible, and as Scripture interprets itself.

The fifth commandment only mentions father and mother because the family is the cell from which all the other relationships of life where authority is exercised grow. When that is understood, we see how the light of God's word in the fifth commandment shines not only upon family life but upon the school, the church, the state and the work place. As we approach the law from our peculiar perspective of the redeemed in Christ and find here a guide for our life, we see how God's word directs us to live before every figure of authority.

The application of this commandment is powerfully revealed in our day against the background of an appalling rejection of authority in every sphere of life. The day of the Lord draws near. For we are told by the apostle in 2 Timothy 3 that a rejection of and defiance toward authority would mark the "perilous times" of "the last days" (vv. 1–2). And Paul wrote not only of the sins of the world, but of those who have "a form of godliness" (v. 5). As we stand before the fifth commandment, therefore, let us hear what Scripture has to say about honoring those in authority.

Steven Key

September 25 — Q&A 104 – Due Obedience

Read: Colossians 3:20.

To the question, "What doth God require in the fifth commandment," the Catechism answers: "That I show all honor, love and fidelity to my father and mother and all in authority over me, and submit myself to their good instruction and correction with due obedience."*

Due obedience is required of a thankful Christian. There is an obedience exercised by those who are not Christians. Asian culture is noted for its honor toward those in authority. Many non-Christian Asians who come to the United States are appalled at the lack of respect for authority that is observed in America today. In many Asian cultures, respect for elders is held as the honorable way of life, and words such as *authority, obedience, order,* and *discipline* are recognized as pillars of society. Yet, even though non-Christians might exercise obedience to those in authority over them, their obedience is not that which is due to God, because they do not acknowledge God as the source of that authority.

We who are in Christ Jesus cannot be satisfied with that kind of obedience. We cannot, because such obedience fails to fulfill the law of love that is at the heart of God's precepts—love for God, which also comes to expression in love for our neighbor.

Still more, there is an obedience that does its duty grudgingly, against one's will—a forced obedience. That is the obedience that we perform when we do what we are told but despise being told what to do. Sometimes we can even obey without complaining, but our obedience is a calculated attempt to please man. It serves only our selfish motivations and attempts to promote self. That also fails to fulfill what is required of us in the fifth commandment.

The expression of thankfulness to God is an expression of love. Due obedience comes to expression in honor, love and fidelity—toward God. We are to live as those who are in Christ. To us for whom Christ has fulfilled the law, the emphasis is now upon the Christian life as a life of sanctification, a life of being in the Lord, and therefore a life by which we express our thankfulness to the God of our salvation.

Steven Key

---

* Heidelberg Catechism Q&A 104, in *Confessions and Church Order*, 129.

September 26 — Q&A 104 – Obedience in the Lord

Read: Ephesians 6:1.

Our obedience to the fifth commandment is obedience in the Lord. That is why this fifth commandment is expounded by the Catechism in the section on thankfulness. Christ holds forth the law now for us who are his! That is how we stand before the law. The law no longer provokes us. The law no longer irritates us with its impossible demands. Christ holds forth the law, saying to us, You are mine. He has redeemed us from the disobedience to authority that brought down the first man—disobedience to God's authority, the authority of his word. He has not only delivered us from the punishment of our guilt; but by the empowering work of his Holy Spirit, he has called us efficaciously to a life of thankfulness. That we learn obedience, that we again acknowledge God's sovereignty, that we submit to his authority, is Christ's redeeming work in us. That is due obedience.

It is God's will that we, who by nature are quite rebellious, learn the sacred act of honoring authority in the family. The foundation is laid in the home with father and mother. What goes on in our homes is of utmost importance. Even though the focus falls upon the calling of the child, parents also are given by God a tremendous calling. Parents must exercise godly authority that requires the honor and obedience of their children. Parents must also teach their children by their own word and example proper honor toward all authority. In the family, we stand at the source of all the other relationships in church, state, school, and society. How the parent (and the father bears the greatest responsibility for this) teaches the child in this matter will have a profound and usually lasting influence on the attitude the child takes with respect to the fifth commandment.

When you as a parent require honor and obedience for God's sake, the child will not forget it. When you hold in esteem your children's teachers, the officebearers of the church, and the magistrate, you teach your children to honor those in authority. This is necessary for the honor and glory of the God who has saved us.

Steven Key

September 27 — Q&A 104 — Honor

Read: Deuteronomy 5:16.

While obedience to the fifth commandment involves honor, love, and fidelity, *honor* is first. That is because authority has to do with a God-appointed office and not merely with a person. Our first concern must not be the person of father or mother or authority figure but rather his or her particular office. God appointed father and mother to be office bearers in the home! God appointed schoolteachers to stand before our children as office bearers in that area. God appointed elders, ministers, and deacons as office bearers in the church. God appointed our government officials, judges, police officers, and so on, as office bearers in society. The same holds true with our employers, our bosses. That is why God tells us to honor them.

We are called to love them too, insofar as that is possible. That may seem somewhat easy for parents who themselves love us, care for us, and provide for our every need. But love is not a mere feeling. Love is the exercise of the will and a spiritual activity. That is why love expresses itself by obedience. Jesus himself said it: "If ye love me, keep my commandments" (John 14:15). There are those who, for Christ's sake, must forsake father and mother, who must disobey unbelieving parents in order to be faithful in their obedience to Christ. Even in such cases, they have the calling to obey the fifth commandment. That includes being respectful to unbelieving parents, explaining why we cannot obey them in a particular matter, showing humility toward them, and living as peaceably as possible with them. We must also show faithfulness toward them, especially when they become old and infirm or in need of help. And if, due to various infirmities, they must receive special care by others, in faithfulness we will brighten their day by our regular visits or calls.

Nor is halfheartedness acceptable with God when it comes to this fifth commandment. He requires that we show *all* honor, love, and fidelity to our father and mother.

On the other hand, if unbelieving parents cast us off, we are not in bondage in such cases. Rather, God has given us a more beautiful expression of those relationships in his own family, the church.

Steven Key

September 28 — Q&A 104 – Submitting to Correction

Read: Hebrews 12:6.

Not only must we submit to the good instruction of our parents but also to their correction. Submitting to correction is not so easy. God himself corrects us. Every Sunday, we come under the preaching of the word, and, in the course of that grand gospel message, we are also disciplined and corrected. We must submit to that correction too. We must turn from our iniquities. God chastens us by his word. But he does so in love. That's what the Bible tells us in Hebrews 12: "Whom the Lord loveth he chasteneth, and scourgeth every son whom he receiveth" (v. 6).

Love corrects. Parents who do not correct show by their permissiveness that they do not love their children. Proverbs 13:24 says: "He that spareth the rod hateth his son: but he that loveth him chasteneth him betimes." Parents, that rod must be used so carefully! But it must be used! In obedience to God and for the proper correction of the child, it must be used. And woe to those who think they know better than God!

But children must not only submit to that good instruction and correction, they must also "patiently bear with" the "weaknesses and infirmities" of their parents.* Honor is required from us no matter the faults, infirmities, and sins of those who are over us. Parents carry many weaknesses, too many to count. But children must patiently bear with their weaknesses and infirmities. That is also the calling of every one of us with respect to those who stand in authority over us.

We are quick to find fault with those who are in authority over us. But we walk in disobedience to God and sin greatly when we refuse patiently to bear with the weaknesses and infirmities of those whom God has appointed to positions of authority over us. What grief we bring to ourselves, what grievous consequences are reaped by such sin against the fifth commandment. Let us learn to exercise patience, remembering how much patience the Lord must exercise with us, in bearing our weaknesses and infirmities.

Steven Key

---

* Heidelberg Catechism A 104, in *Confessions and Church Order*, 129.

September 29 — **Q&A 104 — God-Given Authority**

Read: Hebrews 13:17.

We must never forget that God alone rules. He clothes parents with the authority and with all the responsibilities that come with that position. God rules by parents in the sphere of the home.

God gives authority to office bearers in the church. That is also emphasized repeatedly by Scripture, Hebrews 13:17 and 1 Thessalonians 5:13 being just two examples. Ecclesiastical affairs are under their supervision, and no one may interfere with that.

God is the one who gives authority to the magistrate as well. When we understand that, then we will receive the instruction of Romans 13:1–2, "Let every soul be subject unto the higher powers. For there is no power but of God: the powers that be are ordained of God. Whosoever therefore resisteth the power, resisteth the ordinance of God: and they that resist shall receive to themselves damnation." The apostle wrote this, not about a Christian but a pagan government with ungodly rulers. Nevertheless, for God's sake, we are required to honor and submit to them. That call to subjection is unconditional.

There is a difference between subjection and obedience. When those in authority require of us disobedience to God, we may not obey them. We obey God rather than men. But even when obedience to God requires disobedience to an ungodly magistrate, we submit to the magistrate, subjecting ourselves willingly to the punishment of our disobedience for God's sake, remembering the words of 1 Peter 2:19, "For this is thankworthy, if a man for conscience toward God endure grief, suffering wrongfully."

If we keep these things in mind, then it will be much easier for us to serve God with proper gratitude of heart. Christ our Savior reigns. He reigns over us in our family relationships. He reigns over us in the church. He reigns over us in the workplace and in the state. The purpose in it all, his purpose, is to gather his church, preserve and protect her, unto the final realization of his perfected kingdom. We serve the Lord Christ!

Steven Key

September 30 — Q&A 104 — The First Commandment with Promise

Read: Ephesians 6:2–3.

The reward spoken of in the fifth commandment—"that thy days may be long upon the land which the Lord thy God giveth thee" (Ex. 20:12)—is entirely a reward of grace. After all, it is only by the work of the Spirit of Christ in us that we can possibly show all honor, love, and fidelity to father and mother and all in authority over us. That is only of grace. Apart from that grace, the whole law does nothing but condemn us, provoke us, and harden us in our sin. God so works in his people that they walk in obedience to him and thus enjoy the promised blessing.

What is that blessing? It is not earthly, though it is spoken in an earthly form. For we know that there are many children of God who by grace walk in the way of God's commandment, who yet die young. There are increasing multitudes of disobedient persons who defy this commandment and yet live to old age. Let us not look, therefore, for the fulfillment of this promise in a long earthly life. After all, do we not look for our life in heaven?

This promise is in a form that the Old Testament children of God could understand in all its spiritual significance.

What was the promised land to the children of Israel? It was Canaan. And Canaan was a picture of the promised land, for which, according to Hebrews 11, the people of God looked, even as did Abraham: "For he looked for a city which hath foundations, whose builder and maker is God" (v. 10). God promises us the enjoyment of heaven as we walk in obedience to the fifth commandment. What a thrilling promise! What a blessed reward is set before us, to motivate us in our often difficult calling to honor all in authority.

It is a promise to us and our children, a blessing upon the generations of those who walk in the way of God's commandments. For the obedience of Christ in his chosen people bears precious fruit. It is the fruit of thankfulness offered in the heartfelt prayer, Lord, make me an obedient Christian; and grant me thy blessing.

Steven Key

Lord's Day 40

Q. 105. What doth God require in the sixth commandment?

A. That neither in thoughts, nor words, nor gestures, much less in deeds, I dishonor, hate, wound, or kill my neighbor, by myself or by another; but that I lay aside all desire of revenge; also, that I hurt not myself, nor willfully expose myself to any danger. Wherefore also the magistrate is armed with the sword to prevent murder.

Q. 106. But this commandment seems only to speak of murder?

A. In forbidding murder, God teaches us that he abhors the causes thereof, such as envy, hatred, anger, and desire of revenge; and that he accounts all these as murder.

Q. 107. But is it enough that we do not kill any man in the manner mentioned above?

A. No; for when God forbids envy, hatred, and anger, he commands us to love our neighbor as ourselves; to show patience, peace, meekness, mercy, and all kindness towards him, and prevent his hurt as much as in us lies; and that we do good, even to our enemies.

October 1   Q&A 105 — Murderers by Nature

Read: Romans 13:10.

As we progress to our treatment of the sixth commandment, "Thou shalt not kill" (Ex. 20:13), we must be reminded that mere outward observance of the Old Testament letter of the law will not be accepted by God. "Love is the fulfilling of the law" (Rom. 13:10), and love is essentially an activity of the heart. Mere external conformity that proceeds not from love will be counted as worthless dead works and will receive God's just damnation. God requires a holy, spiritual love. That love must be, first and essentially, love for God. Proceeding from that love must be love expressed toward the neighbor. That means that love for the neighbor is out of the question where there is no love of God in Christ Jesus in the heart.

In that light we are reminded that according to our natures, we are murderers. That becomes even clearer to us when Jesus spells it out with specific application in Matthew 5. The finger of God is pointed at you and me. In that passage, Jesus does not even speak about the actual act of physically murdering someone. Very seldom does a citizen of the kingdom of heaven actually take a life by the shedding of blood. But then, we must not think that because we are the citizens of God's kingdom and do not shed man's blood in murder, we escape the sin of violating the sixth commandment. That is how the Pharisees interpreted this law. They said: "Whosoever shall kill shall be in danger of the judgment" (v. 21). But Jesus says: "But I say unto you, That whosoever is angry with his brother without a cause shall be in danger of the judgment: and whosoever shall say to his brother, Raca [idiot, blockhead], shall be in danger of the council: but whosoever shall say, Thou fool, shall be in danger of hell fire" (v. 22). Very broad is the scope of the sixth commandment. We must see, once again, not only our murderous natures; we must see our salvation in Jesus Christ and the positive way towards which this precept directs us.

Steven Key

October 2 — Q&A 105 — The Righteous Taking of Life

Read: Genesis 9:6; Romans 13:3–4.

Not every killing of a man is murder. Sometimes there is confusion on that matter, especially when it comes to the magistrate's taking of human life. The magistrate is given the sword power by God. The sword is the symbol of the power to put to death. The magistrate must exercise that power in the punishment of the evildoer. "Whoso sheddeth man's blood, by man shall his blood be shed" (Gen. 9:6)—that is the command of God. But that calling does not belong to just anyone to exercise in revenge: "Vengeance is mine… saith the Lord" (Rom. 12:9).

That calling to execute judgment and to wield the sword in punishment belongs exclusively to the civil magistrate. That is not murder, but his calling according to Romans 13. To refuse that calling is to raise a fist in rebellion against the most high God. That does not mean that the magistrate never commits murder when he takes a life. The magistrate also killed Jesus. Pontius Pilate was responsible for the sword power, which he exercised. Throughout history there have been hundreds and thousands of cases where the governmental powers persecuted and killed the righteous. The shedding of blood by the magistrate is only to be used to protect the righteous and for the punishment of evildoers. The taking of the life of a man or woman who has been justly condemned for murder is not wrong in the sphere of the magistrate. It is demanded of them by God.

Nor is the shedding of blood in a righteous war to be accounted murder. Because it is within the calling of the government to protect the good, war may justly be declared in retribution of an attack and to recover what has been unjustly taken away (see 1 Sam. 15:2–3; 30:18–20; John 18:36).

Steven Key

October 3   Q&A 105 — Murder

Read: Exodus 20:13.

Murder is the willful taking of another man's life by one who has no authority to do so.

That deed is, first, the actual killing of a person with or without the use of weapons. It is the destruction of a human earthly life in direct opposition to the revealed will of God. Today, abortion is one of the most open violations of this commandment. But besides abortion, murder has become such a common occurrence in Western culture that there have to be extraordinary circumstances in order for it even to catch our attention. Television glamorizes murder and those who are closely involved with it. The sin of killing by murder is the crassest expression of rebellion against this sixth commandment of God. But it is not the only violation.

The acid test of whether our appreciation for this commandment is merely intellectual, or whether we desire to give God all the glory in the keeping of his commandments, comes when the declaration of God is applied in such a way that it hurts us. When the sixth commandment says to us, "Thou shalt not kill," that ought to wound us very deeply, because in its prohibition and negative form, the sixth commandment points its finger at our own corrupt hearts.

The commandment says, Thou shalt not murder. That is, thou shalt do all within thy power to care for that life that is God's gift, his prerogative to give and to terminate. The Catechism reminds us that this includes "that [we] hurt not [ourselves], nor willfully expose [ourselves] to any danger."* Your life is not your own. Your body is the temple of the Holy Spirit. You have no right to destroy it! You have no right to abuse your body by any means, whether by gluttony, the use of illicit drugs, excessive alcohol intake, or the addictive use of tobacco and smoking, which has been demonstrated beyond any doubt as doing harm to the body.

We need to be honest with the law of God. If we continue to give no regard to the law in its personal application, then the word of James 1:22 comes home to our conscience: "Be ye doers of the word, and not hearers only, deceiving your own selves."

Steven Key

---

*   Heidelberg Catechism A 105, in *Confessions and Church Order*, 129–30.

October 4   **Q&A 105 — Murder with the Tongue**

Read: Matthew 5:21–22.

When it comes to a specific point of application, we very conveniently rationalize away the arrow of God as it strikes us in the words: "Thou shalt not kill." But we have to face that law honestly as it impinges upon the specific point of our own carnal inclinations! Then we must also realize that the sixth commandment not only forbids the act of murder but likewise all causes and occasions leading to it.

Here the commandment uncovers every festering sore in our sinful natures. It uncovers such things as dishonoring or hating our neighbor in thoughts, words, and gestures, as well as in deeds.[*] God counts us as having violated this commandment even when we think evil toward the neighbor. The same is true with evil speech. We kill when we speak evil words that hurt the neighbor like daggers. That sin might be most often seen in children. Children speak very freely. Adults usually are more refined in their sinning—more devilish. We usually don't talk to the neighbors' faces; we talk behind their backs. But children talk very openly. That is beautiful when they are praising God in their openness. But sometimes they very openly hurt with their speech a classmate or brother or sister. That is what Jesus was talking about in Matthew 5 when he said, You want to talk about murder? I tell you, when you call your brother, your classmate, "Raca" (blockhead, idiot, or names like that), you are guilty! That is killing!

And if those charges do not dig deeply enough, our Catechism points to the truth that God abhors not only murder, but "the causes thereof, such as envy, hatred, anger, and desire of revenge; and that he counts all these as murder"![**] Oh, how great is our need for Christ!

Steven Key

---

[*]   Heidelberg Catechism A 105, in *Confessions and Church Order*, 129.
[**]   Heidelberg Catechism A 106, in *Confessions and Church Order*, 130.

October 5 — Q&A 106 – The Causes of Murder

Read: 1 John 3:15.

When the Lord God says, "Thou shalt not kill," he looks not merely at the outward act. He looks at the heart and finds our envy, that terrible and corrupt attitude of our heart that hates to see the neighbor better off than us. In writing to Timothy, Paul mentions envy in the same breath as strife (murder) and railings (words that kill, see 1 Tim. 6:4). Envy, says Solomon, is "the rottenness of the bones" (Prov. 14:30). It is a cancerous growth that not only grows into murder but is murder in its very root.

An unholy hatred is the root of all murderous acts. That hatred is first hatred toward God for placing such a neighbor in my path. That is the terrible attitude of the corrupt, sinful heart. Such hatred characterizes us, always, except by the grace of God.

We must also see the unholy anger that dwells in our hearts. When we are angry for our own cause, angry apart from the conscious love of God, then there is murder in our hearts. When we pay no attention to the injunction of Paul in Ephesians 4:26 to "let not the sun go down upon [our] wrath," then we are sure to awaken in the morning with the scum of murder covering our heart.

Finally, there is the murderous seed that is the desire for revenge. God will take vengeance upon the wicked. That is a terrible thought that should humble us deeply. But when we desire to pay back the wrong that has been done to us, or that we imagine has been done to us, we show that there is murder in our hearts.

The believer has only to look at his own life, and he knows that those seeds of murder, envy, hatred, anger, and desire for revenge, are still very much alive in his sinful flesh. Therefore, the Christian cries out: "God be merciful to me a sinner" (Luke 18:13). But he also prays for grace to fight against those temptations to kill, and he prays for grace to love even as God in Christ has loved him. Is that your life?

Steven Key

October 6   **Q&A 107 — Loving the Brethren**

Read: 1 John 3:14.

Here is the positive calling of the sixth commandment: Scripture calls us to love our neighbor. But first we need to see our calling to love our brothers and sisters in Christ. That love is not a mere sentiment. Love is a "bond of perfectness" between persons (Col. 3:14). Love is the bond that unites persons, so that with all their beings they seek to do good to one another, in "all patience, peace, meekness, mercy, and all kindness."* That love does not exist in darkness, for love is of God. John writes: "Hereby perceive we the love of God, because he laid down his life for us: and we ought to lay down our lives for the brethren" (1 John 3:16).

  Will you see the positive commandment in the words "Thou shalt not kill"? This is it: We must so love the brethren that we are willing to lay down our lives for them. We must seek one another's spiritual and material welfare at the expense of our own, because such is the love by which we have been redeemed: "He that loveth not his brother whom he hath seen, how can he love God whom he hath not seen?" (1 John 4:20).

  Love your neighbor as yourself. Your neighbor is the person whom God places on the pathway of your life. To love him is our calling for Christ's sake. Jesus said: "Think not that I am come to destroy the law, or the prophets...one jot or one tittle shall in no wise pass from the law, till all be fulfilled" (Matt. 5:17–18). Christ loved us. He loved not everybody; but he loved his elect perfectly, while we were yet enemies. On the cross he laid down his life for us who were murderers at heart. Every drop of blood that trickled from his hands and feet was out of his love for us. That is why we must hear the prohibition of the sixth commandment: "Thou shalt not kill." That is why we must also hear the positive demand: "Love thy neighbour as thyself" (22:39). Look at the cross. Hear the gospel. Do you see your calling?

Steven Key

---

* Heidelberg Catechism A 107, in *Confessions and Church Order*, 130.

October 7 — Q&A 107 — Loving Our Enemies

Read: Matthew 5:43–48.

In Matthew 5, it is clear that the love of the neighbor, which God requires, is a holy, spiritual love. It is also clear that the law is indeed of divine origin. For who had ever thought of loving enemies? In opposition to the Pharisees' interpretation of the demand to love the neighbor as yourself, Jesus explains the term *neighbor* and shows that it is so broad as to include our enemies! We are even to love those who hate us, speak evil against us and persecute us (v. 44)! With whomever God in his providence places in our path, we have but one calling: love him. That is the law of God's kingdom, the perfect law of love. That is a profound calling. To love even that neighbor who is our enemy is a love that can only be one-sided. Yet that is our calling, to walk in the love of Christ, also in relation to the neighbor who is our enemy. For did not God love us while we were yet enemies with him?

But then let us also understand, to show love towards such a neighbor is to speak to him of the glorious God of righteousness and truth. We must speak the truth in love, showing patience, meekness, mercy, and all kindness—but also in firmness, declaring and demonstrating from the Scriptures that salvation is only through faith in Jesus Christ our Lord. We do so, recognizing the glorious possibility that even among our enemies, there may be an elect brother or sister.

Steven Key

Lord's Day 41

Q. 108. What doth the seventh commandment teach us?

A. That all uncleanness is accursed of God; and that therefore we must with all our hearts detest the same, and live chastely and temperately, whether in holy wedlock or in single life.

Q. 109. Doth God forbid in this commandment only adultery and such like gross sins?

A. Since both our body and soul are temples of the Holy Ghost, he commands us to preserve them pure and holy; therefore he forbids all unchaste actions, gestures, words, thoughts, desires, and whatever can entice men thereto.

October 8 — **Q&A 108–109 — A Creation Ordinance**

Read: Genesis 2:18.

We now consider the most profound and blessed institution given by God to his people—the institution of holy marriage. The purity of this holy bond must be maintained by us, no matter whether we are married or single, young or old. As we stand before marriage, after all, we stand before the fountain of life as far as human relationships are concerned. To maintain the purity of this fountain, therefore, is critically important and has far-reaching implications. All the more is that true when we understand the significant symbolism of that God-ordained bond. For as Ephesians 5:32 expresses it, marriage is "a great mystery," revealing the amazing and glorious relationship between "Christ and the church." The seventh commandment maintains the sanctity of that holy bond.

Marriage is not a sacrament instituted by Christ but a creation ordinance. Along with the sabbath day, marriage belongs to the treasures established by God for his people at the time of creation. Already then, as Christ emphasizes in Matthew 19, marriage was instituted and established as a precious gift of God, an unbreakable bond which would also serve to reflect the relationship in which man stood to God himself. At the very beginning of time, God created male and female. He created man first, and then in that great act of mercy, he gave man a wife, creating her out of the man. God did so, "and said, For this cause shall a man leave father and mother, and shall cleave to his wife: and they twain shall be one flesh…they are no more twain, but one flesh. What therefore God hath joined together, let not man put asunder" (Matt. 19:5–6). That is Jesus explaining and maintaining that creation ordinance of God.

With all the attacks upon marriage in our day, we must be clear that this institution is not open to reinterpretation. Marriage is not a relationship that man established. Marriage is not a relationship that man can redefine. It is a divinely ordained institution established by God himself at creation, a one man with one woman relationship to serve God's glorious purpose.

Steven Key

October 9 — Q&A 108-109 — One Flesh

Read: Matthew 19:4–6.

In baking bread, separate ingredients are mixed together and become one. Those mixed ingredients are then baked. Once baked, you can never separate those ingredients again. The same is true of marriage. Two persons, a man and a woman, become one flesh. One, by its very definition, is indivisible. Marriage is indissoluble. Though separation of two might take place through sin, and though in the case of adultery, there might even be a putting away, or what we call divorce, even then, there is no dissolution of the marriage bond. Which is why, as Jesus explains, there may be no remarriage among those who are put away or divorced (Matt. 19:9). Marriage is for life. No more than the ingredients of a baked loaf of bread can be separated and restored to be mixed into another loaf, can a married man or woman who have become one flesh be so restored to his or her original single state as to enter another union. Not only is it impossible, but the results of such an attempt can only be a gross perversion of the marriage bond established by God.

This one-flesh relationship is of tremendous significance. For that reason God has also given us the seventh commandment: "Thou shalt not commit adultery" (Ex. 20:14). We approach this commandment as those redeemed by Christ. The power of sin, which also affected our marriages, has been broken by Christ, freeing us from the misery into which we had cast ourselves. So marriage, horribly corrupted by the fall into sin, was brought once again under the discipline of God's loving ordinance. He has done so for our sakes. For that reason, we find in marriage a very special relationship in which we may glorify God with thankfulness for what he has given us in Christ. Even in single life, we see a unique calling to maintain the sanctity of holy marriage, for the significant place God has given it.

Steven Key

October 10 — Q&A 108-109 — Honorable Marriage

Read: Hebrews 13:4.

Scripture tells us that "marriage is honourable in all," a good gift of God (Heb. 13:4). Even in the realm of those who are unbelieving, we may find husbands and wives who are entirely committed to each other, who show that the marriage bond is an honorable institution and who are faithful one to another. In fact, there are those among the children of the world who, to the shame of some church members, show a higher regard for loving and caring for their wives or for submitting to their husbands than do some believers. But the question for Christians is different and deeper than the matter of appearance and outward behavior—even though that is part of it. For us the question is this: Is Christ present in our marriages, and do our marriages conform to his word as expressions of thankfulness to him? That, really, is what lies at the root of the seventh commandment.

Only when husband and wife are faithful as members of Christ, only when Christ exercises dominion over this relationship, is that marriage found in his eyes a bond that reflects the beauty of his grace. And only when we as members of his church uphold and defend that holy institution is there obedience to the seventh commandment.

We sometimes think that we honor God when we refrain from certain wicked activities. But love is the fulfillment of the law. We are not finished with the seventh commandment when we guard ourselves against the physical pursuit of the neighbor's wife and preserve ourselves from adultery and fornication. We are obedient only when love so dwells in our hearts and lives that it crowds out all sinful thoughts, words, and deeds. Love for God and for the neighbor comes to expression by holding marriage in holy esteem and consecrating our marriages and our bodies to the Lord as his temple. So it comes to this: Is Christ present in my marriage? Is Christ present in my perspective of marriage? Is Christ present in my view of single life? Is Christ present in my perspective of my neighbor's wife or daughter? Or, from the viewpoint of the woman, is Christ present in my perspective of my neighbor's husband or son?

Steven Key

October 11 — Q&A 108-109 — Marriage, A Foundational Institution

Read: Amos 3:3.

Christ's presence in our marriages is tremendously important. Marriage is foundational to all of society, including the church. It is the fundamental institution of society. It is the presence or absence of Christ in our marriages that determines in large measure the spiritual welfare of ourselves and our children, of our church and school, as well as our nation and culture. If marriage is sealed in Christ and lived with him and his word at the center, a man and woman assist each other on the way to heaven, glorify their Redeemer, and enjoy marriage as the most blessed relationship God has established. But at the same time, every marriage that is not sealed in Christ, every marriage that is not lived upon the foundation of him who alone is life and whose word alone brings blessing and joy, is a marriage that can do nothing but defile that holy institution that God established at creation. Two must be one, one also in the faith.

The question of Amos 3:3, "Can two walk together, except they be agreed?" is rhetorical, with an obvious answer: Of course not! Notice that the question is not one of permission—may they? It is a question of ability—can they? It is impossible for two to walk together, except they are one in the faith.

The Catechism speaks of "holy wedlock," or purity in single life, which upholds the sanctity of that holy institution of marriage.* Marriage is indeed holy, set apart by God as a special institution for his people. It is a picture of the bond that exists between Christ and his church (Eph. 5:32). The inspired apostle Paul is given to see marriage as a shadow of the heavenly. The bond between a God-fearing husband and his God-fearing wife shows a reflection of the holy and unbreakable bond between Christ and his church. This is our perspective exactly because our Lord Jesus Christ left his Father in heaven to cleave to his bride, indeed, to purchase her with his own precious blood, and thus to become one flesh with her. He did so as a tremendous, even indescribable and unfathomable, act of his love. As he continues his work in us by his Holy Spirit, sanctifying us to his glory, our Christian marriages become reflections of the beauty of that eternal love.

Steven Key

---

*   Heidelberg Catechism A 108, in *Confessions and Church Order*, 131.

October 12 — Q&A 108-109 — Marriage with Love

Read: Ephesians 5:25.

In marriage, the husband represents Christ himself as the head, not only leading and guiding, but also loving his wife, even as Christ loves the church. The husband seeks his wife's spiritual growth and blessing, nourishing and cherishing her, even as Christ sanctifies his bride "that he might present it to himself a glorious church, not having spot, or wrinkle, or any such thing; but that it should be holy and without blemish" (Eph. 5:27). The wife, on the other hand, lives in submission to her husband, serving him, assisting him, reverencing him, living unto him. These things belong to the positive requirement of the seventh commandment. These things mark a sanctified marriage.

In that fellowship of love, the husband and wife also enjoy the physical intimacy of marriage, the sexual union expressive of the intimate love that is theirs as part of that mystery, reflecting the love bond between Christ and the church. It is an act of intimacy that God has given strictly to that holy union between husband and wife, and from which he is also pleased, in the years of our youth, to gather a holy seed, covenant children, showing himself faithful to his promise to establish his covenant with believers and their seed. What a wonder of God's grace is the sanctified bond of holy marriage! Love is the fulfillment of the law!

So highly does God hold the standard with respect to marriage that we are told in 1 Corinthians 6:9–10, "Know ye not that the unrighteous shall not inherit the kingdom of God? Be not deceived: neither fornicators, nor idolaters, nor adulterers, nor effeminate, nor abusers of themselves with mankind...shall inherit the kingdom of God." We read the same in Ephesians 5. The only deliverance from these sins is through the death of Jesus Christ and through repentance and faith in his name. The apostle immediately goes on in 1 Corinthians 6:11 to speak those blessed words: "And such were some of you: but ye are washed, but ye are sanctified, but ye are justified in the name of the Lord Jesus, and by the Spirit of our God."

Steven Key

October 13 — Q&A 108-109 — Maintaining Chastity

Read: Matthew 5:27–28.

Because we are bombarded by various attacks upon the holy institution of marriage, and because the temptations are fierce, God gave us the seventh commandment, calling us to the pathway of righteousness and thankfulness to him. The Catechism says: "Since both our body and soul are temples of the Holy Ghost, he commands us to preserve them pure and holy; therefore he forbids all unchaste actions, gestures, words, thoughts, desires, and whatever can entice men thereto."[*]

The sin of adultery reaches deeply into our sinful flesh, even into our thoughts and desires. That is why all unchaste actions, as well as whatever can entice men to such sinful thoughts and desires, are forbidden us. That is also why Scripture exhorts us to modesty in the way we dress as well as in our speech. For the purity of holy marriage and the sanctity of the Christian life, we may not entice others to sinful thoughts.

Let our youth understand that for this same reason, the modern dance is not fitting for the Christian. Modern dance is usually set to music that by its beat and lyrics is also conducive to lustful thoughts and movements of the body—as a study of music history will reveal. While some will point to the fact that dancing is spoken of in Scripture without condemnation, we ought to remember that such dancing, or literally leaping for joy, without the mingling of men with women, is something entirely different from the artificial movements set to today's music, as the dance now takes place between men and women and often in close contact with each other. Even where some may be unaffected by such activity and contact, most will find unchaste thoughts and desires being incited by these unchaste actions and gestures.

Let us also guard against all vulgar talk about sex. To take that which God has sanctified as a precious gift belonging to holy marriage and make it filthy is to profane the sanctity of marriage. Let us hear the command of Scripture: "Flee fornication" (1 Cor. 6:18).

Steven Key

---

[*] Heidelberg Catechism A 109, in *Confessions and Church Order*, 131.

October 14 — Q&A 108-109 — Marriage Restored by Christ

Read: Ephesians 5:31–32.

Because our marriages are all affected by sin, we must repeatedly be called before the mirror of God's word to repentance and a sanctified walk. It is imperative that we walk godly as husbands and as wives. It is imperative as young people that we see marriage in the light of Scripture and preserve ourselves with a view to that holy state. It is imperative as a church that we uphold the holiness of marriage in our opposition to divorce and remarriage. We must walk in the light of God's word, even if we have to do so alone!

But as we leave this subject, we must also notice God's wonderful preservation of this sanctified bond. The sanctity of marriage has been restored by Christ. Having redeemed us as his precious bride, Christ has given us the motivation to honor marriage. That motivation does not come from the terrible consequences of violating the seventh commandment. Rather, because of our intimate fellowship with God through Jesus Christ, we would not offend him but would live as before his face, to glorify and praise him whether in marriage or single life. So, with Joseph, we flee temptation, saying: "How then can I do this great wickedness, and sin against God?" (Gen. 39:9). God hates all impurity. Because he is my redeemer and my friend, I hate all impurity too. Is that your confession?

We say this because our bodies as well as our souls have been redeemed by the precious blood of Christ. We are not our own but belong unto our faithful Savior Jesus Christ. You do, don't you? Therefore we serve not ourselves, but we walk according to our Lord's will. By that blessed gift of holy marriage, we see God gathering his church and giving us a reflection of that unbreakable, holy bond—his own covenant love embracing us as his bride: "This is a great mystery: but I speak concerning Christ and the church" (Eph. 5:32). May we preserve the purity of that mystery as reflected in our own marriages and those of our brothers and sisters in Christ.

Steven Key

Lord's Day 42

Q. 110. What doth God forbid in the eighth commandment?

    A. God forbids not only those thefts and robberies which are punishable by the magistrate; but he comprehends under the name of theft all wicked tricks and devices whereby we design to appropriate to ourselves the goods which belong to our neighbor, whether it be by force, or under the appearance of right, as by unjust weights, ells, measures, fraudulent merchandise, false coins, usury, or by any other way forbidden by God; as also all covetousness, all abuse and waste of his gifts.

Q. 111. But what doth God require in this commandment?

    A. That I promote the advantage of my neighbor in every instance I can or may, and deal with him as I desire to be dealt with by others; further also that I faithfully labor, so that I may be able to relieve the needy.

October 15 — Q&A 110-111 — Biblical Stewardship (1)

Read: Luke 12:23.

The eighth commandment is short and to the point: "Thou shalt not steal" (Ex. 20:15). But as with all the commandments, so also here the law is very broad in its application. The eighth commandment speaks of our required love towards the neighbor, specifically with respect to our neighbors' earthly possessions. But it also speaks of our own personal use of the possessions that God has given us. It sets before us the positive instruction of this commandment as set forth in Luke 12:13–31, to seek the kingdom of God, knowing that "life is more than meat, and the body is more than raiment" (v. 23).

We also approach the eighth commandment as those who have been redeemed in Christ. We read the ten commandments as they follow the introduction to the law: "I am the LORD thy God, which have brought thee out of the land of Egypt, out of the house of bondage" (Ex. 20: 2; Deut. 5:6). That reality of our salvation is the context in which we approach the law, including the eighth commandment. Hearing the eighth commandment from him who redeemed us from the slavery of sin, we do not attempt to push aside this statute but desire to walk according to the will of God in thankfulness of heart. We see that the redemptive work of Christ embraces all things and necessarily affects our perspective towards earthly possessions. So we seek God's will also concerning earthly possessions.

The eighth commandment is undergirded by a fundamental principle—the biblical principle of stewardship. The eighth commandment requires us to recognize that we are only stewards or managers of God's possessions. The Bible's teaching concerning stewardship emphasizes two things. The first point of emphasis is that God owns all things. That is confirmed in the first two verses of Psalm 24. He who created all things is the absolute owner of all things. There is nothing we can claim as our own. Therefore, when it comes to earthly possessions, we must recognize that everything in our possession is an extension of God's kingly possessions. He is pleased to use certain means to place those goods in our possession. But we are caretakers of what is his.

Steven Key

October 16 — Q&A 110-111 — Biblical Stewardship (2)

Read: Psalm 50:12–14.

The truth that God owns all things is not understood in our day. The disregard of that truth is a fundamental error of all economic systems and philosophies. All forms of economic theory, whether communism, socialism, or capitalism, teach that things belong to man. Although there are other fundamental errors that can be exposed in the economic theories of communism and socialism, excluding God from the equation is a critical fault in current capitalistic theory. This fault is easily explained too. The world, after all, has taken God out of his own creation. They have done so by denying God as the creator. But we confess the truth of Scripture, that he is the creator of all things, the one, only true God: "Through faith we understand that the worlds were framed by the word of God, so that things which are seen were not made of things which do appear" (Heb. 11:3). Because he created, and there is none beside him, it stands to reason that he is the owner of all things.

But this sovereign ownership, which is God's alone, is an ownership that has also been revealed in a most beautiful way. He gave his Son for the deliverance of this his creation. By the deceit of Satan, the whole creation was brought under the power of sin. But God sent his Son to deliver not only his elect church but also the creation from the "bondage of corruption into the glorious liberty of the children of God" (Rom. 8:21). So that when we are told in 1 Corinthians 3:21, that "all things are yours," we do not overlook the connection: "All things are yours…And ye are Christ's; and Christ is God's" (1 Cor. 3:21–23). That means that far from leaving the earth and all material things under the power of sin, Christ has come to pull them away from the grasp of Satan, the prince of this world, and to return them to his heavenly Father—a work that will be seen as complete when he finally accomplishes his purpose and establishes the new heavens and the new earth, where righteousness dwells and where there is no more stealing and usurping of his sovereign ownership (2 Pet. 3:13).

Steven Key

October 17 — Q&A 110-111 — Biblical Stewardship (3)

Read: 1 Timothy 6:10.

The biblical principle of stewardship recognizes God as the owner of all things. But there is a second aspect of this principle of stewardship, namely, that you and I are required to live our whole lives in the recognition that all is God's.

This happens only by our life in Christ and by the work of his Holy Spirit in our hearts. We confessed this when we said in Lord's Day 1 that "I with body and soul...am not my own, but belong unto my faithful Savior Jesus Christ."* That means that the Lord our Savior cares for us also with respect to our physical needs. So Jesus said in Luke 12: 27–31,

27. Consider the lilies how they grow: they toil not, they spin not; and yet I say unto you, that Solomon in all his glory was not arrayed like one of these.
28. If then God so clothe the grass, which is to day in the field, and to morrow is cast into the oven; how much more will he clothe you, O ye of little faith?
29. And seek not ye what ye shall eat, or what ye shall drink, neither be ye of doubtful mind.
30. For all these things do the nations of the world seek after: and your Father knoweth that ye have need of these things.
31. But rather seek ye the kingdom of God; and all these things shall be added unto you.

Redemption in Christ, and more particularly the conscious participation in that salvation through faith, frees us from the slavery of the love of money and the bondage of materialism, so that we no longer have the drive to gain the world at the expense of our souls. The work of the Spirit of Christ in us is a work that instills in us a desire to seek the things above and not the things of this earth. He shows us that the earth is the Lord's, and we are his servants.

But that life of Christ in us always has to fight against the sinful inclinations of our sinful nature, which seeks the things that are below. That also explains the reason for the eighth commandment. In recognition that God sovereignly gives to every man his place and portion, we take that which God has given us and dedicate it to his glory; and we refrain from wrongfully taking to ourselves that which belongs to our neighbor.

Steven Key

---

* Heidelberg Catechism A 1, in *Confessions and Church Order*, 83.

October 18 — Q&A 110-111 — The Thankful Christian's Exercise of Stewardship

Read: Ephesians 4:28.

The eighth commandment, "Thou shalt not steal," implicitly requires us to labor. It is by working that God normally puts in our possession those goods by which we must serve him as stewards. In addition, we faithfully labor in order to have something to give to those in need. Also implied, and stated explicitly throughout Scripture, is our calling to seek first the kingdom of God, even in the application of our stewardship. The fruit of loving the neighbor in our use of the earthly things God gives us is that we relieve those who are truly in need and support wholeheartedly the causes of the kingdom of heaven.

It is indeed the work of Christ in us that fills our hearts with a desire to give to the causes of his kingdom. The thankful Christian will not steal from the cause of Christ and use God's good gifts for his own benefit and pleasure, but he will first give with willingness of heart, knowing by experience that "God loveth a cheerful giver" (2 Cor. 9:7). The apostle, writing in 2 Corinthians 8:2, testified that the churches in Macedonia were faithful in such exercise of stewardship. They are set before us as an example of what ought to characterize us. Though living in deep poverty, they gave liberally for the cause of Christ's church and for those in need. They did so, said the apostle, for this reason: "For ye know the grace of our Lord Jesus Christ, that, though he was rich, yet for your sakes he became poor, that ye through his poverty might be rich" (2 Cor. 8:9).

The thankful Christian, seeing his deliverance from the bondage of sin and death through the precious gift of Christ, honors "the LORD with [his] substance and, with the firstfruits of all [his] increase" (Prov. 3:9). Do we live that way? Do we live with an understanding of the foundational principle of the eighth commandment, that God himself owns all things, and that he is the giver of every good and perfect gift?

Steven Key

October 19 — Q&A 110-111 — Stealing Forbidden

Read: 1 Thessalonians 4:6.

The eighth commandment, and the Catechism's exposition of this commandment, sets before us the grievous violation of this foundational principle in wrongfully acquiring, possessing, and spending earthly goods. Stealing is not only done by those acts punishable by the magistrate. There is also stealing that is done so quietly and without notice that we might still appear in the eyes of others, and perhaps even in our own eyes, as very honest people.

God sees all those sins by which people try to take what belongs to the other, whether by force, or under the appearance of right. He sees those who squander his good gifts as unfaithful stewards. God sees the stealing by healthy-bodied men who do not work faithfully but who take their daily sustenance from others. Paul had to address that, as well as outright stealing, in Ephesians 4:28.

God sees all the unfaithful stewardship in the business world and in the sphere of labor. He sees those executives who draw increasingly exorbitant salaries and bonuses, as if they own the world, while they bleed their workers, cut jobs, and insist on harder work and longer hours. God sees the rich getting richer at the expense of the poor. He has a special word for those rich. It's found in James 5:

1. Go to now, ye rich men, weep and howl for your miseries that shall come upon you…
3. Ye have heaped treasure together for the last days.
4. Behold, the hire of the labourers who have reaped down your fields, which is of you kept back by fraud, crieth: and the cries of them which have reaped are entered into the ears of the Lord of sabaoth.
5. Ye have lived in pleasure on the earth, and been wanton; ye have nourished your hearts, as in a day of slaughter. (vv. 1, 3–5)

But it isn't just the bosses who frequently are found guilty by God of stealing. God also sees those employees who steal from their employers, not putting in an honest day's work for the wages they are paid, who stretch their lunch breaks and coffee breaks, who hold their employers hostage at the hands of their labor unions. God sees.

Steven Key

October 20 — **Q&A 110-111 — Stealing and Covetousness**

Read: 1 Timothy 6:6–9.

Covetousness, the desire to have for ourselves what God has given to someone else, is the heart sin of stealing. Covetousness often comes to expression by frivolous spending without regard to our present obligations. The prosperous and pleasure-mad culture in which we live tempts us to steal. That is exactly what we do when we spend what is not ours to spend.

There is legitimate debt. By that I refer to debt by which we hold equity or goods that have greater value than the debt, which debt also is not impinging upon our proper seeking of the kingdom as the priority in our lives. A man must normally take on debt in order to purchase a house. But he doesn't assume that debt unless he can care for the causes of the kingdom of God first, without hindrance, as well as the needs of his own household in food and clothing and other necessities of life. But there is another form of debt, which is altogether illegitimate, and which Scripture exposes as stealing. That is spending on credit that which is not ours to spend. To spend beyond what God has given us is taking that which is not ours to spend and pretending that we already have it.

In modern culture when so much emphasis is placed on material things, we must guard ourselves against covetousness and remember our biblical calling as stewards! The banks want us to spend and to run up exorbitant finance charges. Clothing stores, electronics stores, and all the other stores want us to spend, and spend freely. Advertising entices us. The possessions of our neighbors instill in us a desire for those same possessions or better. But let us understand the covetousness of our own hearts and pray for the Spirit of grace, that we might fight against this sin of stealing.

Steven Key

October 21 — Q&A 110-111 — The Heart Lesson of the Eighth Commandment

Read: 2 Corinthians 8:9.

The eighth commandment teaches a powerful and blessed lesson to us who are in Christ Jesus. In the first place, this eighth commandment, as all the other commandments, exposes our own sinfulness. It exposes not only our sinful deeds in the failure to exercise faithful stewardship, but more particularly, it exposes the sins of our hearts. How plagued we are with covetousness as it pertains to earthly possessions! How little thought we give to the sovereign mercies of God in what he has given us! How pitifully weak is our exercise of stewardship! How great is our need for Christ! Don't you see? For this stealing that has characterized our lives in many different forms is a sin that calls for the execution of God's righteous justice. But Christ has delivered us from the bondage of this sin too. He did so by bearing the punishment for our guilt, even to the death of the cross. He did so by becoming poor, that we through his poverty might be rich.

Now, by the work of his Holy Spirit, our Lord Jesus Christ has instilled in our hearts a love for him and for the neighbor, a love which also will express its gratitude by seeking God's will concerning earthly possessions. By the wonder of God's grace, we are made servants of God rather than slaves to the world. We have been transformed from being slaves to material things and seekers of earthly possessions that do not last to servants of God and stewards in his everlasting house.

In that light, we see that God's law is sweet. It leads us to the positive calling of "godliness with contentment," which is "great gain" (1 Tim. 6:6). Contentment is the grace of the Holy Spirit in our hearts whereby we are happy in the way in which God leads us. That is ours because we are rich—rich toward God. You are, aren't you? When you see that, then you also confess with the apostle in 2 Corinthians 9:8, "And God is able to make all grace abound toward you; that ye, always having all sufficiency in all things, may abound to every good work."

Steven Key

Lord's Day 43

Q. 112. What is required in the ninth commandment?

A. That I bear false witness against no man, nor falsify any man's words; that I be no backbiter, nor slanderer; that I do not judge, nor join in condemning any man rashly or unheard; but that I avoid all sorts of lies and deceit as the proper works of the devil, unless I would bring down upon me the heavy wrath of God; likewise, that in judgment and all other dealings I love the truth, speak it uprightly, and confess it; also that I defend and promote, as much as I am able, the honor and good character of my neighbor.

October 22 — **Q&A 112 — The Power of the Tongue**

Read: Proverbs 10:19.

It is immediately evident from Proverbs 10 that the tongue is a powerful instrument. It is a power for good; it is also a power for evil. It builds up; it also destroys. It gives expression to wisdom; it also gives expression to utter foolishness and brings destruction. The tongue is a "well of life" when used by the righteous man to give expression to God's truth, but it is a tool of violence when used to oppose the truth (v. 11). A man shows that he is a fool, says the inspired writer, when he uses his tongue to propagate slander and to speak lies (v. 18), and "the mouth of the wicked [speaks] forwardness" (v. 32). But "the lips of the righteous know what is acceptable" before God (v. 32). So the conclusion may be found in Proverbs 10:19, "In the multitude of words there wanteth not sin: but he that refraineth his lips is wise." How careful we must be with the use of our tongues, our mouths. That is the essence of the ninth commandment.

A most destructive sin is the evil use of the tongue. So James wrote in James 3:5–6, "Even so the tongue is a little member, and boasteth great things. Behold, how great a matter a little fire kindleth! And the tongue is a fire, a world of iniquity: so is the tongue among our members, that it defileth the whole body, and setteth on fire the course of nature; and it is set on fire of hell." In the words of our Catechism, the tongue can call down "the heavy wrath of God."* Our consideration of this ninth commandment is a matter of urgency. And our attitude towards this word of God exposes us for what we are. James put it this way in James 1:26, "If any man among you seem to be religious, and bridleth not his tongue, but deceiveth his own heart, this man's religion is vain."

So once again, as those redeemed by Christ, as those who love his word of truth and therefore those who humble ourselves before him, we express our desire. Teach thou us, Father. We desire to walk in the way of thy commandments. For we love thee and would express to thee our gratitude.

Steven Key

---

* Heidelberg Catechism A 112, in *Confessions and Church Order*, 133.

October 23 — Q&A 112 – The Revealer of the Truth

Read: Psalm 25:5.

The tongue is a precious gift from God to show forth his praise and to hold forth his truth. The underlying principle of the ninth commandment is once again found in God himself. God is the God of *truth*. In harmony with the perfection of his own being, God alone determines the truth and works according to that truth: "For the word of the Lord is right; and all his works are done in truth" (Ps. 33:4).

In addition, as David makes clear, God is the God who reveals truth (2 Sam. 2:6). That is why David prays in Psalm 25:4–5, "Shew me thy ways, O Lord; teach me thy paths. Lead me in thy truth, and teach me: for thou art the God of my salvation; on thee do I wait all the day." God's word is truth. It is truth throughout the ages. It is the "scripture of truth" (Dan. 10:21), perfectly reliable and trustworthy. It is breathed by "the Spirit of truth" (John 14:17; 15:26; 16:13), the Holy Spirit. When God sent his Son into the world, his divinely anointed Son who is one with the Father and the Holy Spirit, the Son said: "I am the way, the truth, and the life: no man cometh unto the Father, but by me" (14:6).

It is Christ who reveals to us the infinite perfections of God—his truth, his holiness, his righteousness, his mercy, his love, his grace. By his death on the cross, Christ is the way unto the Father; to the God of truth he leads us, bringing us into the fellowship of his covenant life. There is no fellowship with God apart from the truth. That is why the psalmist sings in Psalm 43:3, "O send out thy light and thy truth: let them lead me; let them bring me unto thy holy hill, and to thy tabernacles." So also we read in Psalm 145:18, "The Lord is nigh unto all them that call upon him, to all that call upon him in truth." To the truth of God, therefore, we must be entirely devoted. God created us to show forth his praise—in truth. So we are to live, and so we are to speak.

Steven Key

October 24   **Q&A 112 — Loving the Neighbor in Truth**

Read: Ephesians 4:25.

The power of the tongue is a precious gift when used not only to praise God in truth, but also to speak the truth in love to the neighbor and to express love for the neighbor. The Catechism expresses our positive calling this way: "That in judgment and all other dealings I love the truth, speak it uprightly, and confess it; also that I defend and promote, as much as I am able, the honor and good character of my neighbor."[*]

That means that when my neighbor is a fellow believer, my speech seeks to encourage him spiritually, to strengthen his faith. Woe to that man who is a stumbling block to the brother. I don't speak, of course, of those offenses that come when a brother refuses to hear the instruction of the Scriptures. As Proverbs 10:17 says: "He that refuseth reproof erreth." When you bring the word of God to a wayward brother and he is offended because he refuses to hear the word with application to himself, that is not your fault—assuming you have spoken the truth in love and with a proper spiritual attitude. Then, his taking offense is not a rejection of you, but of the word. But woe to that man who becomes a stumbling block to the brother by reason of evil speaking or of living a lie. The speech of love is a speech that edifies, that builds up in the faith, that encourages in the truth of God's holy word.

On the other hand, when my neighbor is an unbeliever, the power of the tongue is used to his advantage when I confess the truth of God's word and show my life in harmony with that word of truth. Certainly I am not promoting the honor of my neighbor when I hide the truth from him and ignore the coming consequence of his walk in unbelief. As much as I am able, I am to speak the truth and confess the name of him who is truth. That is the purpose for which God gave me a tongue and the power of speech—to glorify him in truth and to promote that truth also in relation to my neighbor.

Steven Key

---

[*]   Heidelberg Catechism A 112, in *Confessions and Church Order*, 133.

October 25 — Q&A 112 – The Tongue Devastated by Sin

Read: James 3:5–6.

The form of the ninth commandment—"thou shalt not bear false witness against thy neighbour" (Ex. 20:16)—indicates that the tongue has come under the power of our sinful flesh. The ninth commandment, says our Catechism, requires "that I avoid all sorts of lies and deceit as the proper works of the devil, unless I would bring down upon me the heavy wrath of God."[*]

Every form of falsehood is sown by the devil, whose very name means *liar*. Satan kindled that fire of the lie when he came as a serpent to Eve and called God a liar! When Eve responded that if they would eat of the tree of knowledge of good and evil, they would die as God had said, the devil said: "Ye shall not surely die: for God doth know that in the day ye eat thereof, then your eyes shall be opened, and ye shall be as gods, knowing good and evil" (Gen. 3:4–5).

That tells us even more about the lie. The lie is rooted in wicked pride, which seeks to elevate the creature above the creator and which would give the creature the right to determine the truth. It is a common thought in our day that truth is what we make it to be. That philosophy goes hand in hand with the rejection of the Scriptures as the absolute standard of truth and the infallible word of divine authority.

From that first lie of Satan proceeds every form of the lie today and every form of evil speaking. The power of the tongue has been made a power subject to Satan. As we near the end of time, Satan is once again given opportunity to develop his power. He will do so by the success of the lie. The book of Revelation reveals that there is "given unto him a mouth speaking great things and blasphemies," and he is able to deceive the nations, as well as the false church (13:5–8). The tongue, when in the service of Satan, is set on fire of hell. The ninth commandment condemns all forms of lying and deceit as being "the proper works of the devil."

Steven Key

---

[*] Heidelberg Catechism A 112, in *Confessions and Church Order*, 133.

October 26 — **Q&A 112 — Many Lies**

Read: Psalm 119:118.

The lie takes many different forms. False doctrine is the expression of the lie. There is the lie that the Bible has flaws, is not trustworthy in everything it says. That is the very lie of Satan in the garden. There is the common denial of God's absolute sovereignty, his divine directing and governing of all things. There is the denial of creation as set forth in the book of Genesis, the work of God's hands. There is the teaching, contrary to the Bible, that God loves everybody and wants everybody to be saved, if only they will accept him. There are many teachings that deny the application of God's precepts to our lives today. There are many teachings that defile holy marriage, that deny marriage as an unbreakable bond between one man and one woman. The acceptability of divorce, the permissibility of remarriage as the best thing for the happiness of the divorced person, is common and widely accepted in our day, though contrary to the word of God.

It is by the deceit of Satan that there is a muddying or a watering down of biblical concepts. And the fruit is, as the Spirit has spoken "expressly" concerning these last days, that some "depart from the faith, giving heed to seducing spirits, and doctrines of devils" (1 Tim. 4:1). Even as there is evidence of "the wrath of God" upon "all ungodliness and unrighteousness of men, who hold the truth in unrighteousness" and turn it into a lie, we see God's truth held fast. So we are told in Romans 1:18–20.

The lie and the power of the tongue under the embrace of Satan have terrible consequences also in our relationships to others. To bear false witness can take the form of lying about someone or misrepresenting him or her. But it can also come to expression many other ways. To leave out certain facts in order to leave an evil impression is to follow the lie of Satan. To imply evil intentions on the part of someone in whom false motives and evil intentions were absent is to abandon truth. God knows how guilty we have made ourselves by these grievous sins that raise suspicions and evil thoughts about fellow brothers and sisters in Christ. God calls all to repentance.

Steven Key

October 27 — **Q&A 112 — Our Great Need for Purified Speech**

Read: Proverbs 17:4.

As those who come under the accusation of God in Psalm 12:4, we often live echoing the thought: "Our lips are our own: who is lord over us?" Instead of defending and promoting the honor and good character of our neighbor, in accordance with the calling to love our neighbors as ourselves, we hurt our neighbors with our speech and sin against God.

In Psalm 15, the question is brought before God: "Lord, who shall abide in thy tabernacle? who shall dwell in thy holy hill?" And the answer follows: "He that walketh uprightly, and worketh righteousness, and speaketh the truth in his heart. He that backbiteth not with his tongue, nor doeth evil to his neighbour, nor taketh up a reproach against his neighbour" (vv. 1–3). Sometimes there are those in the church who are so caught up in sins of the tongue that they cannot possibly receive a blessing in the sanctuary of God. God will not give them his covenant fellowship or the comfort of his loving presence. And it becomes a vicious circle. As chastisement of their own sins, they receive no blessing from God; so they speak all the more evil of the church, all the while refusing to examine their own wicked attitudes and tongues. So it will continue, until God in mercy awakens them to their utter wickedness, they repent of their repeated backbiting and evil speaking, and they turn again unto the Lord.

The devastation wrought by an evil tongue is a devastation that runs far and wide. This sin explodes its shrapnel into very wide territory. While the Catechism lists rather extensively the various forms in which the tongue shows itself as set on fire of hell, the fact is that the ways of evil are so many that the Catechism finally must sum it up by the expression, "all sorts of lies and deceit,"* so as not to overlook any. It is a simple fact: "If we say that we have no sin, we deceive ourselves, and the truth is not in us" (1 John 1:8). But on the other hand—and how important this is—"If we confess our sins, he is faithful and just to forgive us our sins, and to cleanse us from all unrighteousness" (v. 9).

Steven Key

---

* Heidelberg Catechism A 112, in *Confessions and Church Order*, 133.

October 28 — Q&A 112 – The Wonderful Restoration of the Tongue's Good Use

Read: Proverbs 16:23.

The heavy wrath of God, which must rest upon the abusive and lying tongue, was taken up by Jesus and carried to the cross for all who believe. Having spoken his precious word of truth to us as his almighty power unto salvation, our Lord now fills us with a love for him and for one another. To us who had the name of our father the devil, and who did not hesitate to give others bad names by our gossip and evil speaking, the Lord has given the name of children of God—the very opposite of who we are by nature!

This renewal of life is just as much a part of belonging to Christ as is the forgiveness of sins and justification. It is not possible to claim the work of Christ if our tongues keep on lying, gossiping, slandering, and rashly condemning. It is true—and, oh, the sorrow it causes us—that we do not have perfection here, for we have a continual struggle with the old man of sin in us. We do stumble. But if our tongues are untamed and unbridled, quick to speak evil, how shall we sing with sincerity of heart the words of Psalm 19:14, "Let the words of my mouth, and the meditation of my heart, be acceptable in thy sight, O Lord, my strength, and my redeemer"?

Jesus Christ speaks and works in us to tame the untamable and to break down the works of the devil. What we are unable to do in our own strength is given to us by the power of Christ, when we continually seek his grace and Holy Spirit. In him is mercy and truth. And as we read in Proverbs 16:6, "By mercy and truth iniquity is purged: and by the fear of the Lord men depart from evil." So we shall love the truth, speak it uprightly and confess it. Seeking to glorify God in all things, we shall defend and promote, as much as possible, the honor and good character of our neighbor. This is the way of promoting the well-being of the church of Christ as well. This is the way of God's blessing. May we repent of our evil speaking and seek earnestly to live in thankfulness to our Redeemer.

Steven Key

Lord's Day 44

Q. 113. What doth the tenth commandment require of us?

A. That even the smallest inclination or thought contrary to any of God's commandments never rise in our hearts; but that at all times we hate all sin with our whole heart, and delight in all righteousness.

Q. 114. But can those who are converted to God perfectly keep these commandments?

A. No; but even the holiest men, while in this life, have only a small beginning of this obedience; yet so, that with a sincere resolution they begin to live not only according to some, but all the commandments of God.

Q. 115. Why will God then have the ten commandments so strictly preached, since no man in this life can keep them?

A. First, that all our lifetime we may learn more and more to know our sinful nature, and thus become the more earnest in seeking the remission of sin and righteousness in Christ; likewise, that we constantly endeavor, and pray to God for the grace of the Holy Spirit, that we may become more and more conformable to the image of God, till we arrive at the perfection proposed to us in a life to come.

October 29 — Q&A 113-115 — The Place of the Law

Read: Romans 7:14.

What a difference between the non-Christian and believer when facing the law of God, the well-known ten commandments. For the unbeliever, the law is only the unchangeable demand of the righteous and holy God as creator and sovereign. For you who believe, that same law has become, in and through Jesus Christ, the loving precept, the guide for a thankful life. It comes from the same righteous and holy God as Father and Redeemer. For the unbeliever, that law can only be a matter of crushing responsibility, because he has no relationship to the Christ who alone fulfills that law. For the natural man, that law points to everlasting condemnation, because he must obey that law perfectly, yet he does not obey it because he cannot and will not: "The carnal mind is enmity against God: for it is not subject to the law of God, neither indeed can be. So then they that are in the flesh cannot please God" (Rom. 8:7–8).

But that same law points the Christian to life eternal. It does so because Christ has fulfilled that law for us. We do not have to keep that law in order to be redeemed. By his blood, Christ blotted out all our transgressions; in his life he fulfilled all obedience for us. Therefore, we are no longer under the law but under grace. We are justified by faith, without the works of the law.

Yet, on the other hand, we who believe keep the law by the power of God's mighty grace and the work of his Spirit in our lives. Though only in a small beginning and not yet in perfectness, we strive to walk in obedience to the whole law out of thankfulness for all that God has done for us in Christ Jesus. Because Christ lives in us by his indwelling Spirit, because we are thankful Christians, we are compelled to walk in obedience to that law and shall not enter into glory without it. That is the way it must be, if we are to have any comfort in life and death. For the law does not merely gloss over certain aspects of our outward conduct, but it reaches into the very depths of our being. That is emphasized in the tenth commandment.

Steven Key

October 30 — **Q&A 113 — The Demand for Perfection**

Read: Exodus 20:17.

By the tenth commandment the law reaches into our inmost lives to touch the very thoughts and intents of the heart. As we have seen, each of the ten commandments addresses a much broader area than is initially indicated in the words expressed.

That is why the Catechism, in expounding the law, does not pay attention to the narrow meaning of each commandment but opens it up in its broadest application. It also applies that law very personally: "What doth the tenth commandment require of us?"*

By this approach the Catechism accomplishes three things. First, it examines the tenth commandment itself, calling attention to the spiritual character of the law. Secondly, it compares us with that law and teaches us to understand the reality of our imperfection. Finally, the Catechism speaks of the importance of the law for our spiritual nurture, as it is preached to us and applied to us by the power of the Holy Spirit.

The tenth commandment, as the culmination of the law, demands perfection before the holy God. It requires of us "that even the smallest inclination or thought contrary to any of God's commandments never rise in our hearts; but that at all times we hate all sin with our whole heart, and delight in all righteousness."** Obedience to God is fundamentally a matter of the heart and not merely a matter of outward conformity to his precepts. It is exactly for that reason that Paul wrote in Romans 7:7, "I had not known sin...except the law had said, Thou shalt not covet." Until Paul came to a spiritual understanding of the tenth commandment and saw that the law of God reaches into the deepest recesses of the heart, will and nature, he thought as a Pharisee, namely, that his own outward observance of the precepts of the law marked him as obedient. However, when he saw himself as God saw him, he saw his sin in all those small inclinations or thoughts that arose in his mind and heart, and he understood the bondage to sin and the corruption of his own flesh and the true nature of the law in the light of God's perfect holiness.

Steven Key

---

* Heidelberg Catechism Q 113, in *Confessions and Church Order*, 133.
** Heidelberg Catechism A 113, in *Confessions and Church Order*, 133.

October 31 — Q&A 113 — Called to Perfect Holiness

Read: 1 Peter 1:15–16.

The positive calling of the tenth commandment is set forth in 1 Peter 1:15–16, where the inspired apostle repeats the word of God as set forth in the Old Testament in the last part of Leviticus 11. The apostle sets forth the call to holiness in contrast to that way of life that characterizes us by nature. In contrast to that lust, which is the expression of covetousness, we are to be holy, as God is holy.

As we consider the tenth commandment, we must understand that the law does not merely forbid us from wanting things that we do not have. That, in itself, is not necessarily wrong. We are commanded by Scripture in 1 Corinthians 12:31, for example, to "covet earnestly the best gifts." There are proper desires, virtuous desires, as well as the natural, in-created desires for food and drink.

What the tenth commandment forbids is unlawful desiring, that is, wanting anything apart from God or contrary to his will. That is why Exodus 20:17 speaks of those things that God has given to the neighbor and not to us. That is the perspective as well in 1 Timothy 6:8, where we are called to contentment, "having food and raiment."

Covetousness is essentially idolatry. Thus the tenth commandment ties us back to the first. We have gone full circle! Whoso violates even the least of these commandments, violates them all (James 2:10)! The first commandment, forbidding idolatry, is directed first to our outward lives of worship and confession, and only then reaches into the idolatry of the heart. But the tenth commandment touches especially our hearts' desires in relation to the world and the things of this world. Covetousness, therefore, is principally the same as idolatry of the heart. In fact, Scripture sometimes identifies the two together (Eph. 5:5; Col. 3:5). Positively, our obedience to God must be obedience from the heart. We are to be holy through and through! In accordance with Christ's command in Matthew 5:48, we are called by the tenth commandment to be "perfect, even as [our] Father which is in heaven is perfect"!

Steven Key

November 1 — Q&A 113 — Hating All Sin

Read: Psalm 139:23–24.

If we are to forbid entrance to even the slightest thought or inclination contrary to God's commandments, it is a matter of fundamental necessity that we have an attitude of hostility towards sin in our own lives. Our attitude towards sin must not simply be a neutral attitude, and certainly not a sympathetic attitude; we must absolutely hate all sin. Again, instead of favoring it, or shrugging it off, or even cherishing it and giving it a comfortable place in our hearts and in our lives, we must hate it and seek to sabotage it in every possible way!

This is true of all sins, the Catechism reminds us—the secret and bosom sins, as well as the public and gross sins. While we are often inclined to make distinctions and to downplay our pet sins, Scripture makes unmistakably clear that the tree that bears no fruit is just as ugly and harmful in God's vineyard as the tree that bears rotten fruit. God requires that we hate all sin, even the smallest thought or inclination contrary to his will. There are sins that would seem to be to our advantage, as well as those that are obviously bad and to our hurt. But God requires that we hate them all and flee from them. God demands that we do so with our whole heart.

This must be our attitude, not lethargic nor with hesitation, but earnest! Because all these sins are our mortal enemies, we cannot be relaxed about them even for a moment. No matter where we are or what we are doing, no matter whether we have any support for our position, or whether we are in the workplace where all around us are unbelieving and disobedient colleagues, we dare not relax in our spiritual struggles even for a moment.

We must live with a God-centered focus, delighting in all righteousness. To seek God's glory in all things is our calling. Let all desires and passions be fervently directed towards that which God delights in. This is the Christian's thankful response to the tenth commandment.

Steven Key

November 2 **Q&A 114 – Our Humiliating Imperfection**

Read: Romans 7:14.

The reality of our imperfection comes to its inescapable light when we stand before the tenth commandment. That we commit sin is bad, but that we are sinners in the depths of our beings is worse. This dark background of our lives, this horrible fountain from which our desires arise, and this sinful nature in which those desires grow like weeds on a bad field, only adds to our guilt. In the light of the tenth commandment, we are reminded that we only increase our guilt daily. For when we stand before the commandment and understand that the requirement is to live perfectly and to be perfect before the holy God, we find ourselves utter failures.

Do not lose sight of the fact that we are standing before God's law as the redeemed, those who have been delivered out of the bondage of sin. For nothing in ourselves, but entirely of God's grace, we belong to that elite group of "those who are converted to God."* That does not mean merely that we attend church and have certain convictions. After all, many unconverted people attend church and have certain convictions. But converted people are new creatures in Christ (2 Cor. 5:17). Specifically, as our Catechism explains in Lord's Days 33, we who are converted have "a sincere sorrow of heart that we have provoked God by our sins, and more and more…hate and flee from them."** In addition, we have "a sincere joy of heart in God, through Christ, and with love and delight [we] live according to the will of God in all good works."***

"But can those who are converted to God perfectly keep these commandments?" And the answer is: "No; but even the holiest men, while in this life, have only a small beginning of this obedience; yet so, that with a sincere resolution they begin to live not only according to some, but all the commandments of God."**** This answer is sobering, if not humiliating. Even the holiest men…a small beginning! As far as the sprouting seed is from the full harvest, so distant are we from that perfect obedience to God's commandments. Paul calls himself the chief of sinners, upon whom was bestowed great mercy (1 Tim. 1:15). Peter is the one who cried out: "Depart from me; for I am a sinful man, O Lord" (Luke 5:8). This is the confession of those who are converted.

Steven Key

---

* Heidelberg Catechism Q 114, in *Confessions and Church Order*, 133.
** Heidelberg Catechism A 89, in *Confessions and Church Order*, 121.
*** Heidelberg Catechism A 90, in *Confessions and Church Order*, 121–22.
****Heidelberg Catechism A 114, in *Confessions and Church Order*, 133.

November 3 — Q&A 114 — Pressing Toward the Mark

Read: Philippians 3:13–14.

The reality of our imperfection is not where we stop. In fact, we who are Christ's are very dissatisfied and saddened by this reality of our sinfulness. It is simply impossible to resign ourselves complacently to this imperfection. With the apostle Paul, we "press toward the mark for the prize of the high calling of God in Christ Jesus" (Phil. 3:14). We struggle on in the battle of faith, pressing forward in our expression of gratitude to God, so that with a sincere resolution we begin to live, not only according to some, but all the commandments of God. Does this characterize your life?

The life of those who have been converted to God is not a stagnant pool but a flowing stream. There is no standing still, but progress. So the Holy Spirit of the exalted Christ works. We who are in Christ are partakers of the life of Christ. We are one plant with him. A living plant germinates and buds forth in all directions and grows, bringing forth the fruits that are fitting to that plant. Such life is the driving force behind that sincere resolution that we begin to live not only according to some but all the commandments of God. Our lives must be characterized by the new obedience, the obedience of love, love for God and the neighbor. Spiritual growth is the characteristic of one who is converted, even though his new obedience remains but a small beginning.

That love for God's law and desire to walk in the way of his commandments in thankfulness to him is a love and desire that has been instilled in our hearts and awakened by the Holy Spirit. So even while we lament our sinful nature, we thank God for the wonder of his grace in our salvation. We confess with the inspired apostle in Romans 7:24–25, "O wretched man that I am! who shall deliver me from the body of this death? I thank God through Jesus Christ our Lord. So then with the mind I myself serve the law of God; but with the flesh the law of sin."

Steven Key

November 4 — Q&A 115 — Preaching God's Law

Read: 1 Thessalonians 2:13.

The Catechism concludes its exposition of the ten commandments by reminding us of the importance of preaching that law of God. The authors of the Catechism recognized the need for piercing preaching, preaching that lets no one escape its personal application. They understood that because they were students of the preaching of the prophets, of Christ himself and his apostles. So they taught that when the ten commandments are preached sharply and faithfully, then God will work by his Holy Spirit in the hearts of those who are his, conforming them unto his own image.

Such preaching of the law is necessary, in order that "we may learn more and more to know our sinful nature."* This growing knowledge of our sinful nature is a deepening of spiritual life. The strict preaching of the law exposes our sinfulness and shows us how susceptible we are to wandering and living apart from God.

As our own sinfulness becomes a frightening reality for us in an ever increasing measure, to that same measure we hear more clearly the glad tidings of redemption in Christ. When God exposes our sin by the preaching of his word, he does so not to cast us off but to bind us more and more to himself, drawing us by his grace. So the Spirit works. There is a deepening, therefore, not only in the knowledge of sin, but in the knowledge of our redemption. Christ is found indispensable to us. If we do not enter into fellowship with Christ daily, we wither spiritually. By the preaching, God moves us to fervent spiritual life.

Faithful preaching calls us to a life of true conversion, evidence of the Spirit's work in us. We long to glorify the God of our salvation! The more the preaching of the law finds entrance into our hearts, the more we yearn for the perfection that awaits us. May God soon fulfill our desire for the perfection of holiness, that his glory may be perfectly revealed in us who are the work of his hand.

Steven Key

---

* Heidelberg Catechism A 115, in *Confessions and Church Order*, 134.

Lord's Day 45

Q. 116. Why is prayer necessary for Christians?

A. Because it is the chief part of thankfulness which God requires of us; and also, because God will give his grace and Holy Spirit to those only who with sincere desires continually ask them of him, and are thankful for them.

Q. 117. What are the requisites of that prayer which is acceptable to God and which he will hear?

A. First, that we from the heart pray to the one true God only, who hath manifested himself in his Word, for all things he hath commanded us to ask of him; secondly, that we rightly and thoroughly know our need and misery, that so we may deeply humble ourselves in the presence of his divine majesty; thirdly, that we be fully persuaded that he, notwithstanding that we are unworthy of it, will, for the sake of Christ our Lord, certainly hear our prayer, as he has promised us in his Word.

Q. 118. What hath God commanded us to ask of him?

A. All things necessary for soul and body, which Christ our Lord has comprised in that prayer he himself has taught us.

Q. 119. What are the words of that prayer?

A. *Our Father which art in heaven, hallowed be thy name. Thy kingdom come. Thy will be done in earth, as it is in heaven. Give us this day our daily bread. And forgive us our debts, as we forgive our debtors. And lead us not into temptation, but deliver us from evil. For thine is the kingdom, and the power, and the glory, for ever. Amen.*

November 5 — Q&A 116-119 — The Wonder that is Prayer

Read: Matthew 6:9–15.

The Catechism presents in earlier Lord's Days the two great scriptural truths called sin and grace. It presents sin in all of its terribleness: "I am prone by nature to hate God and my neighbor."* Our first father, Adam, sinned and made all of those born from him guilty and corrupt, worthy of eternal damnation in hell. He was the representative of man for succeeding generations. Besides, each person continues to add to his guiltiness every day. The Bible says that "there is none righteous, no, not one" (Rom. 3:10).

The Catechism presents the one way of deliverance from the wrath of the righteous God. God in his grace sent his Son, the second person of the Godhead, to pay for the sins of those whom God gave to his Son (John 3:16; 17:24). The wonder of salvation that God works for his people is in the way of the offering of Christ's shed blood on the cross. What a wonder God has done—so that all the glory for the deliverance of his people can be given to God alone.

In the third section of the Catechism, we are taught concerning the proper part of thankfulness to God for what he has done for his people. The questions might be asked: What must I do in order to repay God for his great gift? Is his gift given conditionally? Must I do something to contribute towards this deliverance? These questions must be answered. The answer is simple and short. There is nothing that we can do to either contribute towards or earn this salvation! Nor is there any possible thing with which we can repay God for this great work of salvation.

But the fruit of salvation must be seen in the way the Christian lives and walks. He shows thanksgiving in all things before God. The Catechism emphasizes two ways that the Christian shows proper thanksgiving. Scripture teaches that the saved person shows and desires to show true thankfulness by obeying God's law—summarized in the ten commandments. Obedience to the commandments is not a matter of repayment but the fruit of God's work in his people.

The second aspect of thankfulness is prayer. Prayer is the God-given avenue to the very throne of God. Prayer is our hotline to the eternal God. It is the means both to praise God for his greatness and glory and to make petitions for our own needs and cares on this earth.

But how does one pray to God? For what must we ask God? It was the concern of Christ's disciples too. In Luke 11:1, the disciples came to Christ and asked: "Lord, teach us to pray, as John also taught his disciples." Then Christ taught them what is called the Lord's prayer. What a prayer that is! In six petitions, with few words, Christ gives a summary of what proper prayer is and for what we must ask. In a prayer that can be uttered in less than half a minute, Christ shows us the model for and summary of prayer. This we must briefly study in the remaining Lord's Days of the Catechism.

Gise Van Baren

---

* Heidelberg Catechism A 5, in *Confessions and Church Order*, 85.

November 6 — Q&A 116 — Why Is Prayer Necessary?

Read: James 5.

Prayer is necessary, states the Catechism, because it is the chief part of thankfulness and also because God gives his grace and Holy Spirit to those only who ask them of him and are thankful for what they receive.

There is nothing more satisfying to our God than that we pray to him. The Catechism does not state that prayer is the *only* way of thankfulness, but "it is the *chief* part of thankfulness."* It is the fruit and evidence of the work of God in saving his people. So, how do we pray? How often do we pray? This would give us some idea of how thankful we truly are for our salvation.

God gives "his grace and Holy Spirit to those only who with sincere desires ask them of him."**

Many consider prayer as some sort of emergency tool (for example, "break in case of fire"). When one faces sudden and devastating trials, then one will earnestly pray to God. Those on an airplane apparently ready to crash are later reported to be all praying. Others regard "prayer" as a way to express themselves forcibly (for example, "Oh, my God!") Some find it necessary to request hundreds of others to pray for them—as though God will be swayed by numbers. Others believe that if they pray to God for anything, God must surely give that for which they ask.

The Christian prays for such things as God teaches him to ask of him. He is not as a little child who is convinced that if he asks God for a bike, God must give it to him. Jesus taught us to ask for those things necessary for body and soul.

Why should God require that his people ask of him anything? In his providence, has he not eternally determined everything we would receive? He has. However, God has also determined that we would receive these things in the way of asking him for them. God rejoices in our petitions to him. He teaches us important truths. We learn thereby that we are unable to provide for ourselves. We learn that we do not earn anything of him. We learn that God gives graciously and freely. We learn that he often gives more than we could ever think or ask. We learn that his grace to us is only because of what Christ has done on the cross.

Then our hearts overflow with thankfulness to God. Think: the infinite, eternal, and almighty God condescends to do these things for creatures who are less than specks of dust before the Almighty.

Do you desire these things of him? Do you ask in sincerity? Are you thankful for what he provides? If so, you begin to have a proper understanding of prayer.

Gise Van Baren

---

* Heidelberg Catechism A 116, in *Confessions and Church Order*, 134 (emphasis added).
** Heidelberg Catechism A 11, in *Confessions and Church Order*, 134.

November 7 — **Q&A 117 — The Requirements of the Godly Prayer**

Read: Luke 18:9–14.

Prayer is not a matter of man's invention. Prayer is God's gift to his people who are born again and converted. God gives to them a way of access to his throne, so that they can confidently approach him. God expects that this gift be used by them as the highest expression of thanksgiving to him for the salvation that is theirs through Jesus Christ.

It is no wonder, therefore, that the devil would seek to divert attention from this great gift by many ways of deception. The devil seeks to direct his followers to use prayer too—to their gods or idols. The claim is then made that all worship the same god but in different ways. All pray—but prayer comes in different forms.

The devil also seeks to lead the Christians astray with regards to prayer. He seeks to persuade us that if we pray to saints, they can more successfully intercede for us with God; or perhaps prayer to the Virgin Mary, who can approach her son Jesus for us, would be the best way to gain the ear of Jesus.

In prayer, the child of God acknowledges that grace and the Holy Spirit come to him in the way of prayer. We thankfully acknowledge that all this is the gift of God. We cannot purchase these nor earn them. We pray for them, and in this way God also provides.

Prayer must represent a sincere desire for these things. It is not merely a routine exercise out of custom or habit. The Christian prays because he desires earnestly God's grace and the guidance of the Spirit.

Nor is this prayer a matter of a one time request. It might be argued that God knows we need his grace and Spirit before we even ask. Further, we might think that if we ask once, God would not forget that we have asked—and he would then provide. The fact is that we must continually ask for these things (Luke 18:7–8). This is not because God does not understand our request. Rather, God teaches us that we must continually ask so that we never forget that God is the one who provides.

Finally, we show in all that we do that we are thankful for the grace and Holy Spirit he provides. He gives these not merely once, but again and again. Every day we thank him for these.

That is faithful prayer. It is not that of the Pharisee who thanks God that he was "not as other men," but as the publican who cries out: "God, be merciful to me a sinner!" (Luke 18:9–13).

Gise Van Baren

November 8 — Q&A 117 — The Requisites of the Godly Prayer

Read: Romans 3.

What kind of prayer is "acceptable to God…which he will hear?"* That ought to be of concern to us. Remember: we are but specks of dust on the planet Earth, which itself is but a speck in the vastness of the universe. God created and sustains the whole universe. One might quickly be overwhelmed with the very thought of approaching such a God. It would seem far more likely that an ant addresses and seeks to please a human being than we approach the infinite, sovereign God, the creator of all.

But the Bible shows the possibilities, and the Catechism summarizes them. First, prayer must be "from the heart…to the one true God only, who hath manifested himself in his Word."** It must come from the born again, regenerated heart—it cannot come from the heart of the unbeliever. Prayer is not a matter of show or pretense, but sincerity. It must be to the one only true God. It cannot be to God and something else. It must not be to an idol or a god of one's imagination. Proper prayer cannot rest either upon luck, or chance, or upon man's own cleverness in taking care of his own needs.

We must thoroughly know our needs and misery. One does not approach God in prayer only in those situations where he knows not what to do. We are deeply humbled before his divine majesty. We confess that "the good that I would I do not: but the evil which I would not, that I do" (Rom. 7:19). That's quite a confession! There is in the Christian a deep consciousness of his own sinfulness and unworthiness before God. That consciousness arises because he knows his own old nature against which he still struggles. Not only is he so very insignificant in size before the almighty God, but at the same time, he sees rebellion in his members against God.

But out of his regenerated heart proceeds that work of the Spirit by which he confesses his sins daily. He acknowledges his unworthiness. He confesses that he has nowhere else to go than God's throne of grace. His prayer, then, is a confession of his own inability to provide what he needs. He confesses that his God can and does provide—in the way of his calling upon God.

Let us measure our own prayers by this standard.

Gise Van Baren

---

* Heidelberg Catechism Q 117, in *Confessions and Church Order*, 134.
** Heidelberg Catechism A 117, in *Confessions and Church Order*, 134–35.

November 9 — Q&A 117 — The Conviction that God Will Answer Our Prayer

Read: Psalm 115.

There is one large question that comes up in connection with prayer. Will God hear and answer *me* when I pray to him? The Catechism assures us that he will certainly hear and answer us.

Why bring up this question? The Catechism points out our confession that we are not worthy to be heard and answered by God. That is true.

There are related questions which quickly arise in the mind of the Christian. There are those times when our prayers seem to rise no higher than the ceiling, as someone has expressed it. Simply put, the Christian can easily and quickly, but unjustly, conclude that God does not hear his prayer or refuses to hear it. That can often be a very devastating conclusion of the Christian. He might despair of God's mercy and grace.

With the above comes the conclusion that God does not care. He does not answer prayer as he has promised to do. At the least, we might conclude that God is too slow in the answers he gives. We desire an answer *right now*. But the answer does not come. It may be a prayer for a cure from some serious illness. It might be for sufficient funds to pay off one's debts. But God doesn't answer.

Several truths the Christian must remember. Prayers for cures or for seemingly necessary earthly things are not always answered as we might desire. Our prayers must always be with the stipulation: "If the Lord will…" (James 4:15). The fact is that God always sends what is best for his people, for their everlasting welfare in glory. Some requests seem unanswered—for God would teach us patience to await an answer. Has not he taught us in his word: "All things work together for good to them that love God" (Rom. 8:28)? Think of Job. In the loss of virtually everything he had possessed—great riches, many children—he confessed: "The Lord gave, and the Lord hath taken away; blessed be the name of the Lord" (Job 1:21).

The Catechism reminds us that it is for the sake of Christ our Lord that God will hear and properly respond to our prayers. Whether we have health or sickness, riches or poverty, none of these is God's punishment for us. Christ has borne God's wrath, the wrath of hell, for our sins. Our sins are covered by Christ's blood. For Christ's sake, God promises to bless his people in every way. Faith holds fast to that promise of God.

Gise Van Baren

November 10 — Q&A 118-119 — The Model Prayer

Read: Luke 11:1–12.

The disciples had made their request of Jesus: "Lord, teach us to pray" (Luke 11:1). They were aware of the fact that John the Baptist had taught his disciples how to pray. In response, Jesus had given to them the Lord's prayer. Some call it, rightly, the model prayer.

What immediately strikes one is the brevity of the prayer itself. It is striking that the prayer consists of but six petitions. It is a prayer that can be uttered in its entirety in less than thirty seconds.

By this instruction, Jesus did not teach that our prayers ought to be very brief—perhaps no more than thirty seconds. Jesus does condemn long prayers spoken in pretense and made to gain the admiration of men (Matt. 23:14). But Jesus himself could pray all night. Did the perfect Son of God have the need to pray all night? Jesus would have communion with God his Father even as he was ready to offer himself to satisfy God's just demands for payment for the sins of those given him by the Father. Our prayers likewise may be fervent cries to God uttered in times of great need or great distress.

What Jesus does teach is that prayer need not be lengthy to be heard by God. God is not to be swayed by our "much speaking" (Matt. 6:7). A sincere prayer, which is heard and answered by God, might consist of but a few words.

In the Lord's prayer, Jesus sets forth the principle of prayer and the proper content of prayer. We are taught to clearly understand to whom we pray and for what we ask in that prayer. This is the thrust of the instruction of the Catechism in succeeding Lord's Days.

We consider more important questions. Ought we to pray only this prayer? Is it not the perfect prayer? Does it not present to God petitions covering the complete array of what ought to be included in any prayer?

This prayer can appropriately be prayed as Christ has given it to us. In fact, godly parents can teach their very young children to pray this prayer. It is a prayer that they can remember and use for life. It becomes the occasion for parents to remind their children of the requirements of proper prayer.

What a gift is this prayer Christ taught us! We often know not what we should pray for as we ought. Now we are given a simple yet perfect example of what we are to pray for. God grant that his people may learn well from this model.

Gise Van Baren

November 11 — Q&A 119 – For What Do We Pray?

Read: Psalm 116.

In Lord's Day 45, we take a view of the Lord's model prayer in general in the final question and answer. The following Lord's Days will study each part of the prayer itself. An examination of the prayer should give a good idea on how each part of this brief prayer fits in with the whole.

We must remind ourselves first that this prayer was given to us by our Lord Jesus Christ. It is therefore not open to amendment or change. It is not a time-conditioned prayer, which was given for that period of Jesus' day but now must be adapted to our current society. It is a timeless prayer—equally relevant today as it was two thousand years ago.

This prayer consists of several divisions or parts. It consists of an address, of a series of petitions, and of a closing doxology. The remarkable fact is that the prayer, though so very brief, cannot be added to in order to improve it or have parts taken away. It is complete the way Christ has given it.

The address is to "Our Father which art in heaven."* That address is treated more extensively in the following Lord's Day. This is the proper address for this prayer and for the petitions which comprise its body.

There follow six petitions, which can again be divided into two parts of three petitions each. The first three petitions relate to God and our relationship to him. Though brief, these express the basic truths of our proper relationship to God. We could correctly say that the truths of these petitions could not be stated more succinctly than they are. One must be amazed at the beautiful summary that they give concerning God, his kingdom, and his will. The following Lord's Days will explain this further.

The second group of three petitions treats that which pertains to our own needs. Again, one might hastily make some erroneous conclusions. Why should we ask for bread before treating that which is spiritual? One might also wonder at the brevity of the petitions. We might multiply the number of petitions. No doubt other petitions can be presented to our Father. But the model prayer presents all of this in a summary form.

The concluding doxology is recorded in the Matthew account (Matt. 6:13) but not in the Luke account (Luke 11). It is a beautiful concluding doxology. This prayer begins by addressing our Father and concludes with the emphasis, though again so briefly, upon our Father's greatness and glory.

On the basis of the whole prayer we can by faith believe that God hears and answers it. Our prayers, modeled after the principles of this prayer, will likewise be answered. Be assured of it—it is God's promise.

Gise Van Baren

---

* Heidelberg Catechism A 119, in *Confessions and Church Order*, 136.

Lord's Day 46

Q. 120. Why hath Christ commanded us to address God thus: "Our Father"?

A. That immediately, in the very beginning of our prayer, he might excite in us a childlike reverence for and confidence in God, which are the foundation of our prayer, namely, that God is become our Father in Christ, and will much less deny us what we ask of him in true faith than our parents will refuse us earthly things.

Q. 121. Why is it here added, "Which art in heaven"?

A. Lest we should form any earthly conceptions of God's heavenly majesty, and that we may expect from his almighty power all things necessary for soul and body.

November 12   **Q&A 120 — The Address**

Read: Psalm 145.

A prayer is a means of contact with another, with the intent of presenting petitions to him. It is very specific in its address. It indicates that we know whom we address; we know what we will ask of him; and we believe that he is able to give that for which we ask.

In the case of this model prayer, we must be deeply conscious that we are not addressing a mere creature, but rather the sovereign God. In addressing earthly royalty, we would not use crude language (*Hey, you!*), but we would use addresses considered appropriate for royalty (*Your Royal Highness*). Much more ought we to address God with names appropriate to him.

The Bible gives many names of God in Scripture. He is the Holy One of Israel, God Almighty, or Jehovah. There are many similar names indicating the high standing of our God. It would not be improper to use any of these names when addressing our God. The Lord's prayer, however, uses that name most appropriate for God in light of the petitions presented.

It would be very improper for man to alter this name of the Lord's prayer to fit into man's current concept of the male/female relationship. Society would have a gender-free name so that both man and woman are represented. Some address God thus: Our Father/Mother who is in heaven. Thus, God is said to be that being who not only shows the characteristics of an earthly father, but also the softness, love, and concern of an earthly mother. If we are going to honor the fact that Jesus taught us to pray, how dare we alter the address that Jesus teaches here?

We are to address God properly as Father, and our Father for Jesus' sake. We must carefully avoid the politically correct approach of the moment. Let us pray as Jesus taught us in this prayer.

At the same time, let us be sensitive to the amazing truth involved in the name we use. We are addressing the creator and sustainer of the universe. He is the eternal, almighty, sovereign God. We are but creatures of the dust. We are finite, but God is infinite. One might wonder, how dare we even think that we can address this God? Will he not strike us down in anger if we even dare to try to approach him thus? Could one imagine an ant addressing a human being as father? It's preposterous.

But Jesus taught us to call this sovereign one Father. So we will do. This is not some great self-esteem or pride on our part, but our submission to the instruction of our master and Lord.

Gise Van Baren

November 13 — Q&A 120 — Childlike Reverence

Read: Psalm 89:1–18.

When we address the triune God as our Father, we thereby indicate that we are children of his. We must keep in mind what that also means when we address God. We cannot approach God as if somehow he is our equal. We do not seek to make some special agreement with God. Surely we do not approach God as though we are speaking to a servant or a slave. We do not draw up a list of things we want of God and expect that he ought to hear us and provide as we have asked.

Rather, we recognize that we are sons (by adoption through Christ's shed blood), and our Father will give us what is right and good for us. Scripture expresses it thus: "We know not what we should pray for as we ought: but the Spirit itself maketh intercession for us with groanings which cannot be uttered" (Rom. 8:26). It must also be true that we ask with the understanding that only "if the Lord will" can we do what we propose or receive that for which we ask (James 4:15).

The Lord's prayer is Christ's own instruction concerning the necessary things for which we must ask. There are six necessary petitions—each important in its own way. The Christian is not limited to these six petitions. Yet there is a sense that these six petitions include everything essential for our lives on this earth. The Catechism continues to analyze each of these petitions in turn.

But in every prayer and every petition, we address our Father in heaven, which ought to "excite in us a childlike reverence and confidence."* This attitude is seen in children. It is touching to see young children run to their parents. There they believe themselves to be safe. As long as they can hold on to their father's hand, they can be virtually fearless. When they are separated from their parents, they can be filled with fear. The psalmist also compares the father's care for his children with that of God for his people (Ps.103:12–14).

That confidence is also taught in Scripture, which describes God as a high tower into which "the righteous runneth…and is safe" (Prov. 18:10). What comfort, what assurance ought to be ours when we have our heavenly Father to whom we can turn! He protects and provides; he comforts and encourages. Our Father works all things together for good to them that love him.

Gise Van Baren

---

*   Heidelberg Catechism A 120, in *Confessions and Church Order*, 136.

November 14 — Q&A 120 — Sons of God the Father?

Read: John 17.

One great question arises. We've considered how great our Father is (infinite and eternal God) and how small and sinful we are. How is it possible that we be *children* of God? Is not the possibility of such a blessed fellowship and union beyond the grasp of the sinner forever?

Various answers have been given to this important question. It is frequently taught that God loves all, seeks to save all, offers salvation and sonship to all who are willing to accept it. It's a matter of man's choice. But that is a terrible, anti-scriptural conclusion. How could it ever be that the infinite God, who sincerely loves all, and sincerely desires to save all, does not, in fact, finally save all? How can a God of infinite love towards all cast any into hell? If he sent his Son into human flesh to save all, how can it be that any would be lost forever?

A human father will do whatever he possibly can to provide for, protect, and save his children from all danger. Certainly he would not allow his children to die if it were in his power to deliver them! More so it is true that God will save all those whom he sincerely loves. If he sends his Son to save all whom he loves, they shall be saved.

That God is unable to save some of his children is not the teaching of Scripture. Scripture declares the blessed truth that "God so loved the world" that he sent his Son to deliver that world (John 3:16). Jesus limits the scope of the word *world* when he teaches in John 17:9, "I pray for them: I pray not for the world, but for them which thou hast given me; for they are thine." Imagine! God sent his Son into the world to enter human flesh to provide the only way of saving this world (all those given by God to Christ) and bringing them to glory.

So God has ordained that he would adopt unto himself those whom he has eternally chosen as children of God. He is their Father. He who comes to the Father sees in this very action the perfect work of God the Father within him.

So God's people need neither doubt nor fear to come daily, fervently, to their Father. He so loved them that he gave his only begotten Son to atone, to pay for their sins. He will hear the cries of his children and provide for their every need.

What a wonder of grace to have such a Father!

Gise Van Baren

November 15 — Q&A 121 — Our Father Who Is in Heaven

Read: Psalm 115.

The name Father is appropriate to the petitions made in prayer. It reminds us of the parent-child relationships we enjoy. Earthly fathers are expected to make adequate provision for their children. Fathers provide food, clothing, and shelter for them. They also provide protection against storms and people who might want to harm their children. Most children will quickly turn to their fathers for provision and protection.

That earthly relationship is but a picture of the relationship of the child of God to his Father who is in heaven. Jesus teaches us to use this address to show us what we ought to ask of our heavenly Father. Children may not ask for anything or everything but only for the proper things as Scripture presents them.

Scripture uses Father in either one of two ways. Father sometimes has reference to the first person of the Trinity. There are the three persons in one being. The first person of the Trinity eternally generates the second person, Jesus, who entered human flesh to provide the way of salvation by paying for our sins. Jesus, however, does not teach us to pray exclusively to the first person of the Trinity.

Our Father in heaven is the triune God. We address him not through individual persons of the Trinity, but to the three (persons) in one (being). The triune God must answer our petitions. We pray to the Father, through the Son, and by the work of the Holy Spirit.

As is true throughout the prayer, the Christian is conscious that he prays in the communion of the saints: *our* Father. He prays with the whole church of God. He asks not all of these petitions simply for himself, but for the whole body of Christ. It is very important that we remember this as we pray.

The address of the prayer is a beautiful way of emphasizing our close relationship to God. It is almost inconceivable that one so small, and such a rebel, is able to address the infinite God as Father. But it is true, because of the perfect work of Christ on the cross whereby he satisfied the justice of God for the sins of his people. Then the triune God can and does receive us unto himself. Deuteronomy 33:27 speaks of the eternal God as a refuge, "and underneath are the everlasting arms." We have a Father who is both able and willing to provide for his children with every necessary good.

Gise Van Baren

November 16 — **Q&A 121 — Our Father in Heaven**

Read: 1 Kings 8:22–30.

The danger of addressing God as Father is that one might be inclined to visualize God perhaps in the form of a man. The Catechism reminds us that our Father is in heaven. That immediately directs our attention to the fact that there is to be no god of our own imagination. Artists have frequently portrayed God as a very old man with a flowing white beard and long white hair. We ourselves can easily form a mental image of our Father. Therefore Christ taught us to state the fact that he is in heaven.

We even try to visualize heaven. Yet none can see heaven while on this earth. It is a realm different from anything that we now see. It is that place where God is pleased to reveal his glory, wisdom, and might. There, our Father gathers his people who have been purified through the sacrifice Christ made to remove the guilt of their sins. There, we enjoy glorious and everlasting fellowship with God through Jesus Christ our Lord.

Our Father, the triune God, reveals himself in his Son, who has united himself to human flesh. We shall see him in heaven. He reveals to us the triune God, our Father. Jesus also reminded us that God is Spirit (not of some created substance), and those who worship him do so in spirit and truth (John 4:24).

He is infinite—bound neither by time nor space, which are created by him. All of this we confess in our prayers—our Father is infinitely far beyond us. Our Father is in heaven, not as one of many gods but the one true God.

There is another glorious truth that this address teaches us. Our Father has "almighty power," and he can provide "all things necessary for soul and body."* Earthly fathers would likely be ready to give up their lives to protect and deliver their children from terrible dangers. But they are limited in their ability to provide their children with everything that they need.

However, our heavenly Father is both able and willing to give all that his children need. He can and does give them their daily bread through Christ, forgiveness of sin, and life everlasting. Our Father does not always give us what we think we need or what we might desire. But he does hear and answer our prayers. He never fails to give us what we need. Therefore, the Christian is content in whatever God gives.

Finally, in heaven we shall know and understand that whatever he provided us on this earth was exactly what we needed to prepare ourselves for our place there.

Gise Van Baren

---

* Heidelberg Catechism A 121, in *Confessions and Church Order*, 136.

November 17 — Q&A 121 – Only Good Things?

Read: Job 1.

It is very important to remember that whatever God sends to his children, it is always good. What earthly father would give his children only candy for food—and not give carrots and spinach and peas because these are repulsive to his children? What earthly father will only and always praise his children—and never rebuke nor chastise them?

When our heavenly Father sends what we might not like, it is not to punish us for some sin we have committed. Jesus has taken on himself the guilt of and punishment for our sin. That's the wonder of the cross. But God does chastise. We still have the old man, the old nature, as long as we live on this earth. We often need correction from our heavenly Father to remind us of our calling to flee sin and seek righteousness.

Sometimes, we do not see that what we receive is needed—we can think of no specific sin for which God is chastising us. The Bible presents a striking instance of this in the Old Testament saint Job. He had an abundance of material things, much cattle, many servants, and ten children. He was very godly—he offered sacrifices and prayers for his children. Suddenly, God took all of that away from Job. It must have been devastating. Would Job's Father in heaven do that to one so obviously serving God rightly? Yes, God did. It was not to chastise Job but to shape and prepare him for his place in glory.

Satan had challenged God to take all these things away, and then Job would no longer serve God. But Satan was terribly wrong. Job was strengthened in his faith in the way of afflictions. He refused to follow the advice of his wife to curse God and die. He acknowledged God's sovereignty in confessing: "The Lord gave, and the Lord hath taken away; blessed be the name of the Lord" (Job 1:21). Job did not simply confess some dogmatic truth, but he experienced in his heart and life the truth of that confession.

So it must be with God's people. God sends many difficult things in the lives of his people. In Romans 8:28 we confess: "All things work together for good to them that love God, to them who are the called according to his purpose."

That's the confession of faith of the Christian. He knows that whatever befalls him, his heavenly Father knows what is best. God's design must be realized. If we do not understand why something befalls us, we know that finally in glory we shall understand and thank God for what he sends.

Gise Van Baren

November 18 — Q&A 121 — Father Almighty

Read: Matthew 7:7–12.

It is no wonder that the child of God holds his heavenly Father in great esteem. He rejoices in the word from his Father. He loves his law. He rejoices in opportunities to speak to others concerning his Father in heaven. The Christian points out the greatness of his Father: he is the creator and sustainer of the heavens and the earth. He directs the affairs of nations. He continues to gather his children from the four corners of the earth. Not a sparrow can fall and not a hair from one's head can drop without the will of our heavenly Father (Matt. 10:28–30).

He is *my* Father. The Christian enjoys that very close relationship with his Father, of which earthly father-son relationships are but a faint picture. The Christian holds his Father's hand. God guides and directs him in the way he must go. His Father encircles him with his arm. His Father can and does defend him from every enemy. God is closer to his people than a human father could ever be to his children. Our Father guides us by his Holy Spirit. He assures us of the forgiveness of sins through Christ.

It is all so amazing—even unbelievable—if not for the gift of faith. How can it be that one so infinitely great, so almighty, would care for one so finite, and sinful besides, so that he works all things together for my good! His people treasure that relationship above anything that this world has to offer. Material things, earthly prosperity, are as dung compared to this glorious relationship to their Father.

That relationship is established by our Father out of pure sovereign grace. We did not contribute to it nor deserve it—but Christ offered himself to obtain for us the forgiveness of sin and the right to sonship.

Christ now teaches his disciples and us what we ought to ask of our Father. In six short petitions, he teaches what we must ask of our Father, how we must express ourselves, and why we can be sure God will answer our prayers. Though we can bring before our Father all of our concerns, Christ shows us what is absolutely essential for us to bring before him. In presenting our petitions to our Father, we acknowledge our great need. We cannot live before our Father unless he provides that for which we ask in this prayer. Only he is able to provide for us.

In the final Lord's Days of the Heidelberg Catechism, we confront the glorious teaching of Scripture concerning these six petitions.

Gise Van Baren

November 19   Q&A 120-121 — Ask and It Shall Be Given

Read: Matthew 7:7–11.

Children show dependence on their parents and ask them for many things. Dad, can you please fix this? Mom, can you get me a snack, please? It is also true that when children respectfully ask their parents for what they need, loving parents are pleased. They would be hurt if their children did not ask them to provide and went to the neighbor for their needs instead.

God calls us, his children through Christ, to ask him for what we need. As parents would be offended if their children went to the neighbors for food instead of to them, so our heavenly Father is offended when we seek our daily needs from the world rather than from his hand. To do so is a slight to him. He takes pleasure in us coming to him with our petitions, depending on him to provide.

We are to ask God to provide for us, and Jesus shows us what to ask God for in the petitions of the Lord's prayer. We have many books from which we learn things. From the Lord's prayer, we learn how to pray. Jesus included six petitions in this prayer. The first three are concerned with God and his cause in the world. The second three are concerned with our physical and spiritual needs.

In Matthew 7:7, Jesus says: "Ask, and it shall be given you; seek, and ye shall find; knock, and it shall be opened unto you." As we pray regularly for the things we need, the things spelled out in the Lord's prayer, our heavenly Father is pleased to provide these things. Are you praying regularly for the things you need? Are you thanking God for providing gifts in answer to your cries?

Matt De Boer

Lord's Day 47

Q. 122. Which is the first petition?

A. *Hallowed be thy name*; that is, grant us, first, rightly to know thee, and to sanctify, glorify, and praise thee in all thy works, in which thy power, wisdom, goodness, justice, mercy and truth are clearly displayed; and further also, that we may so order and direct our whole lives, our thoughts, words, and actions, that thy name may never be blasphemed, but rather honored and praised on our account.

November 20 — Q&A 122 – God's Glorious Name

Read: Psalm 8.

The first petition of the Lord's prayer is "Hallowed be thy name,"* and thus concerns God's name.

God's name is the revelation of who he is. It is different from our names. Our names are labels that simply help us distinguish one person from another. Our names do not reveal anything about who we are. But God's name shows us exactly who he is. God's name includes his proper names. Psalm 8 uses the name LORD or Jehovah. This means I AM and reveals that God is the faithful friend of his people who never changes. Psalm 8 also uses the name Lord, meaning master or ruler. God's name includes his proper names and his attributes because his attributes also show who he is. Lord's Day 47 lists some of these attributes: "Wisdom, goodness, justice, mercy, and truth."** We can actually say that God is his name, because he is Jehovah, and he is wise, good, just, merciful, and true.

God's name, God himself, is also displayed in all his works. He, for instance, is revealed in his work of creation and providential rule of that creation. Psalm 8:1 says: "O LORD our Lord, how excellent is thy name in all the earth! who hast set thy glory above the heavens." We hear his almighty power in the rumbling of thunder and see it in the flashing of lightning. His wisdom is seen in his design of the bird that flies and swoops to get food. His goodness is evident in the powerful sun that warms us and the rain from above that gives water, food, and life. God's name is displayed in his creation and also in his work of judgment. His judgment on Christ at the cross and his judgment on wicked men today reveal that he is a just and holy God that must punish sin.

In an especially wonderful way, God's name is revealed in his saving work too. Through Christ's death on the cross for our sins, God shows himself to be a just and a merciful God to us his people. In the opening of our blind eyes to see and believe, he reveals he is good and kind. And, through his continued care for us, he shows that he is Jehovah, the unchanging God of truth.

Consider God's name today and bless him.

Matt De Boer

---

*   Heidelberg Catechism Q&A 122, in *Confessions and Church Order*, 136.
** Heidelberg Catechism A 122, in *Confessions and Church Order*, 137.

November 21 — Q&A 122 — The First Petition

Read: Psalm 83.

To hallow literally means to make holy or set apart. To hallow God's name is to set his name apart from what is common and ordinary. Thus, answer 122 says that hallowing God's name is to "sanctify, glorify, and praise" his name.[*]

When we pray, "Hallowed be thy name," we are saying, Set apart and glorified be thy name. We are asking that God cause himself to be glorified in all his works: through his creation, his judgments, and his salvation. We are also asking that God's name be set apart and glorified by us, the church here on earth. Question and answer 122 emphasizes this, saying: "Which is the first petition? *Hallowed be thy name*; that is, grant us, first, rightly to know thee, and to sanctify, glorify, and praise thee in all thy works, in which thy power, wisdom, goodness, justice, mercy, and truth are clearly displayed."[**]

Notice that Asaph made this petition in Psalm 83. As enemies threatened Israel's existence, Asaph prayed not ultimately for his own safety and earthly comfort, but said: "Fill their faces with shame; that they may seek thy name, O LORD...That men may know that thou, whose name alone is JEHOVAH, art the most high over all the earth" (vv. 16, 18). Asaph asked God to bring judgment so that the nations would know that Jehovah is God alone and would then exalt his name.

A prayer for safety, daily bread, forgiveness, and other needs is important, but asking for the hallowing of God's name must be first in our hearts as it was for Asaph. Jesus put this petition first in the Lord's prayer to show us that all our petitions must be made with the goal that God's name be hallowed. This request truly sets the tone for the rest of the petitions. It shows that we must pray for God's kingdom to come and his will to be done, so that his name is glorified. We must pray for daily bread, so that we have strength to praise his name on earth. We ought to pray for forgiveness of sins and deliverance from evil, seeking the exaltation of God's name.

You may be going through a trial right now as Asaph was. Pray for help! But, make the main concern of your prayer God's honor, asking that his name be hallowed through whatever you face. He is worthy of that honor as our Creator and Savior.

Matt De Boer

---

[*] Heidelberg Catechism A 122, in *Confessions and Church Order*, 137.
[**] Heidelberg Catechism Q&A 122, in *Confessions and Church Order*, 137–38.

November 22   Q&A 122 — Ask for Right Knowledge

Read: Colossians 1:1–14.

Lord's Day 47 teaches that when we pray, Hallowed be thy name, we are specifically saying: "Grant us, first, rightly to know thee."* Knowing God is necessary for hallowing his name.

What does it mean to know God rightly? To know God is to understand the truth about him. It is to understand the truth about his works: that he created, rules, judges, and saves his people. Even more, to know God means that you know him personally and experientially as your friend in Christ. John 17:3 says: "And this is life eternal, that they might know thee the only true God, and Jesus Christ, whom thou hast sent." Here, the word *know* does not simply refer to knowing facts, but emphasizes personal, experiential knowledge of God. One who truly knows God knows him as the God of his salvation and thus loves him.

If we do not know God, or if we have a wrong knowledge of him, we will not glorify his name. If, for example, we only know another person superficially, and we make judgments about that person, we will make wrong judgments. When people do not know the truth about God, they speak wrongly of him with their words and do not praise his name. Some, for instance, say God is a monster because of the bad things that happen to people. Others argue that his word is judgmental and hateful. Still others might even go to church occasionally, but they do not know God as a just and holy God. They believe that he is only a loving God who tolerates all lifestyles, so they live in sin. God's word says: "My people are destroyed for lack of knowledge" (Hos. 4:6). We must know the truth about God and know him personally as the God of our salvation if we are going to hallow his name.

What tool does God use to bring people truly to know him? The word! That is part of why we have worship services every week, catechism classes, daily devotions, and Bible studies. The word brings us and our children truly to know Jehovah, his holiness, his work in saving us, and to see his beauty in creation too. This leads to the hallowing of God's name. Even we who have heard the word throughout our lives need to keep hearing it and studying it, for without consistent reminders we can quickly forget God and fail to praise the Lord.

When we pray, Hallowed be thy name, we are praying: "May we first rightly know thee." This was Paul's request for the Colossians (Col. 1:9–10). Make the same petition today and every day.

Matt De Boer

---

*   Heidelberg Catechism A 122, in *Confessions and Church Order*, 136.

November 23 — Q&A 122 – Praise God in All His Works

Read: Job 1.

When we pray, "Hallowed be thy name," we specifically pray that we might know God and then with our mouths praise him for all his works. Lord's Day 47 says: "Which is the first petition? Hallowed be thy name, that is, grant us, first, rightly to know thee, and to sanctify, glorify, and praise thee in all thy works, in which thy power, wisdom, goodness, justice, mercy, and truth are clearly displayed."[*]

Men often praise other men with their mouths when the glory should be going to God. Some inventors and leaders in technology are world famous, and many words are said about them, but men say little about the God who gave them their abilities and the materials they needed for their work. We can even quickly praise certain preachers or others in the church for their faith, prayers, and sacrifice, but not say much about the God who strengthens them.

Or perhaps we praise God for his works, but not for all his works. Sickness, grief, and loneliness also belong to all his works, but it is hard to praise God during those times. We will not do it ourselves.

In the first petition, we are asking that we, and the church everywhere, might be strengthened to praise God in all his works. We are asking that as we see the creation around us, including the inventions men make from it that benefit us, we might not stand in awe of men, but stand in awe of God's power and wisdom and praise him with our mouths. We are praying that as we see people serving God in the church and making great sacrifices for us, we might give praise not to men ultimately, but to God! We are requesting that when we go through sickness and grief, we might be strengthened not to complain about God or remain silent but instead remember the promises of God's word and his faithfulness and say along with Job: "The LORD gave, and the LORD hath taken away; blessed be the name of the LORD" (Job 1:21).

In the first petition, we are asking that we be moved to glorify God for all his works in our prayers, songs, and in our daily conversations with others. We know we can easily be afraid or ashamed to speak of God and his great works to our neighbors, so we are requesting strength to talk about the Lord openly.

Pray these, or similar words, each day: "Hallowed be thy name; grant us rightly to know thee and praise thee with our mouths in all thy works."

Matt De Boer

---

[*] Heidelberg Catechism Q&A 122, in *Confessions and Church Order*, 136–37.

November 24 — Q&A 122 – Glorify God in Your Entire Life

Read: Psalm 19.

When we pray, Hallowed be thy name, we pray that we might not only glorify God in what we say about his works, but also specifically ask that we glorify him with our entire lives. The end of Lord's Day 47 says that in the first petition, we are asking "that we may so order and direct our whole lives, our thoughts, words, and actions, that thy name may never be blasphemed, but rather honored and praised on our account."[*]

So easily we fail to order and direct our lives towards God's mark. God has a target at which all of us must aim our thoughts, words, and deeds, and that target is his glory. However, in our own strength, we do not do this. We seek our own praise, working hard to impress people and to gain success for ourselves. So quickly we backbite and show hatred with our words. Maybe we do wrong deeds in our own private lives as well, listening to and watching things that do not agree with Scripture.

With our sinful actions, we can blaspheme, or make common, the name of God. Someone at work hears our wrong language or observes our private life, and he says to himself, He goes to church? Some God he has. God's name is brought down.

When we pray, Hallowed be thy name, we are asking that we might not blaspheme God's name but instead exalt his name with the way that we think, speak, and act. This is what David asked for in Psalm 19: "Keep back thy servant also from presumptuous sins; let them not have dominion over me: then shall I be upright, and I shall be innocent from the great transgression. Let the words of my mouth, and the meditation of my heart, be acceptable in thy sight, O Lord" (vv. 13–14). Make the same prayer as David today, asking that your thoughts be not focused on yourselves, but on God and giving him praise. Ask that your words not be hateful, self-serving, or empty, but that your words glorify God. Pray that your actions, even when you are by yourself, honor him.

Matt De Boer

---

[*] Heidelberg Catechism A 122, in *Confessions and Church Order*, 137.

November 25 — Q&A 122 – God's Powerful Grace

Read: Isaiah 42.

We will never pray from the heart for the hallowing of God's name if left to ourselves. In Isaiah 42:7, we read that God called his servant, who was the Messiah, "to open the blind eyes, to bring out the prisoners from the prison, and them that sit in darkness out of the prison house." Here it is implied that by nature we are spiritually blind. We do not see the truth about sin, but we walk in it. We are also in the prison of sin, meaning that we are stuck in unbelief and wickedness, never able or willing even to desire the hallowing of God's name. We are interested only in our own glory and not God's.

However, we do seek the hallowing of God's name and pray for it by Christ's gracious work in our hearts. Isaiah 42:6–7 teaches that Christ opens our eyes, bringing us to see the truth about God, about sin, and to turn from sin and to God. The Lord freed Isaiah from the prison of sin so that he even prayed for the hallowing of God's name in verses 11 and 12, and he moves us to make the same prayer today. Let us thank the Lord for his work of salvation in us, a work based entirely on Christ's payment for our sins at the cross.

God strengthens us to pray that his name be hallowed in his matchless grace, and then he graciously answers the request. It is God's eternal will that his name be glorified by us his people, and he is pleased to work in us to glorify his name as we ask for his strength.

Pray the first petition regularly then. Pray silently throughout the day as you are working: "Hallowed be thy name." Pray this regularly with your family too. In that way, you and your children will be aimed in the good way, and our gracious God's name will be praised.

Matt De Boer

Lord's Day 48

Q. 123. Which is the second petition?

A. *Thy kingdom come*; that is, rule us so by thy Word and Spirit, that we may submit ourselves more and more to thee; preserve and increase thy church; destroy the works of the devil and all violence which would exalt itself against thee; and also, all wicked counsels devised against thy holy Word; till the full perfection of thy kingdom take place, wherein Thou shalt be all in all.

November 26 — **Q&A 123 — The Kingdom of God**

Read: Psalm 72.

To understand what we are called to pray in the second petition and to move us to make this petition, we need to know what God's kingdom is.

Somewhat like the United States, a realm that has a leader, citizens, laws, and benefits, the kingdom of God is also a realm with a leader, citizens, laws, and benefits. God rules all things in his power, but when we speak of God's kingdom in the second petition, we are speaking of the realm he rules graciously in Christ.

God's kingdom includes a realm, but central to his kingdom is his rule. That is why answer 123 begins by saying: "*Thy kingdom come*; that is, rule us so by thy Word and Spirit."[*] Christ's rule being the main thing is difficult for us to understand today. When we think of a kingdom, we often first think of the people, the language, and the culture. We do not first think of the rule of the leader. However, in history the rule of the leader was the main thing in the kingdom. King David's rule shaped Israel. Hitler's rule molded Nazi Germany. Kingdoms in the past were so dominated by their leaders that the nations reflected those leaders. What we see in these earthly kingdoms is especially true of God's kingdom. His rule is the kingdom. The kingdom is called the kingdom of God because he is the source of the kingdom and the one who continues to preserve it. He alone brings the citizens into the kingdom and protects them. He makes the laws that the citizens must obey. The benefits the citizens possess come from him.

God presently rules this kingdom in Christ. Psalm 72:8 refers to Christ's coming reign, when it says: "He shall have dominion also from sea to sea, and from the river unto the ends of the earth." Christ came here, died, arose, ascended into heaven, and rules at God's right hand. He has the power and authority because he conquered sin and death by his death and resurrection. Without his death and payment for our sins, there would not even be citizens in God's righteous kingdom. All would have to remain citizens in Satan's kingdom as guilty sinners. However, because of the Lord's death, we believers, and believers from all over the earth, have the right to be citizens of God's righteous kingdom and to live with him.

Let us thank God that he has made us part of his glorious kingdom described in Psalm 72, and that we are ruled by the greatest King, Jesus Christ.

Matt De Boer

---

[*] Heidelberg Catechism A 123, in *Confessions and Church Order*, 137.

November 27 — Q&A 123 — Thy Kingdom Come in Me

Read: Luke 17:20–37.

In Luke 17:21, Jesus says to his disciples: "Behold, the kingdom of God is within you." How was the kingdom within them? God's kingdom is first his rule through Christ. Christ rules spiritually within believers. Thus, in a real sense, his kingdom was within the disciples and is within us believers today.

This came to be by Jehovah's grace. If we were left to ourselves, our hearts would be ruled by Satan. God created man good, but we sinned in Adam, making ourselves guilty. As just consequence for our sin in Adam, God gave us over to Satan so that he rules our hearts. By nature, we can only walk in sin and unbelief and are headed towards hell. However, Christ has taken over our hearts. He gained the right to do this by paying for our sins at the cross. Then, during our lives, at the moment of regeneration, the Lord entered our hearts, removed Satan's rule, and established his power and authority there.

According to answer 123, Christ now rules within us by his word, showing what we are to believe and how we are to serve him. He also governs within us by his Spirit, empowering us to believe what the word says and to obey.

Praying for God's kingdom to come is to pray that he would increase his rule in us as individuals. Answer 123 says: "*Thy kingdom come*; that is, rule us so by thy Word and Spirit, that we may submit ourselves more and more to thee."* We believers already have Christ ruling our hearts, but his salvation has not yet been completed in us. We still each have a sinful nature and struggle to follow God's way in our lives, sometimes holding on to certain sins. When we pray, "Thy kingdom come," we pray that Christ may rule our hearts more and more so we submit to him more and more. We ask that Christ so rule us by his word and Spirit that we believe what the word says and follow it more diligently.

Do you regularly pray for the kingdom to come in you, asking for Christ to increase his rule in you? We who are thankful to Christ the king for bringing us into his glorious kingdom will do so today.

Matt De Boer

---

* Heidelberg Catechism A 123, in *Confessions and Church Order*, 137.

November 28   **Q&A 123 — The Visible Form of the Kingdom**

Read: Psalm 48.

In explaining the second petition of the Lord's prayer, answer 123 speaks of Christ ruling within us individually and then talks about the church. Why? Because Christ graciously rules the church.

God's kingdom is first his rule, and his gracious rule forms a realm. In this realm are citizens, the elect whose hearts he has come to govern. This realm also has a law, God's word. There are spiritual benefits in this realm too. Romans 14:17 says the blessings of God's kingdom are "not meat and drink, but righteousness, and peace, and joy in the Holy Ghost."

Christ's gracious rule forms a realm in which there are citizens, laws, and benefits, and that realm has a visible form. The visible form is the church. The church is the universal assembly of God's elect. Where do we find the church on earth? In local churches where God's word is purely preached. Of course, not everyone in the congregation is necessarily elect. However, the elect certainly do assemble in local churches to worship God. The local, true church is the visible form of the kingdom because everything about the kingdom can be applied to the church. First, the king of the kingdom and the head of the church is the same, namely God who rules through Jesus Christ (Ps. 48). Second, the citizens of the kingdom are the church's members. Third, the law of the kingdom, the word, is the church's law. Last, the spiritual blessings of the kingdom are poured out and enjoyed in the church. In the preaching of the word, the members of the church hear God's declaration that they are righteous in the blood of Christ, and they have spiritual joy and peace.

That the church is the visible form of the kingdom fits with the biblical truth that the kingdom is spiritual, and "not of this world" (John 18:36). The church has a spiritual king, Jesus. In the church, spiritual benefits are poured out.

Let us thank the Lord for bringing us into his kingdom and church and bestowing wonderful spiritual blessings on us through the preaching of the gospel.

Matt De Boer

November 29   Q&A 123 — The Kingdom Is Not Earthly

Read: John 18:28–40.

It is important to see that the church is the visible form of the kingdom, because those who make the visible form wider than the church often make the kingdom earthly, focusing on the earthly. Some Christian colleges today and post-millennialists argue that God's kingdom must come in every sphere of human life, including politics, business, and entertainment. To accomplish their goal, they call Christians to go out and supposedly advance the kingdom by Christianizing culture, being agents of renewal, making Christian laws, and restoring justice and peace to a fallen world. It is good to be a witness, but their goal goes beyond that. Their goal is Christian governments, Christian corporations, and a Christian Hollywood here on earth that conform, at least outwardly, to the morals of Scripture. The idea is that when all this arrives on earth, God's kingdom will have come.

This view is quite prominent, but it is false and dangerous for several reasons. First, it makes the kingdom an earthly kingdom, which runs contrary to Jesus' words and actions in John 18. Second, when one separates the kingdom from the church, church membership and attendance become less important. What becomes more important is conquering for Christ the square inch of Washington D.C. or of the National Football League. This is part of why we see many in the church world so greatly celebrate Christian politicians and professional athletes. Third, making the kingdom earthly is dangerous because it dims the Christian's hope for Christ's return and the full perfection of the kingdom in the new heavens and new earth.

Like many people today, Pontius Pilate thought that earthly kingdoms were what mattered and that the spiritual kingdom Jesus spoke of was unimpressive. Sometimes, we might be tempted to agree. We can begin to think, for instance, that earthly kingdoms are real, but spiritual kingdoms are not. Earthly kingdoms have such great benefits, and the spiritual benefits that Christ the king gives in the church are secondary.

However, the spiritual kingdom of God is real. It truly is the greatest kingdom, and nothing is more important or better than the benefits of righteousness, peace, and joy in the Holy Ghost, benefits bestowed in the church. Having these gifts, we have eternal life in the only eternal kingdom with the best King.

Matt De Boer

November 30   **Q&A 123 — Thy Kingdom Come in the Church**

Read: Psalm 67.

Since the visible form of the kingdom is the church, the second petition is a petition for the church. Answer 123 tells us that when we pray, Thy kingdom come, we are asking that Christ's rule may increase his church.

This is a request that Christ may extend his rule by gathering his church from our children. We are praying that through the preaching of the word, Christ would work powerfully in the hearts of our little children and young people, bringing them to conscious faith and leading them to fight temptation and sin in a dark world.

With the second petition, we are also asking that Christ would gather his church from all nations. This is what the psalmist prayed for in Psalm 67. In verses 1–3, he says: "God be merciful unto us, and bless us; and cause his face to shine upon us; Selah. That thy way may be known upon earth, thy saving health among all nations. Let the people praise thee, O God; let all the people praise thee." The psalmist was asking that God would so bless his covenant people Israel that through them the Gentiles would be brought under the Lord's reign and glorify him.

Do we pray for the increase of the church too? Are we praying regularly that the Lord would touch the hearts of the children in the church through the preaching and through instruction in catechism, at home, and at school? Are we asking often for the kingdom's advancement through missions and the witness of our local church? As those who love our King and desire his glory, we should be!

Matt De Boer

December 1 — Q&A 123 — Thy Kingdom Come Against Enemies

Read: Revelation 12:7–17.

The second petition is a petition for Christ, by his rule, to "preserve and increase [the] church".*

Lord's Day 48 speaks of the church's great enemies and specifically mentions the devil. What an enemy he is! Revelation 12:17, referring to Satan as the dragon and the church as the woman, says: "And the dragon was wroth with the woman, and went to make war with the remnant of her seed, which keep the commandments of God, and have the testimony of Jesus Christ." We all know the powerful temptations he brings to our lives. He finds our weaknesses and then subtly works to try to bring us to sin and to continue in sin thinking it is not a big deal. He does the same to our children.

As answer 123 teaches, the devil also makes "wicked counsels," or plans against God's word. God's word is the foundation of the church, and Satan knows that if he can undermine the foundation, he can destroy us. He uses all the entertainment today to make the preaching seem boring and not worth our time. He works to bring us to the point that we are hardly paying attention at all, not being fed, and waning in love for God and his church. His ultimate hope is to separate us from the church and destroy us.

When we pray, "Thy kingdom come," we are asking that the Lord might preserve the church by destroying the works of Satan and all our enemies. We are looking to Christ to make our enemies' efforts to lead us away from him come to nothing. Essentially, we are praying what David prayed in Psalm 72. He asks for Christ's rule to flourish so that "he shall judge the poor of the people, he shall save the children of the needy, and shall break in pieces the oppressor" (v. 4).

If David was concerned about the defense of the church and prayed for it long ago, we certainly must be concerned for and pray for Christ's rule to defend the church today. We know that when a sports team is behind at the end of a game, the players are desperate and play with a special urgency to come back and win. The devil is working with urgency, especially now that the end is nearing, wanting just one true believer to fall away. Pray regularly for your protection, your family's protection, and the church's protection. Those who love the Lord and desire his glory will do so.

Matt De Boer

---

* Heidelberg Catechism A 123, in *Confessions and Church Order*, 137.

December 2 — Q&A 123 — Thy Kingdom Come to Its Full Perfection

Read: 1 Corinthians 15:12–28.

According to answer 123, the second petition is lastly a petition for Christ's kingdom to come in its full perfection.

This request is necessary because the full perfection of the kingdom has not come yet. "The full perfection" of the kingdom refers to the kingdom in its completed form.[*] This is not an earthly kingdom with Christian leaders that stretches from sea to sea but is something so much better! The full perfection of the kingdom will have come when Christ's rule is complete. There will be no enemies like the devil, for he will have been cast into the lake of fire. Our enemy within, the sinful nature, will have been destroyed. This sin-cursed earth will have passed away, and the elect from every nation will dwell in the new heavens and new earth. Christ will rule within us entirely so that God is "all in all."[**] We will never have carelessness towards the King, but for every member of the church he will be everything always. Every thought, every action, and every word will be to his praise. This amazing, full perfection has obviously not yet been realized.

The petition, Thy kingdom come, partly means, Thy kingdom come in its full perfection. We are asking that Christ return to send all our enemies to eternal destruction, that Christ come to bring his complete rule to our hearts so that God is all in all, and that Christ return to take us all in body and soul to the perfection of the new heavens and new earth.

Wonderfully, God answers and will answer our prayer for the kingdom to come. Lord's Day 48 shows that the full realization of the kingdom is certain when it says that we pray: "*Till* the full perfection of thy kingdom take place."[***] This is based on 1 Corinthians 15. Verse 24 says: "Then cometh the end, when he [Christ] shall have delivered up the kingdom to God, even the Father; when he shall have put down all rule and all authority and power." Verse 25 adds that he will "put all enemies under his feet," meaning that he will put his feet on their necks. The devil, the antichrist, and every person who died in rebellion to the Lord will be thrown into the lake of fire. Even death, "the last enemy," will be destroyed (v. 26). We, and all the citizens of God's kingdom, will be gathered in body and soul into the beautiful new creation, and God will be "all in all" (v. 28). The full perfection is sure, and God is pleased to bring it about as we pray for it.

That the full perfection of the kingdom will take place shows that God will also answer our prayers to increase his rule in us now by his word and Spirit, preparing us for glory. And it shows that he will answer our petition to preserve and increase his church too. God is so gracious!

Matt De Boer

---

[*] Heidelberg Catechism A 123, in *Confessions and Church Order*, 137.
[**] Heidelberg Catechism A 123, in *Confessions and Church Order*, 137.
[***] Heidelberg Catechism A 123, in *Confessions and Church Order*, 137.

Lord's Day 49

Q. 124. Which is the third petition?

A. *Thy will be done in earth, as it is in heaven*; that is, grant that we and all men may renounce our own will, and without murmuring obey thy will, which is only good; that so every one may attend to and perform the duties of his station and calling as willingly and faithfully as the angels do in heaven.

December 3 — Q&A 124 – Praying God's Will Be Done

Read: Matthew 6:10.

About the third petition of the Lord's prayer there is considerable confusion among Christians. What do we mean by God's will? Is God's will, as Reformed Christians teach, always accomplished? If so, why do we need to pray for God's will to be done? Does Jesus teach here that God's will is done in heaven, but not done in earth?

It is important to remember as we consider this petition that the Bible speaks of God's will in different senses. If we understand that, we will see that there is perfect harmony between God's sovereignty and our need to utter this prayer to God.

First, the Bible speaks of God's will of decree. That will is what God has determined to be done in history. Other terms include God's good pleasure or God's counsel. That will of God is always accomplished. No man is able to resist or thwart that will of God. Nebuchadnezzar was compelled to make this confession in Daniel 4:35, "He doeth according to his will in the army of heaven, and among the inhabitants of the earth: and none can stay his hand, or say unto him, What doest thou?" That will of God includes everything that occurs in history, whether good or evil.

That will of God is always performed in heaven and on earth.

Second, the Bible speaks of God's will of command or precept. That will is what God has commanded his creatures, especially human beings, to do. That will is revealed to us in the law of God. That will of God is very rarely performed. None of the wicked ever perform that will, for their lives are walks in disobedience (Eph. 2:2). Even believers attain only a small beginning of this new obedience. That will of God's command is, however, perfectly done in heaven, although rarely on earth.

Sometimes, Christians speak about God's revealed will and God's secret will. Much of God's counsel is secret. We know God has a counsel, but we do not know the details. God's commands are revealed. He reveals to us how we must live. Therefore, our calling is not to pry into God's secret decrees, but to obey God's revealed will—even if our obedience means that we suffer loss, inconvenience, and even persecution.

One more thing we must add to our explanation of God's will. God does not have a will by which he desires things that he has not decreed. Some theologians have misused this *distinction* in God's will to teach a *contradiction* in God's will. It is not true, for example, that God has decreed to save only some, but that he desires to save all. God does not desire things that he knows will never happen, having decreed that they will never happen.

There is a twofold relationship between God's will and our prayers. First, God decrees even our prayers as necessary means to fulfill his purposes; and second, we pray that God would enable us more and more to obey God in his will of command.

Obeying God's will is difficult. Let us pray for grace to obey.

Martyn McGeown

December 4 — Q&A 124 – Father Knows Best

Read: Luke 11:11.

God, who is our Father, has a will. That will is, as we have seen, God's purpose concerning all things—his will of decree—and God's commandments to us—his will of command or precept. About that will, Lord's Day 49 says, it is "only good."*

With respect to his children, God's will is always and only good. God, our Father, delights to shower us with blessings; he delights to show himself the abundant provider, the gracious preserver, and the merciful savior. God's decrees concerning us are good. He has decreed our salvation, our everlasting blessedness. He has decreed that we should be with him forever, beholding his glory in the face of Jesus Christ. Our comfort is that everything that God has planned for us—wealth and poverty, health and sickness, prosperity and adversity—serves our salvation and his glory, and since God has decreed all, none can overthrow his good purpose for us (Rom. 8:28). God's will of command is good for us too. God's law is not grievous but is a good guide for our life. In keeping God's commandments and walking in obedience, we find blessedness, whereas the ungodly who walk in disobedience find misery.

Since God's will is only good, our will is only good insofar as it is in harmony with his will. When God's purposes thwart our happiness, and when God's commands are contrary to our desires, God's will is still good. We struggle often to recognize and confess that. What we see as great evils—hunger, poverty, disease, bereavement, and death—God sends upon us for our good. God never sends trials upon his children out of hatred, ill will, or spite; God never causes us a needless tear; God never gives more than we can bear. We confess this as Reformed believers—the difficulty is in truly believing it.

When we are tempted to despair, we must remember the very simple truth: our Father knows best, and his will is "only good." Do I not have what I want—whether possessions, good health, opportunities, or relationships? My Father knows that I do not need those things right now. He knows best; his will is "only good." Do I have what I do not want—trials, difficulties, disappointments, and pain? My Father knows that I need to pass through this sorrow right now. He has carefully designed this dark valley for me, and he promises to be with me as I go through that valley. His will is "only good."

Jesus illustrates this from everyday life. Even fathers, whom Jesus calls evil, "know how to give good gifts" to their children (Luke 11:13). Will our Father, who is only good, always wise, infinitely powerful and glorious, give evil gifts to his children—stones for bread; serpents for fish; scorpions for eggs (vv. 11–12)?

The problem we have—and this is why we must utter this petition in our prayers—is that we do not *want* our Father's will. We are so self-willed that we want only our own will, which is not "only good." Father, let thy will, which is only good, be done. Father, thou knowest best.

Martyn McGeown

---

* Heidelberg Catechism A 124, in *Confessions and Church Order*, 138.

December 5 — Q&A 124 – Renouncing Our Own Will

Read: Matthew 16:24.

When we utter the third petition, Thy will be done, we are praying thus: May thy will happen; may it come to pass that thy will is performed by us, in us, in our lives. We are not praying that God's decrees will be accomplished—God's decrees are always, infallibly, and effectually accomplished. We are praying that God's commands will be obeyed—by us.

This means that we do not have the natural power to obey God's will. Augustine, the great theologian of grace in the early church, understood this when he prayed: "Give what thou commandest, and command what thou wilt."[*] The unbeliever cannot obey the will of God; indeed, he cannot even desire to obey God. When the unbeliever, who willfully disobeys God, prays "Thy will be done," he is guilty of gross hypocrisy. Let us never pray, "Thy will be done," while we disobey God.

We struggle to utter the words of this third petition sincerely, because we are self-willed by nature. We want *our* will to be done, and only if God's will suits our will do we obey him. We might never utter these words in our prayers, of course, but often our thought is: *My* will be done!

That is why Lord's Day 49 interprets the third petition this way: "Grant that we and all men may renounce our own will."[**] Jesus teaches us self-denial in our prayers. Self-denial is that most difficult of Christian callings. People will give up many things, and they will tolerate a lot even for the sake of religion—but they will not deny *themselves*. Self-denial means that we say no to ourselves. Jesus graphically describes this as taking up our cross (Matt. 16:24). On that cross we are called to crucify ourselves—our desires, our plans, our ambitions, our pride, and everything that would hinder us in performing God's good will.

Can you do *that?* Can I do *that?* That is why we need to seek God in prayer.

When we pray in a way acceptable to God, we say something like this: "O Father, I am so weak, so sinful. I can hardly manage to think a good thought. O Father, the desire is there, the spirit is willing, but the flesh is weak. O Father, give me thy grace and Holy Spirit. Incline my heart to keep thy commandments and to fear thy name. I know that thy will is better than mine, but my flesh wants to assert itself. I find it so hard to give up everything, to account all things as dung, that I might have fellowship with thee. Crucify within me, O Father, the lusts of my flesh, my evil desires, and enable me to perform thy will—not mine—for thy glory."

If you know that struggle—your will versus God's will—then pray the third petition. Let God's will be done in us.

Martyn McGeown

---

[*] Augustine of Hippo, "The Confessions," 10.29.40, trans. J.G. Pilkington, in *The Nicene and Post-Nicene Fathers*, first series, 14 vols., ed. Philip Schaff (repr., Peabody, MA: Hendrickson, 1995), 1:153.

[**] Heidelberg Catechism A 124, in *Confessions and Church Order*, 138.

December 6   **Q&A 124 — Cheerful Submission to God's Will**

Read: Philippians 2:14.

Yesterday, we examined the third petition from the perspective of God's will of command. We pray for strength to renounce our own will and to obey God's will. Lord's Day 49 also addresses the third petition from the perspective of God's will of decree, namely, that we pray for grace to submit cheerfully and without murmuring to God's will of decree. Remember that God's will of decree will happen whether we are cheerful or not, but we must pray for submission.

The sin which Lord's Day 49 exposes is murmuring: "Grant that we…may…without murmuring obey thy will."* Although Lord's Day 49 speaks here about "obeying God's will," it is profitable for us also to apply this to God's decree. Murmuring was the great sin of the Israelites in the wilderness—when they had no water, they murmured; when they had no food, they murmured; when they did not like the leadership of Moses, they murmured. This murmuring was the fruit of discontentment and unbelief—they did not like God's provision, and they did not trust God to provide. God judged his murmuring people. He killed many of them with fiery serpents (Num. 21:6), and the carcasses of the complaining Israelites fell in the wilderness. The New Testament warns us against this sin of murmuring (1 Cor. 10:10).

Murmuring is a temptation for us, which is why we need to pray, Thy will be done. Sometimes, murmuring can be internal, so that we never utter a murmur in our words. The danger is that we become bitter in our spirit—bitter against life, bitter in our circumstances, and bitter against God. At other times, we can utter angry, impatient words, as we struggle to submit to a trial God has sent upon us. We are even tempted to curse God, as Job was. All such murmuring is sin. Satan wants us to question our Father's goodness. We may never do that!

Lord's Day 49 explains this in these words: "That so every one may attend to and perform the duties of his station and calling."** Each person is in a particular position in life *according to the will of God*. It is the will of God that some are married while others (at least for a time) remain single. Submit to the will of God cheerfully and without grumbling, and perform faithfully the duties of marriage or singlehood. It is the will of God that some have children while others (despite longing and praying for children) remain childless. Submit to that will, too, and perform faithfully the duties of your station and calling. God places some in positions of authority, and others he places under those authorities. We may seek in all lawful ways to change our situations, but we must not fret, complain, grumble, doubt the goodness of God, or envy the position of others.

Murmuring against God is a rebellious spirit, and when we sense that spirit within ourselves we must pray: "Father, thy will be done. Break my stubborn will. Break my self-will. Mold my will to agree with thine."

Martyn McGeown

---

*   Heidelberg Catechism A 124, in *Confessions and Church Order*, 138.
**   Heidelberg Catechism A 124, in *Confessions and Church Order*, 138.

December 7 — **Q&A 124 – Praying Without Doubting**

Read: 1 John 5:14.

Some object to the third petition because it seems to express doubt. Such people would argue that we should ask boldly and confidently, and therefore we must not add to our prayers "if it be thy will…" That, they say, neutralizes the prayer—it adds an element of doubt, as if we are not sure whether God will give us what we ask.

However, this is a grave misunderstanding. It is entirely fitting and appropriate for us to add "if it be thy will" to our petitions, simply because we do not know what God's will is.

There are some things for which we do not need to add this petition: Father, forgive my sins. We who have faith in Jesus Christ know that God has promised to forgive our sins. Father, gather, defend, and preserve thy church. We know that God has promised to save his church. Father, destroy the kingdom of darkness. We know that God has promised to do that also.

But there are other more specific petitions for which we have no promise. Perhaps we are praying for the conversion of a friend. We do not know what God's will is, so it is fitting we add "if it be thy will" to our prayer. Perhaps we are at the sickbed of a loved one. Through tears, we beseech God to heal our dear one, but we add "if it be thy will" to our prayer. We do not know the number of the days determined by God for our loved one. What we do know is that God's will for us, even when he takes a loved one in sickness and death, is good.

There is a world of difference between asking in childlike humility and demanding that God give us what we want. Certainly, we come boldly, with confidence, into the very presence of God, but we come to *God*. We cannot demand anything of him; we cannot manipulate him; we cannot by much speaking persuade him to give us what he is not pleased to give.

Another great evil in prayer is to pray for something that God has revealed he will *not* give. That is to tempt God. Our prayers must be according to God's will in this sense too—we must pray for those things which please God. For example, we should pray for grace and the Holy Spirit, but we should not pray that God give us good examination results when we cheat or do not study, or that he prosper us when we steal. Furthermore, we should avoid the pious-sounding sham, "I have been praying about it, and I feel that…" or "Let me pray about that…" When God has revealed that something is *not his* will, we should *not* pray about it—except for grace to resist the way of disobedience. We must never use prayer as an excuse not to obey a clear command of Scripture—that is to mock God in a most shameful manner.

We should make it our business to discover God's will from the Bible, and, having discovered it, we obey. If we struggle with obedience, we pray, Lord, incline my stubborn, foolish, rebellious, sinful will to obey thy commandments. Thy will be done!

Martyn McGeown

December 8 — Q&A 124 — "As in Heaven"

Read: Psalm 103:21.

Jesus in the third petition makes a contrast between the will of God in heaven and the will of God in earth: "In earth, as it is heaven" (Matt. 6:10). The will of God, both of his decree and his command, is always perfectly performed in heaven. There is no disobedience in heaven. Even the disobedience of the devil—remember that Lucifer was dissatisfied with the station and calling God had given him—was decreed by God. The reprobate angels were cast out; among the elect angels, there is no disobedience.

What do angels do? Angels are God's ministers—they are his servants, attending to him. Angels are God's messengers—they are sent to do his bidding, to bring tidings to the earth. Angels are God's hosts—they are his soldiers, who fight in spiritual warfare against the spirits of wickedness and who bring God's just vengeance on the wicked. Angels are God's worshippers—they praise him without ceasing.

Angels also have their own callings and stations. Some are cherubim; others are seraphim. Some are mere angels; others are archangels. Within the angelic ranks there is no envy and no dissatisfaction. No angel ever questions God's will, and certainly no angel refuses to carry out God's will.

Lord's Day 49 reminds us of this and urges upon us the angels for a pattern: "As willingly and faithfully as the angels do in heaven." Psalm 103 teaches us about this: "Bless the Lord, ye his angels, that excel in strength, that do his commandments, hearkening unto the voice of his word…that do his pleasure" (vv. 20–21).

We must contrast the angels' obedience with our obedience. Often we disobey. The angels never disobey. Often our obedience is halfhearted and reluctant. The angels obey God willingly and swiftly. We often murmur against one another, desiring to change our position for theirs. The angels never murmur. When God says to an angel, Go, he goes, and he does not complain that he was sent on an errand. When God commands an angel, Worship me forever, the angel does not get bored with worshipping God. When Gabriel was chosen to bring glad tidings to Mary concerning the coming of Jesus, the other angels did not become envious that they were not sent, nor did Gabriel become proud that he was chosen for such an assignment.

That is the kind of obedience at which we must aim. Lord, make my obedience of thee as eager and faithful as that of the angels. May thy will be done in me and by me as it is in heaven.

Martyn McGeown

December 9 — Q&A 124 – Christ Praying the Third Petition

Read: Matthew 26:39.

Yesterday, we looked at the pattern of willing obedience to the will of God shown by the angels in heaven. But there is one higher pattern—that of Jesus Christ.

Christ came into the world to do the will of God. In the volume of the book of God's decree and revealed in the Old Testament Scriptures was God's will for Jesus Christ (Ps. 40:7–8). So zealous was Jesus for the will of God that he said to his disciples: "My meat is to do the will of him that sent me, and to finish his work" (John 4:34). Never did Jesus transgress the will of God. Never did Jesus even *will* to transgress the will of God.

God's will for Jesus was that he suffer and die for our sins and bear his wrath on the cross. This was eternally decreed concerning him—the serpent would "bruise his heel" (Gen. 3:15); he would be "wounded for our transgressions" and "bruised for our iniquities" (Isa. 53:5); he would be "cut off, but not for himself" (Dan. 9:26); he, the shepherd, would be smitten with the sword of the Lord (Zech. 13:7). When his enemies came to arrest him, Peter tried to defend him, but Jesus responded: "But how then shall the scriptures be fulfilled, that thus it must be?" (Matt. 26:54).

Yet Christ, too, struggled with this petition, more than we ever will. He was not tempted to disobey, but he shrank back in horror at the prospect of drinking the cup of God's wrath. In heaviness of heart, he asked the Father, if it be possible, that the cup might pass from him, but he added those crucial words, "nevertheless not as I will, but as thou wilt" (Matt. 26:39).

In Gethsemane, Christ deliberately and consciously renounced his own will—the will that there might be some other way—to God's will. What self-denial! What submission! What love! What obedience!

Never was the third petition more difficult to utter than in Gethsemane, but he uttered it. And because he uttered it, we have grace to utter it too.

All our self will, murmuring, rebellion, and disobedience was laid on Christ who carried them to the cross and suffered the penalty of death for them. And grace, spiritual strength, and every measure of the Spirit that we possess were purchased for us by the sacrifice of Christ.

From Christ we have an everlasting supply of grace, which we can request from the overflowing fountain of all good. Thus we come to the Father with this petition on our lips: O Father, subdue my will, work thy will in me, let thy will be performed by me. For Jesus' sake. Amen.

Martyn McGeown

Lord's Day 50

Q. 125. Which is the fourth petition?

A. *Give us this day our daily bread*; that is, be pleased to provide us with all things necessary for the body, that we may thereby acknowledge thee to be the only fountain of all good, and that neither our care nor industry, nor even thy gifts, can profit us without thy blessing; and therefore that we may withdraw our trust from all creatures and place it alone in thee.

December 10 — Q&A 125 – Praying for Necessities for the Body

Read: Matthew 6:11.

The Lord's prayer could be divided into two parts, each with three petitions. The first three petitions focus on God—the honor of God's name, the coming of God's kingdom, and the doing of God's will. The second three petitions focus on our needs—our need for daily bread, our need for the forgiveness of sins, and our need for deliverance from evil.

The first of these three is bread. As creatures, we need bread.

Perhaps, we might wonder about this. Is it proper to ask God for such common things as bread, and should we ask for bread before we ask for the forgiveness of sins? We must not think that way. Christ encourages us here to bring our mundane needs to the attention of our heavenly Father. That the prayer which our Savior taught us contains this petition shows us how merciful our Father is. He remembers that we are dust. He remembers that we need bread—physical food—to keep body and soul together. It is not, therefore, unspiritual to pray for mere bread. Without bread, we cannot serve God—we cannot hallow his name, we cannot promote God's kingdom, and we cannot perform his will. In fact, if we do not use our daily bread for those purposes, it would be better for us not to have bread. Unlike the angels, we depend on food, and God permits us, and indeed requires of us, that we ask him for our necessary food.

But we may ask *only* for bread. We may not ask for luxuries with our bread. Christ commands us to ask for bread, because bread stands for the necessities of life. The common people of Christ's day ate a rather simple diet of bread, fish, figs, and olive oil. This was a healthy diet—and certainly enough to live on—but it was not luxurious. In every age, bread is the basic foodstuff of life.

With our bread, other things are implied, which in our age are deemed to be necessities. The basic needs of a human being are four—food, clothing, shelter, and warmth. With these four things we can survive, and with these four things we must be content. In practice, this means that a modern person needs to be able to afford food and drink, rent and basic utilities (such as electricity and heating). Perhaps we could add to that list things like transport (so that we can get to work and to the shops to buy food and other necessities) and medicine when a person becomes ill.

But we must be careful not to add too much to that list. Wants so easily become "needs." A foreign vacation is not a need; a cottage by the lake is not a need; a Mercedes-Benz car is not a need; designer fashion clothes are not needs. We do not ask for luxuries, and when God is pleased—as he often is—to give us luxuries, we are thankful for them, but we do not demand them, nor do we become discontent when God withholds them from us.

We ask for bread. We need bread. With bread we are content.

Martyn McGeown

December 11 — Q&A 125 – God's Providence in Supplying Our Bread

Read: Genesis 3:19.

Did you ever consider how bread comes to our tables, and therefore how God answers our prayers to give us our daily bread? In the Old Testament, for some forty years, God caused bread miraculously to fall out of heaven for his people, but he does not supply manna in that manner today. When we ask God for bread, much is implied.

First, in our prayer for our daily bread, we ask God to prosper the entire economy for the sake of God's people, so that we can eat and be supplied with the necessities of life. God has created us as interdependent creatures. God's providence governs everything that is involved in bringing the humble loaf of bread to our tables. In many nations today, agriculture is a multibillion-dollar industry, but other industries are involved too.

Even in Jesus' day, this was understood. The farmer relied upon the weather. If the weather was too wet or too dry, or if there were pests, such as locusts, caterpillars, cankerworms, and palmerworms (Joel 2:25), the harvest would fail. That we have modern inventions does not make us immune from famine. If the farmer's crop fails or is insufficient, there can be no bread. Therefore, part of our prayer "Give us this day our daily bread" includes a prayer for good weather—not so we can enjoy ourselves at the beach, but so that we can eat.

Modern farmers have other concerns too. The oil industry, for example, which supplies the fuel to run the machinery to harvest the grain, is necessary for bringing bread to us. Then there is the transportation industry, by which the grain is brought to factories to be made into bread, and by which the prepared bread is transported to the shops, where the consumer buys it. Therefore, we need to pray for the smooth running of society, so that the bread can reach us.

Indeed, without a flourishing economy there will be insufficient employment, and people will not be able to work to earn the money necessary to buy bread. "Give us this day our daily bread" is not answered by God dropping pre-sliced bread on our tables out of heaven!

Second, in our prayer for daily bread, we ask God to supply us with jobs, so that especially the husbands and fathers may support their families. It is God's will that we eat in the way of our working: "In the sweat of thy face shalt thou eat bread" (Gen. 3:19); "If any would not work, neither should he eat" (2 Thess. 3:10). Therefore, the Christian husband and father must pray, Father, give me work, work sufficient for me and my dependents, work sufficient for me to help the poor; and Father, give me diligence in my work, and the physical and mental ability to work.

A lazy man may not—must not—pray: "Give us this day our daily bread." He must repent of his sloth, and "with quietness…work, and eat [his] own bread" (2 Thess. 3:12).

Let us remember all that is involved in bringing bread to us and pray accordingly.

Martyn McGeown

December 12   **Q&A 125 — Our Daily Bread**

Read: Luke 11:3.

The fourth petition does not simply concern bread, but *daily* bread.

This reminds us that we must pray every day for our bread. Daily bread means enough bread measured out in an amount sufficient to feed us for one day. Christ is teaching us in this petition to look to God every day for a fresh supply. We never get to the point where we become self-sufficient. We must never make the mistake of the rich fool in the parable who said: "Soul, thou hast much goods laid up for many years; take thine ease, eat, drink, and be merry" (Luke 12:19). He did not pray for daily bread; he did not even pray for yearly bread!

The Israelites learned the lesson of daily bread in the wilderness. Every day, God supplied fresh manna from heaven, but only enough for one day. God commanded the people to gather only enough for one day, and he warned the people that they may not store it up or hoard it. The only exception was the sabbath day—then they could gather enough for two days to avoid working on the Sabbath. The Israelites disobeyed. Some tried to hoard the manna, but it bred worms and stank. God did this to teach them that they must rely on him daily for their needs. The Israelites were slow to learn.

We also find it difficult to learn this lesson, because most of us do not live from one day to the next wondering where the next meal will come from. Most of us have cupboards and freezers stuffed with provisions that could last for weeks and even months. We find it difficult, therefore, sincerely to pray for daily bread, but that does not change the petition: God might give us more than daily bread, but Christ instructs us to pray *only* for our daily bread. The danger we have is that, whereas we gladly receive an abundance from God's hand, we become accustomed to plenty and will become discontented and grumble when God reduces our rations later.

Nevertheless, we must not feel guilty when God gives us more than daily bread. We must not squander it foolishly, but be wise, faithful stewards of it. It is not wrong for us to use prudent foresight—to buy our groceries in advance and to plan for the more distant future—but we must not hoard God's provision selfishly and live like misers. Even in our affluent society, we *do* live on daily bread—how easily we can lose everything we have stored up for the future: a thief, a power cut, a fire, a flood, and it is all gone!

Do not, in an age of abundance, lose sight of this truth: we rely on God for every morsel of food *every day*. The wise man Agur understood this: "Give me neither poverty nor riches; feed me with food convenient for me: lest I be full, and deny thee, and say, Who is the Lord? or lest I be poor, and steal, and take the name of my God in vain" (Prov. 30:8–9). God knows exactly how much food we need each day. Let us trust him and pray.

Give us this day our *daily* bread!

Martyn McGeown

December 13 — **Q&A 125 — Seeking God's Blessing with Our Bread**

Read: Proverbs 3:33.

As soon as our children are old enough to utter the words, we teach them a simple prayer: "Lord, bless this food and drink. Forgive my sins. For Jesus' sake. Amen." So familiar is this prayer to Reformed families that it is often called "Lord, bless."

This is a good and appropriate prayer. In this prayer, we teach our children that their food will not profit them without God's blessing. That is why we ask God to bless our food and drink. Lord's Day 50 expresses this idea: "That we may thereby acknowledge… that neither our care nor industry, nor even thy gifts, can profit us without thy blessing."*
Therefore, the important thing is not so much the food, but the blessing with the food.

But what is a blessing? The word is so commonplace in our Christian vocabulary that we can lose sight of its meaning. The word *bless*, both in the Hebrew and Greek language, means to make a pronouncement upon someone or something. It means especially, therefore, to speak good concerning or good upon someone or something. A blessing is a good word. Specifically, a blessing is God's good word, his speaking good upon or concerning something or someone. For example, God blessed man when he first made Adam and Eve: "So God created man…And God blessed them, and God said unto them, Be fruitful" (Gen. 1:27–28); and God blessed the Sabbath: "And God blessed the seventh day, and sanctified it" (Gen. 2:3). God spoke a good word upon them.

Now, the blessing of God is the blessing *of God himself.* Ultimately, only God can bless—your food can nourish you, but it cannot bless you; your house might shelter you, but it cannot bless you; your clothes might keep you warm, but they cannot bless you; your friends and family might comfort you and give you companionship, but they cannot bless you. And whom God blesses, he saves. God's blessing is not like a lucky charm or a well-meaning wish that nice things might happen to us. God's blessing is the effectual, powerful word of his favor, pronouncing good upon us and causing us to be blessed.

Therefore, when we pray in connection with the fourth petition, Give us this day our daily bread, and when we teach our children: "Lord, bless this food and drink, we are asking God so to use the food which he gives us that it might profit us spiritually, that it might do us good—real, spiritual, eternal good."

And we pray that with confidence. God has promised to bless us; God delights to bless us; God will not withhold his blessing from us. All things (including our bread) serve our salvation and work together for our good (Rom. 8:28).

With his blessing—*only* with his blessing.

Martyn McGeown

---

* Heidelberg Catechism A 125, in *Confessions and Church Order*, 138.

December 14 — Q&A 125 — Our Bread Unprofitable Without His Blessing

Read: Psalm 69:22.

Lord's Day 50 in a very striking manner makes a distinction between God's gifts and his blessing. In other words, Lord's Day 50 acknowledges that a person can receive gifts from God's hand but with those gifts *not* receive God's blessing. This has very important implications for the question of what God gives to the wicked—for the doctrine of common grace.

The doctrine of common grace is that God has a favorable attitude towards the wicked, that he blesses the wicked. This favor or blessing (grace) which God supposedly has for the wicked—that is, the reprobate wicked, whom God has eternally rejected from salvation—manifests itself in the good gifts which God gives the wicked in this life. Nobody can deny that God gives the wicked many good gifts. Often, he gives to the wicked more than he gives to his own children, but it does not profit the wicked without his blessing.

Remember what God's blessing is—the effectual word of his favor (grace) speaking good concerning, and pronouncing good upon, his people. How, then, could God bless the wicked? How could God speak good concerning, and pronounce good upon, the wicked? The Bible teaches a sharp distinction between God's people and the wicked. God loves, blesses, and has favor upon his own people, but God hates, curses, and is angry with the wicked. This is a hard saying—something fearful—but we believe it. "They that be cursed of him shall be cut off" (Ps. 37:22); "The curse of the Lord is in the house of the wicked" (Prov. 3:33); "Depart from me, ye cursed" (Matt. 25:41).

If the blessing of God is wonderful, the curse of God is awful, but just.

The curse of God is the opposite of his blessing. To curse means to speak evil concerning or upon something or someone, or to speak against something or someone. God's curse is not the word of his favor or his grace but the word of his disfavor or his wrath. God's curse is upon the wicked—and that curse makes even those gifts, which God gives the wicked in his providence, serve their condemnation.

That is the prayer of imprecation in Psalm 69, a prayer which is on the lips of Jesus as he hangs on the cross. Jesus prays against the enemies of God, that God might curse them. That curse will make "their table become a snare before them" and make a trap "that which should have been for their welfare" (v. 22). Paul quotes this in Romans 11:9. Therefore, for the wicked, the abundance of good things—food, clothing, shelter, money, health—which they receive from God's hand only serves to destroy them. Those good gifts are the means whereby God places the wicked on "slippery places" that he might cast "them down into destruction" (Ps. 73:18).

The issue, therefore, is not how many gifts God gives a person, but why and with what attitude and purpose God gives them. If you are found in Jesus Christ, all things are a blessing to you. If you are not a believer in Christ, flee to him—lest he curse you even in your gifts!

Martyn McGeown

December 15 — Q&A 125 — Eating Our Food Under the Cross

Read: Galatians 3:14.

God will not bless the wicked—even in the good gifts he sends them. God will not curse his people—even in the afflictions he sends them. But how can we account for this difference? How can we confidently pray for daily bread with God's blessing, when we are as wicked and depraved as the reprobate are? What right have we to expect that God would bless us?

The wicked man has no right to the bread that he receives. He lives as an unwelcome guest in God's house, which is this world. God feeds such a man, but not out of love. The wicked man uses the good gifts of the world, but he has no right to them. Every morsel of bread that he eats he steals. Furthermore, the wicked man uses the goods of this world against God and in the service of sin. The wicked man is unthankful for the gifts of God, does not use them to serve his creator, and does not even acknowledge the giver of every good and perfect gift. Thus the wicked man demonstrates his awful wickedness, and God is justified in condemning him.

But what about us? Do we not also sin as we eat and drink? Should we not therefore also expect to be cursed in our daily bread? The truth is that something as earthly and commonplace as our daily bread comes to us from the cross. We have no right to eat our bread with God's blessing without the cross. We can eat our daily bread in good conscience only because our sins have been forgiven in the blood of our Savior. Otherwise, we would be in exactly the same position as the wicked man whose daily bread is a curse to him. What a humbling and sobering thought—I have this morsel of food, and I may eat it with the assurance of God's blessing, not because I deserve it, not because I worked for it, but because Christ shed his blood for me to have it. "That we may thereby acknowledge [our Father] to be the only fountain of all good, and that neither our care nor industry, nor even [his] gifts, can profit us without [his] blessing."*

Christ was cursed so that we would be blessed—even in the eating of our daily bread. The effectual and powerful word of God's wrath (God's curse) was directed towards Christ. God pronounced evil upon Christ; God spoke against Christ; God spoke evil concerning Christ. The blessed Son of God was cursed because of our sins. Christ took upon himself our guilt and placed himself in the position of cursing. God turned his face against Christ and thrust him away from himself into unspeakable misery. Christ's soul had to taste the bitterness of that curse. "Christ hath redeemed us from the curse of the law, being made a curse for us: for it is written, Cursed is every one that hangeth on a tree" (Gal. 3:13).

Think about that as you eat your daily bread. Then you will begin to understand how even our food comes to us from the cross of Christ. We eat under God's blessing—let us pray confidently for it.

Martyn McGeown

---

* Heidelberg Catechism A 125, in *Confessions and Church Order*, 138.

December 16   **Q&A 125 — Acknowledging God the Only Fountain of All Good**

Read: James 1:17.

In the fourth petition, Christ reminds us that God, who is our Father, is the source of all good things, even of our daily bread. Prayer, as we saw already in Lord's Days 45–46, is a confession of our utter dependence upon God. If we did not need things, we would not pray. That we pray is proof that we need things and that God is the only source of the things that we need.

We need to be reminded—daily—of this dependence upon God.

Lord's Day 50 mentions other things that might distract us from trusting God.

First, our care. Our care is our worry. Jesus commands us: "Take no thought for your life, what ye shall eat, or what ye shall drink; nor yet for your body, what ye shall put on. Is not the life more than meat, and the body than raiment?...your heavenly Father knoweth that ye have need of all these things" (Matt. 6:25, 32). Paul writes: "Be careful for nothing; but in every thing by prayer and supplication with thanksgiving let your requests be made known unto God" (Phil. 4:6). When we worry, we waste valuable energy on a fruitless pursuit. When we are tempted to worry, let us pray.

Second, our industry, or simply, our work. We imagine that by working hard, we earn our own bread, and we hardly acknowledge that it comes from God. He gives us the opportunity and the ability to work. We must not trust in our own work—for salvation or for our daily bread.

Third, the creature. The fourth petition is designed so that we might "withdraw our trust from all creatures and place it alone in [God]."* We are naturally prone to trust in the creature instead of in God. This is a form of idolatry, and how easy for us it is! We see the creature, and we forget that the creature is but an instrument—a secondary cause—in God's hand. When the creature fails, we are prone to panic. We must therefore turn to God before the creature fails. We must withdraw our trust from every creature—including ourselves. God must not be our last resort, but the one to whom we turn at all times.

Prayer is an acknowledgement or a confession. We have nothing; we need both natural and spiritual gifts. God alone can and does give these things to us. He is the "only fountain of all good."** We deserve nothing at all, but he is pleased to give them to us for Jesus' sake.

Father, give. This is never a demand, but a humble cry to God, who knows our needs and richly supplies them. Father, give. This is not a loan that we ask of God, but a free and unmerited gift. And when Father does give, we thank him for his gifts.

And, as we receive our daily bread, we receive his blessing, and in that blessing we are strengthened to serve him through the bread that we receive.

Father, thou only fountain of all good, give us this day our daily bread—with thy blessing.

Martyn McGeown

---

*   Heidelberg Catechism A 125, in *Confessions and Church Order*, 138.
**   Heidelberg Catechism A 125, in *Confessions and Church Order*, 138.

Q. 126. What is the fifth petition?

A. *And forgive us our debts, as we forgive our debtors*; that is, be pleased for the sake of Christ's blood, not to impute to us poor sinners our transgressions, nor that depravity which always cleaves to us; even as we feel this evidence of thy grace in us, that it is our firm resolution from the heart to forgive our neighbor.

December 17 — **Q&A 126 — Necessary to Pray for Forgiveness**

Read: 1 John 1:9.

The fifth petition concerns forgiveness of sins. It is sometimes disputed. If Christians are already forgiven, so the argument goes, why do we need to pray for the forgiveness of our sins? Such objectors contend that we need only to ask God for forgiveness once—at the point of our conversion—and we never need to pray for forgiveness again.

But this is a mistake. The saints of God have always felt the need to utter this petition, and we understand our need also. This is not because we fear that God will not forgive or because we doubt that God has forgiven us. Rather, we pray because we are confident of God's forgiveness—God is our Father, and, as we shall see, we have good grounds for our prayer—and because we desire to have the joyous experience of forgiveness in our hearts and lives.

It is not enough that we *be* forgiven. When we utter this petition, we desire to *know* that we are forgiven. We desire, as the publican, to go down to our houses justified (Luke 18:14). We desire to be conscious of our justification.

Besides that, while it is true that all of our sins are forgiven finally and completely, we keep falling into sin; we keep incurring guilt; and we daily increase our debt. Jesus likens our situation to a man freshly washed who, while walking in this world, gets his feet dirty. He requires a regular foot bath (John 13:10). The life of the Christian is one of daily turning from sin in repentance and daily turning to God in Christ in faith. Thus the Christian is one who is a sinner, yet forgiven; forgiven, yet sinning.

So far is it the case that a daily forgiveness of sins is not necessary, that a daily forgiveness of sins is more necessary and more urgent than daily bread. That the petition for daily bread precedes the petition for the remission of debts does not mean that forgiveness is less important. Better to be a starving beggar than to be deprived of the forgiveness of sins! Remember poor Lazarus: he longed for the crumbs that fell from the rich man's table, but he had something that the rich man, who fared sumptuously every day, did not have. Lazarus had the forgiveness of sins (Luke 16: 19–26).

In the way of uttering this petition, Forgive us our debts, we receive that blessing also. What a necessary petition this is! Without the forgiveness of sins, the holy God is a terror to us. Without the forgiveness of sins, we are barred from the kingdom of God. Without the forgiveness of sins, we cannot even begin to fulfill God's will. Without the forgiveness of sins, our daily bread is a curse to us.

How miserable to be without the forgiveness of sins! How blessed to know that God forgives our sins, even ours!

Martyn McGeown

December 18 — Q&A 126 — Our Debts

Read: 2 Kings 4:1.

In the fifth petition of the Lord's prayer, our sins are called debts. A debt is an obligation to pay something we owe, but which we have not paid. To be a debtor who is unable to pay puts a person in a very difficult situation—he is at the mercy of his creditors. In the ancient world, creditors were not known for their mercy.

The widow in 2 Kings 4 was in such a predicament. Her husband had died, leaving her responsible for the household debt. The creditor was hounding her for the money she owed, but she had no source of income. Moreover, the interest (usury) on the debt was steadily increasing. Her cruel creditor demanded that she make full payment, and if not, he threatened to sell her and her family into slavery and confiscate her possessions. Thus she cries unto Elisha the prophet: "Thy servant my husband is dead; and thou knowest that thy servant did fear the Lord: and the creditor is come to take unto him my two sons to be bondmen" (v. 1). By a miracle, Elisha provided the widow with the means to pay back her creditors (vv. 2–7).

Thus we see how miserable debt is. It causes anxiety, sleepless nights, fear when the mail arrives or the telephone rings. Sometimes when debt spirals out of control, a person's house will be repossessed. In former days, there were debtors' prisons for delinquent borrowers.

We are spiritual debtors before God. We owe God an amount that we have not paid and that we cannot pay. Our debt is not money—God has no need of money. Our debt is a debt of love.

As human beings, who were created in our first father in the image of God, we are obligated to love our creator. We owe God lifelong, perfect obedience in love. In short, we must love God with our whole heart, soul, mind, and strength. We must devote everything we have to the service of God. That obligation is upon us every moment of every day. Adam and Eve before the fall gladly performed that obligation—without sin. But when Adam and Eve fell—and when we fell in them—they (and we) ceased to perform that obligation. In fact, because of the fall, they (and we) became totally corrupted and depraved, so that they are spiritually unable and unwilling to fulfill that obligation.

However, as Lord's Day 4 taught us, while the fall destroyed our ability to obey, it did not destroy our obligation to obey. When a person has taken out a loan, but then his financial circumstances change for the worse, the bank does not relieve him of the obligation to pay back the loan. So God does not relieve mankind of the obligation to love him—God is still glorious; God is still worthy of all praise and devotion from his creatures.

Alas, we cannot pay. Therefore our prayer is—and can only be—Forgive us our debts.

Martyn McGeown

December 19   **Q&A 126 — The Misery of Indebtedness**

Read: Psalm 130:1–3.

Psalm 130 uses two powerful illustrations of the misery of debt. The more we understand them, the more we appreciate the great blessing of forgiveness, and the more we understand the urgency of our prayer, Forgive us our debts.

The first illustration is that of a drowning man, sinking ever deeper into the depths of the sea. Great is the terror of the man gasping for breath as he is sucked under the water to his death; he panics, desperately trying to tread water to keep himself afloat. That sea in Psalm 130 is not a physical sea of deep water but a powerful symbol of sin. The idea is of the depth of depravity or the ocean of guilt in which a person is perishing. In desperation, the psalmist cries out to the only one who can save him, Jehovah his God.

The second illustration is that of a guilty man before the judge: "If thou…shouldest mark iniquities" (v. 3). The psalmist's iniquities are on his mind and conscience. They are deviations from the law of God—the twisted, perverse, fallen nature of mankind, and all of the sins that proceed from that corrupt nature. Picture the judge sitting at the bench, with his pen in his hand. Will he mark the iniquities of the psalmist? Will he mark *our* iniquities? To mark iniquities means to write them down and to treat us on account of them. What an awful possibility—that God could mark our sins against us and then punish us because of them!

If God did that—marked our iniquities—he would be perfectly just to do so. We do owe him obedience, and we have not paid. We do deserve to be punished, and we have not undergone that punishment, punishment which awaits the wicked in hell, whose debts are not forgiven. The thought is fearful—who shall stand? The answer is solemn—no one would stand, because there is none righteous.

The awful truth is that the majority of people live in the world unconcerned about the debt that they owe. They have no consciousness of sin. They have deceived themselves that their sins are not at all serious and that God will not take sins seriously. They see no need to pray the fifth petition. Blind and dead they are in their sins!

But the child of God knows his sin. He knows that he sins daily, and that his sins are serious. Thus he is urgent in his plea: "Lord, hear my voice: let thine ears be attentive to the voice of my supplications" (Ps. 130:2).

Are you drowning in debt? Does your conscience condemn you before God's judgment throne? Pray to your Father: "Forgive us our debts."

Martyn McGeown

December 20 — Q&A 126 – Forgive!

Read: Micah 7:18.

What do we mean—and what do we ask God to do—when we ask: "Forgive?"

Forgiveness, along with grace, mercy, and blessing, are common words in a Christian's vocabulary, but we lose much of the sweetness of these words by our imprecise and vague ideas of these great truths.

The word *forgive* in the Bible, especially in the Old Testament, means to lift up or to carry away. The idea is of a heavy, crushing burden. We struggle under a heavy load of guilt and shame, but God lifts that burden and carries it away, so that we experience blessed relief. That is the teaching of Micah 7:18, "Who is a God like unto thee, that pardoneth iniquity?" The same truth is celebrated in Psalm 32:1, "Blessed is he whose transgression is forgiven." Another word for forgiveness, also found in Micah 7, is *to pass over* ("passeth by the transgression of the remnant of his heritage" (v. 18)). The idea is not to look at sin, not to regard it, and therefore not to treat the sinner according as his sins deserve. It is the opposite of marking transgression, which we considered yesterday in Psalm 130. A third Old Testament word for forgive is *to cover*, also found in Psalm 32 ("whose sin is covered," v. 1). Again, the idea is that God covers over sin so that he does not see it—he covers it over by means of a sacrifice. In that sense, he blots it out.

In the New Testament, the most common word for *forgive* means to send away or to release. In terms of debts, to forgive means to send the debt away, to remove from the debtor—from us—the obligation to pay. Imagine the relief of a debtor who receives a message from the creditor—I have removed from you the obligation to pay. You no longer need to concern yourself with the debt. I have wiped your debts clean. Jesus speaks of this in Luke 7:41–42, "There was a certain creditor which had two debtors: the one owed five hundred pence, and the other fifty. And when they had nothing to pay, he frankly forgave them both." That is forgiveness, except here the debt is sin, and the one who forgives is God.

Therefore, we see what we are asking in the fifth petition.

We are not asking that God should ignore our debts and pretend that we do not have any debts. We are not asking God to deny his own justice. Not that! We are asking that God not make us pay in full what we owe him—we are asking that someone else pay for us instead. We are also not asking that God give us more time to pay him back what we owe him. We are not promising that, if God be lenient, we will do better in the future. We are not trying to bargain with God. Not that! We confess the debt, but we are asking that, seeing we can never pay, God not make us pay. That is a bold, almost a staggeringly impudent request—but we make it on good grounds.

And the wonder is that God not only forgives—relieves us of the obligation to pay, sends away our debt, carries away the burden of our sins—but that he does so by sending his Son to pay our debt, and sends the Spirit into our hearts to assure us that we are forgiven.

Let us pray, then, with confidence, Forgive us our debts!

Martyn McGeown

December 21 — Q&A 126 – Impute Not to Us Poor Sinners

Read: Psalm 32:2.

Lord's Day 51 interprets the petition "Forgive us our debts" as "be pleased for the sake of Christ's blood, not to impute to us poor sinners our transgressions."[*] Thus, Lord's Day 51 interprets the fifth petition, rightly, in terms of justification.

Impute is a legal term that we encountered in Lord's Day 23. It means to reckon something to the account of another, so that legally that thing belongs to the person to whom it has been imputed. In Scripture, guilt or innocence (unrighteousness or righteousness) can be imputed or money can be imputed to a person's account. For example, in Philemon 18, Paul writes: "Put that [Onesimus' debt] on mine account," that is, impute it to me, so that I become legally obligated to pay for it.

A debtor might echo the words of Lord's Day 51 to his creditor, Impute not to me, a poor debtor, the obligation to pay what I owe. But here the debt is not money, but sin (or the obligation to perfect obedience and the obligation to satisfactory punishment for imperfect obedience, which we have not paid and which we cannot pay). Thus, the one praying the fifth petition asks, Impute not to me, a poor sinner, my transgressions nor my depravity.

Clearly, this is a petition for mercy, not a petition based on what we deserve. If God did impute our transgressions to us, he would be just. They are, after all, *our* transgressions, not his. Similarly, if a creditor insisted on payment from a delinquent debtor, he would be just to impute debt to his debtor. The clearing of a debt is mercy, not something a debtor can demand.

Two things we ask God not to impute to us. First, we beseech God not to impute our transgressions to us. Do not account us guilty before thee for all of our sins—our lies, our thefts, our murders, our idolatry, our blasphemy, our disrespect toward our parents, and so many more sins in thought, word, and deed. Do not mark those sins against us with a view to punishing us for them. What a bold request to make before the judge! Second, we beseech God not to impute our depravity to us. Do not account us guilty before thee for "that depravity which always cleaves to us."[**] We are polluted, wicked, and depraved by nature, but, Lord, do not hold that against us. An even bolder request!

But there is more. In not imputing guilt to us, God gives us something even more wonderful. It is one thing not to be guilty—to be exempt from punishment. It is quite another to be positively righteous—to stand before God as spotless and holy as God himself!

In this fifth petition we ask for Christ's righteousness, about which we will learn in our next meditation.

Martyn McGeown

---

[*] Heidelberg Catechism A 126, in *Confessions and Church Order*, 139.
[**] Heidelberg Catechism A 126, in *Confessions and Church Order*, 139.

December 22   Q&A 126 — For the Sake of Christ's Blood

Read: Romans 5:9.

In the fifth petition, we ask not only that God would send away our sins, that he would remove from us the obligation to pay, but also that, in not imputing to us poor sinners our transgressions and sinful natures, he would account us positively righteous in his sight.

To understand the enormity of that request, consider an earthly example. A poor widow owes a creditor ten thousand dollars. Which widow would have the audacity to make this request of her creditor: "Do not make me pay the ten thousand dollars. Remove from me the obligation to pay back that money. And credit to my account the positive balance of one million dollars?" That is what we ask—in spiritual terms—in the fifth petition.

Forgive our debts. Cancel them; send them away; tear them up. Make it so that we do not have to pay. But, Father, do not stop there. Go further! Credit to our account perfect obedience, so that we become positively and legally worthy of eternal life. Let us stand before thee as those who have never had any sin, who have never sinned, and who have kept the law perfectly.

That is implied in Lord's Day 51. When we ask God not to impute to us poor sinners our transgressions and sinful natures, we mean, do impute something positive to us. And all of this is based on the work of Christ: "For the sake of Christ's blood."[*]

In Scripture and in the Catechism, Christ's blood stands for everything in his life, and especially in his death, which he has accomplished for our salvation. Christ's blood is his death on the cross, where he personally took legal responsibility for our debts—for the debt to God's justice which demanded our punishment; and for the debt to God's law which demanded perfect obedience and righteousness.

The debt that we owe has been paid. Nothing has been ignored or overlooked. When God sends the burden of guilt away from us and lifts it off our shoulders, it is because he has placed it on another, namely on his Son, Jesus Christ. When God is pleased not to impute to us poor sinners all our transgressions and our sinful natures, it is because he imputed that guilt to another—and Jesus Christ paid the full penalty. When God no longer demands from us perfect obedience to his law, it is because he already demanded and has received to his satisfaction that perfect obedience from his own, only begotten, dearly beloved Son, our Lord and Savior, Jesus Christ.

Thus we see that on the last day, God's record books will be perfectly balanced. Every sin will be punished; no debt will be ignored; no transgression will be overlooked. Some will be forgiven, and others will be eternally condemned.

What will God see when he looks at your record? Will he mark your iniquities against you? Will he see the mark: "Balance outstanding"? Or will he see stamped in blood, Paid in full. Fully satisfied? Believer, your debt is paid; unbeliever, you must flee to Christ, lest on the last day you be found a debtor!

Martyn McGeown

---

[*]   Heidelberg Catechism A 126, in *Confessions and Church Order*, 139.

December 23 — Q&A 126 – Our Firm Resolution to Forgive

Read: Matthew 5:7.

The fifth petition has two parts. "Forgive us our debts," we have considered that. "As we forgive our debtors," this we must still consider.

We are debtors to God, but our neighbors are debtors to us. How we treat those who sin against us speaks volumes about the forgiveness we have received—or claim to have received—from God. We must carefully understand the relationship between our forgiveness of our neighbor and God's forgiveness of us. One is not the condition of the other. God does not promise to forgive us on condition that we forgive our neighbors. Rather, our forgiveness is the fruit of God's forgiveness—if we have received forgiveness, we will forgive our neighbors. If we do not forgive our neighbors, we show by that wicked behavior that we have not received God's forgiveness.

To illustrate this great truth, Jesus told a parable. A debtor owed his lord ten thousand talents—an enormous sum! The creditor commanded that he be sold with his wife and children and all his possessions. Terrified, the debtor asked for mercy: "Have patience with me, and I will pay thee all" (Matt. 18:26). The lord mercifully forgave him his debt—ten thousand talents! However, immediately after leaving the presence of the merciful lord, the erstwhile debtor meets another servant who owed him a hundred pence—a paltry sum, especially in comparison to the ten thousand talents that he owed his lord. The fellow servant begs for mercy, but his cries are not heard, and he is cast into prison until he pays the debt (vv. 28–30). The situation comes to the attention of the master, who, in punishment for the debtor's refusal to forgive, delivers the debtor to the tormentors (v. 34).

From this parable we learn a few important truths about forgiveness. First, in comparison to the enormous sum we owe God, our neighbor who wrongs us owes us very little. Second, one who has a cruel and merciless attitude toward his penitent neighbor shows that he was never forgiven by God. Third, the forgiveness of our neighbor must take the same form as the forgiveness we receive from God. We must send away the neighbor's sins; we must resolve not to treat him as his sins deserve. We must declare to our neighbor who sins against us and asks for forgiveness: "I forgive you. I forgive you because Christ forgave me. Your sins against me I will remember no more."

That is hard—it means we swallow our pride; we take a loss, because we relinquish the right to revenge and the right even to remember that sin or to hold a grudge. But how much harder was it for Christ to forgive us—he bled and died to procure our forgiveness!

Thus, forgiveness is the blessed fruit of forgiveness. Forgiven sinners forgive other sinners, or as Lord's Day 51 puts it: "We feel this evidence of thy grace in us, that it is our firm resolution from the heart to forgive our neighbor."*

Have you sinned against your brother? Seek forgiveness. Has your brother apologized to you? Forgive him, even as God for Christ's sake has forgiven you.

Martyn McGeown

---

* Heidelberg Catechism A 126, in *Confessions and Church Order*, 139.

Lord's Day 52

Q. 127. Which is the sixth petition?

A. *And lead us not into temptation, but deliver us from evil*; that is, since we are so weak in ourselves that we cannot stand a moment; and besides this, since our mortal enemies, the devil, the world, and our own flesh cease not to assault us, do thou therefore preserve and strengthen us by the power of thy Holy Spirit, that we may not be overcome in this spiritual warfare, but constantly and strenuously may resist our foes, till at last we obtain a complete victory.

Q. 128. How dost thou conclude thy prayer?

A. *For thine is the kingdom, and the power, and the glory, for ever*; that is, all these we ask of thee, because Thou, being our King and almighty, art willing and able to give us all good; and all this we pray for, that thereby not we, but thy holy name, may be glorified for ever.

Q. 129. What doth the word *Amen* signify?

A. *Amen* signifies, it shall truly and certainly be; for my prayer is more assuredly heard of God than I feel in my heart that I desire these things of him.

December 24   **Q&A 127 — The Prayer for Deliverance from Evil and from the Evil One**

Read: Galatians 5:13–21.

With this meditation we begin the consideration of the sixth petition of the perfect prayer that the Lord Jesus Christ himself has taught us. To understand the urgent need for this petition, we need to understand our need as Christians for deliverance from the twofold power and destruction of our sin. The fifth petition of the Lord's prayer teaches us to pray for deliverance from the guilt of our sin. Sin makes us guilty before God. That we are guilty before the righteous and holy God means that we deserve to be condemned by him. Our sins are so serious that they make us worthy of God's everlasting judgment of hell fire. In praying the fifth petition, we pray that the atonement that Jesus offered for us on the cross might cover the guilt of our sin and be applied to us personally. We pray that the perfect righteousness of Jesus Christ might be imputed to us by his wonderful grace, even as we believe in him and trust in him.

The sixth petition of the Lord's prayer teaches us to pray earnestly for deliverance from the power and corruption of our sin. Born from fallen Adam and Eve, we have inherited a totally depraved nature. The corruption of sin makes us ugly, abominable, and loathsome in the sight of God. We cannot possibly live in the presence of the holy and blessed God as long as we are corrupt and wicked. Even as born again believers, we have a sinful nature against which we must wrestle all our life long. We will not be fully delivered from our corrupt sinful nature until our vile bodies are put in the grave, and we are raised again with new bodies, wholly delivered from the corruption of sin and gloriously changed to be fashioned after the glorious body of Christ. Paul speaks of this in Philippians 3:21. The child of God who has the Spirit of Christ in his or her heart desires to be made more and more holy, until finally he or she is made perfect as God is perfect and holy as God our heavenly Father is holy.

The remaining corruption of our sin is a power of evil in our very nature. We are called to struggle against this sinful nature. We are not to yield to the inclination of our sinful nature for even a moment. The presence of this sinful nature is the cause of an ongoing mighty spiritual battle within us. When our Lord taught us to pray the sixth petition, Deliver us from evil, he was making us aware of the reality of this sinful nature in us and the power of this sinful nature to destroy us. We cannot deliver ourselves; we need the help of our God. Experiencing the reality of this struggle within himself, the inspired apostle Paul cried out: "O wretched man that I am! who shall deliver me from the body of this death?" (Rom. 7:24).

The words of the sixth petition of the Lord's prayer can also be translated according to the original language of the Bible as "the evil one." So then in this petition we are praying for deliverance from the power of the devil himself, who is the author of all evil. Not only is he the author of all evil in the world, but he is also the author of the evil within our sinful natures. This is a fearful reality. In Ephesians 6:12 the inspired apostle Paul warns us that "we wrestle not against flesh and blood, but against principalities, against powers, against the rulers of the darkness of this world, against spiritual wickedness in high places."

In the sixth petition we are taught of the great need for deliverance from the power of the devil in our lives. Do you know the great urgency of this prayer to God?

Arie den Hartog

December 25 — Q&A 127 — The Prayer for Deliverance from a Threefold Enemy

Read: Ephesians 6:10–18.

The sixth petition reminds us that we are engaged in spiritual warfare with a threefold enemy. These three enemies are working together for our spiritual ruin and destruction. To understand the urgency for praying this petition every day, we need to know this threefold enemy.

It is easy to imagine that our greatest enemy is a physical enemy. We might imagine our greatest enemy to be some human person that hates us and wants to destroy us physically. We might imagine him or her to be a fellow student at school who is trying to make greater educational and career achievements. We might imagine our enemy to be a person in society trying to ruin our reputation and turn attention to himself. We might imagine our enemy to be a fellow worker in our occupation trying to get an advantage over us, a higher salary, or a promotion in the company. We might imagine our greatest enemy to be any person who competes with us for riches, glory, and honor in the world. We might imagine that our enemy is some fearful, even unknown, criminal.

The word of God tells us we have a far greater enemy. We are engaged with this enemy in a spiritual warfare for our eternal soul. Peter tells us in 1 Peter 5 that the devil is real and has great power. He goes about like "a roaring lion…seeking whom he may devour" (v. 8). He is the great deceiver who tempts us to sin against God and his commandments. He wants us to leave the Christian religion altogether, to rebel against God, and to join the world in its enmity against God. He may come to us "in sheep's clothing," but in fact inwardly he is a ravening wolf seeking to tear us apart and devour us (Matt. 7:15).

In the sixth petition we pray for spiritual knowledge and discernment, so that we can recognize the works of the devil and his temptations. We pray for spiritual strength to fight against the devil and his whole dominion of demons and evil devices. The devil is very powerful. He cannot be resisted nor overcome by human or earthly might, but only by spiritual strength and power. We need to receive this spiritual strength from God the Father, Jesus Christ, and the Holy Spirit. The Holy Spirit is given to us and works in us to overcome our sin, resist the devil, and to triumph over him.

The devil uses the world to tempt us and entice us to sin. The devil tempted Jesus with the deceitful words, that if only Jesus would bow down to him, the whole world would belong to Jesus and be his inheritance (Matt. 4:9). The devil has many devices in this world to tempt us. This is all the more true in our time. He can use the modern-day media of the movie theater, the computer, and the worldwide internet. By these means the devil places in our minds and hearts the desires and thinking of the world's philosophy. The devil may seek to attract us to a life of immorality with the promise of its sinful pleasure and the satisfaction of the lusts of our sinful nature. The temptations of the devil are very powerful. We need to realize this. We can only resist and overcome the devil by the power of God.

Our third enemy is our own sinful nature. We have this sinful nature even as Christians. Deeply residing in this nature are all kinds of inclinations, desires, and lusts for sin. The devil, by using the wicked world, can appeal to that sinful nature and lead us into sin and away from God, and to our own personal spiritual ruin. How needful is the prayer of the sixth petition for every Christian!

Arie den Hartog

December 26 — Q&A 127 — We Cannot Stand Against Our Mortal Enemies Even for One Moment

Read: 1 Peter 5:6–11.

The sixth petition which our Lord taught us in his perfect model prayer is an urgent petition. We must never begin a single day without earnestly praying this petition. A petition earnestly prayed to God arises out of the heart of the child of God who is fully aware of the danger he is in and the power of the enemy. We will hardly see our need of praying the sixth petition if we do not understand or live in the fearful consciousness of this.

The Catechism speaks of three enemies that are engaged with us in a constant spiritual battle. These enemies are "mortal enemies."* A mortal enemy is one who purposes to kill and destroy us completely. The devil's purpose is not to entertain us but to destroy us. He deceives man into imagining that sin is pleasure that can be enjoyed without consequences, without the judgment of God. After he has completely deceived a person, he blinds and leads him to his own ruin and destruction. The destruction that he leads men to is not merely personal ruin, shame and trouble in this life, but the awful and eternal destruction of hell.

To pray the sixth petition, we must be conscious of our complete dependence on God and his grace, strength, and salvation. No one else but God alone can save us from the enemy.

The devil is very powerful. He is not almighty, as God is. But he is very powerful. Furthermore, his mode of operation is deceit. The Bible speaks of the wiles of the devil. The wiles of the devil are his subtle tactics. Peter speaks of the devil going about "as a roaring lion…seeking whom he may devour" (1 Pet. 5:8). If he is not able to make us fall into sin by using one approach, he will try other approaches until he has fully accomplished his treacherous purpose to destroy us.

On the other hand, we are weak in ourselves. Our weakness is due to the reality of our sinful nature. In fact, we have no power at all to deliver ourselves from the devil and sin, because our sinful nature fully agrees with the devil and is wholly given over to the philosophy and deceitful temptations of the world. The Catechism states that we cannot even stand for one moment against the devil. We are in great need every day, every moment, of the power, grace, and Spirit of God to deliver us.

The wonderful truth of the gospel is that Christ has triumphed over the power of the devil and all the powers of sin and temptation in the world.

Christ merited the grace and power of salvation as our Lord on his cross. This power was first given to Christ when God raised him up from the dead and set him at his own right hand, far above the principalities and powers in this world and in the world to come.

When we pray the sixth petition of the Lord's prayer, we must think of the blessed truth that Christ now works this power in us and makes us partakers of his own victory over Satan and the power of evil. Jesus gives this great power and triumph to all of his saints who earnestly call upon him in faith and prayer.

Arie den Hartog

---

* Heidelberg Catechism A 127, in *Confessions and Church Order*, 139.

December 27   Q&A 127 — The Prayer for Deliverance from Temptation

Read: James 1:12–21.

Temptation is a strong appeal to our sinful natures to draw us away from God and to lead us into a life of evil. This evil is presented as though it were actually something good, something that can give us innocent pleasure and satisfaction. On the other hand, remaining faithful to the Lord and his commandments is presented as something evil and burdensome. The devil, working in temptation, presents the way of the Lord as though following this way will in fact cause us to miss some great good and pleasure in our lives in the world, or perhaps pass by opportunities for great riches, real lasting glory, or honor in the world.

The words of this petition present some difficulties to our understanding. These words do not mean that God is the author of temptation. We know that God does not tempt us with sin. James tells us this: "Let no man say when he is tempted, I am tempted of God: for God cannot be tempted with evil, neither tempteth he any man" (James 1: 13).

The wording of the sixth petition does teach us that God is sovereign even over temptation and does sometimes give us over to temptation to chasten us for our own sin of pride or self-reliance. There are some classic biblical examples of this. David was led into the temptation of numbering Israel so he could become proud and trust in the greatness of his own armies to deliver Israel from the evil of all enemies. Peter was led into the great evil of boasting in himself that he was actually stronger than all the other disciples of the Lord. He was led into the temptation of denying his own beloved Lord and falling grievously.

The devil alone tempts us. He tempts us by appealing to the evil lusts that reside in our sinful nature. Read what James has to say about this. The devil can tempt us only when we are "drawn away of [our] own lust, and enticed" to agree with him in his temptation (James 1:14). If God does not deliver us from temptation, the lust of our own sinful natures will bring us down to death. The devil constantly assails us with temptation, virtually from the moment we awake in the morning to the time we close our eyes and sleep. He tempts us in every sphere of our lives, even while we are in church.

We yield to temptation long before we fall into sin. Let no one imagine that as long as temptation has not led us into actually doing some great evil in our lives, we have not yet fallen. One of the crucial things we must understand about sin is that sin begins with the heart and the thoughts of our minds. As soon as we have given in to temptation in our hearts and begun to desire that which the devil presents to us in a temptation, we have already fallen. If we continue in this desire, it will lead us to sinful purposes and plans, and finally to sinful works in our lives. These evil works will bring upon us the wrath and judgment of God.

When we yield to temptation, the world mocks us and at times even blasphemes the name of God. Jesus Christ, who has saved us by his great love for us, is deeply grieved, and his name, which we as Christians bear, is dishonored. When we are led into temptation, we are for a time estranged from God in our lives and can no longer experience the great blessings of salvation and communion with him. We need to pray daily that God will deliver us from all temptation!

Arie den Hartog

December 28 — Q&A 127 — Strengthen Us by Thy Holy Spirit

Read: 1 Thessalonians 5:12–23.

In the sixth petition of the Lord's prayer, we are taught to pray for the strength of God to deliver us from evil and from the evil one. This strength comes to us through the work of the Holy Spirit in us.

The Christian life is a constant spiritual warfare. Every true child of God knows this. The devil and the world in which we live constantly oppose us. We may not even for one moment yield to our enemies. If we do so, in the thoughts and intentions of our hearts, as well as in our words and deeds, we bring shame to the name of the Lord. Furthermore, yielding in this warfare will result in damage to our Christian life. We should be greatly concerned about this. The reason why the sixth petition is often not prayed is that many Christians are not concerned enough about the issues just mentioned. In this, they show that their love and devotion to God is weak. If we love God, we will desire to be delivered from all remaining sin and to be made perfectly holy as God our Father is holy.

In prayer, we acknowledge God to be our God. This God is the blessed triune God, Father, Son, and Holy Spirit. God the Father desires in his great love that we are perfect in our soul, body, and spirit as he is. Jesus the Son of God gave himself as a sacrifice for sin, not only to blot out the awful guilt of our sins but to deliver us from the power and corruption of sin.

It is noteworthy that in the entire Lord's prayer the first person plural is used. We do not pray only for ourselves. We pray also for our fellow saints. Jesus gave himself in order to cleanse not only certain individuals who were given to him in the love of his heavenly Father, but also his beloved church. The purpose of our Lord Jesus Christ was that his beloved church might finally be presented in heaven as his glorious bride without spot and blemish, perfectly holy and exceedingly glorious.

We are delivered from the power of sin and spiritual warfare against evil and the devil by the Holy Spirit. Christ works in our hearts by the Holy Spirit. No other power can deliver us from the power of sin, only the wonderful, mighty, sanctifying power of the Holy Spirit.

In the sixth petition we earnestly pray for the ongoing work of the Holy Spirit in our hearts. We pray for his constant strengthening work in us. How wonderful is his power! He is the mighty power of God, and with him is the blessed hope of final and glorious deliverance from sin and the devil.

As long as we sincerely pray the sixth petition, we need not despair in the midst of the ongoing battle with sin. Our final victory will definitely be accomplished through the mighty operation of the Spirit of Christ in our hearts.

We long for the glorious perfection of the work of God in our hearts and complete victory over all sin. For this we pray earnestly, confident that the Lord will indeed hear us, actually deliver us, make us perfect, and save us to give us everlasting life and glory.

Arie den Hartog

December 29 — Q&A 128 – Praises to the King of Kings

Read: 1 Chronicles 29:11–17.

Jesus teaches us in the Lord's prayer always to make God central in our prayers, and then also in the whole of our lives. In his perfect model prayer he teaches us in the very first petition to pray for the hallowing of the name of God, so that his name might be glorious in all the earth.

God should be central in our prayers. This is not commonly the chief concern of prayers made by Christians, and sometimes also not in our own. Many Christians, and we also, sometimes make our own needs the concern of our own prayers. Central to many of our sinful prayers is the demand that God give us what we want ourselves, as though God must listen to our every demand and serve our every need.

All of our prayers must praise God's greatness and glory. Our prayers must always be centrally about God, his kingdom, his sovereign will, and the glory of his name.

The conclusion of the Lord's prayer is often called a doxology. A doxology is an exalted expression of praise and honor to God. All glory, honor, and power belong to God. In our prayers we acknowledge the truth of God and desire that this truth be always revealed in the world. When David had finished preparing for the building of the temple, he stood before the nation of God's chosen people and praised God with a doxology similar to the one found at the end of the Lord's prayer.

God is king over all the universe. He created the universe by his almighty power. He created all the creatures in this vast universe for his own pleasure and glory. Do we sincerely know this to be true, and do we show in our whole life that we truly believe this? All creatures must serve the glory of God, but only man can do this as a moral and rational creature. He can do this consciously and willingly, knowing the greatness of God, his creator and sovereign Lord. If we believe that the universe as a kingdom belongs to God alone and we owe the service of our whole life, our obedience, and attribution of glory to God alone, we pray for this. We must not give this praise and glory to any other.

In the doxology of the Lord's prayer, we also confess that God has given the kingdom to his beloved Son Jesus Christ. After Christ's death on the cross, resurrection from the dead, and exaltation to God's right hand in heaven, God bestowed the kingdom on him. Because of the unity of the Father and the Son, the kingdom belongs to God alone. The dominion over this kingdom is exercised, realized, and revealed in its glory in the beloved Son, Jesus Christ. In Revelation 19, Jesus appears in a vision that prophesies of his final coming at the end of the world in triumph and glory. He has the name "KING OF KINGS, AND LORD OF LORDS" (v. 16). This is the truth concerning Jesus that we shall know perfectly in heaven and express continually before him in songs of praise and adoration.

Prayer is the highest expression of praise to God when we pray with knowing and sincere hearts. Of course, all of our activity must be in harmony with this profound truth. The psalmist in Psalm 115 says it well when he declares: "Not unto us, O LORD, not unto us, but unto thy name give glory, for thy mercy, and for thy truth's sake." (v. 1)

Let us pray that all our prayers might be in adoration, worship, and consecrated love for God.

Arie den Hartog

December 30 — Q&A 128 – The Blessed Assurance We Have in God Through Prayer

Read: John 15:7–16.

In our last meditation, I emphasized that our Lord taught us to conclude our prayer with a doxology of praise. The doxology of the Lord's prayer is an exalted one. We confess in our prayer that the kingdom, power, and glory belong to God forever and ever. This God is our God for Jesus' sake. When we pray, we must not do so in doubt and unbelief, but in the full confidence of faith and with blessed assurance in our hearts.

Believing this doxology to be absolutely true, we have the ground for confidence and assurance in our God. The Catechism comments on the doxology of the Lord's prayer. When we pray to God as our almighty King, we are assured that he is able and willing to give us all good things. What an amazing thing this is!

God is the absolutely sovereign king of the entire universe, being over all creatures great and small, ruling over all things, so that all things finally serve his purpose and good pleasure. There is no power in all the universe that is not under the control of God. Not even the devil or the whole host of wicked powers in the world are outside God's control. God is sovereign over all the mighty forces of nature. We often feel ourselves to be powerless against the mighty forces of nature and all the powers of darkness. We cannot stand against them, and we greatly fear their destructive power in our lives. But we have confidence in our God.

We pray for the reality of this confidence in our hearts, and God answers prayer. We are not to be afraid or anxious about any part of our lives in the world, no matter how dark our lives seem or how powerful our enemy might be. God is king over all forever and ever.

God is almighty in his power. There is nothing too hard for him. He does whatsoever he pleases, and he is able to work all things for our good and final salvation. There is no power, no matter how great and seemingly overwhelming to us, that can resist the power of God successfully. There is no enemy, no trial, or no trouble so great that he cannot or will not deliver us from it.

Not only is God almighty to save us from enemies and the greatest forces in the universe that might otherwise threaten our destruction, we can also be sure that he is willing to save us. His love for us in Christ assures us of this.

The doxology of the Lord's prayer assures us also that God is eternal. "Before the mountains were brought forth, even from everlasting to everlasting" he is God (Ps. 90:2). He never changes. We are constantly changing. The world in which we live is constantly changing and this can be distressing for us. Nothing in this world is certain. But our God is absolutely steadfast. He is the unchangeable and the steadfast rock of our salvation.

God never changes in his own infinite glory, majesty, and goodness. We are dependent on his goodness and faithfulness. We are born as helpless infants, entirely dependent on others to care for us and protect us. We grow, if the Lord wills, to the age of youth and strength. A few years later we grow old and weak. God remains forever the same, faithful and almighty to accomplish our final salvation and glory.

Arie den Hartog

December 31   Q&A 128 — Amen

Read: Psalm 41.

The last word David used in his prayer in Psalm 41, and the last word we say in our prayers, is much more important than we might realize. We might think "Amen" simply means the prayer is done. Finally, I can eat or go play. However, the term does not merely mean that prayer is over. *Amen* literally means *truly*. When used at the end of prayer, the idea is, What I prayed for shall truly and certainly be. What I prayed for will really happen. Thus, when said from the heart, *Amen* is a confession of faith, expressing confidence in Jehovah, the confidence that he requires for prayer.

How confident are we believers that God will answer our prayers? Question and answer 129 says that with this word *Amen*, we are each saying: "My prayer is more assuredly heard of God than I feel in my heart that I desire these things of him."[*] We do have a strong desire for the things we asked for, for forgiveness for our awful debts and deliverance from terribly addictive sins. Yet our confidence that God will hear our prayer is even stronger than our want for these things.

How can we be so sure God will hear and answer? Recall that when we pray the petitions of the Lord's prayer, or similar words, we believers are asking for things God has promised to grant us in Christ, things like daily bread, forgiveness, and deliverance from evil. The God of truth will certainly answer our prayers for these necessities that he has promised to provide. Sometimes, we also ask for things that we are not sure it is God's will to provide, like physical healing. With the term *Amen*, we are saying, It shall be that God will grant healing if it is his will. I am confident he will give what is best.

If you are struggling today with any doubts about God answering your prayers for your needs, remember that Jehovah always keeps his promises, and remember to dwell on the cross. The King who loves us so much that he sent his only begotten Son to pay for our sins will provide our necessities now and forever.

Say *Amen* then from the heart at the end of your prayers, believing that God will give what you need for Jesus' sake. Speak this word to God's glory! Jehovah is indeed praised when we express our confidence in him.

Consideration of the word *Amen* is actually a very fitting way to end our journey through the Heidelberg Catechism. We speak in prayer about many things we need from God and things we can become anxious about, from the money needed to pay bills to our struggles with sin and Satan. Now, we end the Catechism with the word *Amen*, a word that reminds us that God will truly and certainly give us all the things we need, even all the gifts of eternal salvation we heard about throughout the Catechism. This is more sure than I feel a desire for these things in my heart. What a comfort! Go forward with that comfort, praying regularly to the glory of our heavenly Father.

Matt De Boer

---

[*]   Heidelberg Catechism A 129, in *Confessions and Church Order*, 140.

LIST OF CONTRIBUTORS

Allen J. Brummel, minister of Calvary Protestant Reformed Church (Hull, IA).

Matt DeBoer, minister of Edgerton PRC (Edgerton, MN).

Arie den Hartog, emeritus minister in the PRCA and minister-on-loan in Singapore.

Herman Hanko (1930–2024) served as a minister in the PRCA and then as a professor of church history at the Protestant Reformed Theological Seminary (1965–2001). He authored many books, including *When You Pray*, *Portraits of Faithful Saints*, and *Contending for the Faith*, all published by the RFPA.

Steven Key, emeritus minister of the PRCA. For the RFPA, he authored *Living Joyfully in Marriage: Reflecting the Relationship of Christ and the Church*.

Jason Kortering (1936–2020) was a minister in the PRCA. From 1992–2006, he was called to missionary labors in Singapore, India, and Myanmar. You can read more about his ministry in *Say Among the Heathen the Lord Reigns: Evidences in Southeast Asia*, by Jean Kortering.

Dennis Lee, minister of Kalamazoo PRC (Kalamazoo, MI).

Martyn McGeown, minister of Providence PRC (Hudsonville, MI) and author of several books, including *The Savior's Farewell: Comfort from the Upper Room* and *Grace and Assurance: The Message of the Canons of Dordt*, all published by the RFPA.

Gise VanBaren (1932–2019) was a minister in the PRCA and a prolific author of theological articles and pamphlets.

YOU MIGHT ALSO LIKE

"Though we shall grow in the knowledge of God into all eternity, we shall never reach an end of our search for the riches of God's blessed being. Everlasting life is not long enough to exhaust the riches of the knowledge of God. Though we know what the Scriptures say of God, our knowledge of God is less than a thimbleful of water in comparison with all the oceans and seas on the earth. Yet, we know him—know him as our Friend, our Redeemer, our covenant God! What a wonder, for he shows us enough of himself for us to live in warm covenant fellowship with him. Let us exalt his holy name."

— excerpt of January 6 meditation, *God is Incomprehensible*

Through daily readings, thoughtful meditations, and heartfelt singing, you'll find in this book the comfort and guidance you need as you weave your pilgrim way through the sacred songbook.

Whether you're seeking solace in times of trouble, longing for a deeper connection with God, or simply craving a moment of stillness in your day, this devotional will nourish and strengthen you with the riches of the gospel of our Lord Jesus Christ.

These devotions flow from the heart of a man who devoted his life to ministry and to the needs of the saints in his care. Vos writes, not as a technical commentator, but as a pastor who wants to communicate to his readers the same awe and comfort that he experienced while reading those doctrinal and practical masterpieces which are the Psalms. Above all, Vos' desire is to point his reader to the ultimate fulfillment of the Psalms: the God of *peace* as revealed in the Lord Jesus Christ, the only one who can fully sympathize with his saints in all circumstances.

All books available at **rfpa.org**,
or by calling the Reformed Free Publishing Association
at **616-457-5970** or emailing **mail@rfpa.org**

Our Mission

To glorify God by making accessible to the broadest possible audience material that testifies to the truth of Scripture as understood and developed in the Reformed tradition.

Reformed Free Publishing Association
1894 Georgetown Center Drive
Jenison, MI 49428-7137
Website: rfpa.org

www.ingramcontent.com/pod-product-compliance
Lightning Source LLC
Chambersburg PA
CBHW072217240426
43670CB00038B/1618